Nihon Ki-in's Dictionary Series

DICTIONARY of BASIC FUSEKI

Rin Kaiho

Volume 3

3-4 Point Openings

Published by Yutopian Enterprises
2255 29th Street, Suite #3
Santa Monica, CA 90405
1-800-YUTOGO-3
yutopian@netcom.com, yutopian@aol.com
http://www.webwind.com/go

ISBN: 1-889554-89-8

Translated by Robert Terry

Editing, Diagrams, and Layout by Craig R. Hutchinson

Proof Assistance by Anthony Blagrove, James Bonomo, Larry Gross

First English Printing January 2008

Printed in Japan

FOREWORD

Leaving aside the era during which the practice was for both sides to place stones in the corners prior to the game, the history of the 3-4 point opening is limited to the rich source material of old game records that have been passed down to the present age since the Edo Period [1600-1868].

It was touched upon in the Star Point Section of Volume I, but there is a strong flowing element to the opening, and putting this into systematic classifications is extremely difficult. In the present work, the focus is on the first move played on the 3-4 point and the diverse combinations that are manifested with it, while openings with the first move played on the 5-3, 5-4 and 3-3 points, etc., are also referred to, but within the long history of development of go, it has only been at most one hundred and ten odd years since this material has been incorporated into a system with a field of vision that encompasses the whole board. Representative of that is black's 1, 3 and 5 at 3-4 points, in short, the Shusaku Style, but before that, both black and white would occupy the 3-4 points in diagonal corners together, the so-called true opening method, and to that extent as well as the fact that at that time the structure of the opening was in a primitive form, means that opening strategies relevant to later generations did not appear.

Although the openings at the start through the middle of the Edo Period pioneered schemes and tactics in regards to localized patterns, black's first move of 1 at the 3-4 point was principally met with the immediate knight's move attack on the corner with white 2, aiming at brute force fighting, skillful players who could strike out with originality in the opening in any direction of the board did not appear on the scene. However, Meijin and Honinbo Dosaku, whose excellence towered above his generation in terms of vision of the game and move order analysis, left opening conceptions that are worthy of study today, and one's attention is directed to the considerable influence he has exerted on the formation of stones of later generations.

The superior nature of the Shusaku Style theory goes without saying, but making a corner enclosure with 1 and 3, or diagonal 3-4 points, or facing 3-4 points, etc., that is, just how to combine 3-4 points in the opening in order to achieve superiority is a question that each generation works out according to its needs, and the way that it struggles with it makes for one of the interesting facets of the analysis. For instance, how black worked out a conception of using the 5-3 or 5-4 point in order to expand influence, or the first time this appeared in play, or else the conjecture of when the feeling was born that the immediate attack on the corner with white 2, which was so prevalent during the early years of the Edo Period, should be avoided. Coming down to the twentieth century, the parallel pattern and 3-3 point, etc., each were born against a particular background, and exploring that, or the matter of taking up a higher stance, is something that an opening dictionary could not possibly consider a wasted effort.

Naturally, in this work attention was lavished on analyzing the vicissitudes of new developments in contemporary go, but at the same time, a sounding pole has been dipped into the long current of four hundred years of go's opening history, and the crystallized blood and sweat of the pioneers has been taken up to see the form in which it has affected the present day and the influence that it has exerted. By plunging the scalpel into that side of the matter, an attempt has been made to carve the composition of this dictionary in deep relief.

If a just little bit of that effort can be sensed, there is no greater happiness that this writer could hope for.

May 1978

Rin Kaiho

This work, *The Dictionary of Basic Opening Positions, Volume II* published by the Nihon Ki-in in May 1978, was revised and enlarged upon the occasion of being reprinted.

August 1996

Nihon Ki-in Editorial Division

TRANSLATOR'S NOTES

Amateur players are often told that the way to improve is to develop full board perception. They are criticized for focusing too much on local situations. But the size of the whole board can be overwhelming, and, anyway, how does one go about "studying" full board play?

Well, here the reader has a guide to full board play, one that has been noticeably lacking in the English language go literature up to now. It has been written by a master of full board perception, the inimitable Rin Kaiho, enhanced with the scholarship of top writers, and supplemented with detailed analysis of myriad positions. One can scarcely conceive of a better overall guide to the game of go.

But a note on the text. The trend in English language go literature has been to eliminate technical jargon and Japanese terms. This translation continues along that line. Except for very specific words for which there can hardly be substitutes, such as sente, hane, etc., English words have been used as far as possible. This has made for some awkward constructions sometimes, but the reader should understand that in a similar way the original text may seem awkward to the average reader in Japan.

Then there were words that caused much contemplation. "Honte" is an example of one word that defies adequate translation. "Real play" is traditionally given as the English equivalent, but what does it mean?! (And strong go players might be stymied by a request to define the word themselves!) Finally, the conclusion was reached that the expression "true play" sounded closer to the original. Other words are translated as they have been in the past, such as skillful finesse for "tesuji." (But the word "suji" has been translated as tactic.) It is hoped that the reader will sympathize with what must be done to accomplish the leap of interpretation that accompanies a translation such as this.

Thickness is another difficult word to translate. Not so much because of the word itself, but in the nuances in its meaning. For many players, especially at the kyu level, the idea of playing for thickness, rather than for territory or capturing stones, is difficult to understand. For the sake of such players it has been thought worthy to use the terms "thickness and strength" together, or to say that one side or another makes a "thick and strong" play. Two words must take the place of the single Japanese word, but this concept is so important in go that it must be conveyed to the reader. Stronger players might shrug, but weaker ones can always use the helpful reminder that the extra word gives. (It should also be understood that the word "influence" is often used in a synonymous sense with thickness.)

Go is not an easy game to understand. One needs the help of experienced players to advance. I have been lucky to gain access to brilliant minds such as

Rin Kaiho's, and I try to pass on the insightful analysis of such minds whenever I can.

Bob Terry, Long Beach, 2002

EDITOR'S NOTES

The traditional Japanese word "nirensei" will be used to identify the occupation of two corner star points on one side of the board.

The traditional Japanese word "sanrensei" will be used to identify the occupation of three star points on one side of the board.

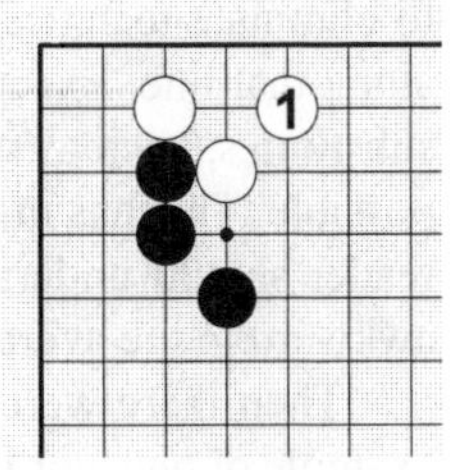

I call white's three stone shape a tiger and write "White plays a tiger link at 1" instead of "White connects with a tiger's mouth play at 1" or "White connects with a hanging connection at 1".

I take full responsibility for the final result. Please send any comments or suggestions to Yutopian Enterprises. Your critique will be much appreciated. Enjoy!

Craig R. Hutchinson

Star Point Openings

Table of Contents and Index

Section 1

Shusaku Style

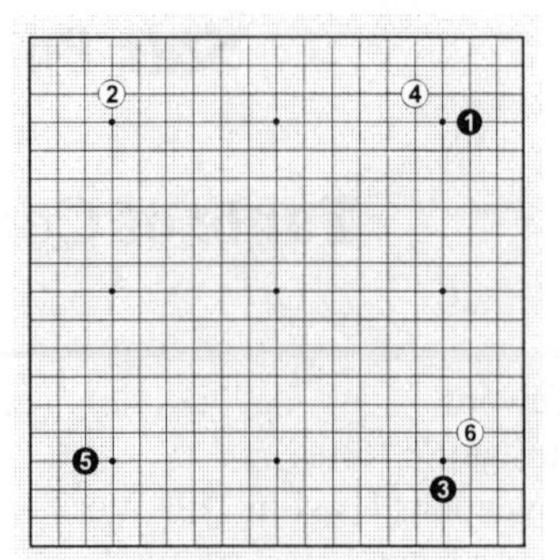

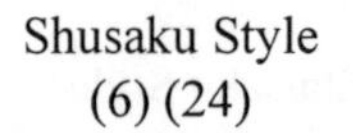
Shusaku Style
(6) (24)

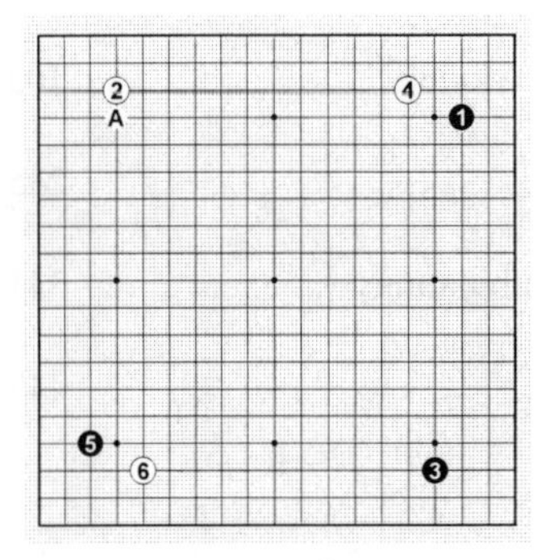

Shusaku Style (Including 2 at **A**)
(16) (62) (72)

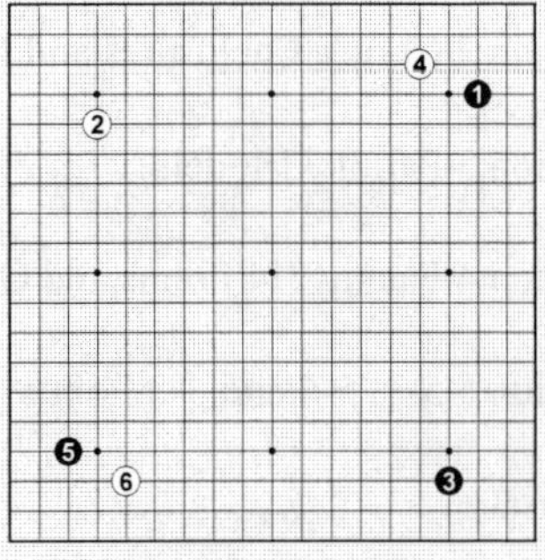

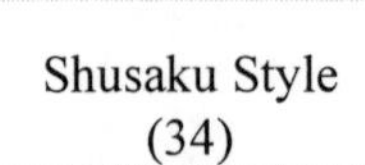
Shusaku Style
(34)

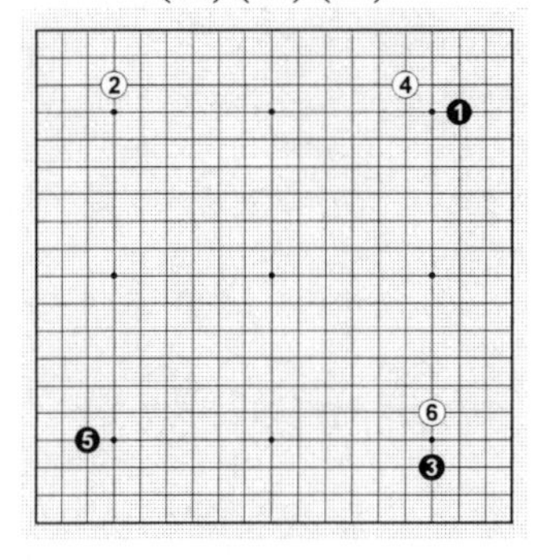

Shusaku Style
(42) (50)

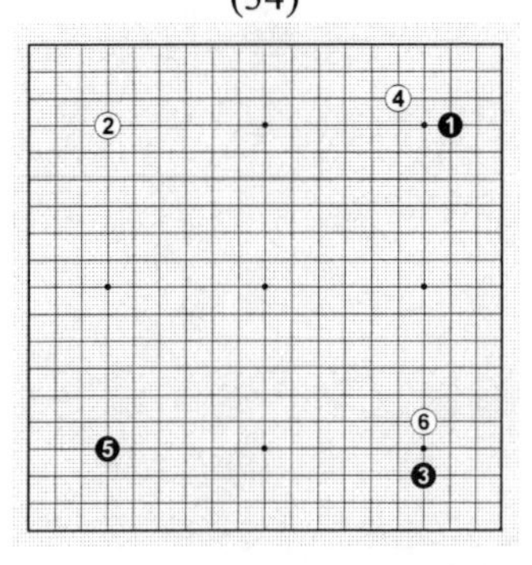

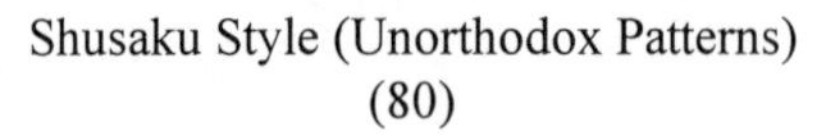
Shusaku Style (Unorthodox Patterns)
(80)

Section 2

Corner Enclosures and Diagonal Models

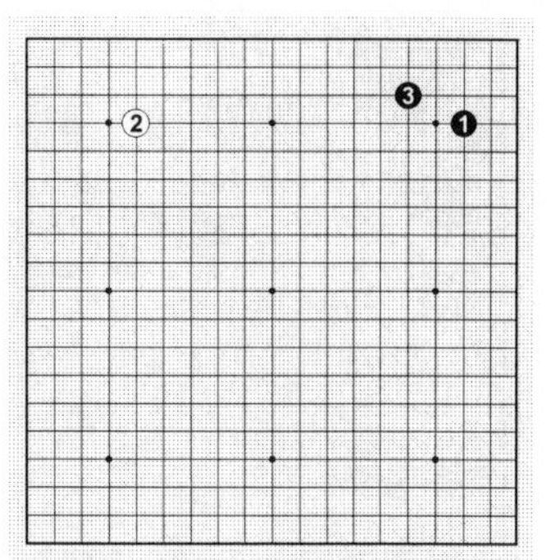

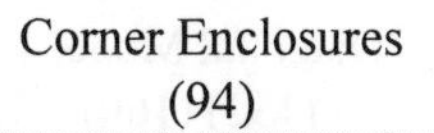

Corner Enclosures
(94)

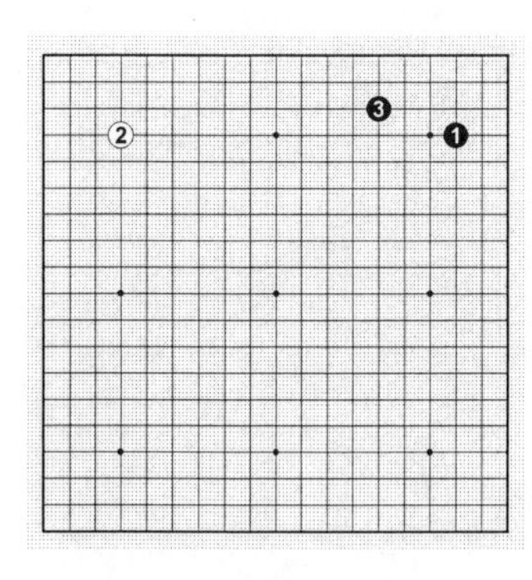

Corner Enclosures
(102) (128)

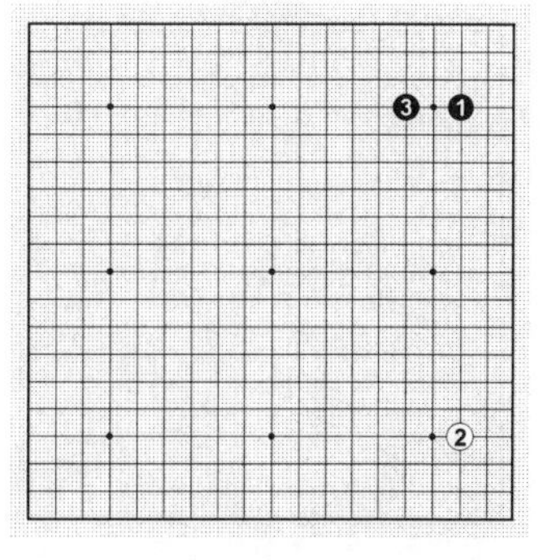

Corner Enclosures
(110)

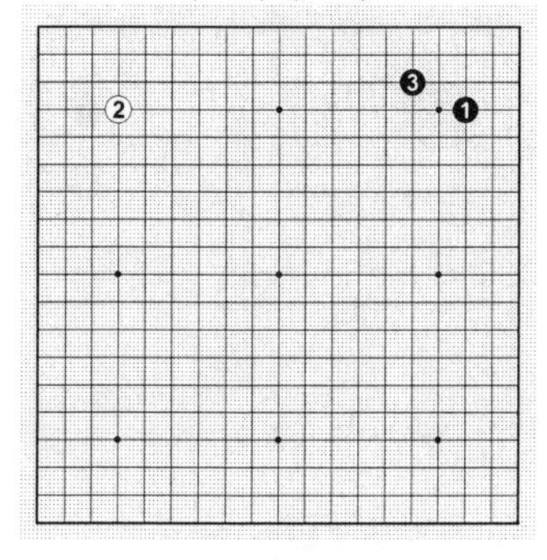

Corner Enclosures
(120) (136)

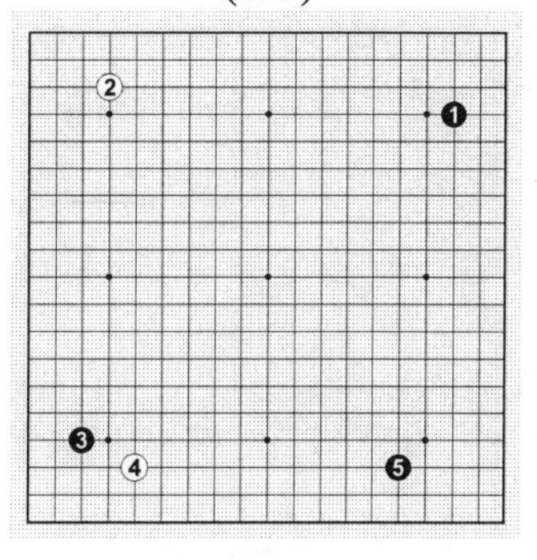

Diagonal Model 1
(144)

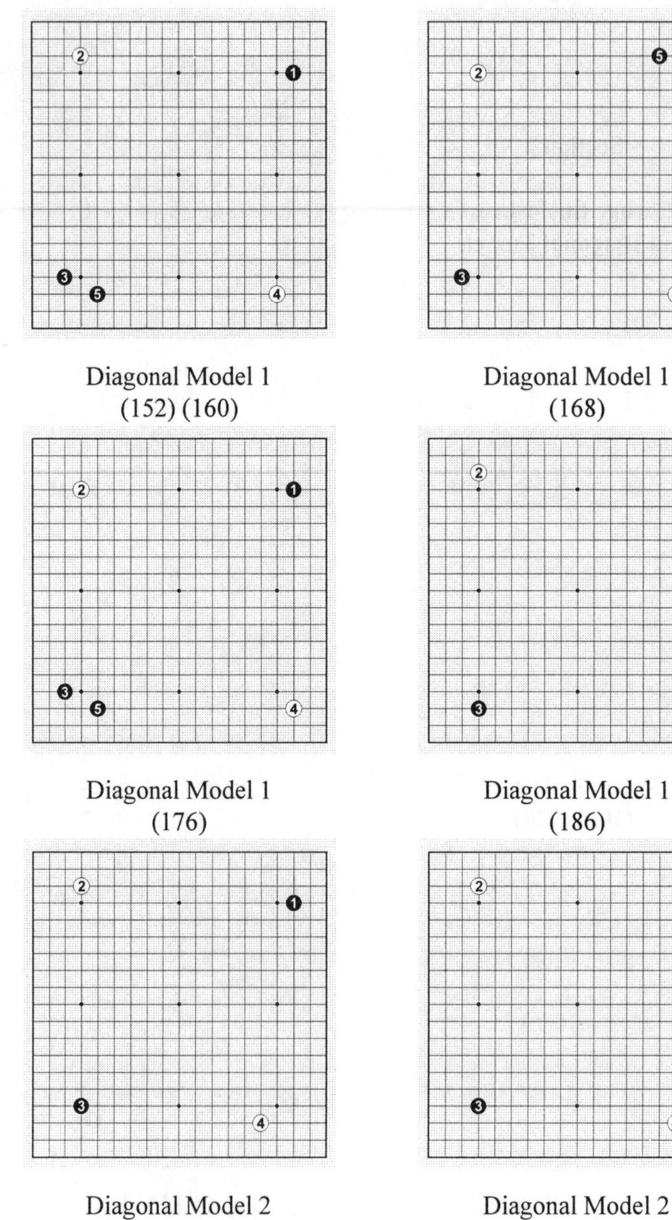

Diagonal Model 1
(152) (160)

Diagonal Model 1
(168)

Diagonal Model 1
(176)

Diagonal Model 1
(186)

Diagonal Model 2
(196)

Diagonal Model 2
(204) (212)

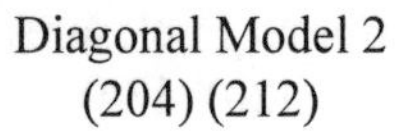

Section 3

Parallel Models

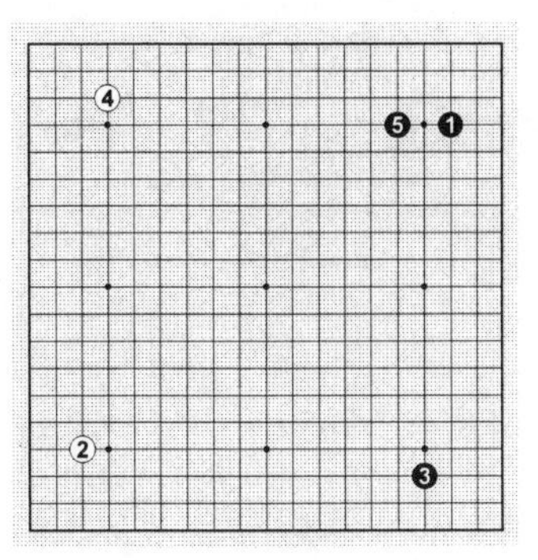

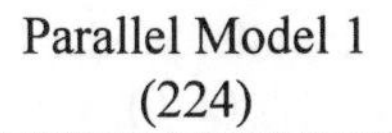

Parallel Model 1
(224)

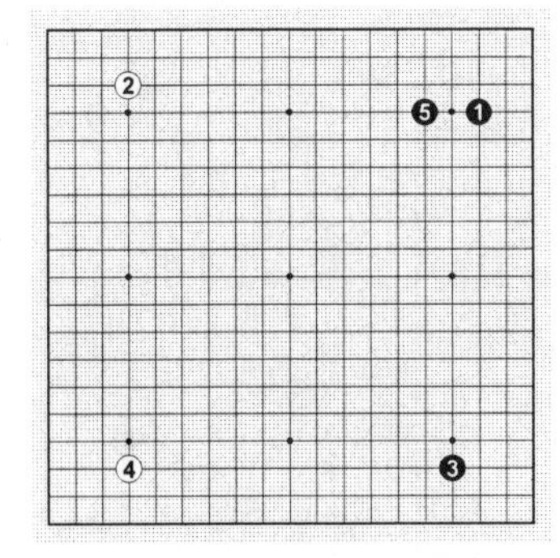

Parallel Model 1
(232)

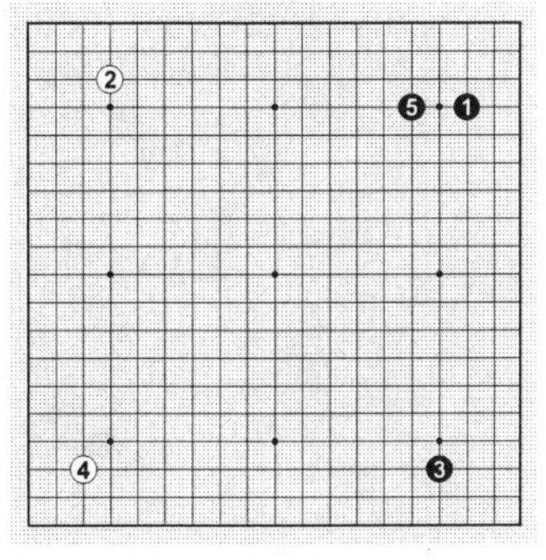

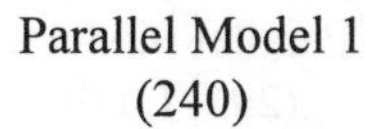

Parallel Model 1
(240)

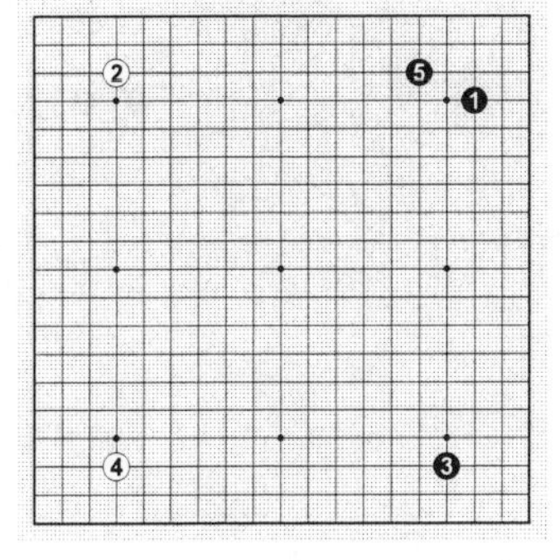

Parallel Model 1
(250) (258)

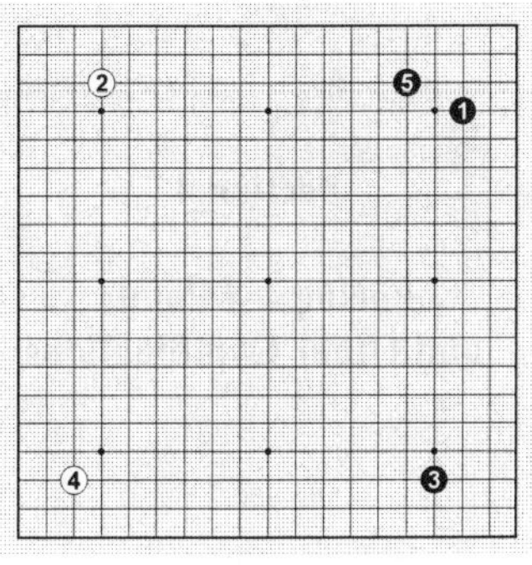

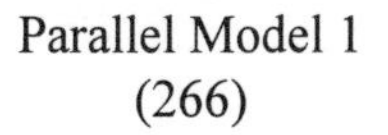

Parallel Model 1
(266)

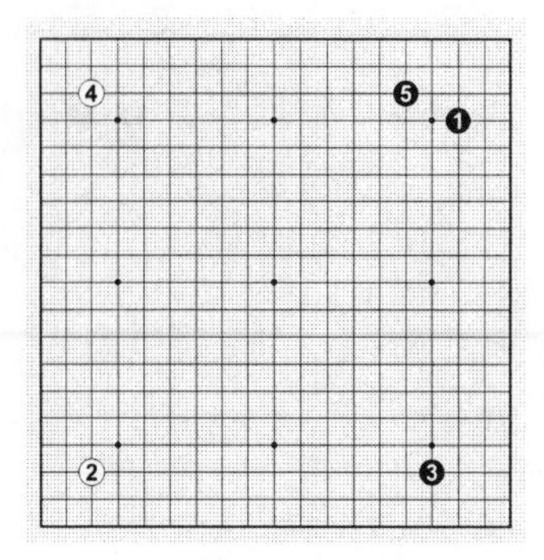

Parallel Model 1
(276)

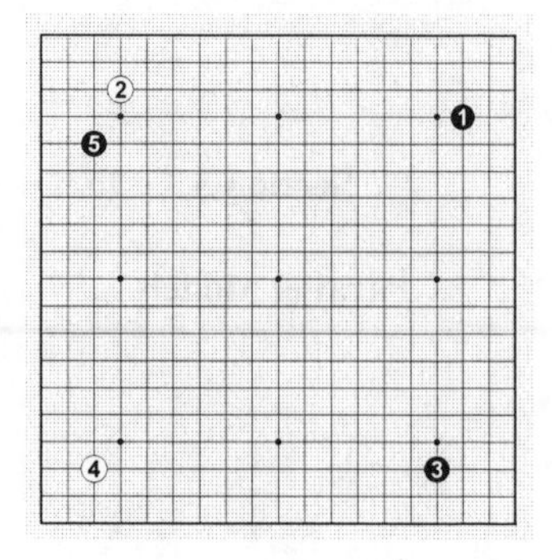

Parallel Model 1
(284)

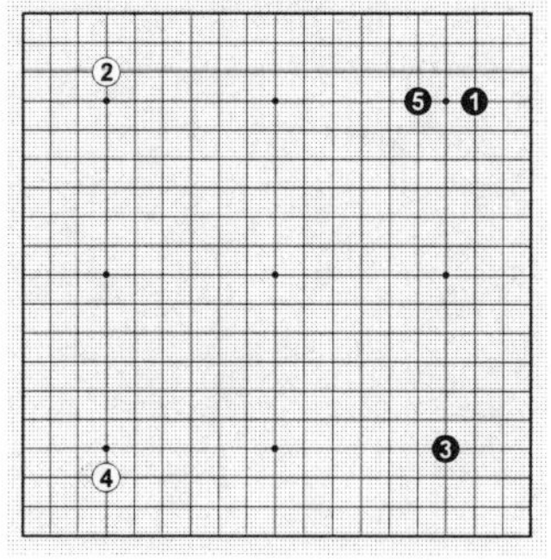

Parallel Model 2
(292) (300)

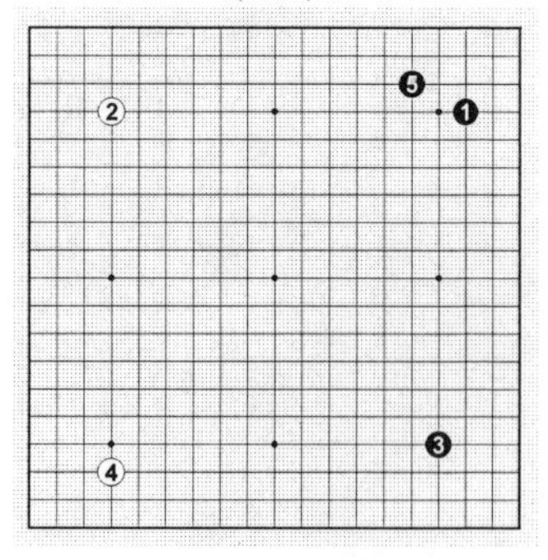

Parallel Model 2
(308) (318)

Section 4

**Facing 3-4 Points
and Other Combinations**

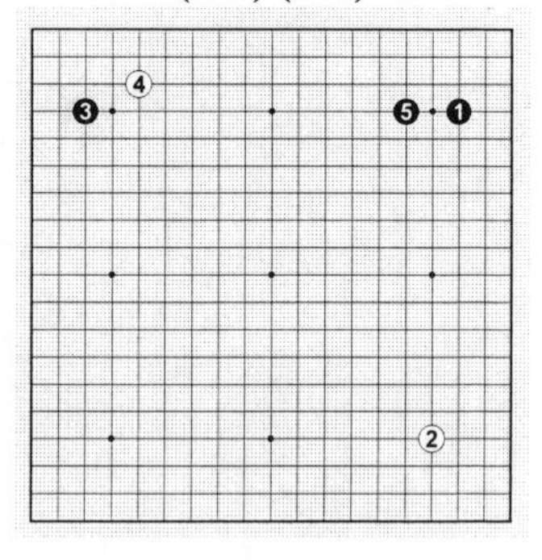

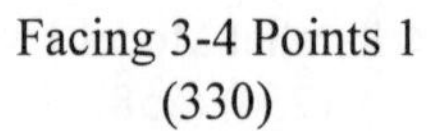

Facing 3-4 Points 1
(330)

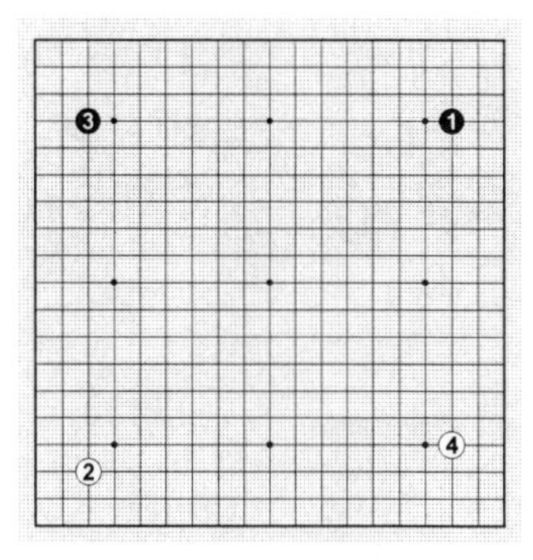

Facing 3-4 Points 1
(338)

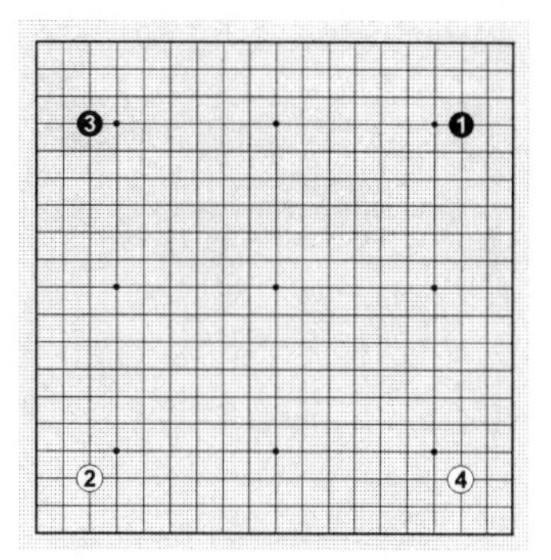

Facing 3-4 Points 1
(346)

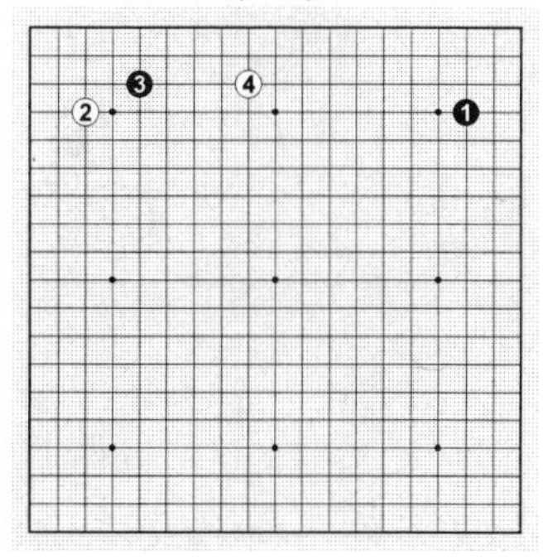

Facing 3-4 Points 2
(354) (364)

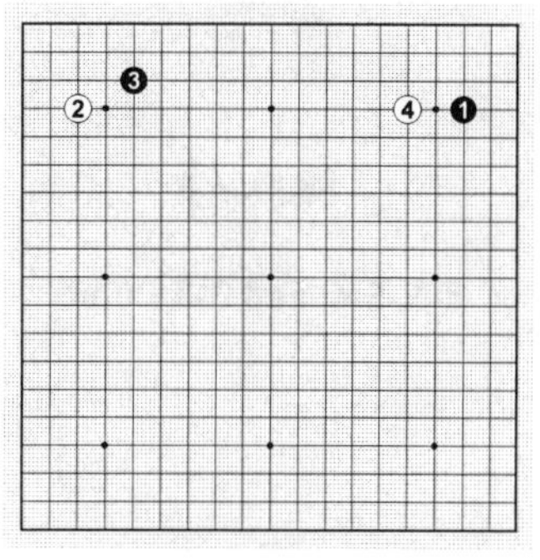

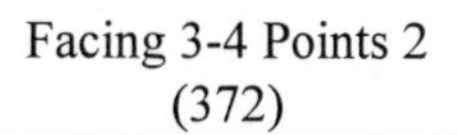

Facing 3-4 Points 2
(372)

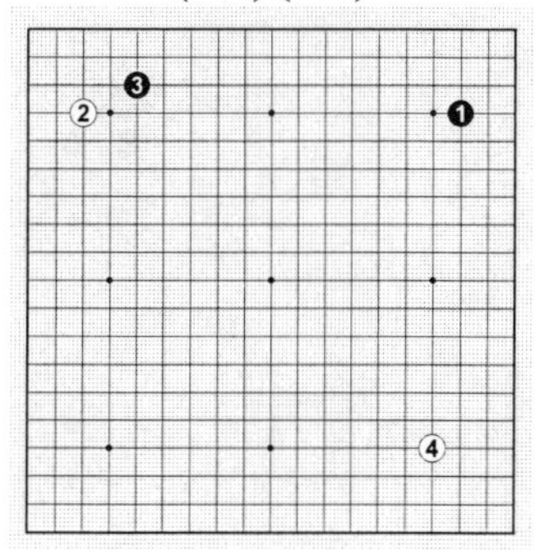

Facing 3-4 Points 2
(382)

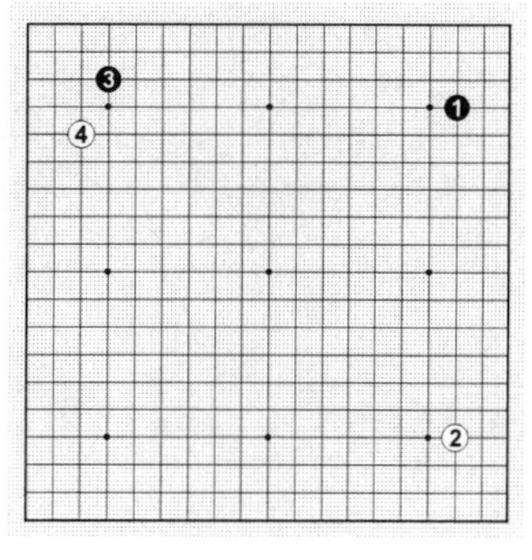

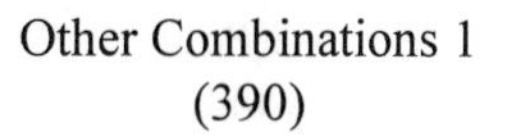

Other Combinations 1
(390)

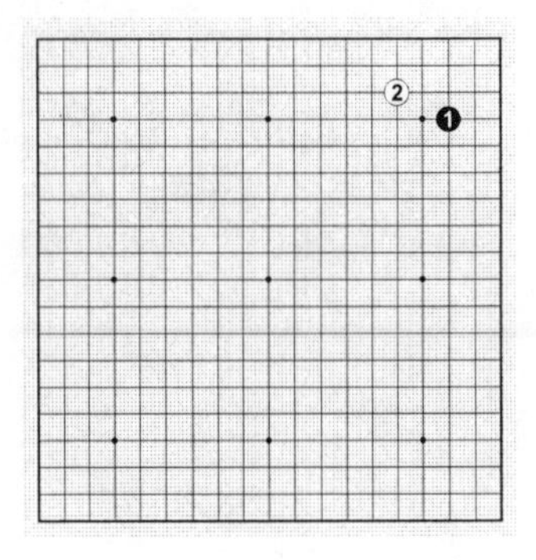

Other Combinations 2
(400)

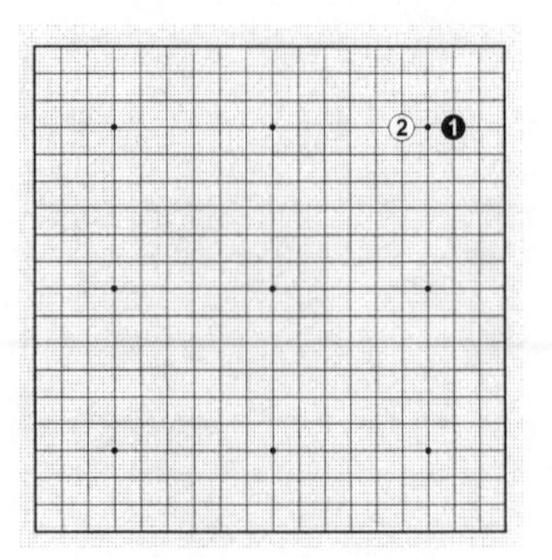

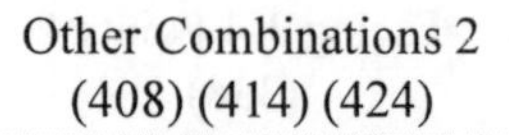

Other Combinations 2
(408) (414) (424)

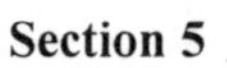

Section 5

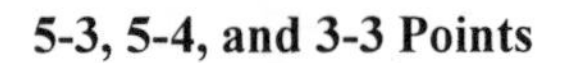

5-3, 5-4, and 3-3 Points

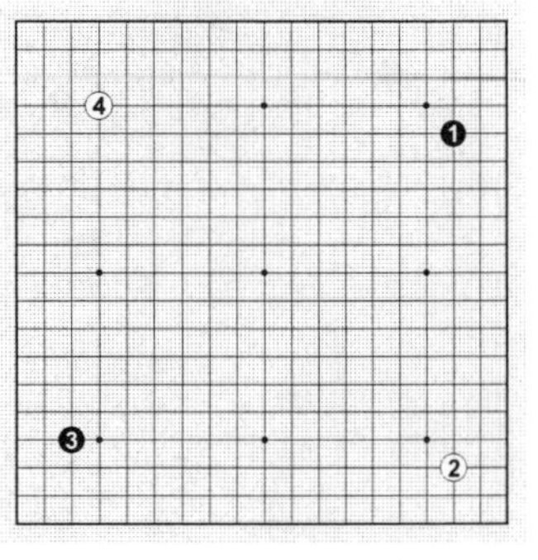

5-3 Point
(436)

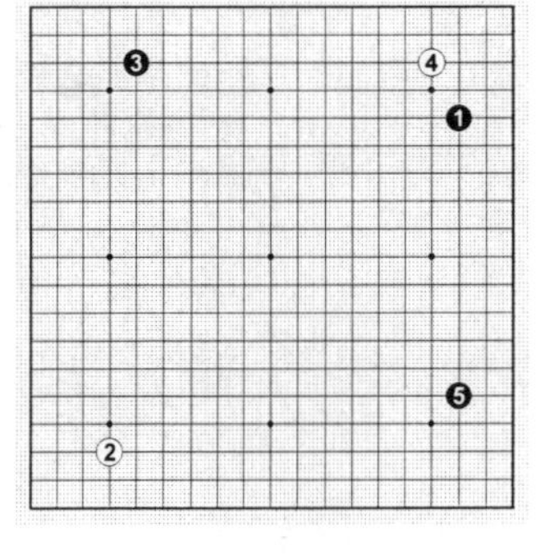

5-3 Point
(444)

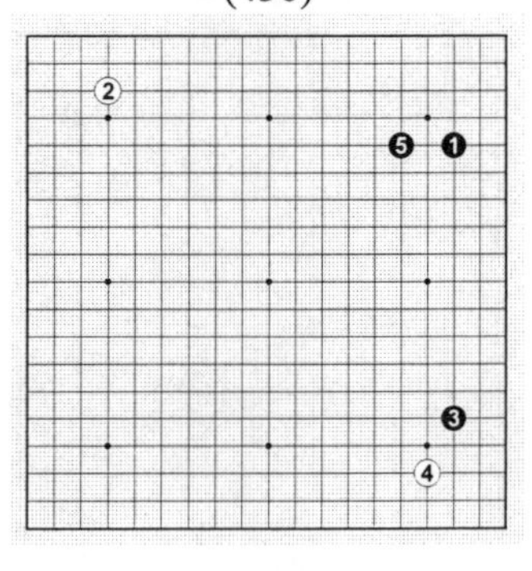

5-3 Point
(452)

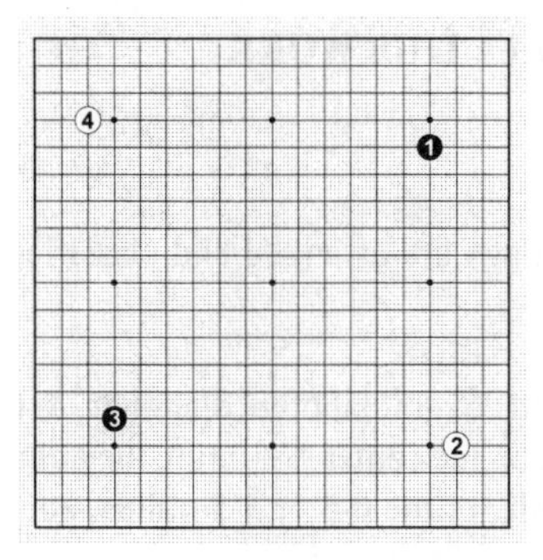

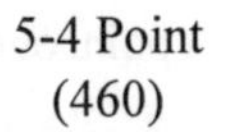

5-4 Point
(460)

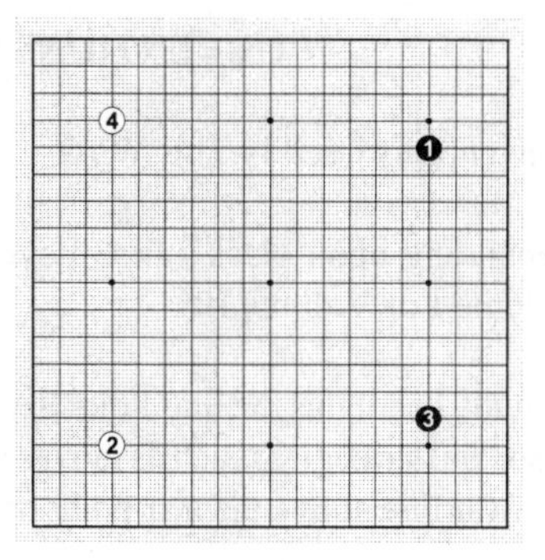

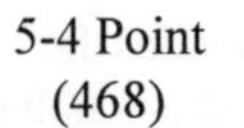

5-4 Point
(468)

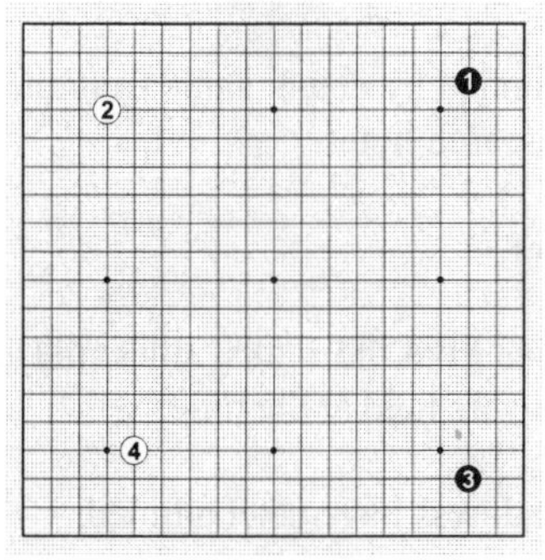

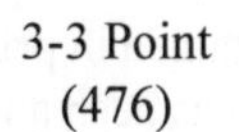

3-3 Point
(476)

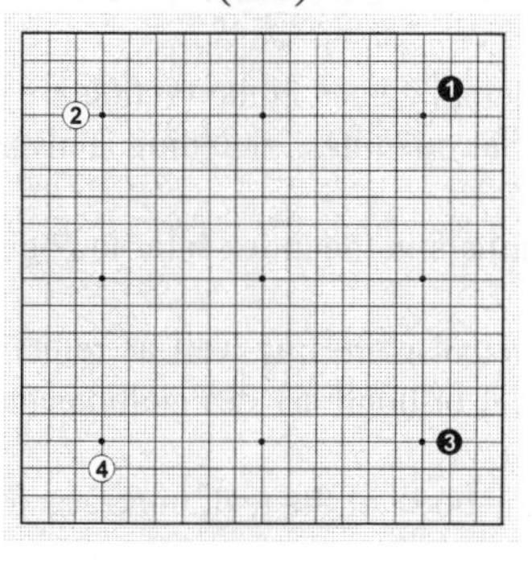

3-3 Point
(484)

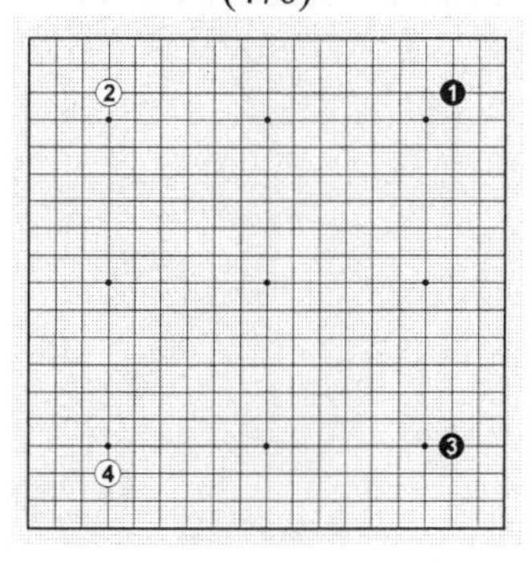

3-3 Point
(492)

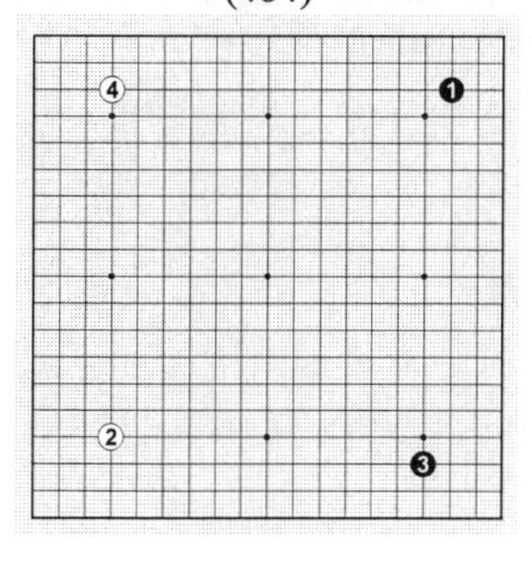

3-3 Point
(500)

CONVENTIONS USED IN THIS WORK

Conventions Used in This Work

Depending upon black's first move, openings are arranged and classified in Volume I or Volume II.

Volume I contains the Star Point Section and covers star point openings, as well as special strategies (such as moves played on the center star point, the point on the fifth line above the star point on the side, or the 6-5 or 5-5 points, etc.)

Volume II contains the 3-4 Point Section and covers 3-4 point openings, as well as 5-3, 5-4 and 3-3 point moves, etc.

Principal games in the section are supplemented by actual game examples of similar openings, including analysis and research notes.

Numbers in the index refer to page numbers.

Principal games as well as reference games give the ranks, titles, personal names or honorary designations that the players held at the time.

In the body of the text, honorary forms of address have been omitted.

For the sake of convenience in locating analysis contained in principal games, an appendix covering both Volume I and Volume II has been added at the end of this manual.

SECTION 1

SHUSAKU STYLE

THE FOUNTAINHEAD OF THE SHUSAKU STYLE

As an opening of recent times which has had a profound influence on contemporary go, the Shusaku Style is one of the model patterns, the theory of which was established in the waning years of the Edo Period. Representative of the opening play up until that point were games between Genjo (11th hereditary Honinbo) and Chitoku (8th hereditary Yasui) contested in the time period from 1789 to 1830. Those were the so-called true method openings, but in that pattern, both white and black occupies diagonal 3-4 points, and from there the game develops from the corner to the side, a localized opening fighting method. The theory of full board development through opening configuration had yet to be created.

The Shusaku Style pushed the theory of a forced win for black to the fore, and was an epochal opening that systematically dealt with the board from all angles. With the first, second and third plays distributed in a circulatory pattern on 3-4 points and the seventh a diagonal play in the upper right corner, or else a one point corner enclosure in the lower right or left, the intention was to maintain the advantage of playing first. The special feature was that the direction of white's corner attacks was steered in a uniform manner, a solid strategy to develop while engaging those attacks to minimize complications.

It is not clear who originally made the 1, 3 and 5 plays of the Shusaku Style. Here the context of the course of progress leading up to the establishment of this opening method of Kuwahara Shusaku (1829-1862; 14th hereditary Honinbo successor) is traced through game figures.

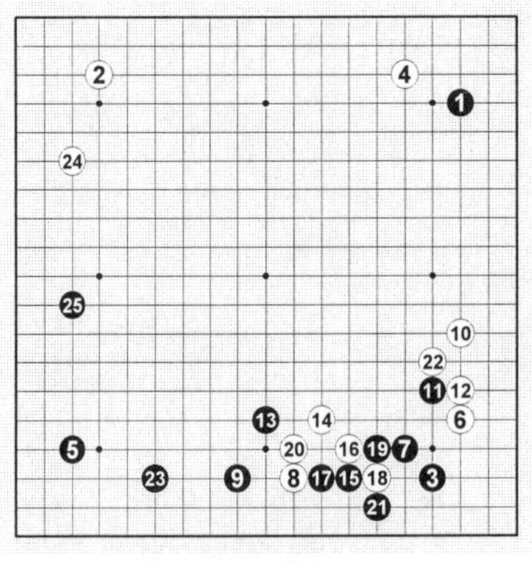

Reference Figure 1

Reference Figure 1 - [Castle Game; 1809; White: Inoue Inseki (9th hereditary Shunsaku); Black: Hayashi Tetsugen (10th hereditary Monnyu)] This is not sufficient evidence to designate this player as the originator, but Hayashi Tetsugen (10th hereditary Monnyu) experimented with the 1, 3 and 5 opening in this Castle Game, and when white attacked the corner at 6, black made the diagonal play at 7 in this corner.

From 1789 through 1830, the go world was at the height of prosperity, and in 1809 the House of Honinbo leadership passed from the 10th

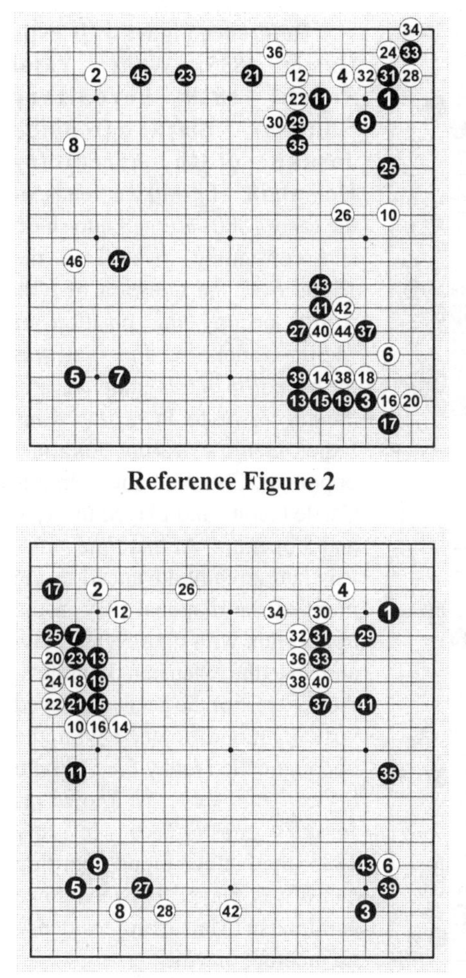

Reference Figure 2

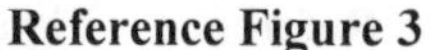

Reference Figure 3

hereditary Honinbo Retsugen to the 11th hereditary Honinbo Genjo. The next year, 1810, one of the opponents in this game, Shunsaku Inseki, passed away to be succeeded by Insa, the 11th hereditary Inoue. At length, Tetsugen became the 10th hereditary Hayashi and made Funabashi Gemmi of the House of Honinbo the successor of the House of Hayashi. All of this was hectic trends of the time.

In 1805, Tetsugen became the successor to the House of Hayashi at the age of 21 and 2 dan in strength, and began appearing in Castle Games. Far from being top class, he played with a two stone handicap and did not have notable success within the House of Hayashi, so the go world took little note of his opening in this game. However, it is interesting that twenty years before the birth of Shusaku, and 34 years before it was formally introduced, he originally played the Shusaku Style and left the record of it in this publicly played game.

Reference Figure 2 - [1813; White: Kadono Jowa (Meijin, 12th hereditary Honinbo); Black: Hattori Rittetsu (11th hereditary Inoue, Genan Inseki)] Four years after that, 16 year old Genan Inseki, known as Rittetsu, played the Shusaku Style against his opponent, Jowa. The one point corner enclosure of black 7 and diagonal play of 9, etc., embodied the progenitor of the Shusaku Style. Genan was young with a reputation of being brilliant, so this experiment no doubt became a topic of conversation of the day.

Reference Figure 3 - [1826; White: Yasui Sanchi (8th hereditary Chitoku); Black: Inoue Inseki (Genan)] With black 7, the game became one in which all corners were attacked. In relation with 7, 9 was an interesting play, and this game became one of Genan's triumphs.

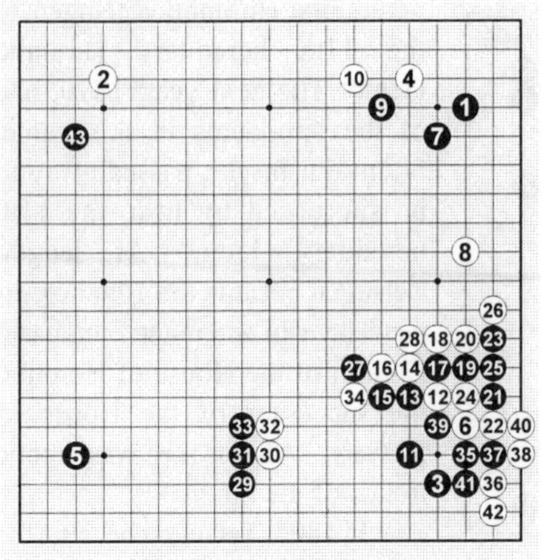

Reference Figure 4

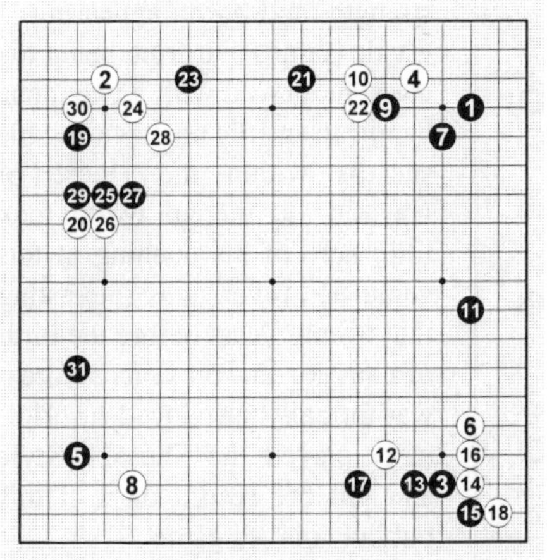

Reference Figure 5

Reference Figure 4 - [Castle Game; 1835; White: Yasui Senchi (8th hereditary Chitoku); Black: Honinbo Josaku (13th hereditary Honinbo)] The hidden feuds of the early 1800s erupted into sharp and continuing discord in the 1830s over the question of who would occupy the position of Meijin-Godokoro, and that was the backdrop of this game. Josaku, the successor to Jowa, faced his father Genjo's worthy longtime opponent, Chitoku Sanchi, in this Castle Game, and played the 1, 3 and 5 opening. At that time, analysis had already advanced to the point of the diagonal play in the upper right with the seventh play, and up to the extension of white 8, the progress of the game displayed virtually no difference with the opening called today the Shusaku Style. This game is known as Josaku's masterpiece. In July 1835, the famous blood vomiting game was played between Jowa and Intetsu (Matsudaira residence go meeting place).

Reference Figure 5 - [Nijubango, Game 6; 1843; White: Kadano Chuzaemon (12th hereditary Inoue, Setsuzan Inseki); Black: Kuwahara Shusaku (Honinbo successor)] The year that he was 15, Shusaku used this opening for the first time, following which he began to devote his energy into systematically developing the practical application of the Shusaku Style. The diagonal play of black 7, the fencing-in tactic of 9, and then the pincer at 11 on the right side, made ideal shape, and this is the basic pattern of the Shusaku Style. While avoiding complications, his theory of fighting in actual games was designed to take the lead over the whole board in the opening, and this smart way of thinking and outstanding results bowled over the go world. Gradually, he forged his way to the top position of the strongest

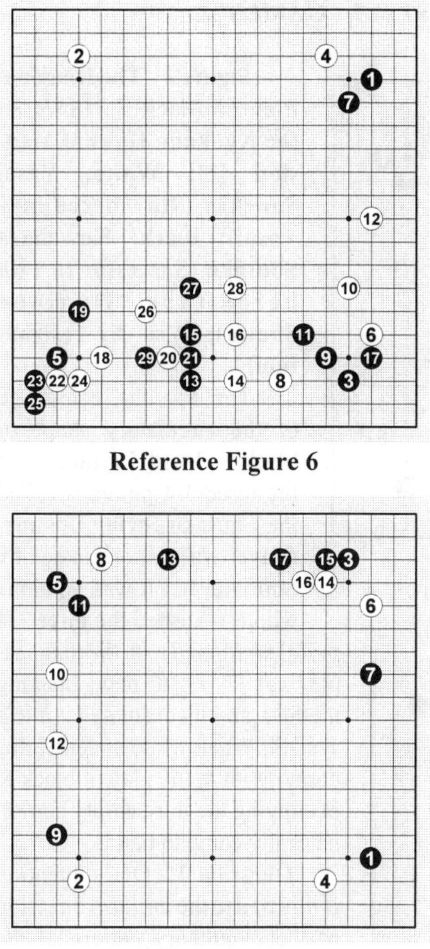

Reference Figure 6

Reference Figure 7

player active. Regardless of the extant game records of his predecessors and hints that he might have received, it must be said that to be able to systematize that theory was, after all, due to his talent and effort.

In 1846, Shusaku played against Genan Inseki in Osaka and experimented with the Shusaku Style. That game record is shown in **Reference Figure 2** on page 35, in which he incurred a painful position while playing against Genan's Taisha joseki, but cut through the difficulties in the game with the exquisite play known as the "ear-reddening play," winning the game and widespread fame. Seeing black playing the Shusaku Style, Genan must have thought about the schemes and maneuvers that he had come up with when he was young and had mixed feelings.

Reference Figure 6 - [1847; White: Honinbo Shuwa; Black: Kuwahara Shusaku] He played 1, 3 and 5 in this game against his teacher, Shuwa. In response to the diagonal play of black 7, white 8 and 10 bespeak painstaking effort to counter the Shusaku Style. In fact, Shuwa was a player who enjoyed using the Shusaku Style.

Reference Figure 7 - [White: Honinbo Sanetsu (2nd hereditary Honinbo); Black: Doetsu (3rd hereditary Honinbo)] Putting aside the question of the time period, between 1648 and 1658, the 1, 3 and 5 opening appeared in a teacher/student game contested by the 2nd and 3rd Honinbo. It can only be characterized as surprising that this maneuver was used in the early days of the Edo Period [1600-1868].

SHUSAKU STYLE - GAME 1

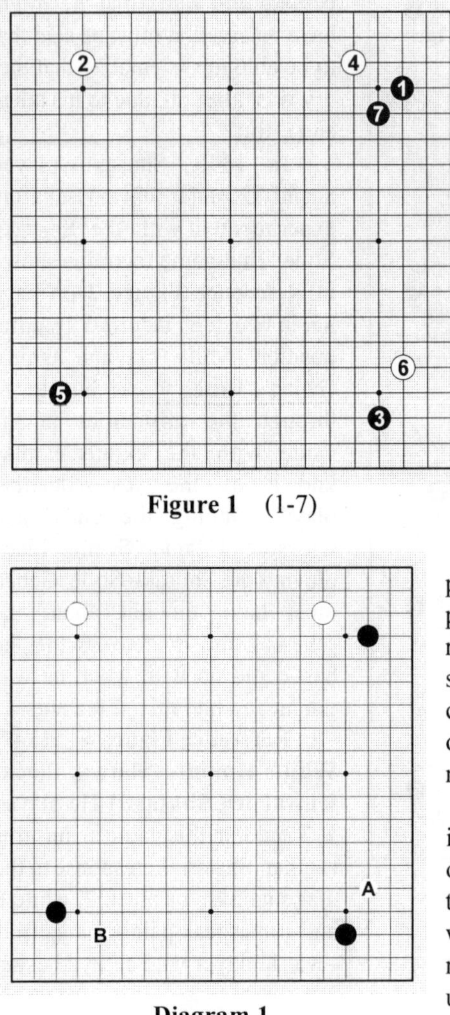

Figure 1 (1-7)

Diagram 1

Figure 1 - The Diagonal Play of Black 7 [1847; At the Kyukaiin Hanshu Mansion [?]; White: Yasui Sanchi (9th hereditary Yasui); Black: Kuwahara Shusaku (Successor to 14th hereditary Honinbo Shuwa); Wins by resignation]

The opening comprised of the circulatory shape of black 1, 3 and 5 arranged on the three 3-4 points is called the Shusaku Style. This maneuver was not originated by Shusaku, but it was he alone who established the three 3-4 points combined with the diagonal play of 7 as a new opening method, and incorporated it into a system. When white attacked this corner with 4, the play of black 5, occupying the third empty corner, naturally came to hand.

Diagram 1 - One's attention is directed to the uniform direction of the circulatory pattern of the three 3-4 points. This restricts white to a corner attack at **A**, or **B**, making it easy for black to come up with a strategy to counter those plays, a feature that makes this opening formation a superior one.

Then, in response to white's attack on the corner at 6, the diagonal play of black 7 is designed to be solid, and is a play that has the implication of avoiding complications. In the contemporary game, the burden of the komi on black means that 7 is more often aggressively played as a pincer against white's stone at 4, but in those days if black could win by 3 points it was fine. So the thing

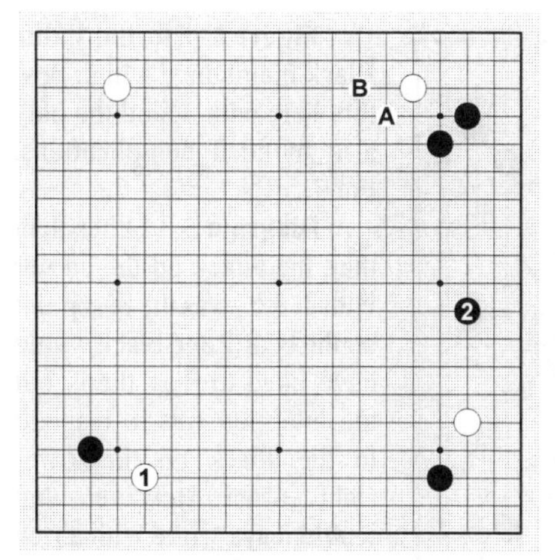

Diagram 2

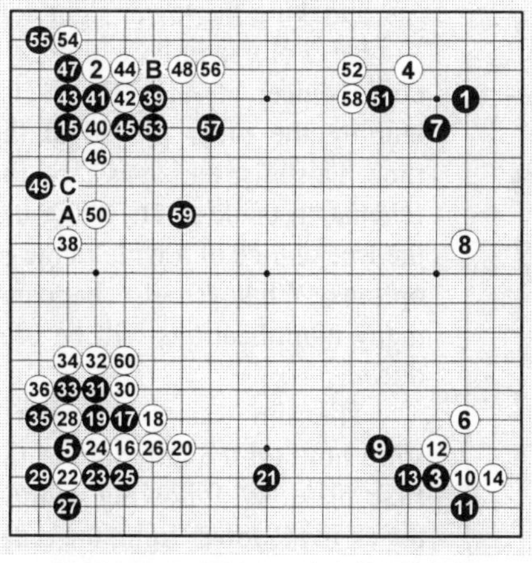

Reference Figure 1 (37@28)

most desired was to avoid allowing white the scope to initiate complicated maneuvers.

Diagram 2 - In regards to this diagonal play, if white turns elsewhere to play, such as at 1, the black extension at 2 is ideal, combining a pincer with a territorial play. This is the best point on the board. Black can play the fencing-in tactic at **A** in exchange for the white defensive play at **B**, making that build up and the distance between 2 great.

Reference Figure 1 - [1846; White: Inoue Inseki (11th hereditary Inoue, Genan); Black: Kuwahara Shusaku (Honinbo successor)] Black attached at 17 and drew back at 19, then the pincer of 21 was a painstaking play of Shusaku's. The plays through 37 comprise a contemporary joseki. For white 38, a connection at 60 would obviously invite the extension of black **A**. White 48 was interesting. Here, if **B** was played, black 53, white 56 and black **C** would ensue.

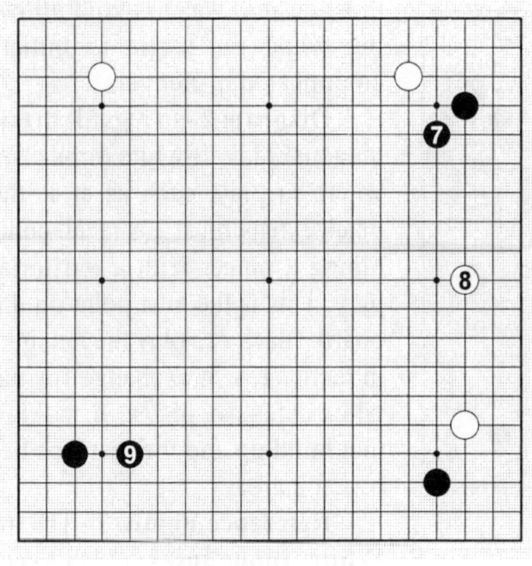

Figure 2 (7-9)

Figure 2 - Eternal Value Black maintained a high posture here with 7, and the play also avoided complications. For 7,

Diagram 3 - Other than that, the attack on the corner with 1, etc., was the best point on the board, and black would have liked to play there, but the intention was to respond to the attack on the lower right corner. However, that would leave white with a rich selection of options to use in conjunction with the stone attacking the lower right corner. For example, white could pincer at **A** or **B**, or else employ the often played at the time Taisha joseki at **C**, or the fencing-in tactic at **D**. White has the free choice of a wide range of options. Whatever else happens, many complications will be produced.

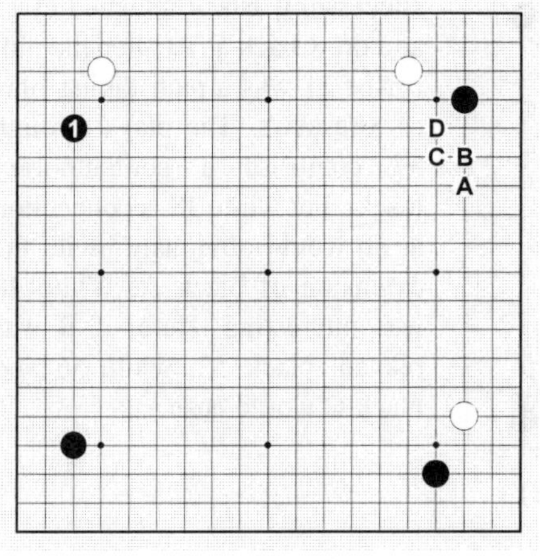

Diagram 3

The aim was to preserve a solid hold on the initiative of the first play, so following white's attack in the lower right, the diagonal play of black 7 was the most simple and direct.

"After this, no matter how much the technical skill in go progresses, as long as the game is played on a 19 by 19 line board, this diagonal play will never be bad."

These have been passed down as the words of Shusaku.

Although the advent of the komi altered the nature of the opening, this play has eternal value, and the truth of that statement is unchanged.

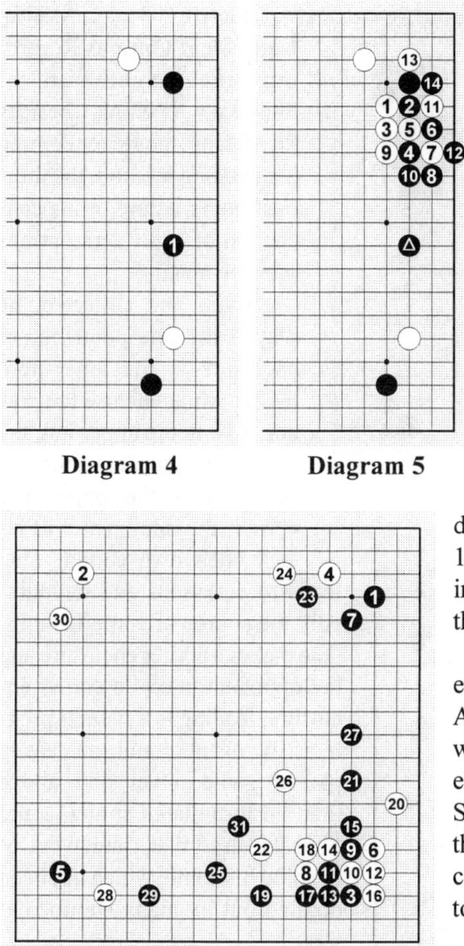

Diagram 4

Diagram 5

Reference Figure 2

Diagram 4 - Not playing the diagonal play and immediately making the pincer of black 1 was indeed not impossible, but the continuation in the next diagram was possible, so this is not correct shape.

Diagram 5 - In olden times, Dosaku (Meijin, 4th hereditary Honinbo) often used this maneuver, making the fencing-in tactic of white 1, then the atari of 7 and 9, and the forcing tactics of 13 and black 14. This joseki is not satisfactory. Black ▲ is a duplication of effort with 8 and 10. First black diagonally, gaining a higher posture, then making the pincer is correct.

Since the pincer is ideal, the extension of white 8 was ideal. Almost all of go is played this way. Here black made the corner enclosure at 9, a typical play of Shusaku's. One's eye is drawn by the attacking play in the upper left corner, but it was deemed all right to permit white to play there.

Reference Figure 2 - [1849; White: Ito Showa; Black: Kuwahara Shusaku (Honinbo successor)] Here is an example of the black diagonal play of 7 answered by the Taisha fencing-in tactic of white 8. The plays through black 27 comprise the usual joseki, but in distinction to the Genan Inseki joseki on page 35, the maneuvers here show no special scheme by white, who thereby fell into difficulties. The surrounding black stones worked effectively.

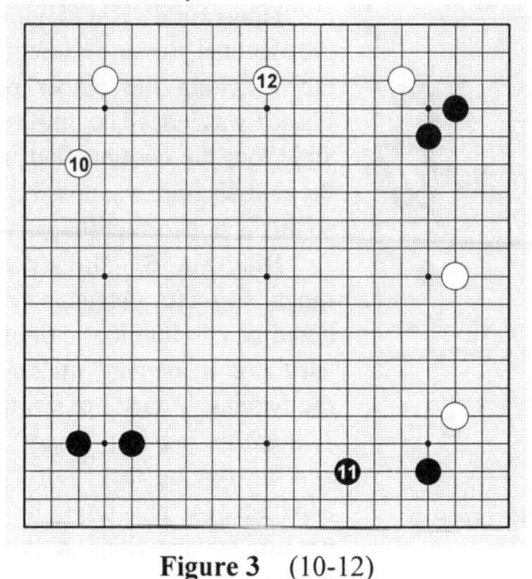

Figure 3 (10-12)

Figure 3 - Skillful Equivalent Options Regarding the excellence of Shusaku's opening, besides the details above concerning his opening method, the thoroughgoing nature of his conception of equivalent options must be noted.

Calm and collected, he played the one point corner enclosure in the lower left, letting white enclose the corner at 10 in the upper left, the so-called equivalent option. If one attacks the opponent's corner, the opponent will attack one's own corner. That leads to variations and undoubtedly the source of complications. One makes a corner enclosure and the opponent makes a corner enclosure, leading to a natural progress of events, and an easily played game. Over and above that, he formulated strategy, and Shusaku used that framework to develop his game, which has been pointed out by many commentators.

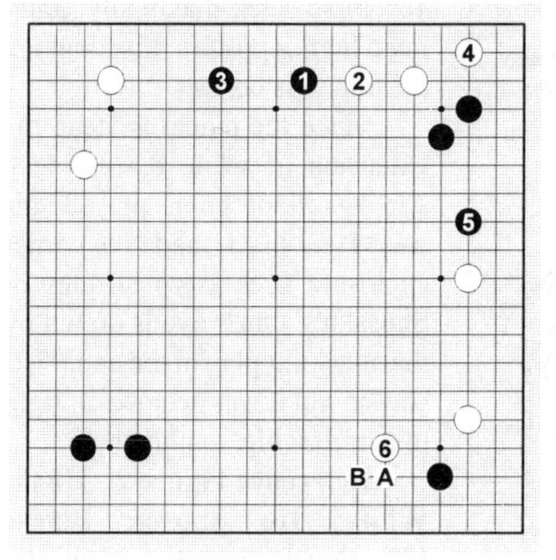

Diagram 6

Then, black built the position with the two point extension at 11 in the lower right, allowing white to take the big point on the upper side, which was not small. That also set up the next equivalent option.

For black 11, more intense players might consider that instead of this play,

Diagram 6 - Splitting the upper side at 1 would also make a pincer on white's stone. It was natural for black to think of the follow-up to the diagonal play at 7, but after white 2 and 4, black ends in gote with 5. Then white plays the Taisha play at 6, or else has the option of playing schemes at **A** or **B**, etc., in the lower right. Black disregarded the obvious big point and played his own way. This is the kind of skill that cannot be imitated.

There was a meaning to the two point extension of 11.

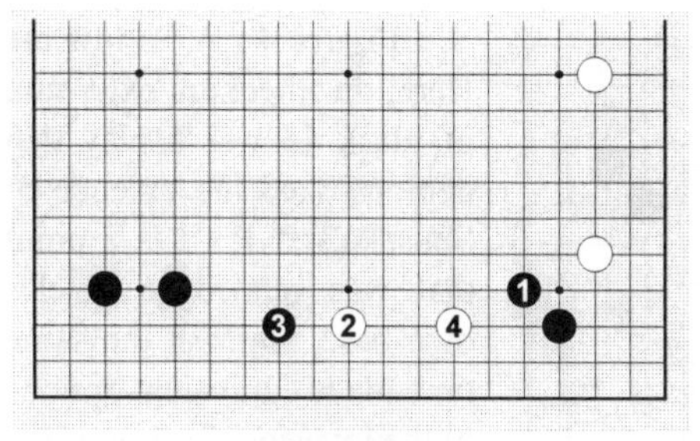

Diagram 7

Diagram 7 - The diagonal play of 1 was also possible, but that allows white to make a base on the lower side at 2 and 4. To prevent that, black played the good two point extension in the figure.

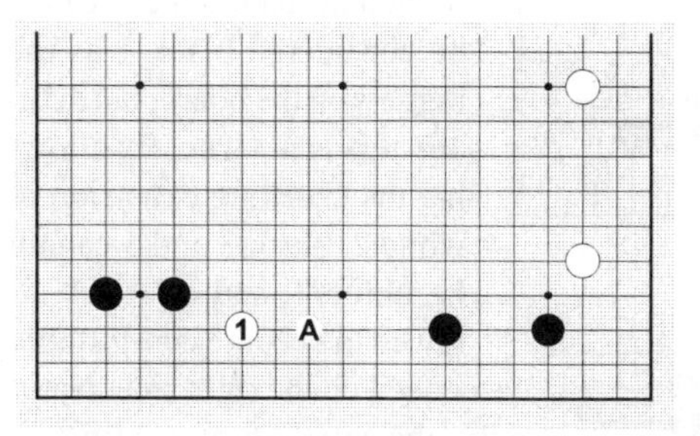

Diagram 8

Diagram 8 - Once the two point extension is in place, white has no way to attack the corner except with the attack at 1. As shown in the following figure, black can look forward to attacking with the pincer at **A**.

Hopefully the reader can see the strategy developing play by play.

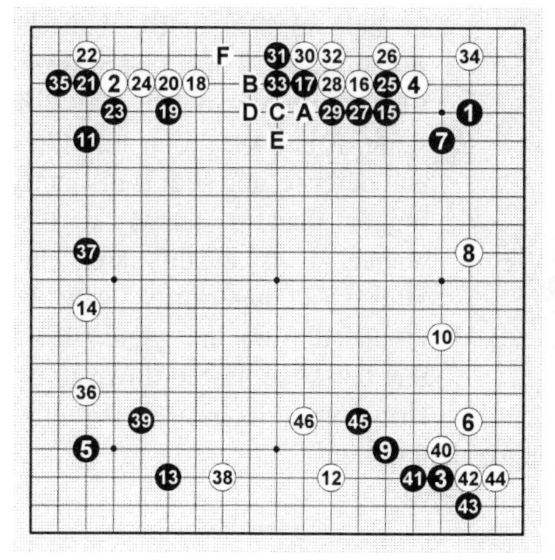

Reference Figure 3

Reference Figure 3 - [1851; White: Honinbo Shuwa (14th hereditary Honinbo); Black: Kuwahara Shusaku (Honinbo successor)] In this game, black made the knight's play at 9, permitting white to surround territory at 10, then attacked the corner at 11. Black made the exchanges from 19 through white 24, then embarked on a strategy with 25 through 31. If white used 32 to cut at 33, black would play **A**, white 32, black **B**, white **C**, black **D**, white **E** and black **F**, and white is badly off since the groups on both sides are under attack.

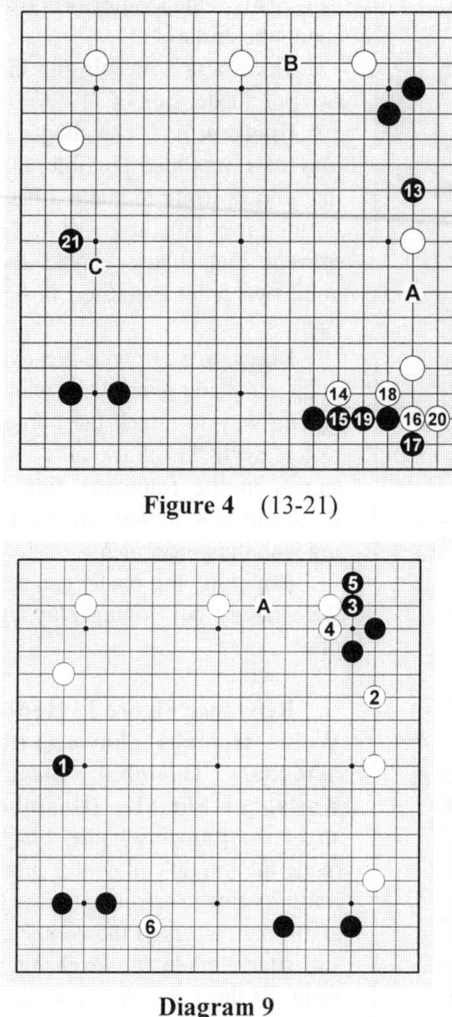

Figure 4 (13-21)

Diagram 9

Figure 4 - A Solid Line Here, the checking extension of black 13 was a play that demonstrated the essence of Shusaku's style. It is a point that was related to black's own base, while at the same time made equivalent options of the invasions at **A** and **B**.

Diagram 9 - The big point that catches the eye may be considered black 1 as the biggest on the board, but actually this is not true. By allowing the checking extension of white 2, black 3 and 5 cannot be omitted, and white is allowed to become comfortably ensconced on the right side. Naturally, the invasion at **A** remains, but once black has descended at 5, one way or another white would be able to deal deftly with the situation. More than that, it is terrible to allow white to play 2 in sente. It is a key point for attack and defense, and so it is distinctly bigger than it seems at first glance. It is in this area that Shusaku's superiority can be glimpsed from the game record that has been passed down to us. However, at its basis, it was supported by a way of thinking about equivalent options.

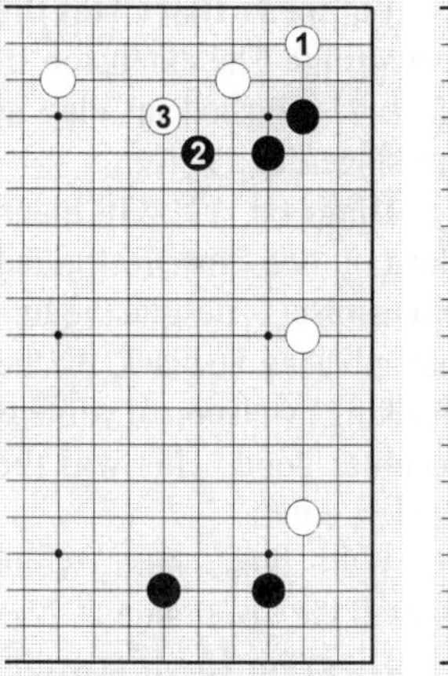

Diagram 10

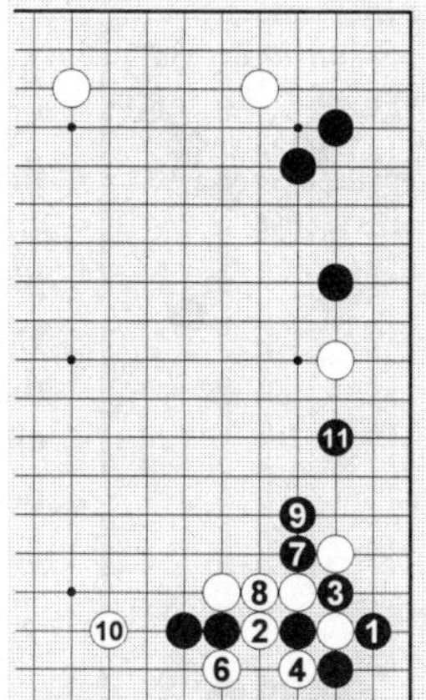

Diagram 11 (5below 3)

Diagram 10 - If black did not defend at 3 and 5 in the previous diagram, the slide of white 1 would be severe. Black 2 is answered by white 3, making territory while attacking, and also accumulating other smaller advantages, gaining more compensation than was given up. Black must avoid this continuation.

Once black made the checking extension, white had to immediately alleviate the threat of an invasion on the right side, and therefore made shape here with the skillful finesse of 14 through 20.

Diagram 11 - Instead of the connection of black 19, the hane of 1 is not unseen in actual games, but how should one evaluate the variation through 11? In the local context, this is playable for white.

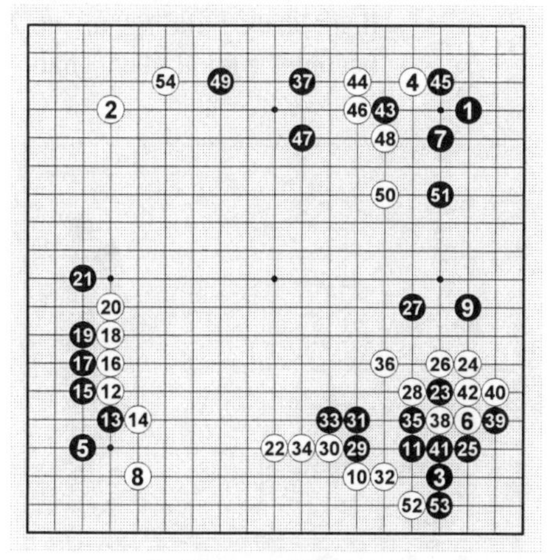

Reference Figure 4

The descent of white 20 was the true play. If white rushed to make the extension at **C**, considering the invasion of black **A**, the hane of 20 next would be severe.

With the lower right corner settled, black headed for the big point of 21 for the first time. This was a sufficient round of plays.

Reference Figure 4 - [Oteai Ranking Tournament, Spring Session; 1927; White: Suzuki Tamejiro 7 dan; Black: Iwamoto Kaoru 6 dan] Black was given the pincer of 9 so that white could play the Taisha play at 12. Iwamoto: "Since there was a star point stone in the upper left, I thought that jumping to black 21 was not bad." Suzuki: "For 35, I thought that black would play the fencing-in tactic at 36. White would find it difficult to live here."

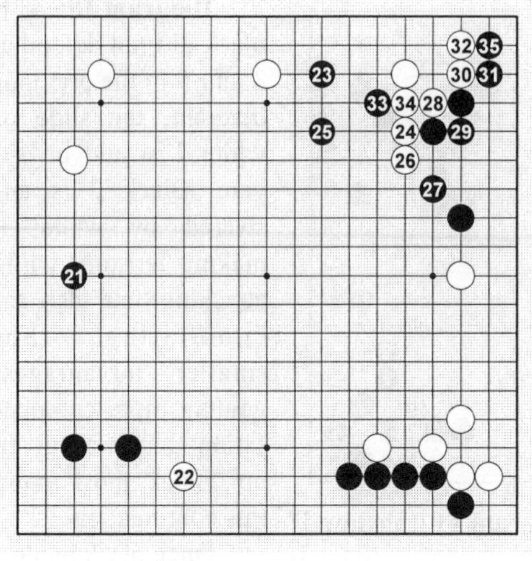

Figure 5 (21-35)

Figure 5 - Black Has the Advantage The extension of black 21 finished up play at this stage.

Diagram 12 - If black plays a one line restrained extension at 1, despite the further advance at black **A**, the checking extension of white **B** becomes good. This was the last big point.

Well then, here white entered the lower side at 22.

Diagram 13 - If possible white would like to surround territory on the upper side, but then black building up at 2 becomes a good play. That

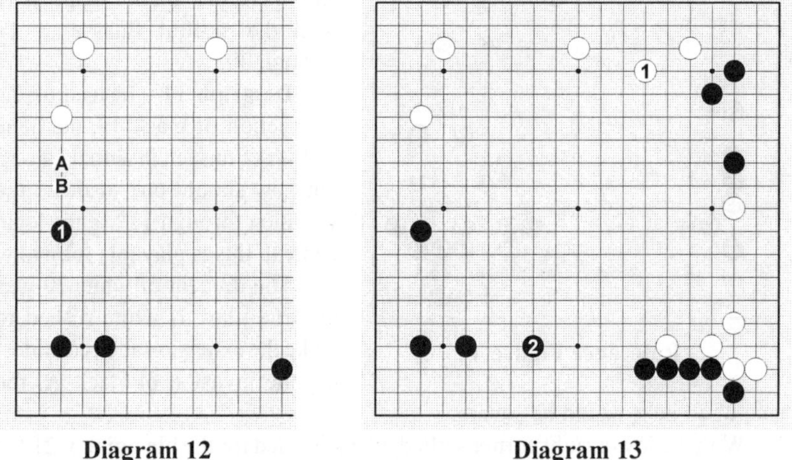

Diagram 12

Diagram 13

means that black's extensions on both sides of the one point corner enclosure are ideal, so this strategy of mutually surrounding territory from white's standpoint is akin to nonsense.

In that case, black must invade at 23, giving black another equivalent option. Following that, white is driven out under attack, making this a successful invasion by black.

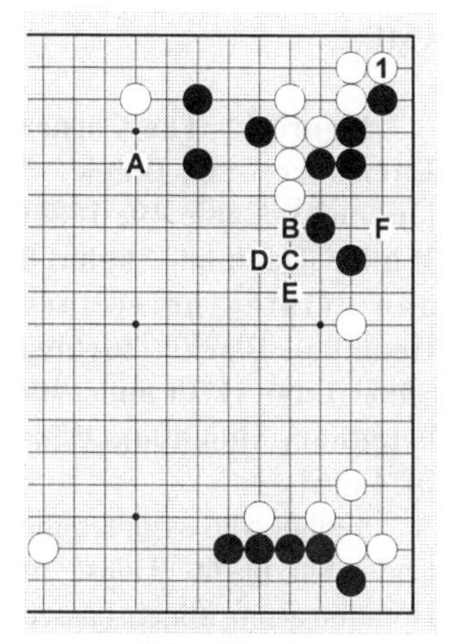

Diagram 14

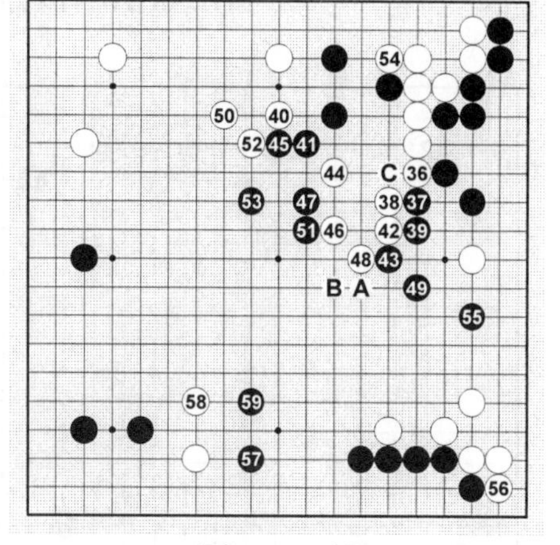

Diagram 15

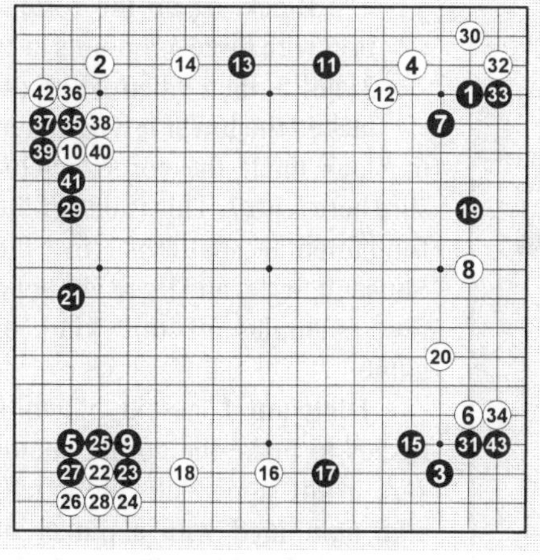

Reference Figure 5

Diagram 14 - For 35, black itches to play at **A**, but allowing white to block at 1 turns the tables of attack and defense. After that, white **B**, black **C**, white **D**, black **E**, and white aims at the placement of **F**.

Diagram 15 - Here is the further course of the actual game. For 54, white would have liked to surround the right side, but doing so would permit black to block at 54, aiming at cutting tactics with black **A**, white **B** and black **C**. Black took control of the stone on the right side with 55, making black's advantage obvious. When white played 56, black attacked with 57 and 59.

In this game the logical nature of Shusaku's play was striking.

Reference Figure 5 - [Oteai Ranking Tournament, Autumn Session; 1930; White: Maeda Nobuaki 4 dan; Black: Go Seigen 3 dan] This was the young Go when he first came to Japan. The Shusaku Style was a forte of his and he compiled a good record with it. The opening from black 11 through white 14 is often played. When white played 22, black took sente with 23 and the following plays, then turned to play 29. Go: "I thought that by making the checking extension here black was not bad off."

SHUSAKU STYLE - GAME 2

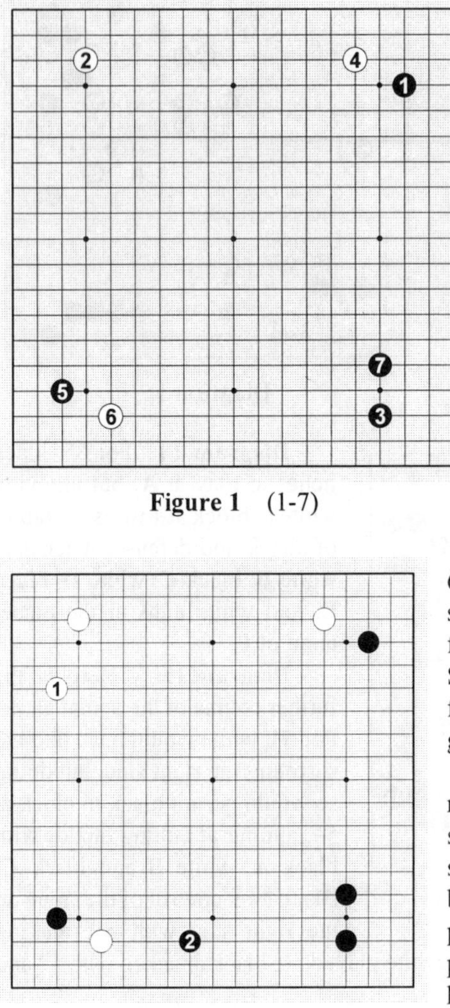

Figure 1 (1-7)

Diagram 1

Figure 1 - The Corner Enclosure of Black 7 [Jubango, Game 10; 1886; White: Honinbo Shuho 8 dan (18th hereditary Honinbo); Black: Tsuchiya Shuei 7 dan (17th and 19th hereditary Honinbo); Wins by 4 pts.]

Shuho, who assumed the leadership of the House of Honinbo from Shuei, passed away just two months later, and this was his last game.

Black set up the formation with three 3-4 points at 1, 3 and 5, then when white attacked the lower left corner at 6, black made the corner enclosure here with 7. This is one of the fundamental patterns in the Shusaku Style, and there are not a few examples of this kind of game.

Diagram 1 - Next, if white rushes to make the corner enclosure in the upper left, the extension combined with a pincer of black 2 is ideal, on a par with the pincer made after the diagonal play in the previous game, or perhaps even has a value greater than that. White will have trouble dealing with the lower side.

It is sufficient to let white take the initiative in the upper right corner.

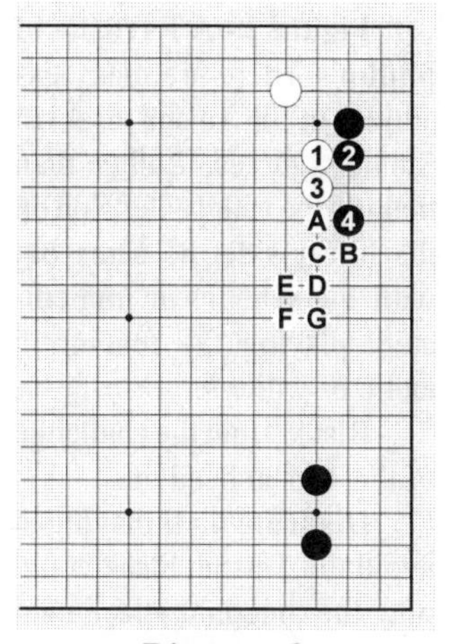

Diagram 2

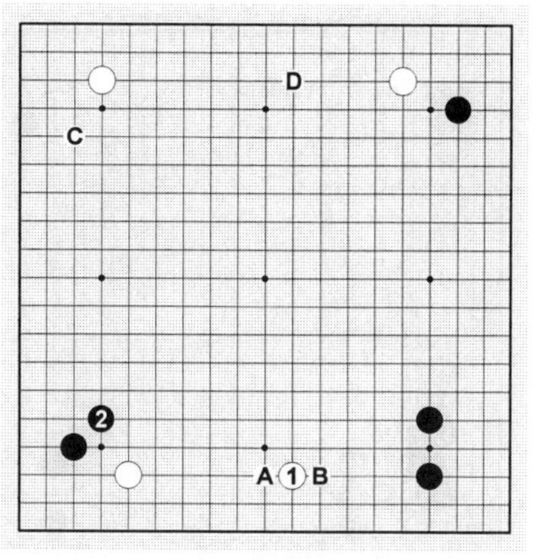

Diagram 3

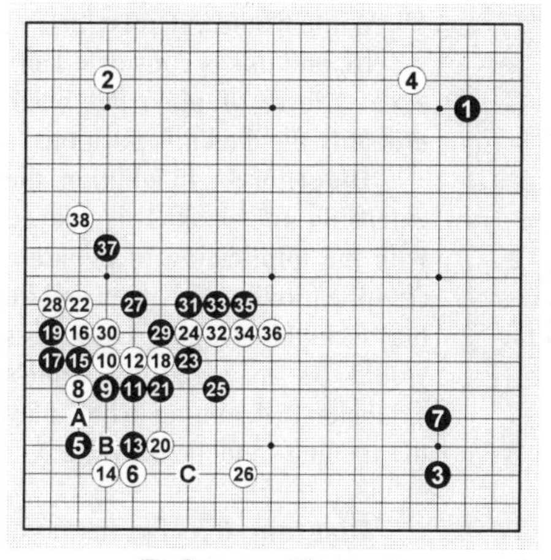

Reference Figure 1

Diagram 2 - If white plays the fencing-in tactic at 1, black 4 is good, and after that if white plays **A**, black **B** and pushes at white **C**, black replies with **D**, white **E** and the two-step hane of black **F**, or **F** can also be used to pull back at **G**. It is difficult for white to adopt the strategy of white 1 and the following plays.

Diagram 3 - If white were to make an extension on the lower side, it would probably be at 1 or else at **A**. If **A**, black can make the checking extension at **B**. Black links out with diagonal play at 2, and if white encloses the corner at **C**, black will probably pincer at **D** on the upper side. Naturally, 2 aims at invading white's position on the lower side, although the timing of that is a problem.

Reference Figure 1 - [1847; White: Honinbo Shuwa (14th hereditary Honinbo); Black: Kuwahara Shusaku (Successor to Shuwa)] White made the one point pincer at 8. At 16, white could capture two stones with **A**, black **B**, white 16, black 17 and white 19, but black would torment the corner with **C**, then turn to hane at 18, leaving white badly off. The plays through 26 probably comprised a new pattern at the time.

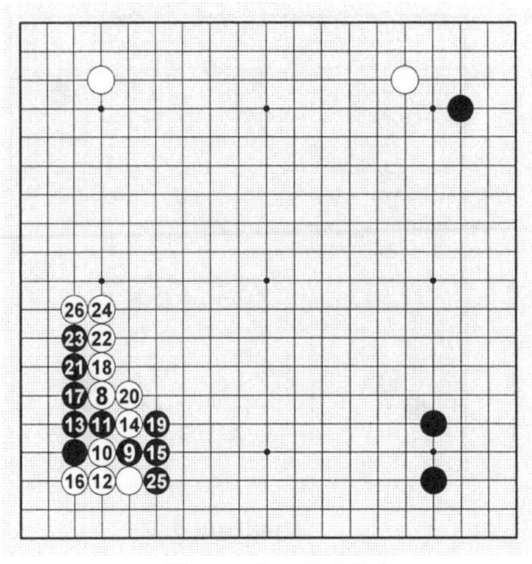

Figure 2 (8-26)

Figure 2 - A Favorite of Shuho's There are many examples of the Taisha joseki in Shuho's games. Rather than making the usual extension on the lower side, he came out with the scheme of immediately playing the fencing-in tactic of white 8.

Black 9 met the challenge of the Taisha head on.

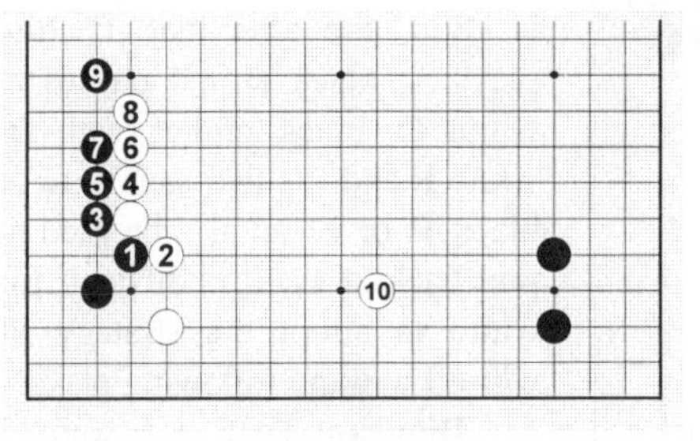

Diagram 4

Diagram 4 - If playing to avoid the Taisha, black could play the diagonal attachment of 1, followed by 3, leading to the plays up to the jump of 9. White would extend widely at 10, and this is considered an equal course of play, but black probably disliked this position.

Diagram 5 - In addition, the extension of black 1 is played with the implication of avoiding complications, and then white plays 2 and black jumps to 3. This would be answered by white's extension to 4, aiming to next play the fencing-in tactic of white **A**.

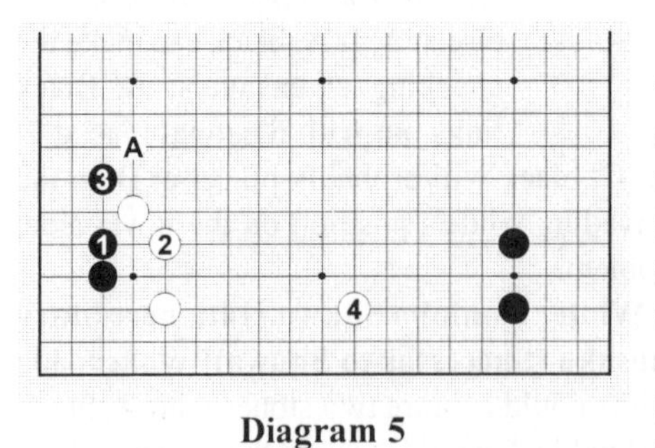

Diagram 5

Diagram 6 - Furthermore, when white cuts at 14, black plays atari on the outside at 1 and 3, and the sequence through 9 is one that is often seen in games from olden times. However, in the local context this joseki is considered somewhat disadvantageous for black since white makes the extension to 10. In contemporary games this maneuver is not often encountered. In this case, black allowing white to extend to 10 is terrible.

White played for the variation that starts by extending to 18.

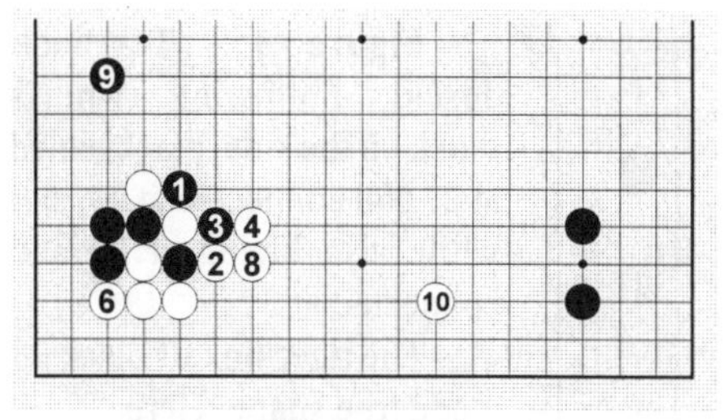

Diagram 6

Diagram 7 - With this play, connecting at 1 leads to the basic pattern of the Taisha with the plays through 8, but the corner enclosure in the lower right works effectively, giving black an easy position. It is here that white had to come up with a workable scheme.

Diagram 7

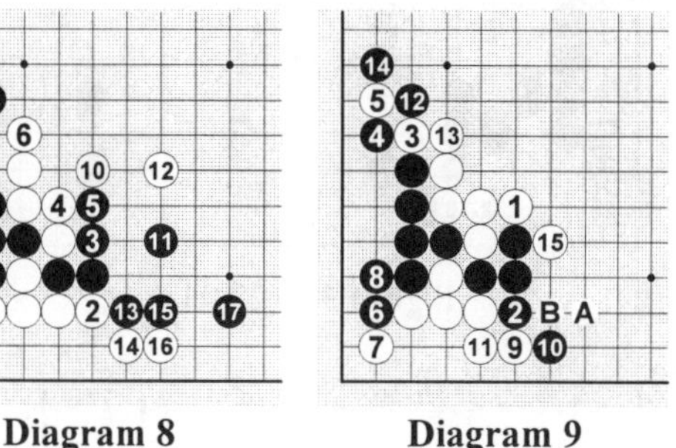

Diagram 8

Diagram 9

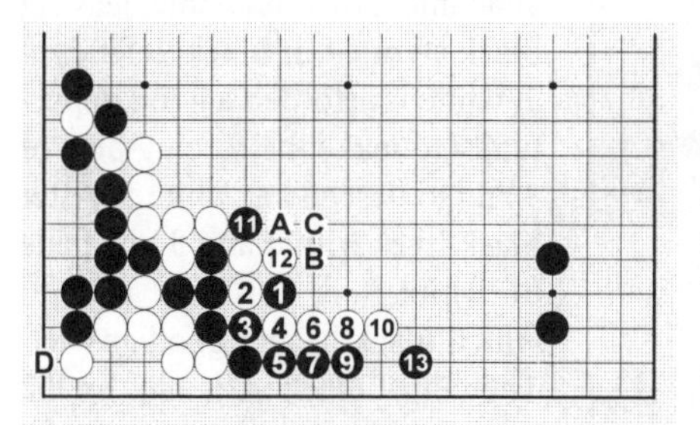

Diagram 10

For the atari of black 19,

Diagram 8 - Dodging with the knight's play at 1 is the usual method of answering in the modern age. Black makes shape with the sequence through 17.

After extending at 24, white blocked at 26, but for 22,

Diagram 9 - White could have also turned at 1. But after 15, white would not have captured with **A** or **B**, but,

Diagram 10 - In this game, black could jump to 1, and play effectively with the sequence through 13. Playing black **A**, white **B** and pushing at **C** is good for black, and since black can hane at **D** as well, this position is tenable.

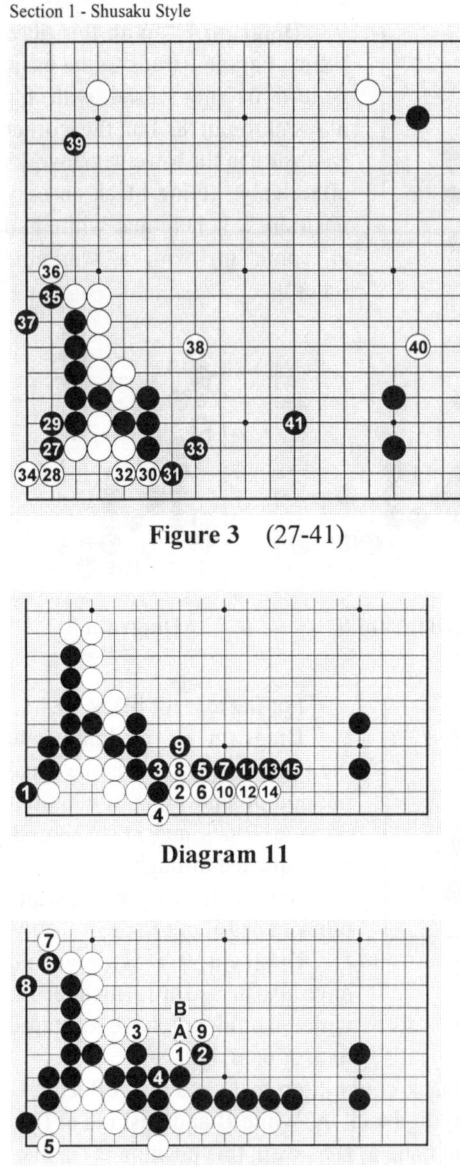

Figure 3 (27-41)

Diagram 11

Diagram 12

Figure 3 - Textbook Joseki Following white's block on the side, black haned at 27 and connected at 29, and white also haned at 30 and connected at 32.

The tiger link of black 33 made true shape. Here,

Diagram 11 - If black rushes to attack the corner with the hane of 1, since the ladder is unfavorable, white cannot cut on the outside, but having white connect underneath with 2 and 4 is no good. It seems that it is not good for white to press several times in a low stance with 6 through 14, but next, **Diagram 12** - White has the good tactic of the clamp attachment of 1 available, leaving black stymied. If black defends at 2, white is afforded a good opportunity to make the forcing play of 3 and to descend at white 5. After black lives with 6 and 8, the hane of white 9 is a stylish play to which black has no good answer. The cut of black **A** is met by the return atari of white **B**.

Black waited for white 34, then haned at 35 and connected at 37.

Here, white 38 was an essential strategic point, and up to this point one of the textbook patterns in this joseki was played.

The play at 38 was one that could not be omitted, because if white neglects to play it,

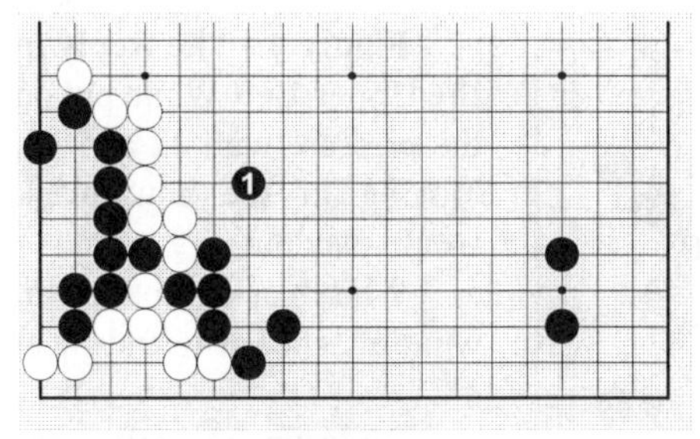

Diagram 13

Diagram 13 - The knight's play of black 1 becomes ideal, turning the tables regarding the relationship of influence. The thickness and power as well as the breadth of the position on the lower side becomes good, and from the perspective of the whole board this is a point that could not be missed.

With 39, black attacked the upper left corner. If white was allowed to play one more play here, it would have been impossible to invade the area. White attacked the corner once with 40 in exchange for black 41.

White's course of play in the upper left was difficult.

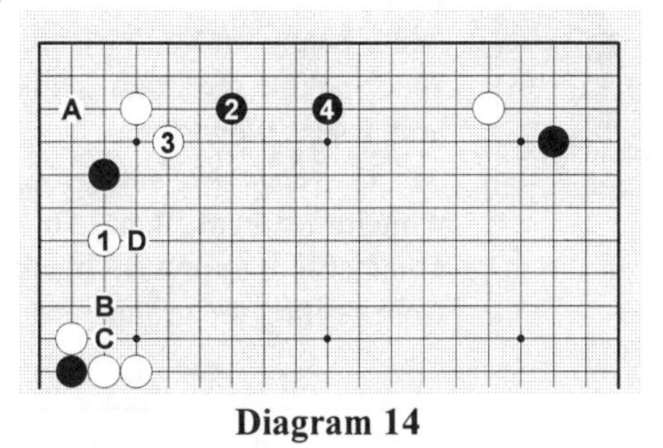

Diagram 14

Diagram 14 - Here, it was hard for white to pincer at 1. After playing 2 and 4, black could slide at **A**, so this would not yet be secure territory. Black **B** forces white **C**, and the potential of an attachment of black **D** also exists.

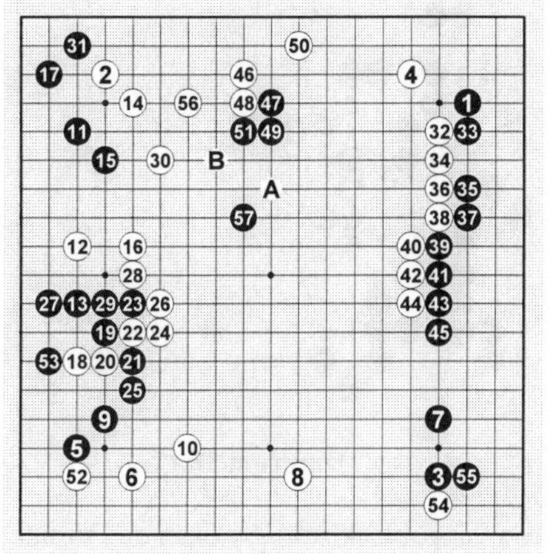

Reference Figure 2

Reference Figure 2 - [Jiji Newspaper Tournament; 1905; White: Tamura Hoju 6 dan (Meijin, 21st hereditary Honinbo Shusai); Black: Karigane Junichi 5 dan] When black made the corner enclosure with 7, white surrounded territory with 8 and 10. White 32 and the following plays put into effect a resolute territorial framework strategy. Black defended through 45, confident of being able to make an erasure. White 46 was a terrible blunder. Playing the high play of 48 was suitable. With 47 through 57, black easily neutralized the territory, making white's strategy a failure. For 56, even if white attacks at **A**, black can survive with the diagonal play at **B**.

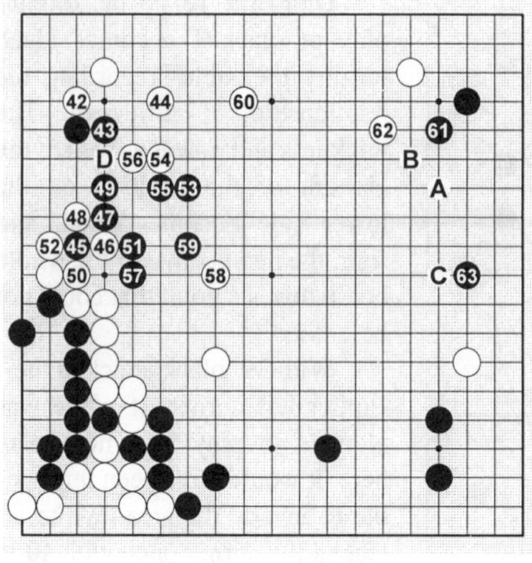

Figure 4 (42-63)

Figure 4 - The Reply in the Upper Left White put on the pressure with 42 and 44, looking to see how black would play out.

When black peeped at 45, white attached at 46 and cut at 48.

Diagram 15 - By connecting at 1, white is forced to let black jump to 2, making white heavy on the left side. Black poking the knight's link at **A** is also worrisome.

In reply to black 53, white thrust in at 54 and 56, going all-out to prevent black from settling the group here.

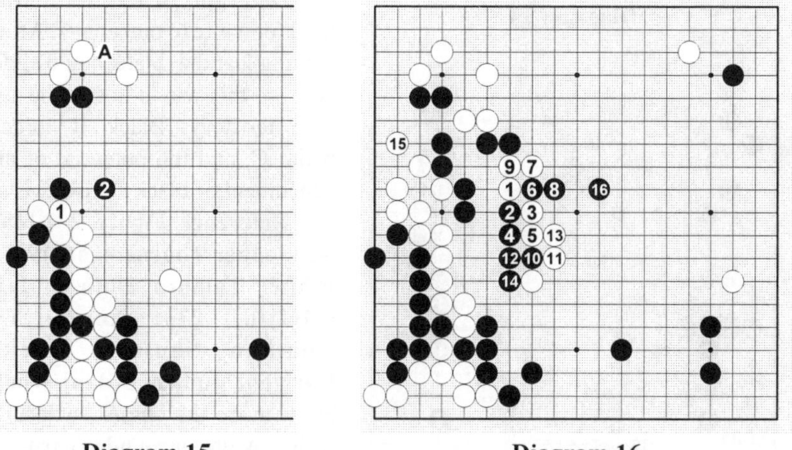

Diagram 15 **Diagram 16**

Since just defending was not promising, black strongly extended straight outward at 57 to counterattack.

The single blow of white 58 answered by the defensive play of black 59 was par for this situation. For 58,

Diagram 16 - White would like to go as far as to play at the vital point of 1, but black would attach at 2 and extend at 4, and it would not work out well. White 5 would allow black to cut at 6, and when white plays 7 and 9, the hane

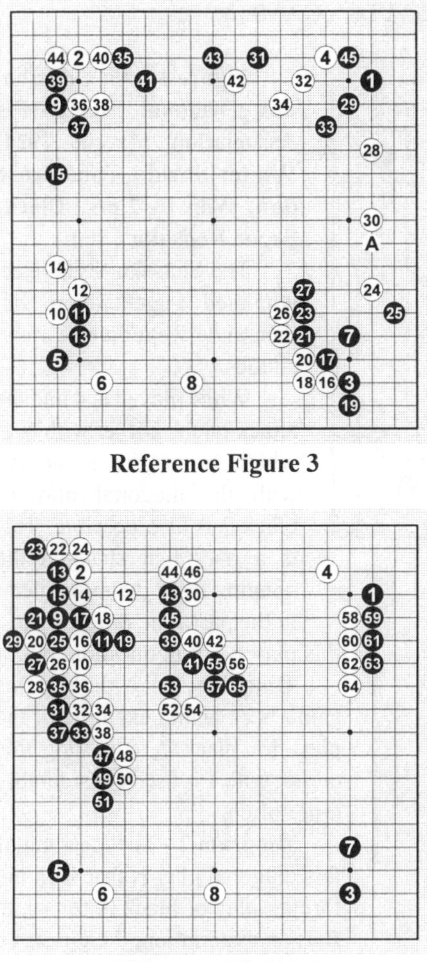

Reference Figure 3

Reference Figure 4

between the stones of black 10 initiates a severe counterattack. The plays through the black jump at 16 follow, leaves white's five stones in the center floating, and nothing is accomplished.

White surrounded the upper side with 60, putting the attack on black's group in the upper left in abeyance for the moment to see what would happen next.

The diagonal play of black 61 was solid, played with the upper side in mind.

White made the knight's play at 62, aiming to turn the upper area into a territorial framework. One is inclined to doggedly play like this.

After black 63, white played the sparkling plays of **A**, black **B** and the attachment of white **C** to deal deftly with the situation.

White was left with the play at **D**, so the game was yet to be decided.

Reference Figure 3 - [Oteai Ranking Tournament, Autumn Session; 1938; White: Kubomatsu Katsukiyo 6 dan; Black: Fujisawa Kuranosuke 4 dan] During this time, Fujisawa often used the Shusaku Style. Fujisawa: "Instead of attaching at 11 and drawing back at 13, now I would probably make the diagonal play at 13." Other than defending at 25, black could make the pincer at **A**, but thought that it would let white put on pressure with 29.

Reference Figure 4 - [9th Annual Go Championship; 1956; White: Fujisawa Shuko 9 dan; Black: Otake Hideo 6 dan] While using the Meijin Title Match - [of 1964] joseki in the upper left, 22 is usually played as the jump at 43. The attachment with white 40 and extension at 42 let black connect underneath on the left side so as to put the upper side in order.

SHUSAKU STYLE - GAME 3

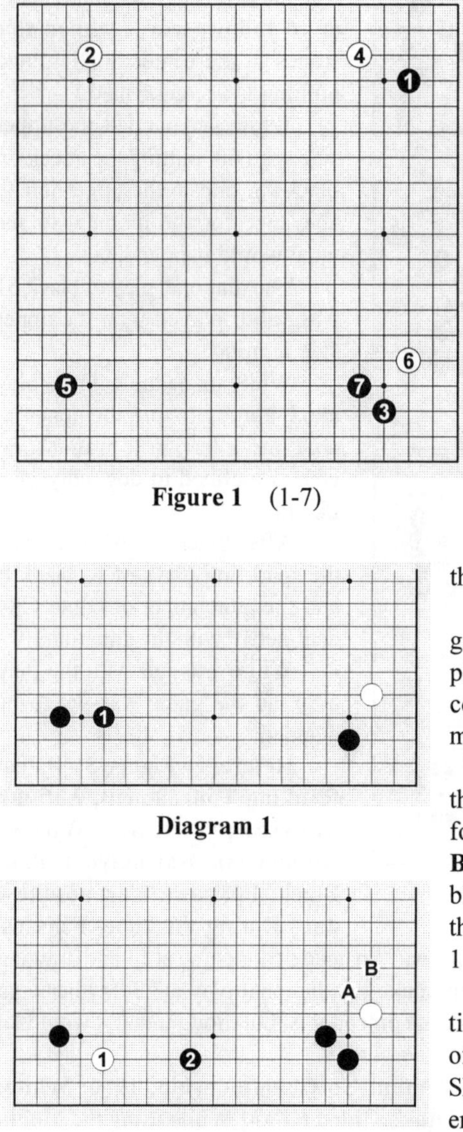

Figure 1 (1-7)

Diagram 1

Diagram 2

Figure 1 - An Unorthodox Diagonal Play [Hisei Association Match; 1924; White: Suzuki Tamejiro 6 dan; Wins by 2 pts.; Black: Segoe Kensaku 6 dan]

The Shusaku Style overwhelmed a generation, but then underwent diverse vicissitudes.

White played at 4 and the attack on the corner with 6, at which point the maneuver with the diagonal play of black 7 is also possible. This is a play that changed the opening logic that prevailed in the past. The propriety of this play is not in question, but,

Diagram 1 - Although this game is an actual example of the play, for black 7, enclosing this corner with 1 is used considerably more often.

Diagram 2 - The meaning of this diagonal play is that with the forcing play of black **A** for white **B** as an assumption, the pincer of black 2 may be said to constrain the white attack on the corner with 1 in advance.

However, viewing the situation in terms of the opening logic of the diagonal play of the Shusaku Style made on the seventh play in order to maintain the advantage of playing first, this diagonal play gives white scope to initiate schemes against the upper right corner, so on the surface it can be described as irregular.

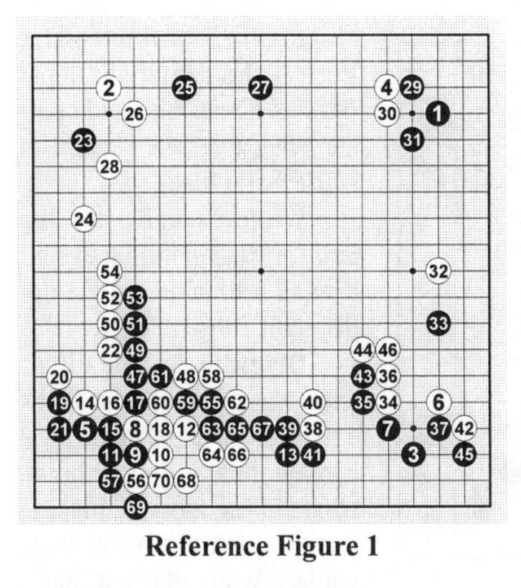

Reference Figure 1

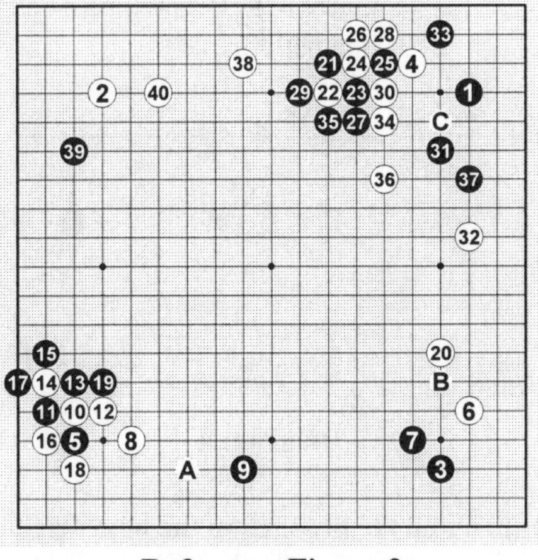

Reference Figure 2

White has a rich assortment of plays to initiate complications, from the upper side to the fencing-in tactic in the upper right, so this should be understood as a way for black to see what will be tried and then counter it. As demonstrated on the left, it is not as if there are no examples of this.

Reference Figure 1 - [1904; White: Honinbo Shuei 8 dan (Meijin, 17th and 19th Honinbo); Black: Tamura Hoju 6 dan (Meijin, 21st Honinbo Shusai)] Black made the diagonal play at 7, and when white attacked the corner with the high play at 8, played 9 and the following plays through the pincer of black 13. "In regards to this scheme, a definitive evaluation cannot be made," according to Shuei. The fight with black 47 and the following plays is also seen in contemporary go, and the result through white 70 repays close attention.

Reference Figure 2 - [Jiji Newspaper Knock-out Tournament; 1907; White: Nozawa Chikucho 3 dan; Black: Takabe Dohei 4 dan] This is one game from Chikuzo's ten straight knock-out wins. From the diagonal play of 7, black made the pincer of 9. One is inclined to advance as far as **A** with 9. White 20 prevented the fencing-in tactic at **B**. For white 28, playing atari from above at 30, followed by black 34, white 28, black **C** and white 29, or else 35 was better.

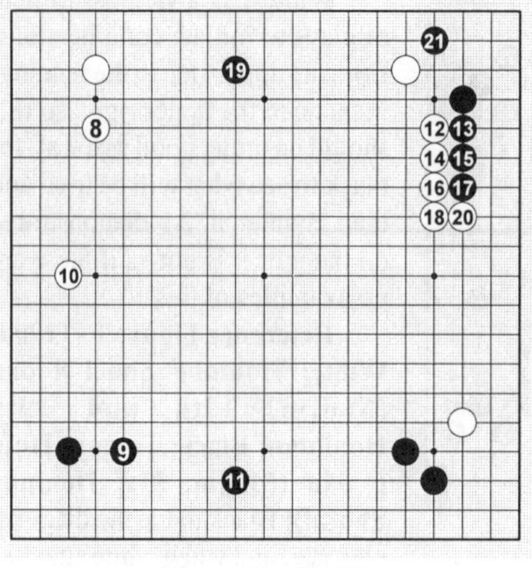

Figure 2 (8-21)

Figure 2 - An Excessive Push Both sides left the upper right as it was and made corner enclosures in tandem at white 8 and black 9.

White occupied the big point at 10, still failing to contrive to start action in the upper right corner. Here,

Diagram 3 - The difference was between the black extension at 1, and in the local context this is a big point. Next, black aims at making the checking extension at **A**, while if white plays **B**, black jumps to **C**, developing a box-like pattern.

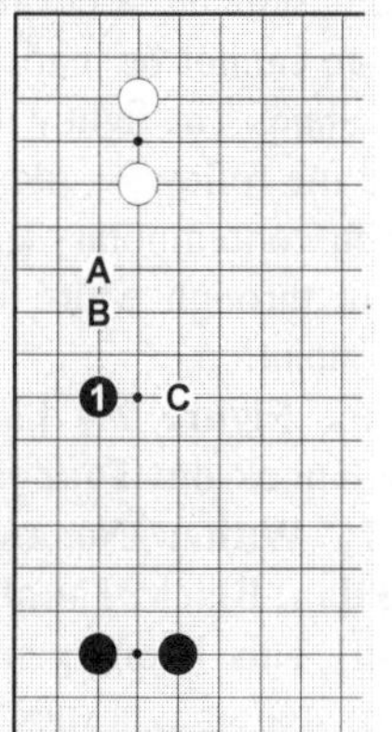

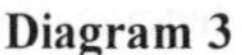
Diagram 3

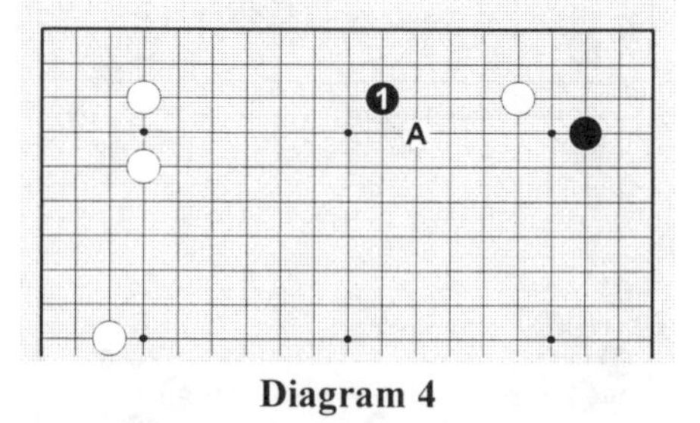

Diagram 4

If white wants to avoid the problem of the upper right, this is the biggest point on the board.

Making the extension on the lower side at black 11 was calm and collected but,

Diagram 4 - Here, shouldn't black pincer on the upper side at 1? If thinking in terms of contemporary fashion, the two point high pincer at **A** is also feasible. Black tries as hard as possible to get white to play out in the upper right, and that is perhaps another strategy.

In the end, white made the fencing-in tactic at 12. Black pushed four times, from 13 through 17, then split the upper side at 19. Black probably planned to play this way from the start.

Instead of pushing at 15,

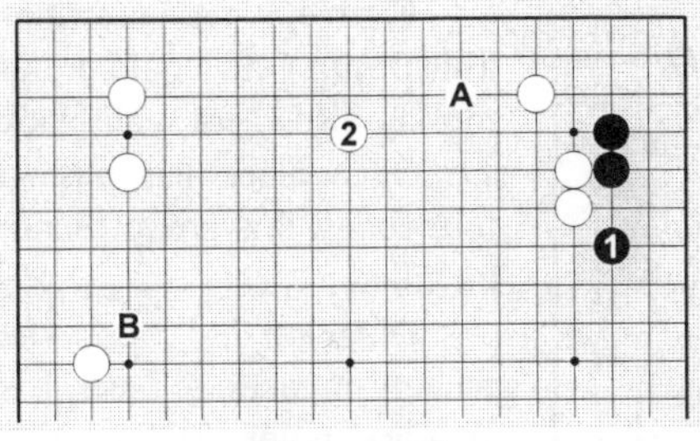

Diagram 5

Diagram 5 - It was also possible to jump at 1 in accordance with joseki. It may be understood that the extension of white 2 is ideal and so that prospect was distasteful, but even given this position, the invasion of black **A** and erasure at **B**, etc., are available, so it is not as if this is impossible.

The block of white 20 was, for all intents and purposes, a play that had to be answered.

Here, black made the knight's play at 21, but if black was going to defend like this, stopping with the third push of black 15 and,

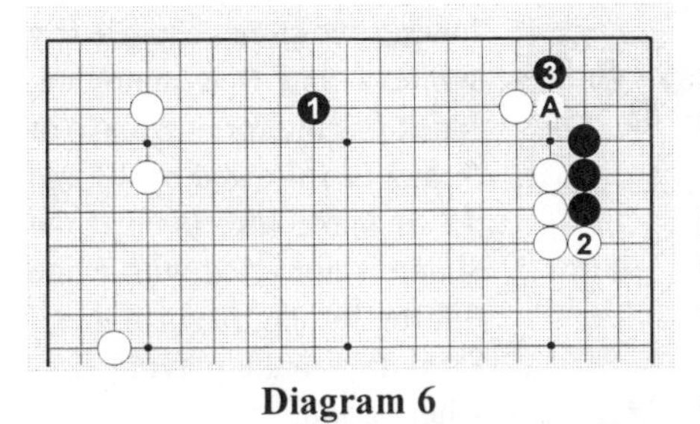

Diagram 6

Diagram 6 - Splitting the side with black 1 is usual. When white plays 2, black defends the corner with 3, or else at **A**, and in the present age this play is the way to respond.

If black pushes four times, it is common sense to omit defending at 21 and play elsewhere. Since every push increases white's thickness, today there are few examples of this maneuver.

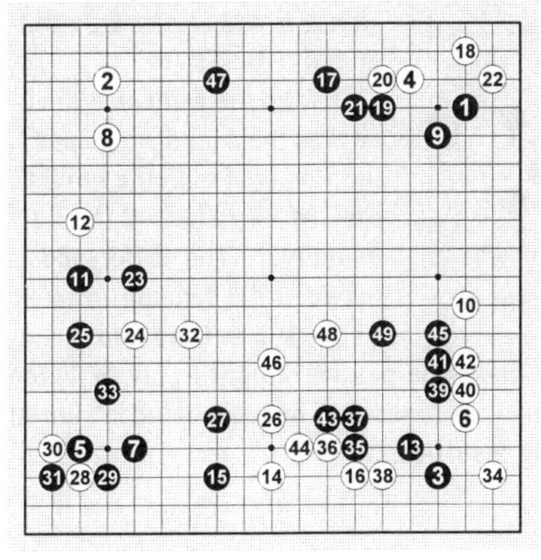

Reference Figure 3

Reference Figure 3 - [1871; White: Murase Shuho 7 dan (18th hereditary Honinbo); Black: Honinbo Shuwa 8 dan (14th hereditary Honinbo)] In response to the attack on the corner of white 6, there are not a few examples of black making the corner enclosure at 7. When white made the corner enclosure at 8, black turned to play the ideal diagonal play at 9. Black 17 and the following plays, and the way of fixing the shape in the lower left area are illustrative of the calm and collected style typical of Shuwa in his later years.

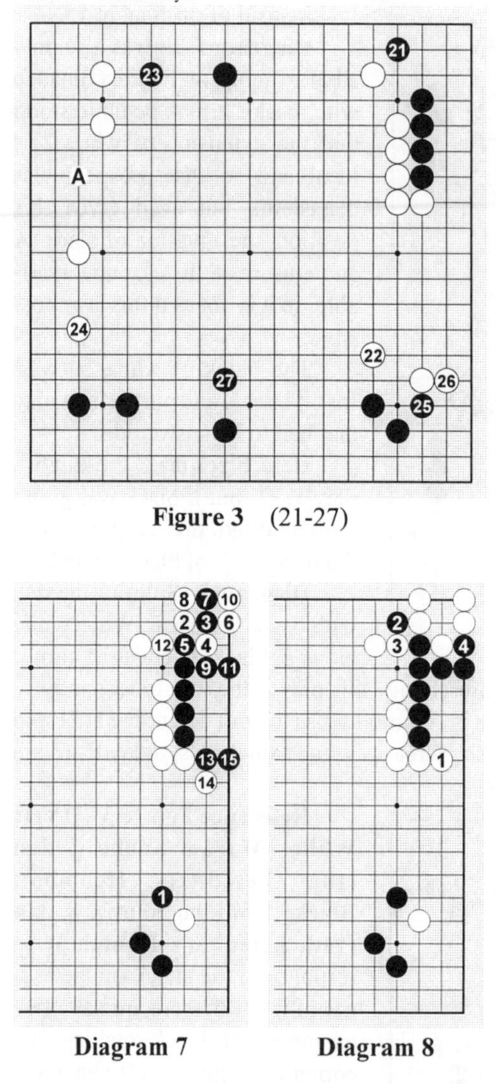

Figure 3 (21-27)

Diagram 7 **Diagram 8**

Figure 3 - A Questionable Jump One would prefer to play elsewhere with black 21. Once black has pushed four times, this group cannot be killed.

Diagram 7 - The fencing-in tactic of black 1 is an ideal point. Sliding with white 2 is met with the attachment of black 3, and though having two stones captured by white 4 and 6 is annoying, black has the forcing plays of 9 and 11 followed by 13 and 15 to make life. Even if the shape is not fixed with white 12, the forcing plays in the local area make playing elsewhere good.

Diagram 8 - For 12 in the previous diagram, if white descends at 1, black hanes over the stone with 2, then thrusts in at 4, and the three stones in the corner are obliterated. Black lives.

With the right side thickness as the backdrop, expanding this area with the knight's play of 22 is indeed the only maneuver. The difference is between the fencing-in tactic of black 1 in **Diagram 7**.

Diagram 9 - If this is used to make the passive knight's play of 1, the thickness that was so carefully built up goes to waste. The scale of the territorial framework is small, this extent being insufficient.

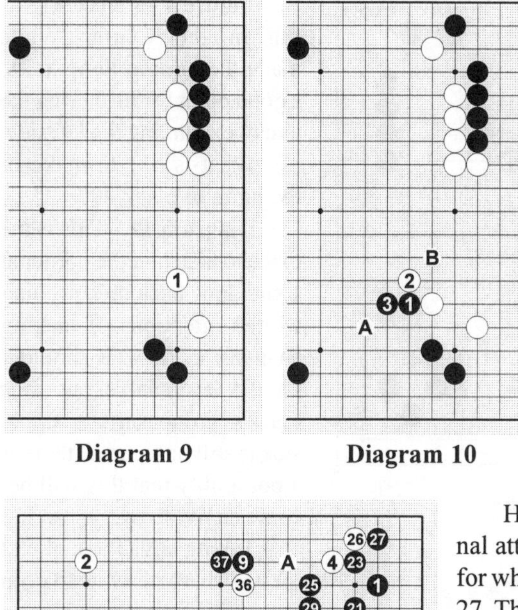

Diagram 9 Diagram 10

Black made the extension at 23, and white also developed on the left side. These were identical two point extensions, but each had a different meaning. Black established a base for the group, while white took territory, in short, a question of boundaries. Each extension had a distinctive aim.

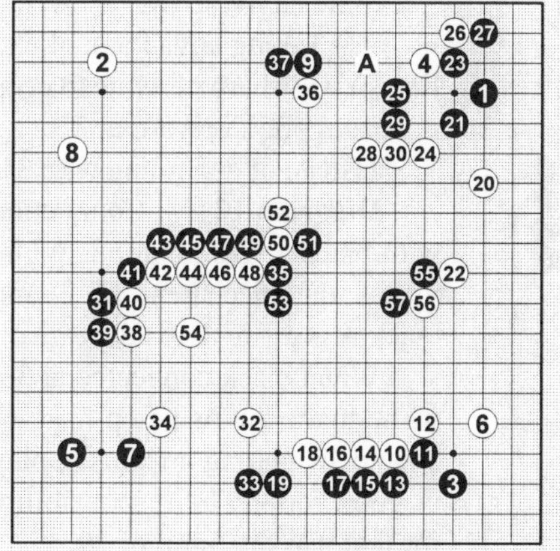

Reference Figure 4

Here, black made the diagonal attachment of 25 in exchange for white 26, then black jumped to 27. This was a calm attitude for an attack, but it was questionable.

Diagram 10 - Playing black 1 and 3 to expand the lower side was another strategy, or for 1, black could make the preparatory play at **A**, aiming to next make the erasure play at **B**. Or else, the invasion of **A** in the figure was also possible. Black 27 seems like a slack play.

Reference Figure 4 - [Honinbo-Hoensha Elimination Match; 1918; White: Honinbo Shusai, Meijin; Black: Hirose Heijiro 6 dan] Following the corner enclosure of 7, black made the pincer at 9. Shusai's comment was that, "For 19, black should have played elsewhere, as the diagonal play at 23. Black 23 at 25 followed by white **A** and black 23 was the correct order of plays."

The give and take with white 38 through black 53 was masterful, with black deftly dealing with the situation.

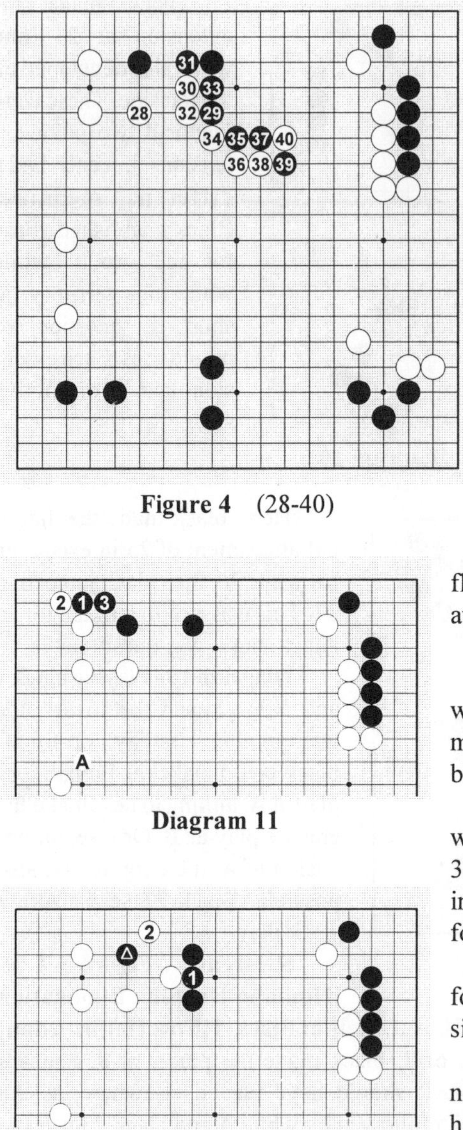

Figure 4 (28-40)

Diagram 11

Diagram 12

Figure 4 - Fierce Fighting in the Center White made the turning jump at 28, a good point for furthering the aim of expanding the left side.

What is one to make of the jump of black 29?

Diagram 11 - This is the place to attach in the corner at 1 and draw back at 3, probing white's intentions. If making an invasion, for 1 the shoulder hit at **A** is available, but since black's group on the upper side is still unsecured, there is a possibility that this will become an overplay.

Taking advantage of that flaw, it was sharp of white to peep at 30 and press upward at 32.

Instead of defending with 31,

Diagram 12 - Connecting with black 1 was no good. White makes the placement of 2 and black ▲ is difficult to take care of.

When black connected at 33, white made the two-step hane of 34 and 36, getting impetus to play in good form. The responsibility for that was the jump of 29.

White pushed at 38, trying to force black to answer submissively.

Diagram 13 - Here, the connection of 1 makes the shoulder hit of black 2 perfect. After white 3 and 5, black turns at 6, and this erasure in the midst of white's deliberately built up thickness neutralizes it.

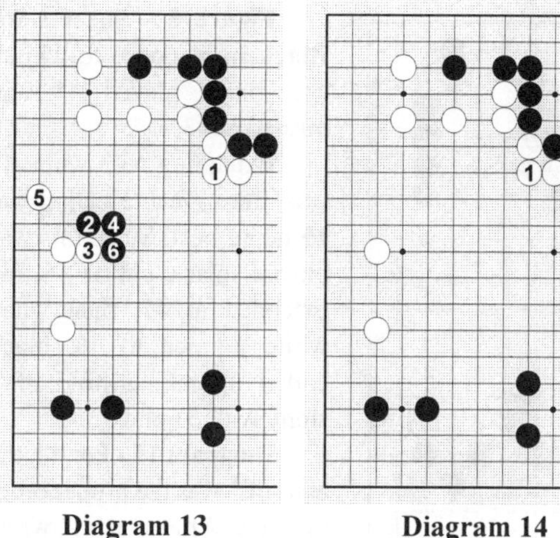

Diagram 13

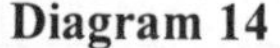

Diagram 14

White expected that for 39, black would extend at 40.

However, black put up stiff resistance with the hane at 39. Not being outdone, white cut at 40, and they were both swept up in a raging battle.

But the cut of white was quite overbearing.

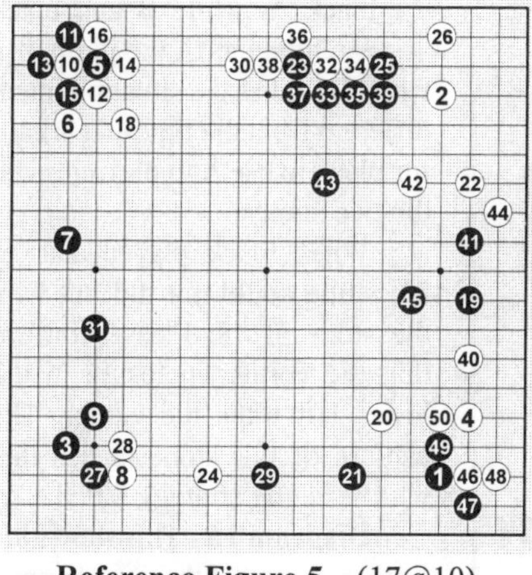

Reference Figure 5 (17@10)

Diagram 14 - Here, wouldn't a play like the connection at 1 be sufficient? Black would also connect at 2, with the pending question being how the left side would be enclosed, but this way black is given no impetus, making it a wide open game.

In the figure, a melee burst out.

Reference Figure 5 - [8th Annual Honinbo Title Match, Game 5; 1953; White: Takagawa Shukaku, Honinbo; Black: Kitani Minoru 8 dan] Black 1 was played at a different starting point, but with 3 and 5 the Shusaku Style results. Kitani often played the first play some place other than the orthodox upper right corner. For 7, black first made the three point pincer, then the diagonal play at 9. Surrounding territory with 31 was done out of distaste for a white invasion.

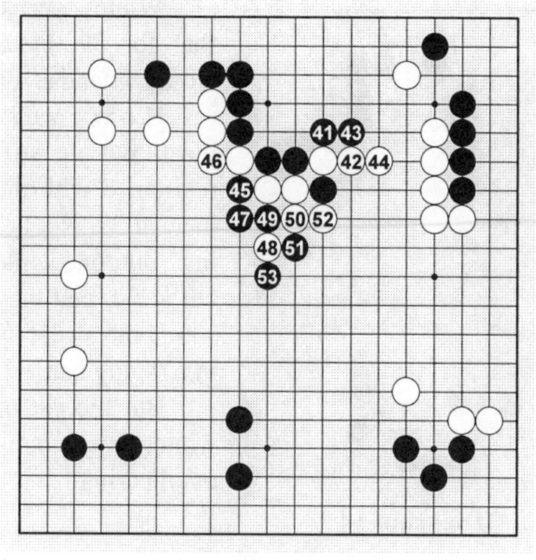

Figure 5 (41-53)

Figure 5 - Success for Black In response to white's cut, black played 41 and pushed at 43.

Extending with white 44 was questionable, **Diagram 15** being best. Since this was played, black cut at 45 and extended at 47, then when white jumped to 48, black ended up taking hold of a stone with 51 and 53.

Diagram 15 - For 44, the atari of 1 was the proper order of plays. After black 2, white extends at 3, and after next black **A**, white **B** and black extending at **C**, the jump of white **D** makes the situation much different from the figure. It is hard for black to use **A** to play out with the two stones.

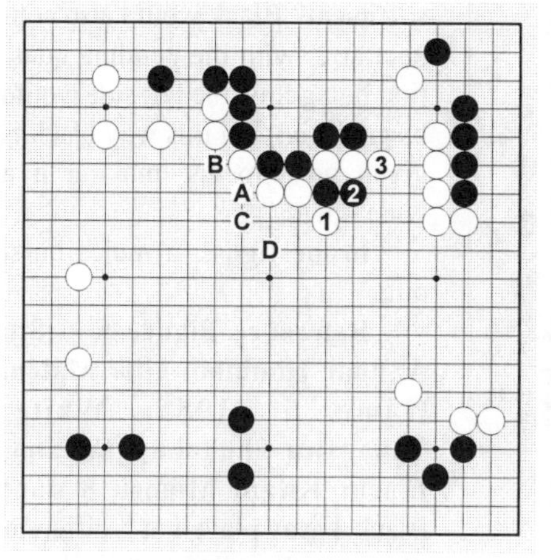

Diagram 15

When black played atari at 53, white could not run out with the stone at 48. Please confirm that the corner enclosure in the lower left traps the ladder. The capture of this stone means that white's center strategy failed.

Diagram 16 - This shows the further course of the actual game.

White peeped at the corner enclosure with 54, but had no alternative other than to play for a swap with 56 and 58.

If black used 55 to connect at 56, white's running out with the stone in the center becomes possible. That is the reason that black pressed at 55.

When white cut at 58, instead of the atari of black 59,

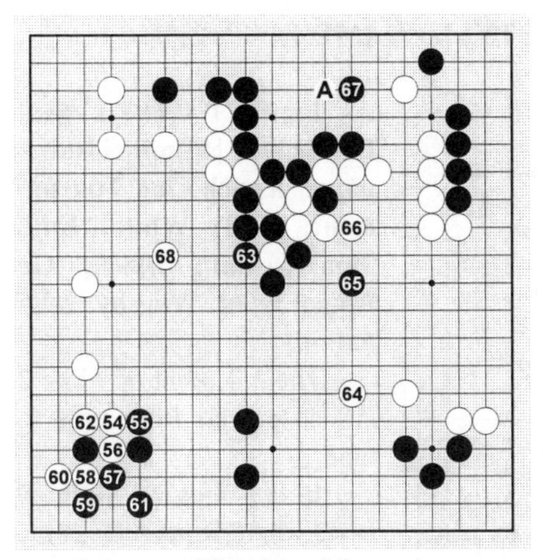

Diagram 16

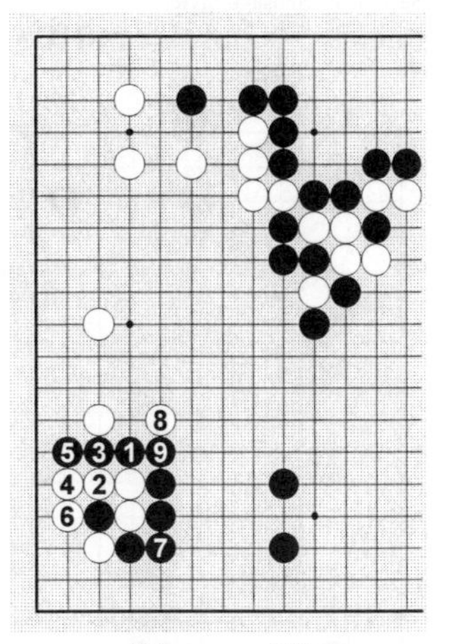

Diagram 17

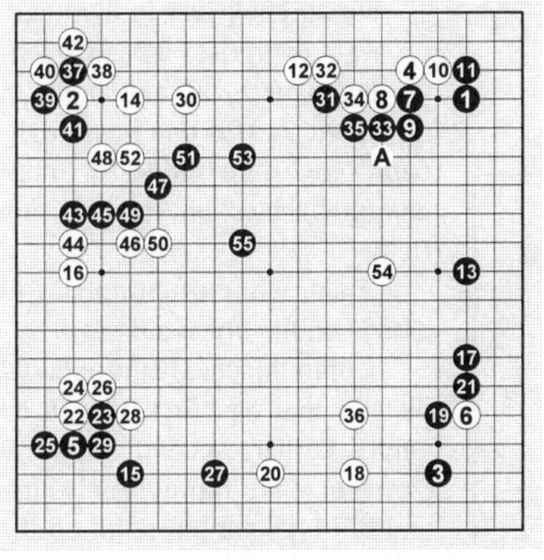

Reference Figure 6

Diagram 17 - It was also possible to play atari from above with 1, leading to the connection of 7, and this way was better. Next, in reply to the peep of white 8, it is fine for black to connect at 9, since the stone at 8 does not break the ladder, which one must pay attention to.

Black made a tiger link with 59 and 61, then white took grasp of black's stone with 62.

Black 67 was big in terms of avoiding the white forcing play at **A**. However, white then jumped to the good point of 64 and enclosed territory with 68, getting a substantial position. It must be judged that it will not be easy of black to secure the win of this game.

Reference Figure 6 - [1st Annual Meijin League; 1961; White: Fujisawa Shuko 8 dan; Black: Kitani Minoru 9 dan] Black 7 and 9 were unusual. According to Go Seigen, for white 12, playing 33, black **A** and white 32 was promising. Black 13 was a Kitani style play that did not rush ahead. White 30 provoked controversy, with the consensus being that 50 was better.

SHUSAKU STYLE - GAME 4

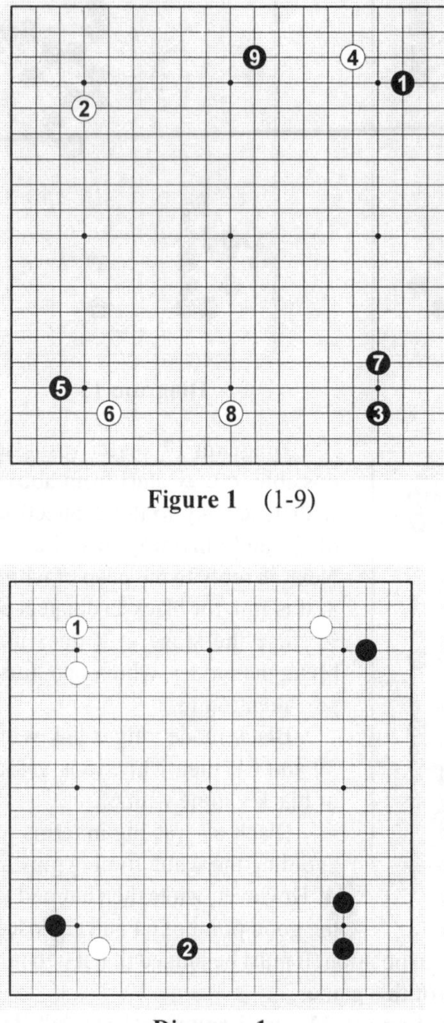

Figure 1 (1-9)

Diagram 1

Figure 1 - The Urgent Lower Side [Yomiuri Newspaper Knock-Out Tournament; 1931; White: Kato Shin 6 dan; Black: Go Seigen 3 dan; Wins by resignation]

The 5-4 point of white 2 is also played from time to time.

In the Shusaku Style, in cases where white attacks the upper right and lower left corners with 4 and 6, the black corner enclosure in the lower right comprises a basic opening pattern, as explained in Game 2. This one point high corner enclosure is ideal for maintaining balance on the left and right.

Then, white often hurries to extend on the lower side at 8.

Common sense in the opening dictates that one first play in an empty corner, second, attack a corner or make a corner enclosure, and third, take a big point on the side, but in this case it breaks down.

Diagram 1 - If a corner enclosure is aimed at, it would be done with white 1 in the upper left, but this play would let black make the combined extension and pincer of 2, a key point for attack and defense, and so from white's standpoint, this cannot be undertaken. This is one example of situation where a big point on the side takes priority over a corner enclosure.

One should understand the extension at 8 being in this opening virtually essential. In addition, 8 also makes schemes against the lower left corner

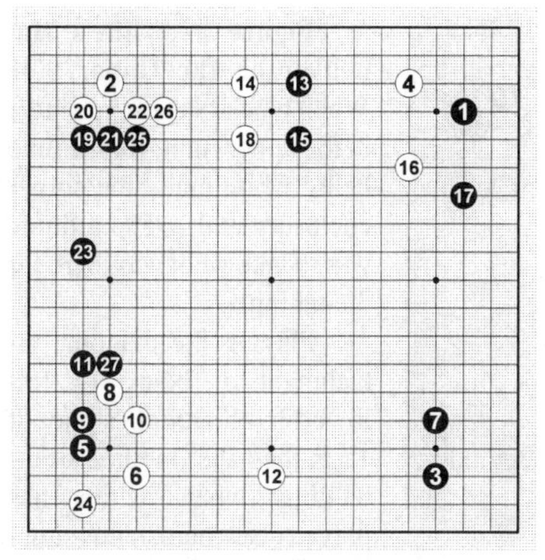

Reference Figure 1

possible. The three point pincer of black 9 was also quite a point. Attacking the upper left corner would have given white scope for machinations.

Reference Figure 1 - [1837; White: Yasui Shuntetsu (9th hereditary Sanchi); Black: Tsuchiya Shuwa (14th hereditary Honinbo)] This is the Shusaku Style played by his teacher Shuwa several years before Shusaku began playing the 1, 3 and 5 opening. When white attacked the corner with 6, black made the corner enclosure at 7, falling in with the model. After 8 and 10, white rushed to make the extension at 12.

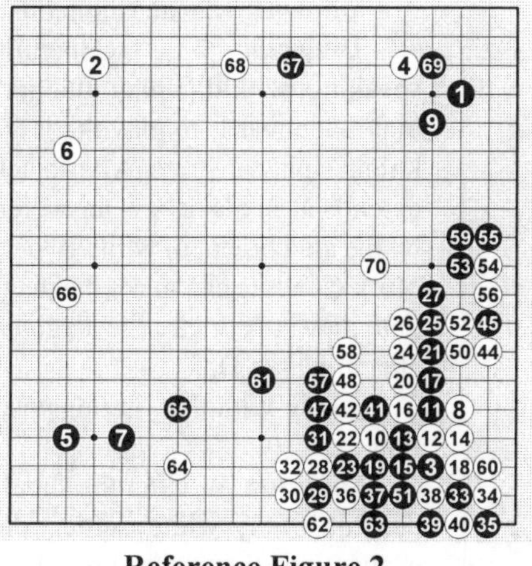

Reference Figure 2
(43, 49@33, 46@40)

Reference Figure 2 - [1846; White: Inoue Inseki (11th hereditary Inoue, Genan); Black: Kuwahara Shusaku (Honinbo successor)] This is the famous "ear-reddening play" masterpiece played by the 17 year old Shusaku. The game was one in which black made the corner enclosure here at 7, but what is striking is the skillful maneuvering by Genan Inseki in the Taisha joseki in the lower right. The ear-reddening play was played afterward at black 127. It was that outstanding handiwork that enabled black to ride out a difficult game.

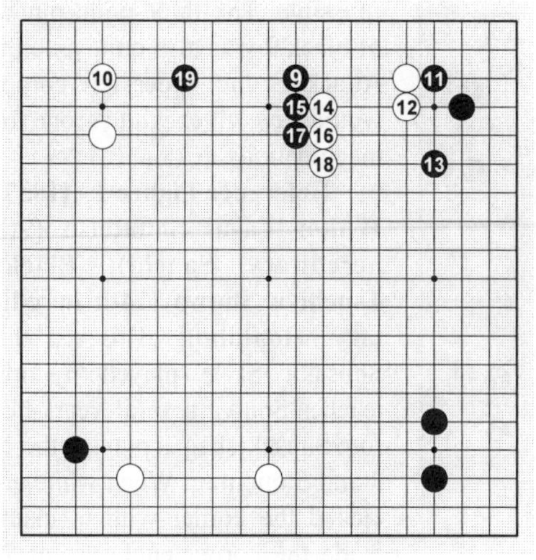

Figure 2 (9-19)

Figure 2 - White's Maneuver on the Upper Side When black played the pincer in the upper right, for the time being white made the corner enclosure at 10. The attitude was to take what was there for the taking.

Playing the diagonal attachment of black 11 followed by the knight's play of 13 is the usual method of attacking when white has played elsewhere in this situation.

White's maneuver with the shoulder hit of 14 and the following was questionable.

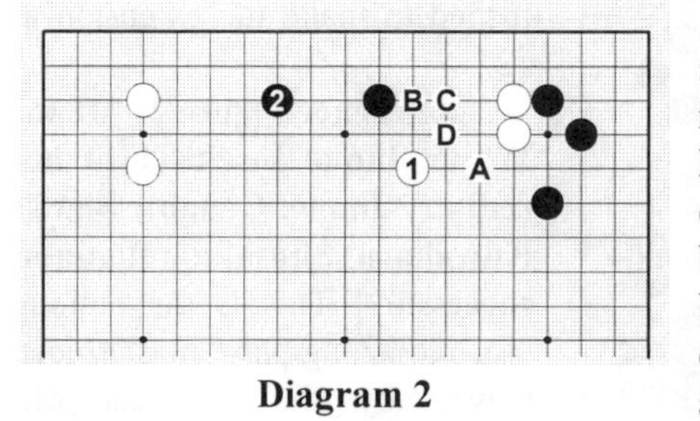

Diagram 2

Diagram 2 - Generally speaking, with this play, the normal maneuver is to play the large knight's play at 1, etc. After black extends at 2, black **A** is answered by the attachment of white **B**, or if black **C**, white can make the diagonal play at **A** or else the diagonal attachment at **D**.

Along with that, in this position,

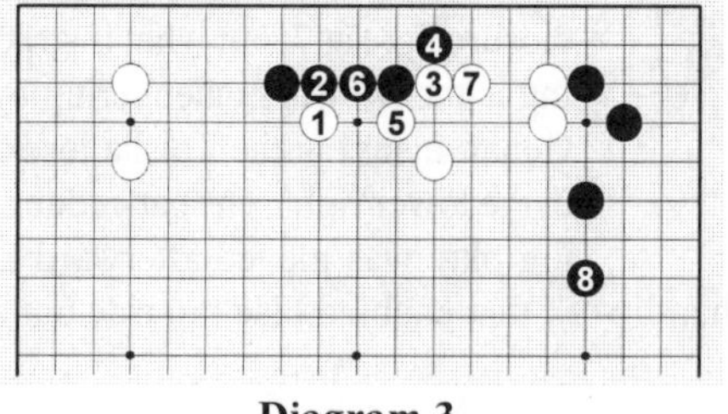

Diagram 3

Diagram 3 - After the shoulder hit of 1, white settles the group with the plays through 7, and then black jumps to 8, with the whole sequence regarded as joseki.

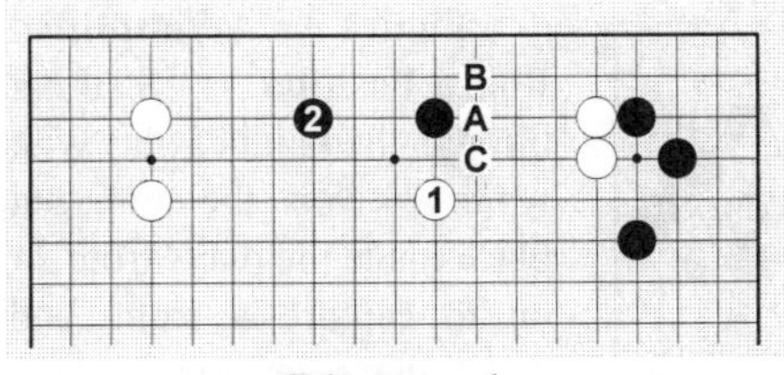

Diagram 4

Diagram 4 - White advancing to 1 with a cap, is also possible. After black 2, white **A**, black **B** and drawing back at white **C** comprises one pattern.

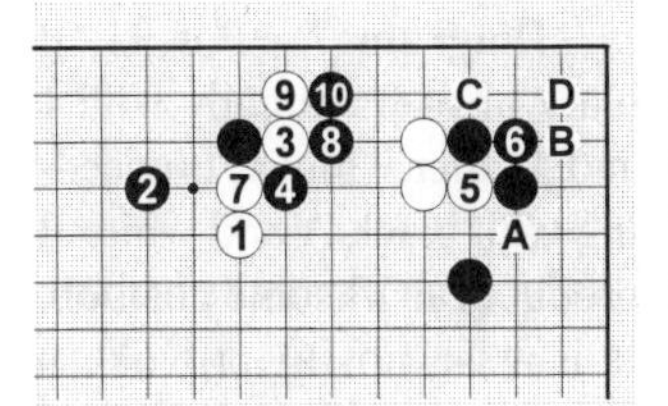

Diagram 5

Diagram 5 - Leaving aside the question of whether it is suitable for this game, in reply to white's cap at 1, black can also defend with the knight's play at 2. When white attaches at 3, the hane out of black 4 produces the large scale joseki in the next diagram. Thrusting between black's stones with white 5 is a good play, and,

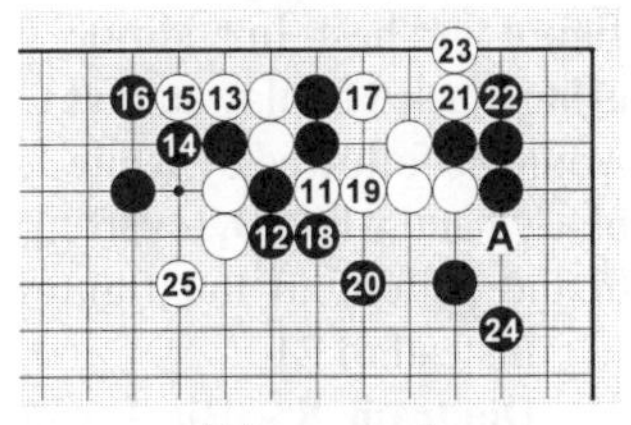

Diagram 6

Diagram 6 - The sequence proceeds through 25. Black 24 is played to safeguard against the hane over black's stone at **A**. If black 6 in the previous diagram is used to draw back at **A**, the variation with white 6, black **B**, white **C**, black 8 and white **D** will result.

White 14 and the following plays were made with the idea of striking through the knight in the upper right corner shown in the next figure, but permitting black to make ideal shape with 19 was somewhat questionable. There are cases where a loss incurred earlier in the game is not compensated for.

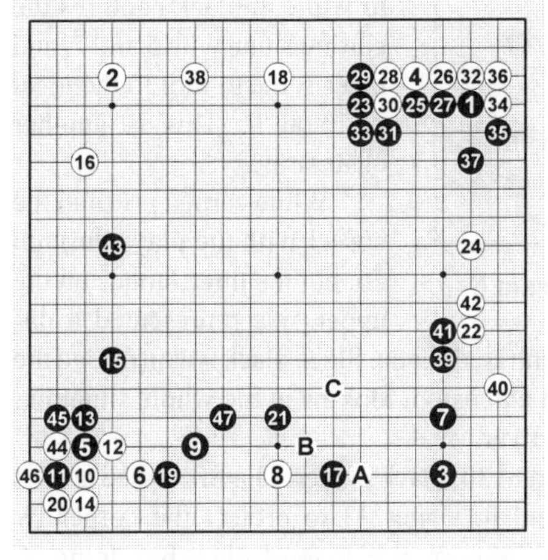

Reference Figure 3

Reference Figure 3 - [10th Annual Go Championship Final, Game 1; 1966; White: Magari Reiki 8 dan; Black: Fujisawa Shuko 9 dan] When white extends at 8, immediately invading with black 9 is the contemporary pattern. For white 16, the extension at **A** was the leisurely maneuver. Black 21 was ideal, and if white played **B** right away, black would play out at **C**. After surrounding white with 47, the board position was in black's favor.

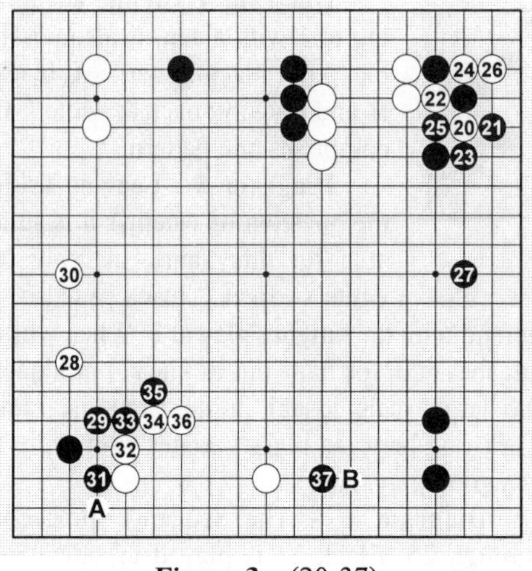

Figure 3 (20-37)

Figure 3 - A Simplified Board Position Striking through the knight's play with white 20 was the aim, but black made the plays from 21 on to capture a stone and make the extension at 27 a clear strategy to dodge complications.

Diagram 7 - For 21, if black answers directly with 1 and 3, after white 4, proceeding with black **A** and white **B** produces an irksome position. It is wise not to provoke a fight where white is thick and strong, so playing as in the figure was best. In addition, using black 3 to play atari at **C** would be followed by white 3, black 4 and white **D**, reverting to the pattern in the figure.

Instead of 21,

Diagram 8 - Black can also defend at 1. In response to white 4, black captures the cutting stone with 5 and 7, and takes sente to turn to the ideal point at 9. This is another clear strategy.

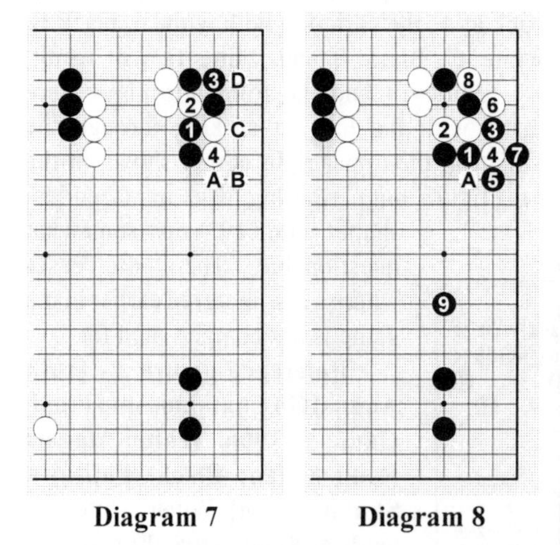

Diagram 7 **Diagram 8**

White earned profit in the corner with the plays through 26, but the three stones on the upper side represented a duplication of effort with an overconcentrated shape. Since black was afforded the good shape made by the three point extension, looking at the whole situation, this was decidedly not a great maneuver.

When white developed with 28 and 30, black played 31 and pressed at 33,a sequence that had a strategy behind it. Using 33 to protect the corner by descending at **A** would have been the normal course of play, but doing so would let white make the extension at **B**, taking the final big point.

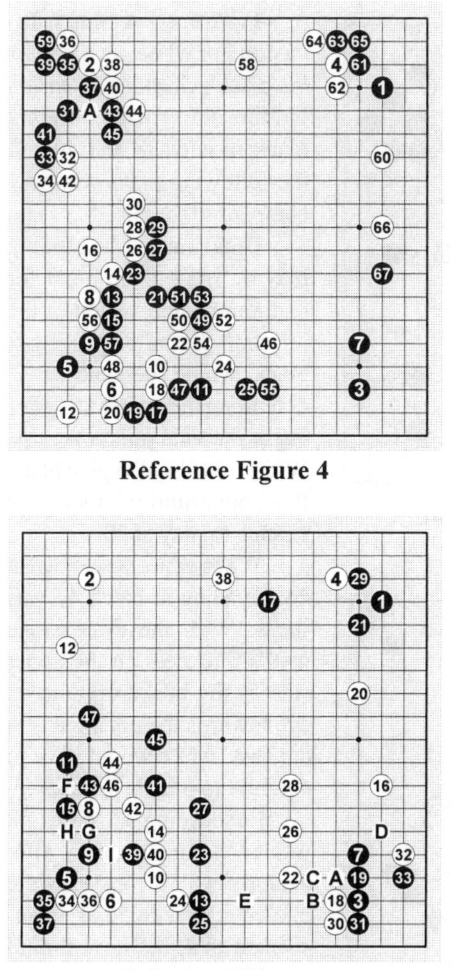

Reference Figure 4

Reference Figure 5

Disliking that, black provoked white to play 34 and 36, in order to beat white to the punch with 37, a typical quick developing ploy of Go's. Taking into consideration the situation on the upper side as well, up to here black's board position was an easy one to play.

Reference Figure 4 - [10th Annual Go Championship; 1966; White: Kano Yoshinori 8 dan; Black: Fujisawa Shuko 9 dan] After black 9 and white 10, the checking extension of black 11 was played out of fighting spirit. White was not allowed to make an extension on the lower side, and black was able to play a new pattern with 13 and the following plays. If white used 42 to atari at **A**, black would cut at 42, initiating a swap. Turning at 59 was a key point in this game which aimed at maneuvering on the upper side.

Reference Figure 5 - [19th Annual Nihon Ki-in Championship; 1971; White: Shimamura Toshihiro 9 dan; Black: Miyashita Shuyo 9 dan] Black made the checking extension at 13, denying white an extension on the lower side. The connection of black 19 was the proper play. If this was played at **A**, white **B**, black 31, white **C**, black **D** and white **E** would be unsatisfactory for black. Playing white 38 at 43, followed by black **F**, white **G**, black **H** and white **I** would have solidified the position, and been thick and strong. Black played 39 through 45, attacking in good form.

Figure 4 - A Sharp Invasion For white, after enduring black's checking extension on the lower side, sealing black in with 38 and 40 and the following plays was only compensation. For 38,

Diagram 9 - The capping play of 1 is a good point for restraining an invasion of the left side, but after playing it black would descend at 2, defending the corner and aiming at the vital point of **A**. White, not about to give black this opportunity, took the chance to play at 38.

When white descended at 46, invading at black 47 was sharp. With the three stone wall's thickness on the upper side as the backdrop, and an eye towards the potential of a cut at **A**, white would have to struggle to handle this play.

Descending at white 48 was a forcing play, then, after exchanging 50 for 51, white played atari with 52 as an answer to that, but how should one evaluate this?

Figure 4 (38-57) (45@40)

Diagram 9

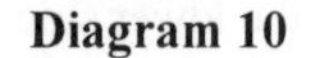

Diagram 10

Diagram 10 - Couldn't white have jumped at 1, interrupting black's connection? Even if black plays out with 2 through 12, white connects at 13, and rather than attacking, black's five stones are a burden. White would welcome this continuation.

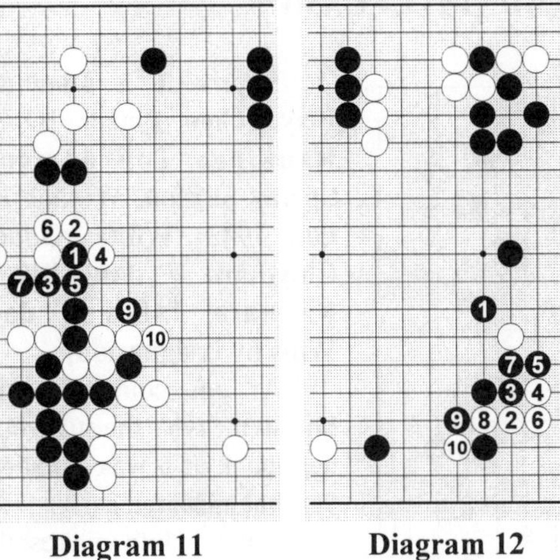

Diagram 11 Diagram 12

Diagram 11 - Instead of playing at 6 in the previous diagram, black could take hold of two stones with the attachment of 1 and block of 3, but capturing white's two stones is small. On the contrary, this does damage to black's two invading stones, so black would not be satisfied with this divvying up.

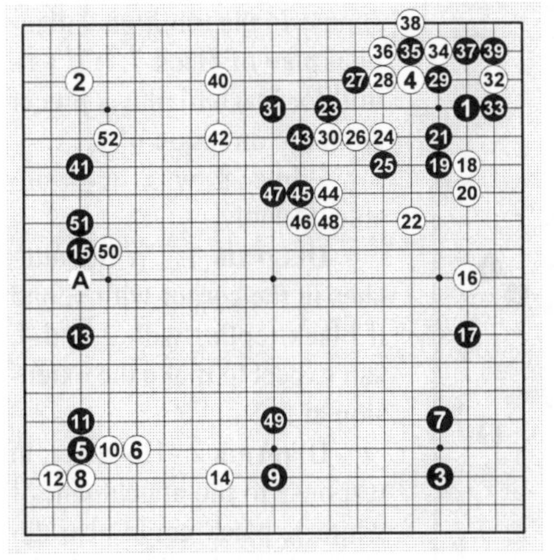

Reference Figure 6

Letting black connect with 53 represented failure on white's part.

When white invaded at 54, black locked up with 55.

Diagram 12 - Even if black seals white in with 1, white plays 2 through the cut at 10 to profit in the corner.

Black embarked on an attack with 57, an easy one to press forcefully. In this game, one senses the overflowing genius of the young Go Seigen.

Reference Figure 6 - [1971; 9th Annual 10 Dan Title Match, Game 4; White: Otake Hideo, 10 Dan; Black: Hashimoto Utaro 9 dan] When white attached at 8, black used 9 to play first on the lower side. If 15 was omitted, the checking extension of white **A** would have been severe. Instead of black 27, playing 29, white 35, black 27 was correct.

SHUSAKU STYLE - GAME 5

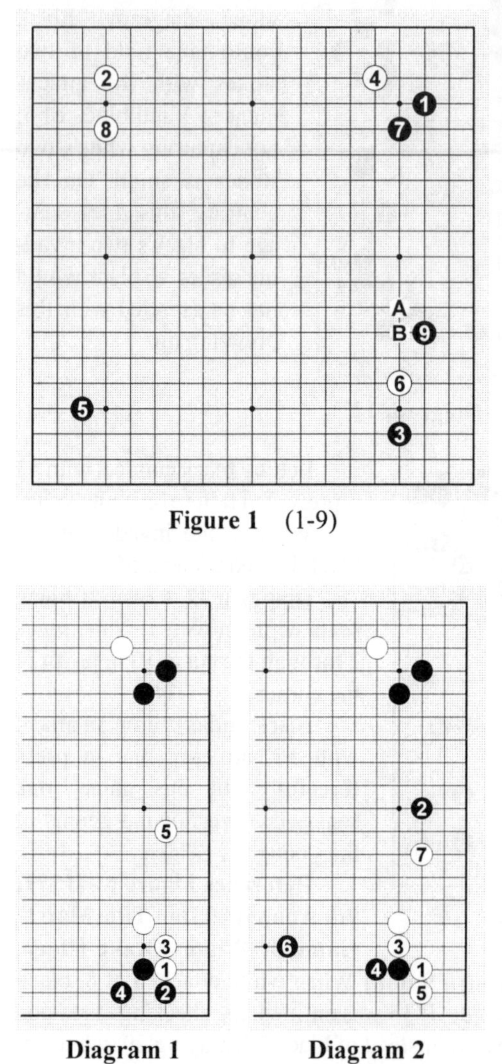

Figure 1 (1-9)

Diagram 1

Diagram 2

Figure 1 - Diagonal Play, Then Pincer [Oteai Ranking Tournament, Spring Session, Winner Final; 1943; White: Onoda Chiyotaro 7 dan; Black: Kajiwara Takeo 4 dan; Wins by resignation]

As one counter to the Shusaku Style, the high corner attack of 6 was a maneuver that appeared early.

When white makes the corner enclosure at 8 in response to the traditional diagonal play of black 7, it is natural for black to play a pincer from the direction of 9.

White 8 was questionable. Usually,

Diagram 1 - White attaches in the corner with 1, and if black replies with 2 and 4, can expect to make the extension at 5.

Diagram 2 - However, in response to the attachment of white 1, black could also develop the right side with the play at 2, and considering the diagonal play in the upper right, black must be thirsting to play this. After white 3 through 7, black makes the large knight corner enclosure in the lower right with 6, or else attacks the upper left corner, etc., each play leading to a different game. In addition, for 3, white can also proceed with a clamp attachment at 4 - **[Reference Figure 5]** or else not play in this corner at all, and consider attacking the lower left corner.

Black made the tightest pincer possible with 9. In a present day game the two point pincer at **A**, or else one point pincer at **B** would probably be chosen.

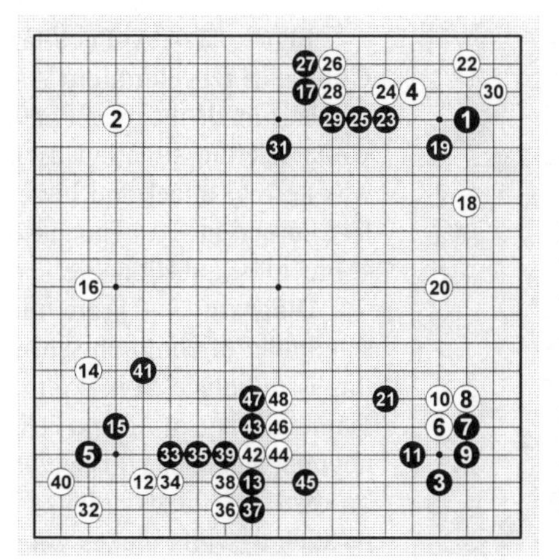

Reference Figure 1

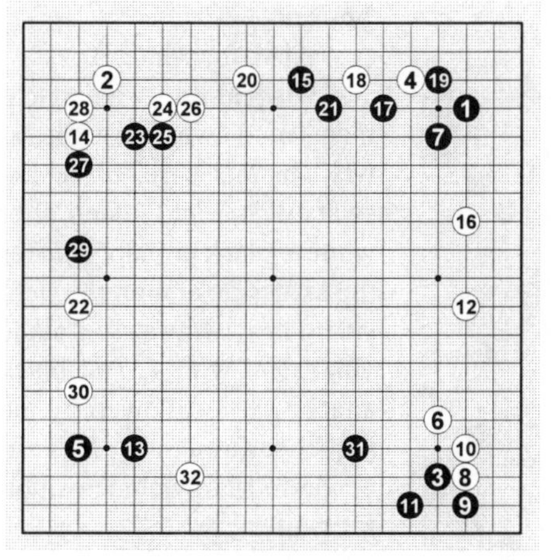

Reference Figure 2

Reference Figure 1 - [Shizokai Game; 1899; White: Tamura Hoju 5 dan; Black: Hirose Hirajiro 4 dan] White attacked the corner with the high play at 6, and black 7 through 11 was immediately played. The three point pincers at 13 and 17 were questionable since white got ideal shape with 18 and 20. When black expanded the position with 41, white cut at 42 and played through 48 to fight.

Reference Figure 2 - [Oteai Ranking Tournament, Spring Session; 1931; White: Kubomatsu Katsukiyo 6 dan: Black: Onoda Chiyotaro 6 dan] White attached at 8 and made the plays through the extension of 12, whereupon black made the corner enclosure with 13 in the lower left. When black made the three point pincer at 15, white left to extend at 16, so black sealed white in with the usual plays from 17 through 21. White put up resistance with extensions 20 and 22.

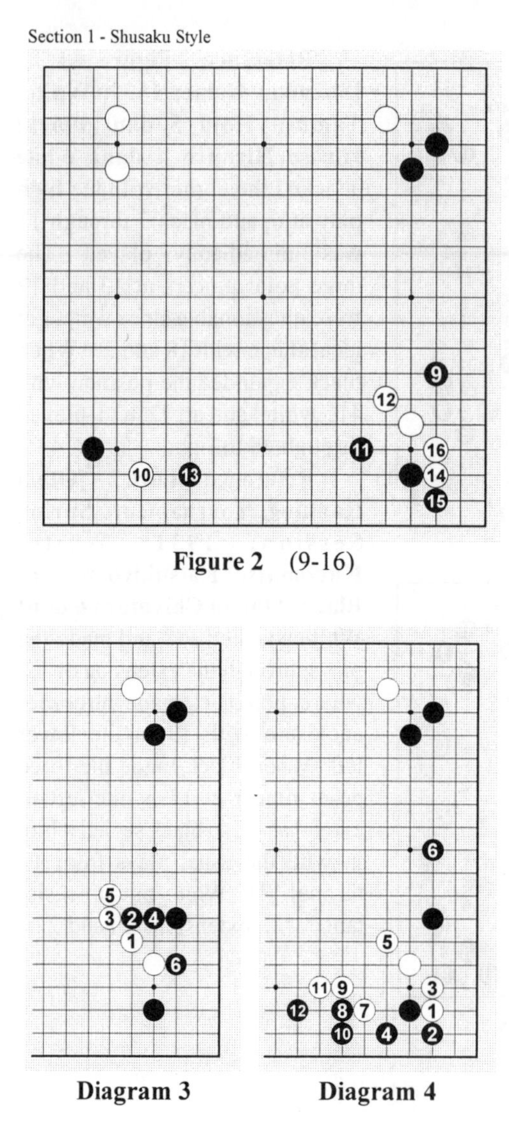

Figure 2 (9-16)

Diagram 3 **Diagram 4**

Figure 2 - A Peculiar Course of Development After black made the pincer at 9, white left the situation as it was here to attack the lower left corner at 10. This also seems to be questionable.

Diagram 3 - From the standpoint of common sense, this is the place to make the diagonal play of 1, and it is not imaginable that this would be bad. If black plays 2 through 6, white makes good shape by extending straight out at 5, getting a playable position.

Also, for white 10,

Diagram 4 - The attachment of 1 was possible as well. In this case, black answers with 2 and 4, and after white 5, black probably makes the extension at 6 on the right side. Then, white strikes at the vital point with 7, and black attaches at 8 followed by the sequence through 12. This can be viewed as a viable position for white.

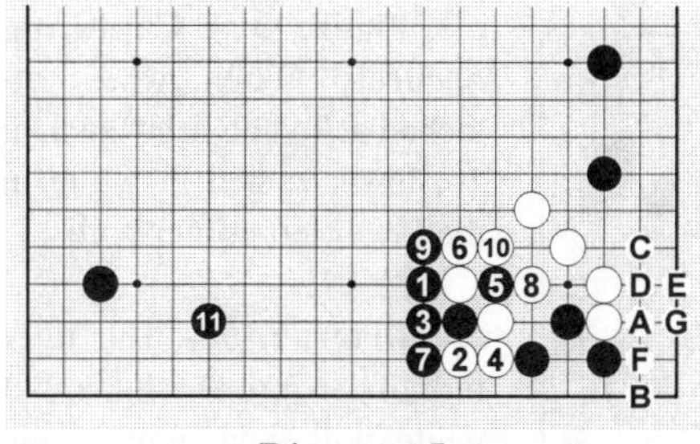

Diagram 5

Diagram 5 - According to Kajiwara, black 10 in the previous diagram should be a hane at 1. After white 2 through 8, black presses upward at 9 and then turns to play at 11. If this took place, black is developing rapidly. In the corner, afterward black is left with the tactic of playing the hane at **A**, followed by white **B**,black **C**, white **D**, black **E**, white **F** and black **G**, so the corner is still not inviolable.

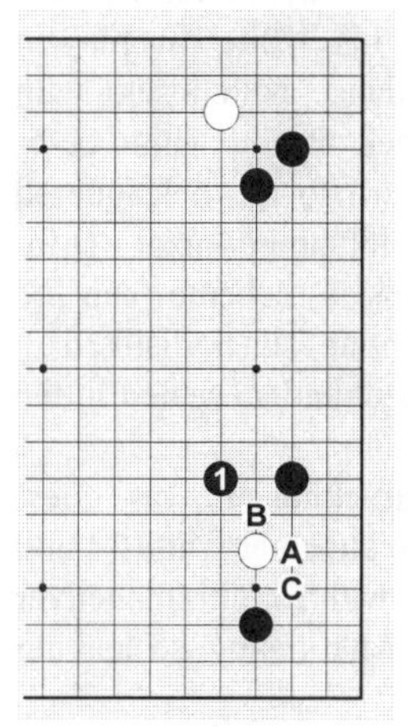

Diagram 6

Since white played elsewhere, it was natural for black to attack white here with 11. However, if the intention is to emphasize the right side,

Diagram 6 - Jumping at 1 is superior, with great distance between the diagonal play in the upper right, and depth. Using 1 to attach at **A**, with white **B** and black **C** to follow is small in scope.

Black made the knight's play at 11, so white replied with the diagonal play at 12, and then black went for the pincer at 13.

White attached at 14 and drew back at 16, a course of opening development not often seen.

Reference Figure 3 - [Oteai Ranking Tournament; 1951; White: Fujisawa Shuko 6 dan; Black: Kajiwara Takeo 6 dan]

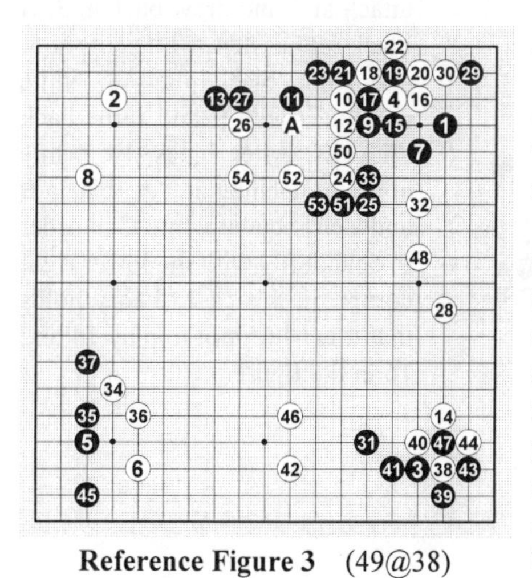

Reference Figure 3 (49@38)

Although white did not attack the lower right corner, black made the diagonal play at 7, with the plan that if white did attack the lower right, black would pincer. Black 15 was in keeping with Kajiwara's taste, played with the reasoning that once white had pressed at 12, a pincer at black 28 would not be suitable. The play at 16 showed that white was swayed by black's plan. With this, white 26, black 27 and then the attachment of white **A** would have made shape. Black took a good point at 51.

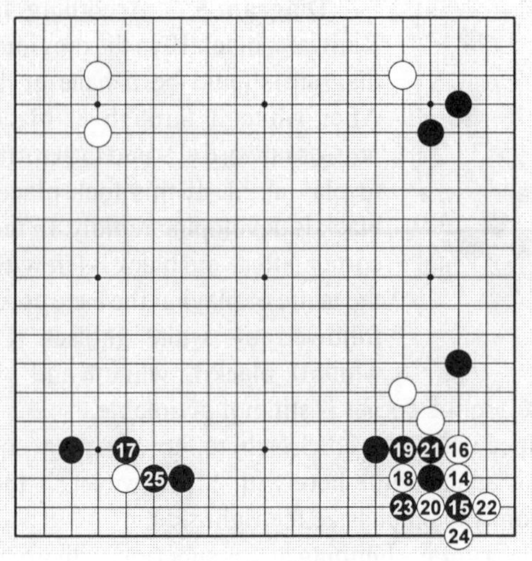

Figure 3 (14-25)

Figure 3 - Capturing Securely When white attached at 14 and drew back at 16, black sealed in white in the lower left corner with 17.

At 17,

Diagram 7 - The tiger link of 1 is proper shape, but white will then employ the fencing-in tactic of 2, and black 3 may be anticipated. After this, white can play in accordance with joseki with **A**, black **B** and white **C**, or else turn to the beleaguered lower left and jump at **D**, or perhaps a scheme can be thought up. Black disliked this prospect and so sealed in the lower left.

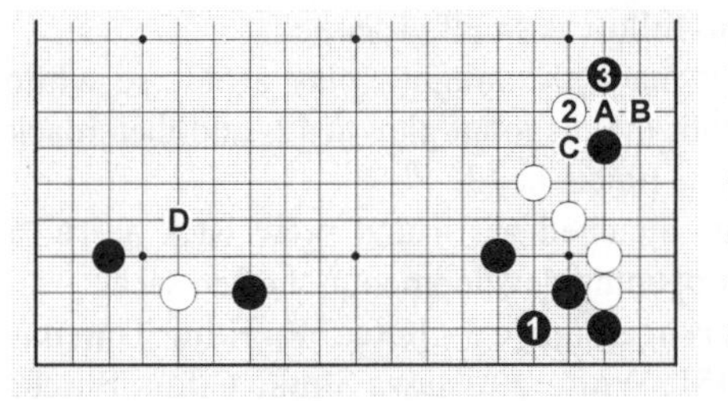

Diagram 7

Backtracking, it was questionable to attach at white 14 and draw back with 16. This maneuver was somewhat heavy, so leaving that area,

Diagram 8 - It was better to attach at 1 and draw back at 3. If black replies at 4, white cuts at 5, and when black plays 8, white continues with 9 and turns back with 13. After black 14, white aims at attaching at **A**, black **B** and a crosscut at white **C** in order to deal deftly with the lower right corner. In this case, theory holds that it is better not to play 14 and 16 in the figure.

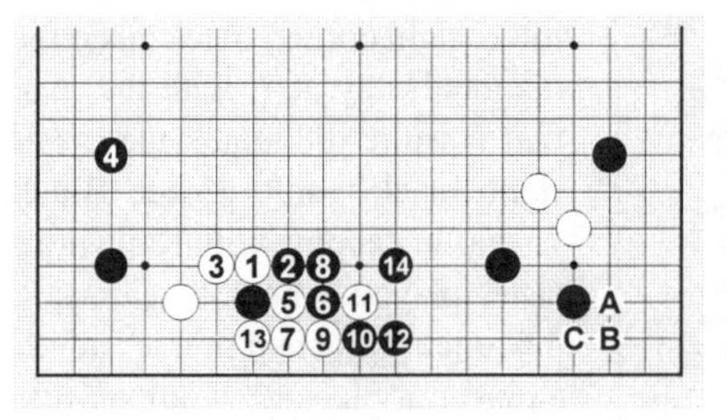

Diagram 8

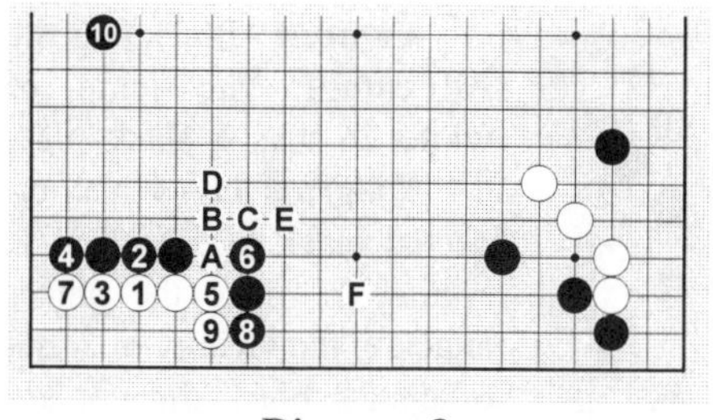

Diagram 9

White had aimed to strike through the knight's play with 18, satisfied to take the corner with the sequence from black 19 through white 24. At 18,

Diagram 9 - If white lives in the corner with 1 through 9, black makes the extension at 10, developing a territorial framework centered around this position. Next, even if white plays **A**, black **B**, white **C**, black **D**, white **E** and black **F**, the stones that have playd out have, on the contrary, become a burden. It is hard to say that white is well off.

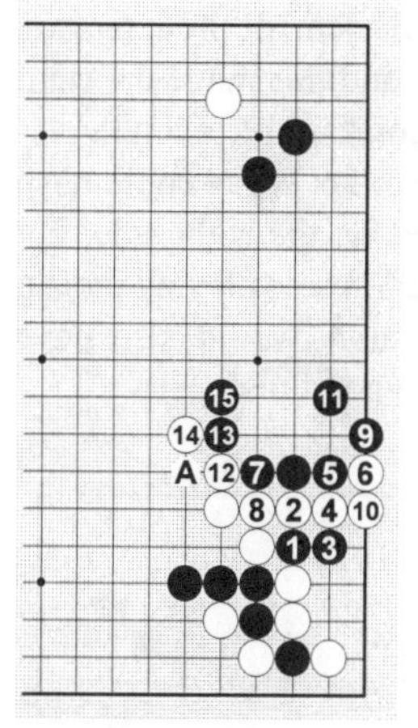

Diagram 10

The exchange of the atari of black 23 for white 24 was not good according to Kajiwara.

Diagram 10 - It was better to cut on this side with black 1, and after white 2 and 4, black blocks at 5 and then plays 7, putting the emphasis on the right side. With the plays up to 15, there is the cut at **A** to aim at next, so this position is promising for black.

With 25, black securely captured this corner.

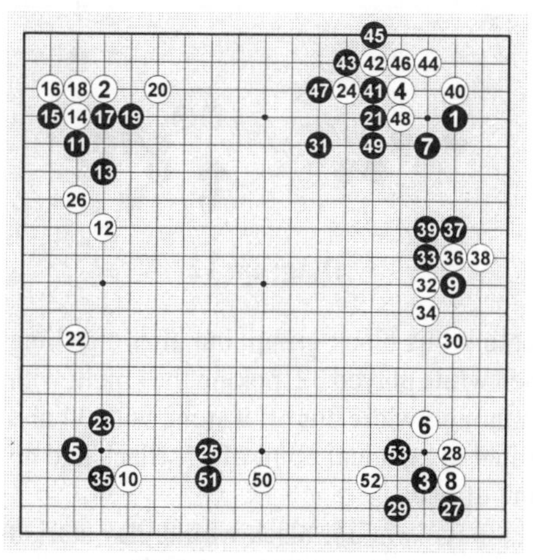

Reference Figure 4

Reference Figure 4 - [1951; 6th Annual Honinbo Title Match, Game 7; White: Sakata Eio 7 dan; Black: Hashimoto Shou, Honinbo] White attached at 8, and black made the pincer at 9. White left this area alone for a while, putting the left side in order with 12 through 26. Black played the thick and strong plays on the upper side from 41 through 47, and white concentrated on the lower side with 50 and 52.

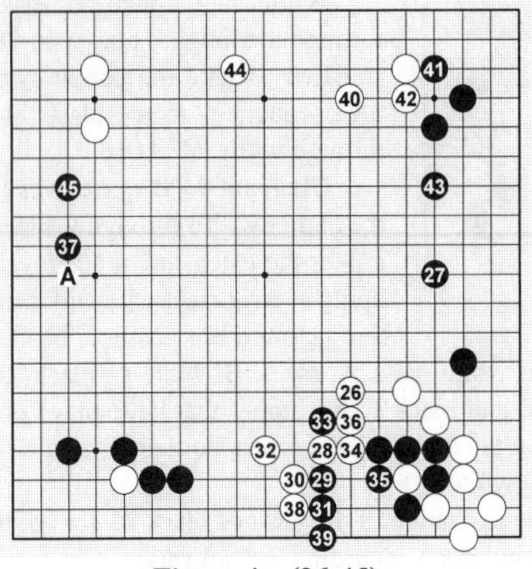

Figure 4 (26-45)

Figure 4 - Black Has the Advantage The jump of white 26 was a slack play.

Diagram 11 - White expected black to defend at 1, aiming to make the pincer attack in the vicinity of 2, but of course black did not answer in line with white's desires.

Black made the extension at 27, and this made the right side comfortable overall.

For 26, white could have played on the right side, but on the left side playing the big point at **A** would also have been a good play.

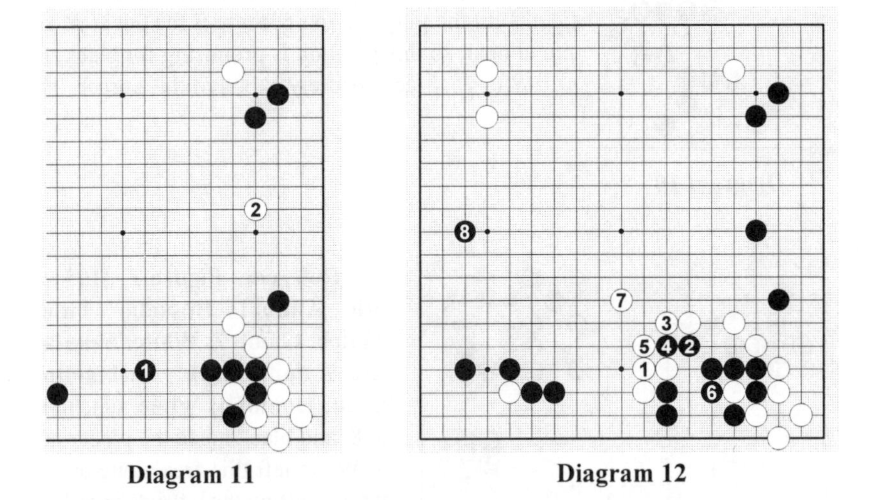

Diagram 11 **Diagram 12**

With 28, white set about tormenting this black group, but after attaching at black 29 and descending at 31, when white played 32, poking the knight with black 33 was a good strategy. Even though white cut off a stone with 34 and 36, black lived in sente here, and turned to the ideal point of 37. Black had no cause for dissatisfaction with this line of play.

For 34, if white had substituted the reply at 36, black would play atari at 34, forcing white to connect in bad shape, which would be painful.

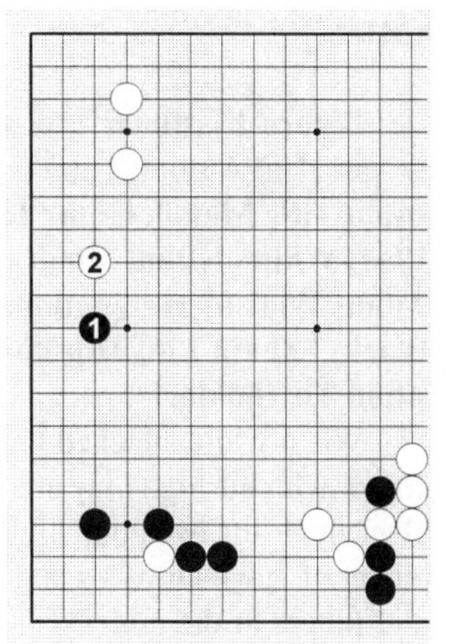

Diagram 13

Instead of the tiger link of 32,

Diagram 12 - If white solidly connects at 1, black puts a flaw in white's shape with 2 and 4, then makes life with 6. When white reinforces with 7, black turns to 8 on the left side, which is felicitous.

Here, getting the value out of every single play was big, and one should pay close attention to the pains taken in order to take sente. White became thick and strong in the lower right corner, but played three more stones than black. Black was satisfied to take compensation for that by turning elsewhere.

Diagram 13 - In addition, black did not play 37 beneath the star point at 1 to hinder a white extension at 2. Black threw a twist of a scheme into this extension as well.

When white made the knight's play at 40, black calmly played 41 and defended the side with 43. Even though white was allowed to make the extension at 44, black considered that being able to turn to the checking extension of 45 was good. From a full board perspective, black has developed the right and left sides on a large scale, while white has only the upper side and the lower right corner, plus the thickness in that vicinity with which to counter black. That thickness has little scope for working effectively, so black's lead cannot be doubted.

Reference Figure 5

Reference Figure 5 - [13th Annual Honinbo Tournament; 1957; White: Yamabe Toshiro 8 dan; Black: Kajiwara Takeo 7 dan] In response to black's pincer at 9, white attached at 10, and with white pressing at 22 and the following plays, a new pattern result. Using white 22 to capture at 27, with black then playing at **A** would be joseki, but dissatisfying for white. Pressing at 27 was the lifeline for black, since drawing out at 29 with this play would let white push through at 31, creating difficulties. White 32 was a fine skillful finesse. For 34, white should have jumped to 40.

SHUSAKU STYLE - GAME 6

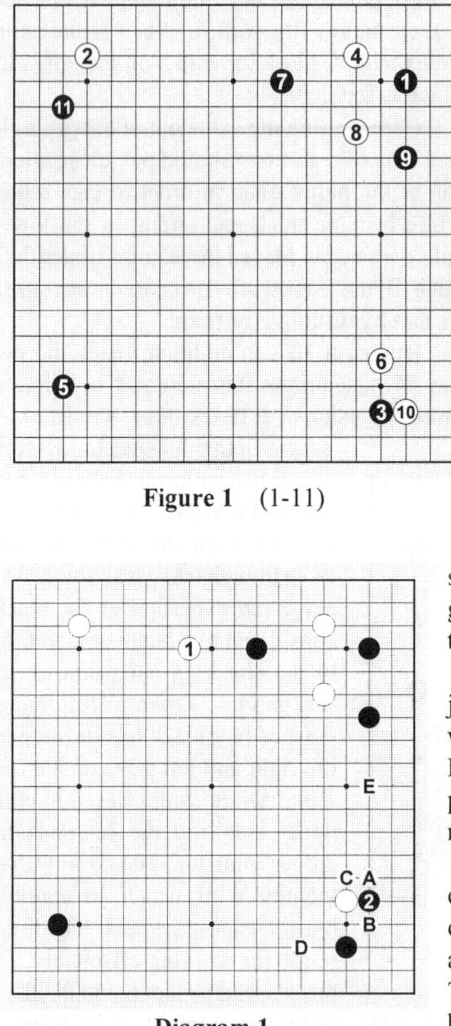

Figure 1 (1-11)

Diagram 1

Figure 1 - Black 7 as a Pincer [2nd Annual Top Position Title Match, Game 1; 1957; White: Kitani Minoru 9 dan; Wins by resignation; Black: Sakata Eio, Top Position Titleholder]

When white attacked the corner with the high play at 6, black made the two point high pincer of 7, which was a popular pincer in the mid-1950s, taking center stage in conjunction with the Shusaku Style. The traditional defense with 7 as a diagonal play from black's standpoint was not suitable in games with komi, so this aggressive maneuver gained favor. This is one aspect of the severity of the modern game.

In response to the two point jump of white 8, black defended with the two point extension at 9. From the era of this game to the present day, this representative maneuver has not been rejected.

White attached at 10. Kitani commented, "Here, if white pincers at 1, I thought black would attach at 2, which I disliked"
The reasoning was that if white blocks at **A**, after black **B**, white **C**, black **D** and white **E**, these stones are aiming at black's low extension. That was distasteful.

White attached at 10, but instead of immediately fixing the shape in this corner, black attacked the upper left corner with 11. Although there was no komi in this game, this was an aggressive maneuver, and illustrates black's way of thinking in not wanting to fix the position in the area of the lower right corner and the right side.

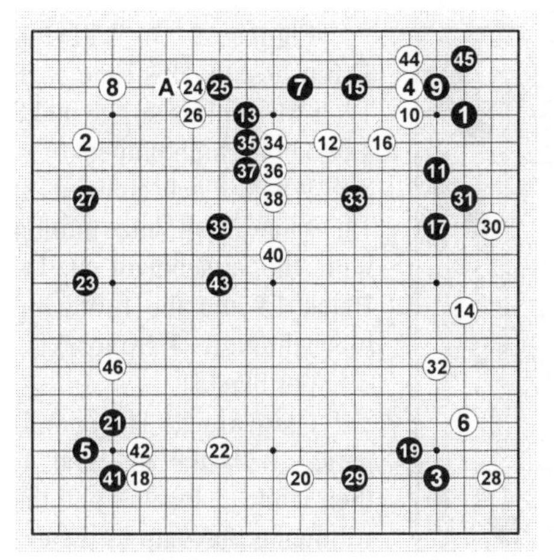

Reference Figure 1

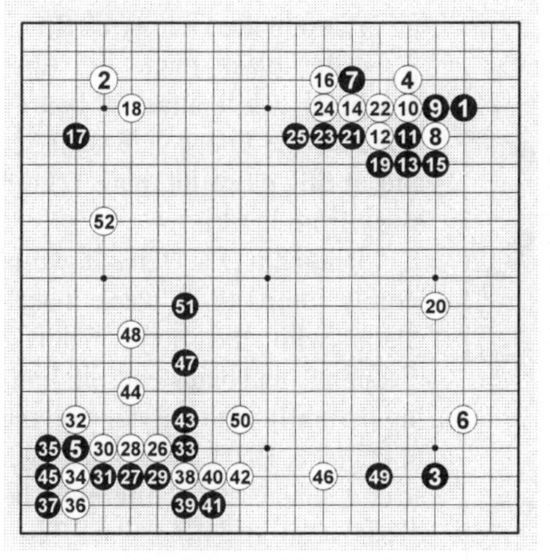

Reference Figure 2

Reference Figure 1 - [Mancho Newspaper Tournament; 1910; White: Nozawa Chikucho 4 dan; Black: Kita Fumiko 3 dan] After white 6, black made the three point pincer at 7, but during this era this maneuver was not often seen. The knight's play of black 13 displayed an attacking attitude. Here, if black made a two point extension at 25, the maneuver with white 13 and the following plays in **Diagram 3** on page 50 was possible. That was avoided and next the aim was to make the checking extension at **A**.

Reference Figure 2 - [Jubango, Game 4; 1928; White: Nozawa Chikucho 7 dan; Black: Suzuki Tamejiro 7 dan] Black made the one point pincer at 7, and the joseki with the fencing-in tactic of white 8 through 16 was played. Pushing with black 19 and the plays through 25 was a thick and strong maneuver. In the lower left, the large avalanche joseki with the attachment of black 37 is classified as an old pattern. Ambitious play overflowed the board in this game.

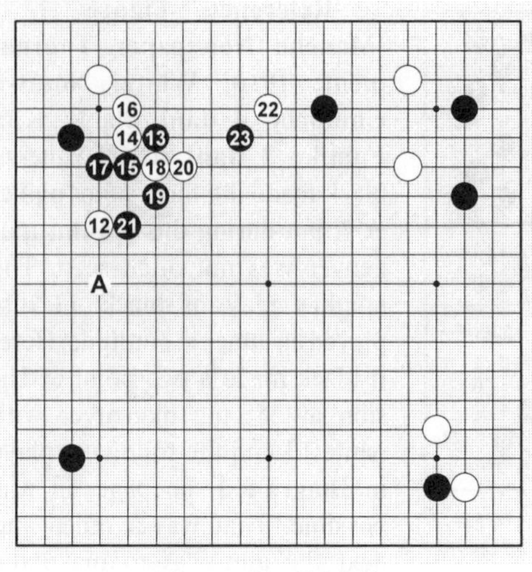

Figure 2 (12-23)

Figure 2 - Varying From Joseki This time with 12, it was white's turn to make a two point high pincer.

When black jumped at 13, white went into motion with the attachment at 14. Black 15 and the following plays through 21 are joseki.

For black 17,

Diagram 2 - The continuation with the jump at 1, then white 2, black 3 and the following plays up to the extension of 7 was also possible. If white uses 6 to capture at **A**, black will probably develop in the vicinity of **B**.

After black made the tiger link at 21, white attacked black's stone on the upper side with 22, and at this point the play veered away from joseki.

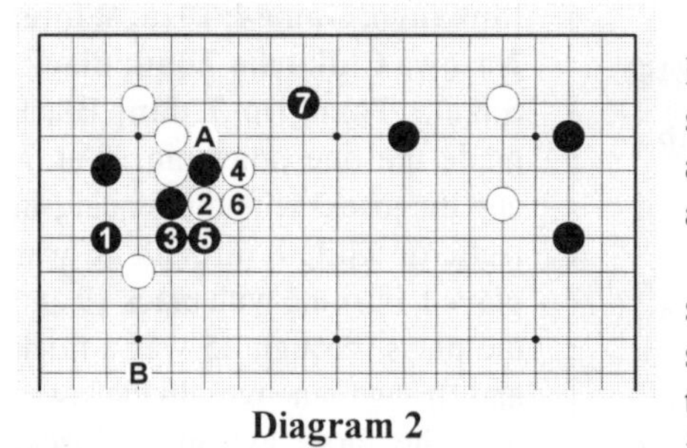

Diagram 2

Diagram 3 - Here, if white simply jumps to 1, black makes shape with the plays from 2 through 8, and black ends up linking naturally with the stone on the upper side. Black has a thick and strong shape, and white must be dissatisfied at letting black have things so easy.

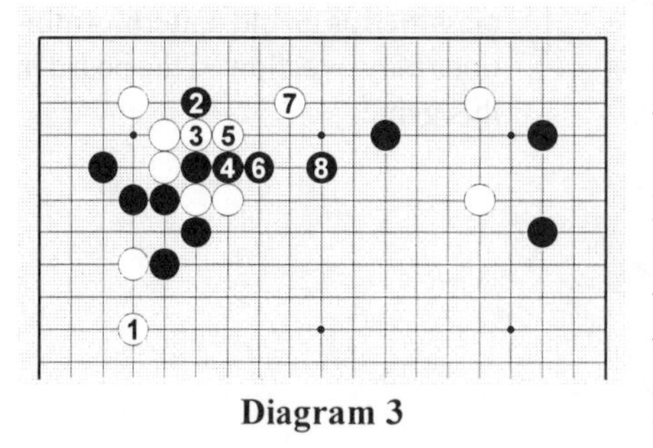

Diagram 3

Diagram 4 - On the other hand, if white takes control of the stone with 1, the hane of black 2 is the obvious response, and even if white then makes the checking extension at 3, black jumps to 4. White's play falls short of packing a real punch.

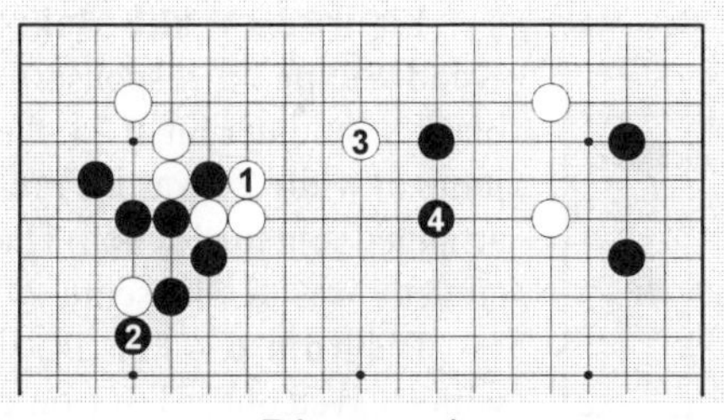

Diagram 4

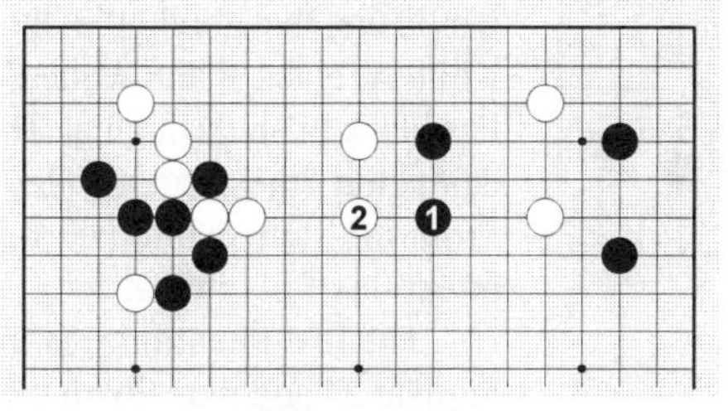

Diagram 5

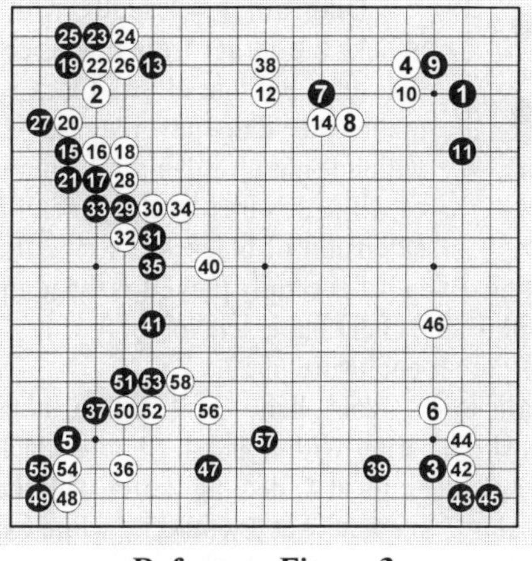

Reference Figure 3

White essayed the expansive play at 22 in order to see how black would play out, and according to that reaction, could determine when to turn to the jump at **A** on the left side. This was a juncture that white met painstakingly, and the scheme that resulted is an edifying model for players aspiring to improve.

Diagram 5 - If black jumps to 1, white also jumps at 2, building territory to the greatest extent possible.

Since letting white surround that area on such a large scale would be terrible, black made the shoulder hit at 23 to play out, countering white's designs. Naturally, black aimed at pulling out the single stone. This was a sharp idea typical of Sakata.

When the existing joseki is deemed insufficient, one must pursue a variation that fits the situation. From this figure through the next, the originality of the schemes of both players and their technical prowess in skirmishing may be called splendid, and from that perspective the game is a masterpiece worthy of admiration.

Reference Figure 3 - [13th Annual Honinbo Title Match, Game 2; 1958; White: Takagawa Shukaku, Honinbo; Black: Sugiuchi Masao 8 dan] In answer to white 8, black made the plays at 9 and 11, an unprecedented maneuver. When black invaded at 19, white thought long and hard for more than two hours before blocking at 20, and made shape with the plays through 40. The sharp demarcation of territory enclosed in tandem on the upper side and left side is the feature of this game.

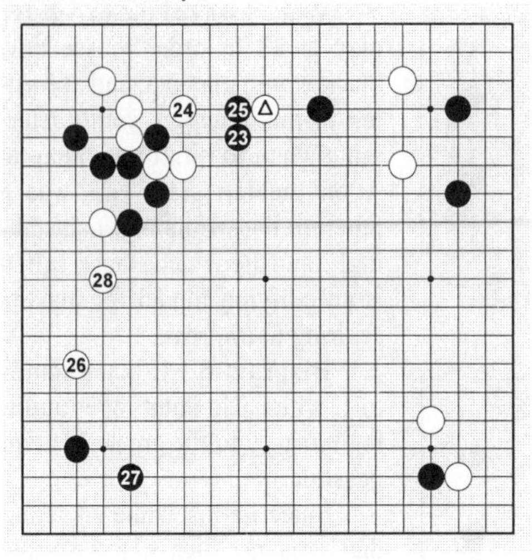

Figure 3 (23-28)

Figure 3 - White Makes Good Shape In response to black's shoulder hit at 23, the jump of white 24 was the prearranged course of action. The strategy was to take sente.

Diagram 6 - For 24, if white played out at 1, it would permit black to pull out the single stone with 2, which would not be good. Playing white **A**, black **B** and white **C** lets black push through at **D**, damaging the two stones. From the start, white had no intention of playing at 1.

The real intention was to jump at 24 and play 26 on the left side. This 26 was another painstaking play.

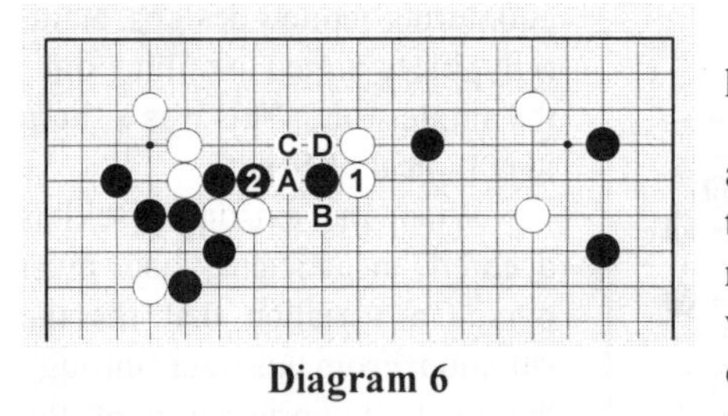

Diagram 6

Diagram 7 - Usually white attacks the corner from this direction of 1, but that allows black to make the diagonal play at 2, which is not promising. The jump of white 3 is met by the checking extension of black 4, leaving the stones floating. Even if 1 is simply played as the jump at 3, black plays the checking extension of 4.

For the corner enclosure of 27,

Diagram 8 - If black hanes at 1, white takes action against the corner with 2 and 4. Should black play 5 and 7, white cuts at 8, dealing deftly with the situation. Using 7 to connect at 8 would let white cut at 7, taking the corner.

Diagram 9 - Playing 5 in the previous diagram at 1, followed by 3, gives white ideal shape with the plays through 8.

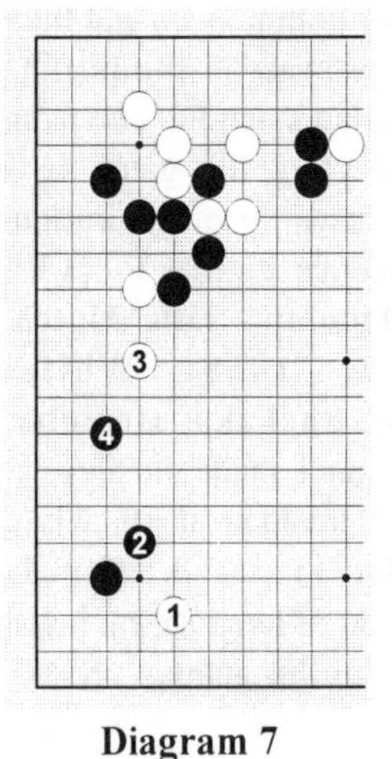

Diagram 7

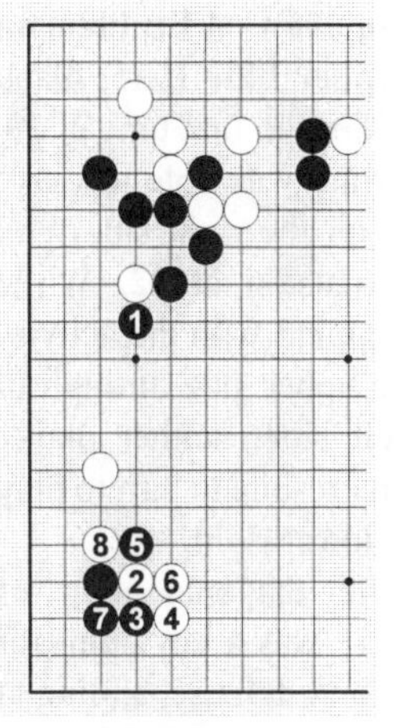

Diagram 8

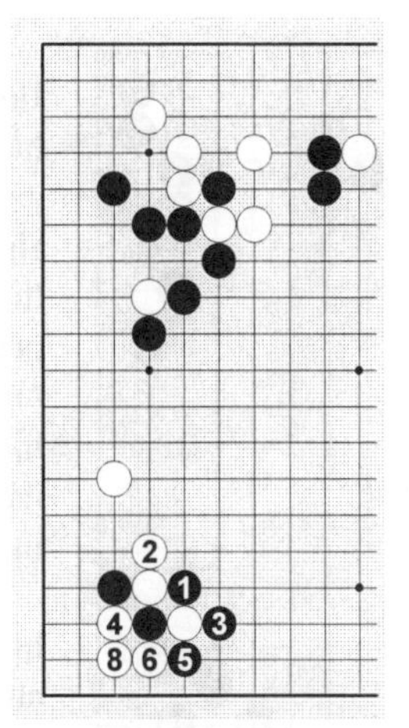

Diagram 9(7 below 1)

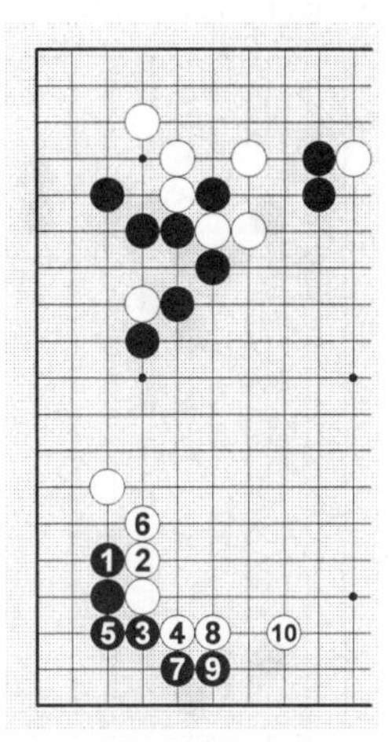

Diagram 10

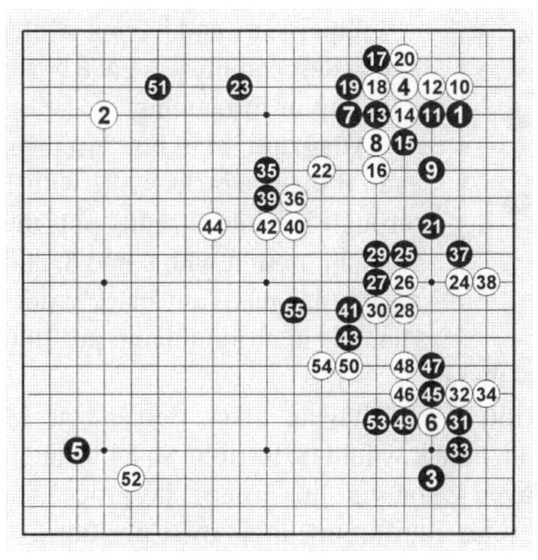

Reference Figure 4

However,

Diagram 10 - In reply to white's attachment, extending at black 1 is cool-headed, and the division with the plays through white 10 may be expected.

On that point, a question lingers concerning black 27. By letting white develop in good form with 28, black made a concession.

Even though black was able to take control of white Δ, explosive elements remain there, and the initial stage of the opening can be considered in general as successful for white.

Reference Figure 4 - [Mainichi Newspaper Sanbango, Game 1; 1958; White: Takagawa Shukaku, Honinbo; Black: Go Seigen 9 dan] Black made a one point high pincer at 7, and the plays through 21 resulted in a new pattern. Afterwards, in the 1964 Meijin Title Match contested by Sakata and Fujisawa Shuko, this "Meijin Title Joseki" appeared and was given that pseudonym. A fierce battle erupted with the plays through 45, representing success for black's strategy. Consequently, with 44, white should have jumped to 53, defending against the cut.

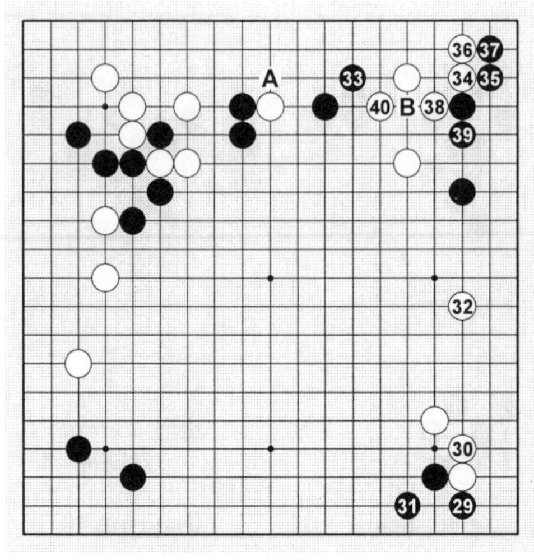

Figure 4 (29-40)

Figure 4 - A Problem on the Upper Side Here, black haned for the first time at 29, and white was able to make shape on the right side with the extension at 32. While preoccupied with the activity on the upper side through to the left side, neither player had any respite to turn to play in the lower right.

The diagonal play of black 33 was a key point for attack and defense, aiming at white's weaknesses while protecting black's own group. There were tremors on the upper side, and having white aim at descending at **A** gave black a feeling of foreboding.

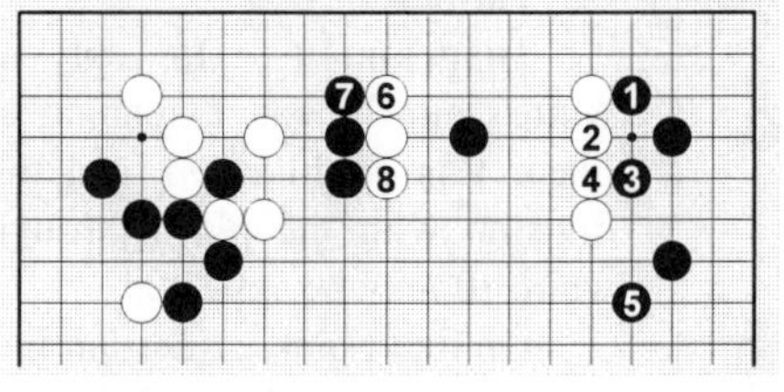

Diagram 11

Diagram 11 - For instance, even if black attacks white with 1 through 5, white abruptly puts the stone in motion with 6 and 8, and all the danger is on black's side. Black is in absolutely no position to dictate matters.

For white's part, having black descend at 34 instituting an attack would be terrible, so 34 through 40 were played to stabilize this group. Play proceeded with both sides reinforcing their own positions, a natural flow of stones.

For 37, black could have played 38, white **B** and black 37.

Also, instead of descending at 36,

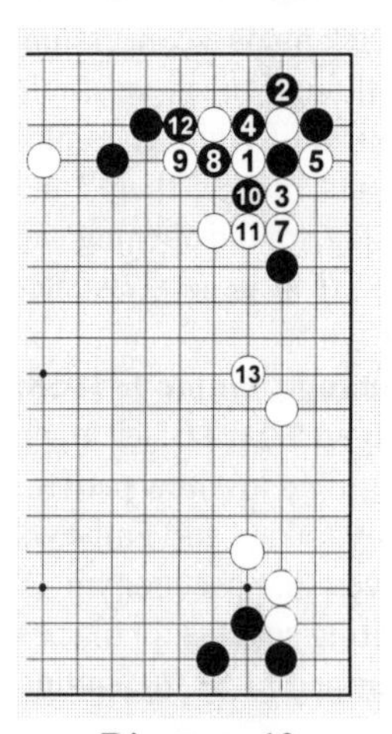

Diagram 12
(6 below 2)

Diagram 12 - White could have first expanded outward with 1. If black makes the return hane at 2, the plays from white 3 through black 12 produce a good swap, and by next making the diagonal play at 13, white consolidates the right side.

Both sides secured their own bases, and play proceeded with the motto being to avoid coming

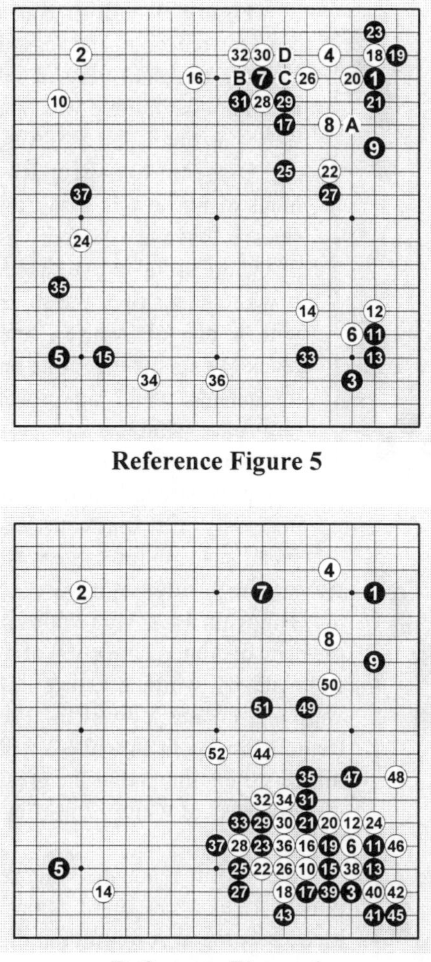

Reference Figure 5

Reference Figure 6

under attack. That is the point to be learned here.

White made the diagonal play at 40, a play that was essential for the stability of these stones.

Reference Figure 5 - [6th Annual Oza Title Match, Game 3; 1958; White: Handa Dogen 8 dan; Black: Fujisawa Hosai 9 dan] When white made the corner enclosure at 10, black attached at 11 and drew back at 13. The knight's play of white 14 was light, in order to meet the needs of the position. However, in the present era, this would probably be played one line to the left as a large knight's play. For 22, white failed to conform with the usual method of playing the extension at **A**. Playing black 31 at 32 would lead to a melee after white **B**, black **C** and white **D**.

Reference Figure 6 - [14th Annual Honinbo Tournament; 1959; White: Yamabe Toshiro 8 dan; Black: Fujisawa Shuko 7 dan] After the fencing-in tactic of white 10, extending at 12 was a new play. Since the right side was played out, white did not block here. When white attacked the corner with 14, black 15 through the cut of 21 was severe. Instead of white 22, the solid connection of 26 made shape. Black 23 was the vital point, and through 49, black got an advantageous result.

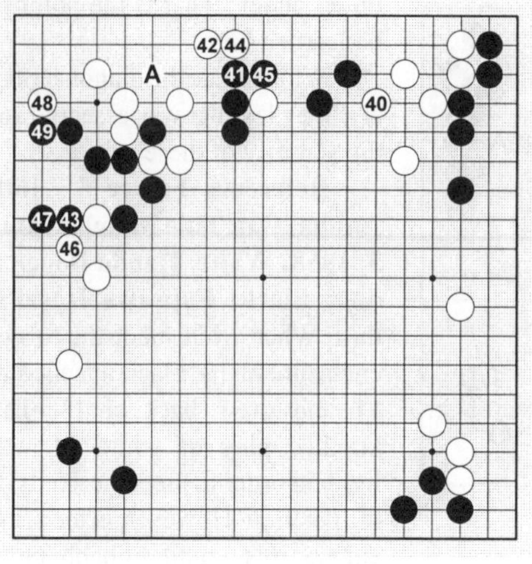

Figure 5 (40-49)

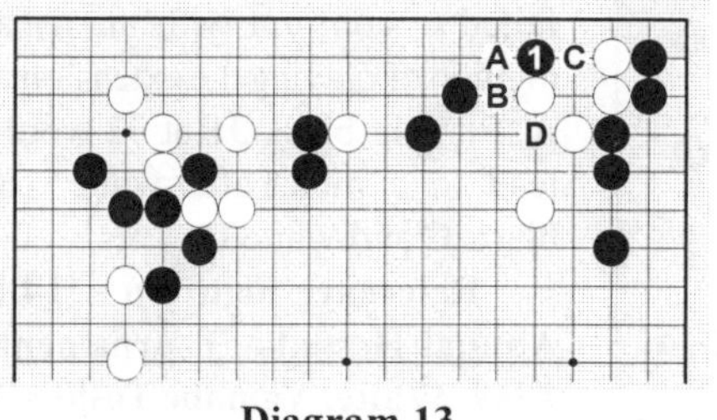

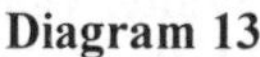
Diagram 13

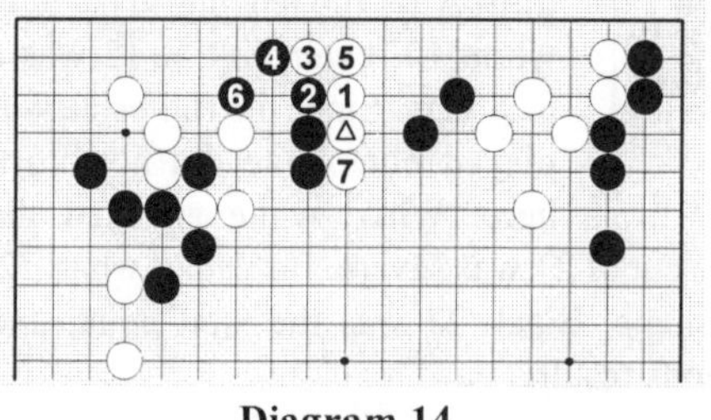

Diagram 14

Figure 5 - Both Sides Set Down Roots The reason that the diagonal play of 40 could not be omitted was that if the position is left as it was,

Diagram 13 - The attachment of black 1 is a skillful finesse that clearly deprives this white group of eye shape. If white hanes over the stone with **A**, black **B**, white **C** and black **D** cuts off the stone on the outside, which represents failure for white.

Now when the white group is strengthened, it is necessary for black to descend at 41. In the same way, leaving the position as it was,

Diagram 14 - After white 1, the hane of 3 and connection of 5, followed by white pressing upward at 7 creates a problem. The tremors issuing from white Δ will not be stilled, indicating the great effectiveness of white 22 in **Figure 2**.

Now white made the knight's play at 42 as a safeguard against black peeping at **A** to pull out the single stone, as well as to aim at a placement in the corner. In terms of territory also, this was by no means a small play.

Black viewed 41 as a forcing play answered by 42, and then played at 43, aiming to stabilize these stones.

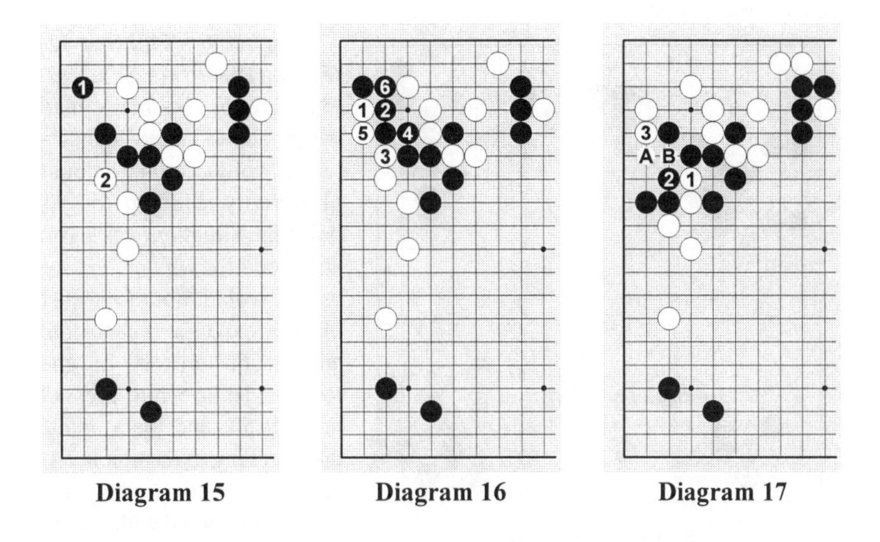

Diagram 15 Diagram 16 Diagram 17

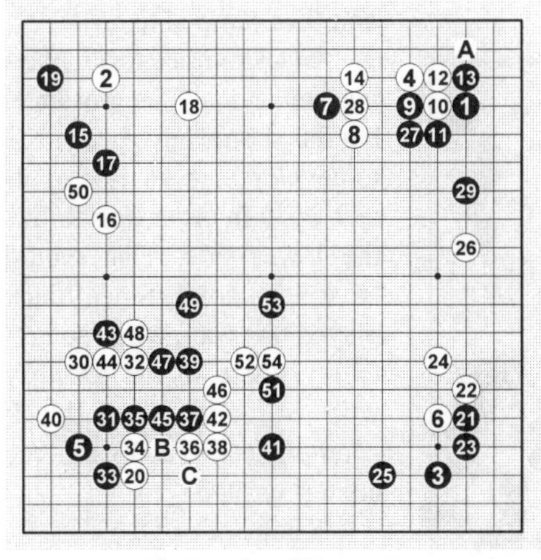

Reference Figure 7

Diagram 15 - For 43, black would love to make the knight's play at 1, but the diagonal play of white 2 makes good shape, and black has no counter for it.

Diagram 16 - Letting the position remain at that invites the severe attachment of white 1, and if black replies at 2, white presses in closely with 3 and 5.

For that reason, attaching at 43 and descending at 47 were big plays, and at this stage, neither side could neglect to set down roots in this area.

The knight's play of white 48 became a forcing tactic when black answered at 49, but black had no choice but to defend here. If this was not played,

Diagram 17 - White 1 followed by the push at 3 leave black stripped after white **A** and black **B**.

Reference Figure 7 - [23rd Annual Honinbo League; 1967; White: Kato Masao 5 dan; Black: Rin Kaiho, Meijin] White 8, black 9 and the following plays make up a pattern that was played at the time. Black 29 defended against white playing hane at 29 and cutting at **A**. Black 33 at **B**, followed by white **C** and black 33 would have been a leisurely maneuver.

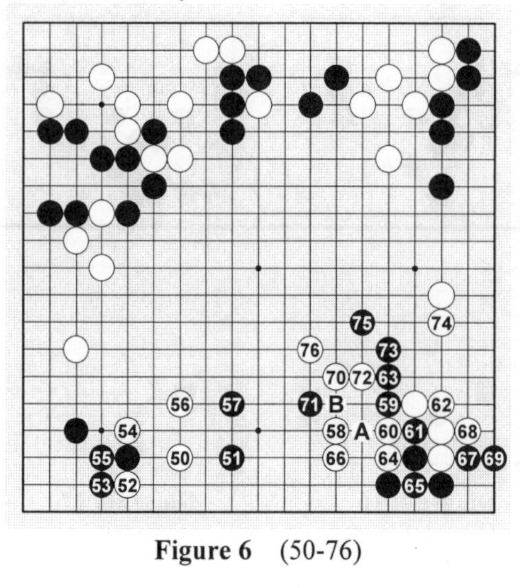

Figure 6 (50-76)

Figure 6 - Fighting Ignites on the Lower Side Various groups of black and white stones lived concurrently with a certain amount of territory, and up to this point the situation was passably good for white.

It would not do to let black make a substantial amount of territory on the lower side, so white pressed in with 50, and black made the checking extension at 51. After this, hostilities began.

White forced with 52 and the clamp attachment of 54, and then jumped to 56.

Black jumped to 57, playing tenaciously as possible, but this should have been used to develop at **A**, or else to attach at 59 in order to stabilize the lower side. That would have been solid. Since black played this way, white sought to lay waste to the territory with 58, and when black counterattacked at 59, a fierce contest ensued.

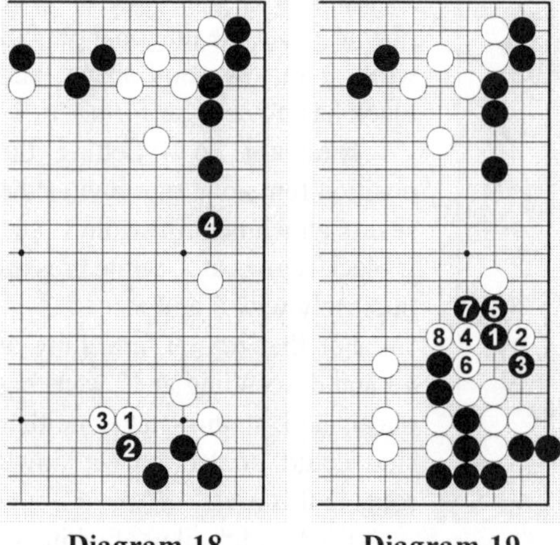

Diagram 18 **Diagram 19**

Kitani: "For 58,

Diagram 18 - It was better to play the knight's play at 1."

That is what he said, but in that case, black will probably answer at 2 and then make the checking extension at 4. If it is played this way, the game would clearly become a leisurely one.

Simply extending at black 63 made shape. Then, white ataried at 64 and put the shape in order with 66. Black 67 and 69 were the plays to make at this juncture, and the sequence up to the jump of white 70 comprised one pattern.

Black peeped at 71 to try to dictate the direction of play. If white connected at **B**, black would then aim to attach at 74. Instead of 71,

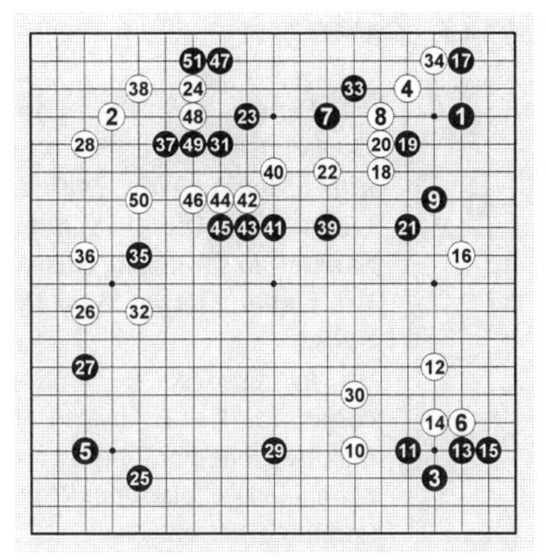

Reference Figure 8

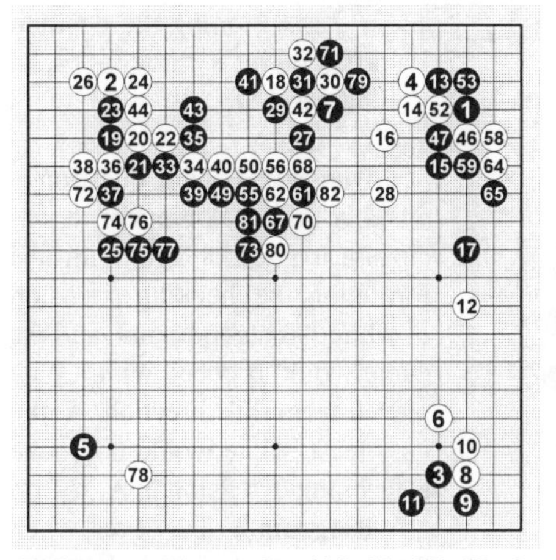

Reference Figure 9 (45, 51, 57, 63, & 69 at 31; 48, 54, 60, & 66 at 42)

Diagram 19 - If black invaded at 1, the sequence through white 8 would follow, with the outcome unclear.

Both sides made diagonal plays with black 75 and white 76, leading to a difficult fight, and depending upon the later fighting, the prospects in the game would sway back and forth. This was a titanic contest of strength.

Reference Figure 8 - [3rd Annual Pro Best Ten Title Match, Game 2; 1966; White: Takagawa Kaku, 10 Dan; Black: Rin Kaiho, Meijin] Black answered white 8 with the large knight's play at 9, seeking a variation. For white 22, common sense dictates that the pincer at 23 should have been made, but playing leisurely and banking on the komi was the Takagawa style. Instead of 28, white could have considered making the fencing-in tactic at 31. With 41 and the following plays, black's strategy was to play for a clear and simple position.

Reference Figure 9 - [3rd Annual Pro Best Ten Tournament; 1966; White: Otake Hideo 7 dan; Black: Rin Kaiho, Meijin] White 30 was an energetic play, but drawing back at 41 was the true shape. A difficult board situation that hinged on a ko fight was the upshot. With the swap up to 71, black had no cause for dissatisfaction.

SHUSAKU STYLE - GAME 7

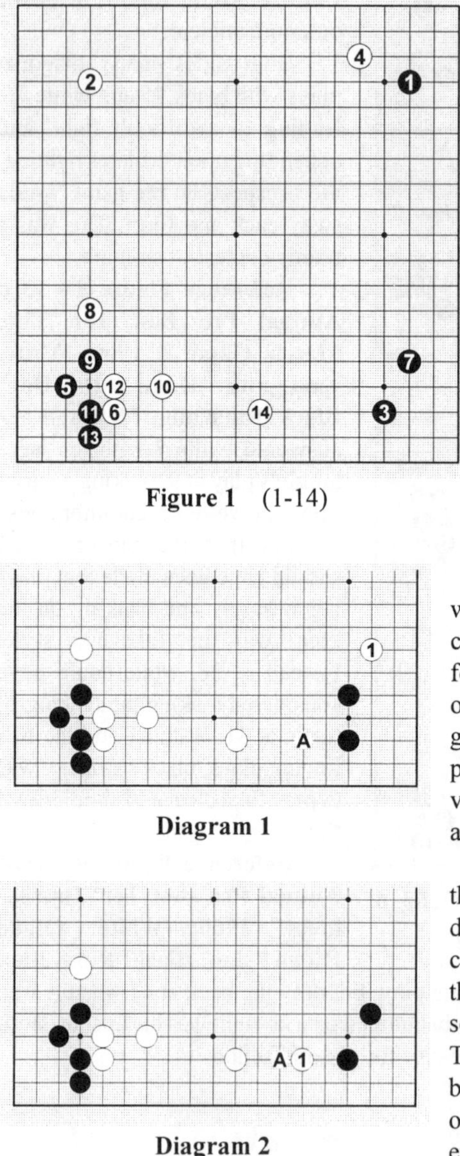

Figure 1 (1-14)

Diagram 1

Diagram 2

Figure 1 - The Low Corner Enclosure [5th Annual Meijin Title Match, Game 2; 1966; White: Sakata Eio, Honinbo; Black: Rin Kaiho, Meijin; Wins by 5 pts.]

In response to white's corner attack at 6, instead of making a one point high corner enclosure, black made the knight corner enclosure at 7. The idea is to consolidate the corner with this single play.

Envisioning the position after white 8 through 14, in that case,

Diagram 1 - The question is whether this one point corner enclosure is good or not. With this formation, the checking extension of white 1 is a good point, and the game would proceed with a play played from this direction. At the very least, white would not make a checking extension at **A**.

Diagram 2 - However, when the corner enclosure is low, the difference is that between the checking extension of white 1 and the checking extension of black **A**, so it becomes an urgent point. There is no particular necessity for black to defend against this. As opposed to the one point corner enclosure, there is no severe checking extension on the right side, and it has the strong point of defending the corner with one play.

It is true that in the Shusaku Style, the one point corner enclosure is one of the basic patterns, but along with the vicissitudes of the ages, one cannot fathom what changes will occur later on in the maneuver in regards to different formations. Localized maneuvers are refined in small increments, and in this way the opening evolves.

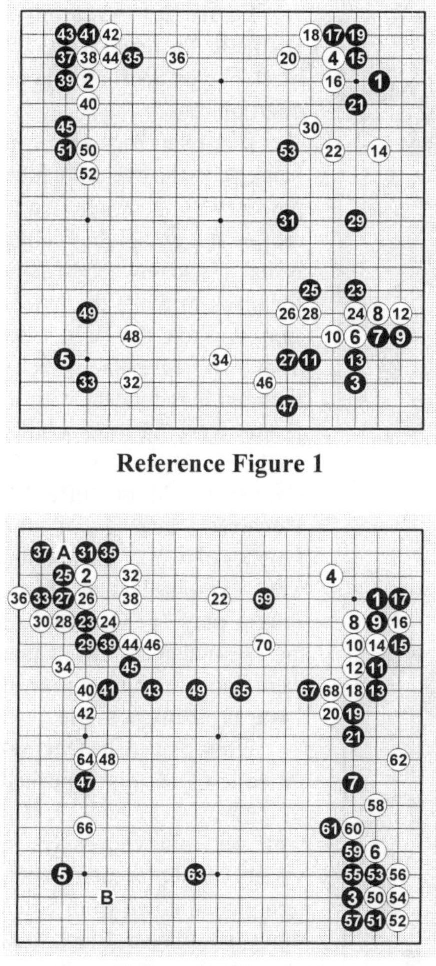

Reference Figure 1

Reference Figure 2

Reference Figure 1 - [5th Annual Honinbo Title Match, Game 5; 1959; White: Takagawa Shukaku, Honinbo; Black: Kitani Minoru 9 dan] White's high attack on the corner with 6 was met by black 7 and 9, restrained plays typical of the Kitani style. The pincer of white 14 was answered similarly, black 15 and the following plays securely defending the corner, and then black 23 and the rest challenged the breadth of the right side. Black took four corners and then confronted white's influence.

Reference Figure 2 - [11th Annual Oza Tournament; 1963; White: Shimamura Toshihiro 9 dan; Black: Rin Kaiho 7 dan] When white attacked the corner at 6, here is an example of black making a pincer at 7 in relation to that corner. White immediately played the fencing-in tactic of 8, and expanded the upper side with 22. With 32, white rejected the joseki cut at **A** and initiated a strategy to establish a position on each side of the corner. It would have been sufficient for black to use 69 to make a corner enclosure at **B**.

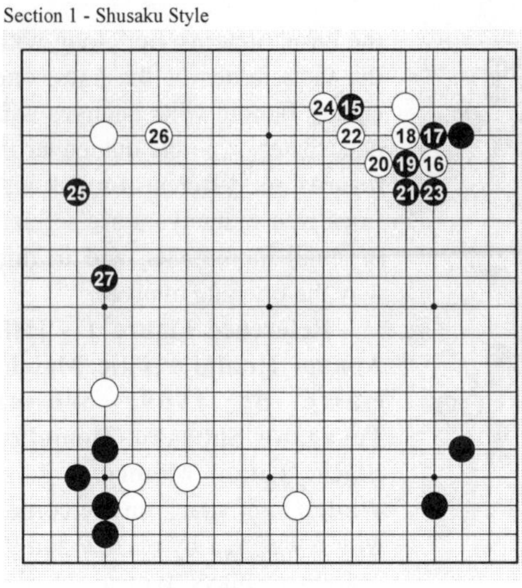

Figure 2 (15-27)

Figure 2 - Avoiding a Difficult Pattern With 15, black played the forceful one point pincer.

Diagram 3 - Here, if black plays the two point high pincer with 1, when white replies at 2 and 4, the feeling is that it is somewhat difficult for black to make the extension at 5 on the right side. That is because black ▲ is low and is redundant with it. If this were the high corner enclosure at **A**, the circumstances would be different. However, instead of the knight's play of 3, the opinion was expressed that black should play at the corner of the position at **B**, and if that were done, the high pincer of 1 was probably possible.

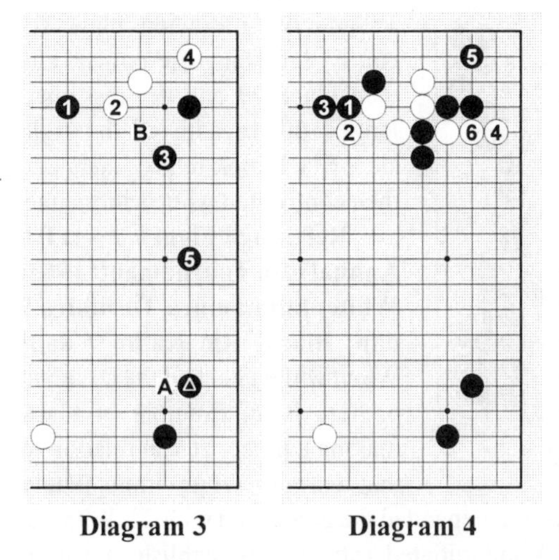

Diagram 3 **Diagram 4**

White played the fencing-in tactic of 16, black pushed through with 17 and 19, and with the following plays, a variety of a representative pattern passed down from olden times was played. Black took control of a stone with 23, even though the feeling is that it falls in with white's desires by permitting the block of white 24, conforming to a peaceful maneuver.

Diagram 4 - At 23, the joseki starting with the hane of 1 and continuing through 6 was also possible, but this is an impenetrably difficult pattern, and I was not all that confident playing it.

The fact is that I wanted to avoid variations and play simply.

Black attacked the corner with 25 and developed on the left side with 27. White 26 had no choice but to defend at 26. Here,

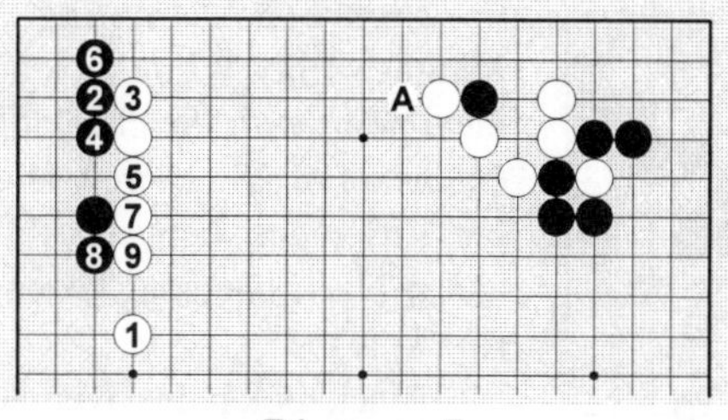

Diagram 5

Diagram 5 - If white pincers at 1, black enters the 3-3 point with 2. White creates thickness through 9, but black has the clamp attachment of **A** with which to make an erasure of the upper side, and one way or another will deal deftly with the situation. White found this distasteful.

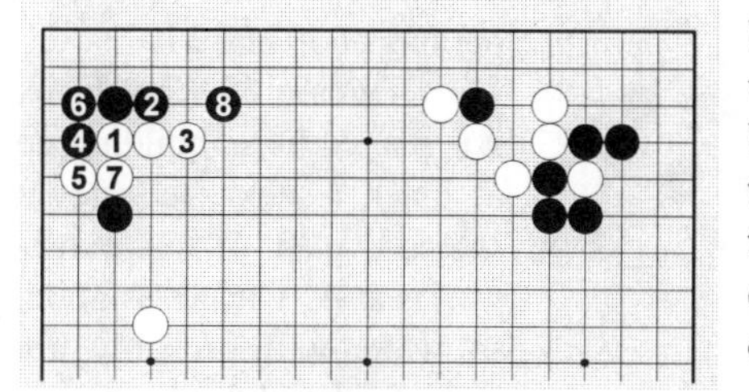

Diagram 6

Diagram 6 - In response to black's play at the 3-3 point, if white blocks on this side with 1, black 2 through 8 expose the mistake in direction. In this position, the protruding sword point of 8 erases the upper side to white's displeasure.

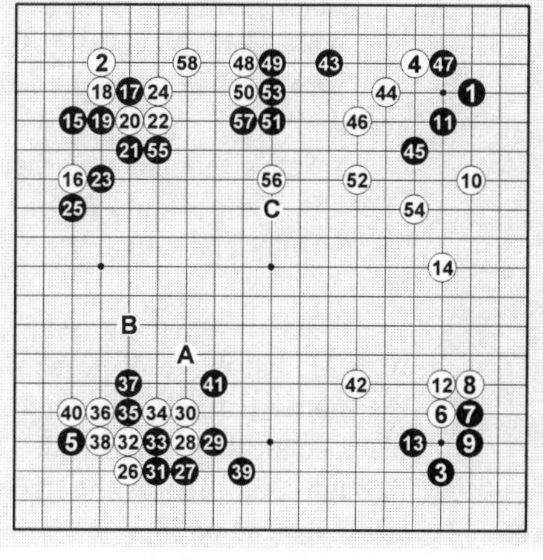

Reference Figure 3

Reference Figure 3 - [14th Annual Oza Title Match, Game 1; 1966; White: Rin Kaiho, Meijin; Black: Sakata Eio, Honinbo] Examples of the knight corner enclosure in the lower right are treated in the Reference Figures of the next game, but here other formations used in the Shusaku Style are introduced. The plays through white 14 comprise one such pattern. The same joseki as in the present game was played in the upper left corner. For 40, it was possible to play **A** and black **B**, but the strategy was that giving up the three stones was all right. For 55, it was urgent for black to play 57, white 58 and black **C**.

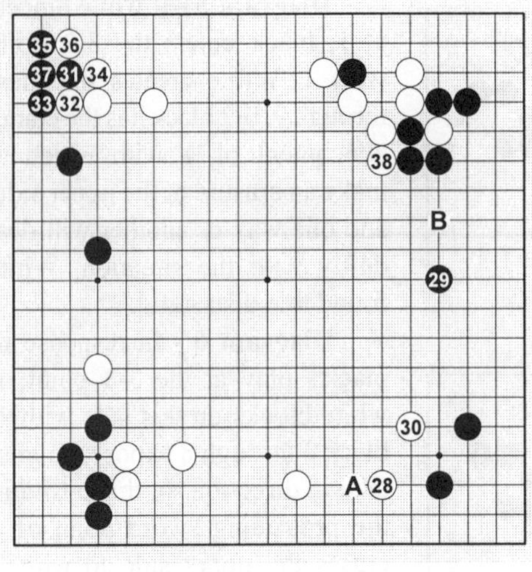

Figure 3 (28-38)

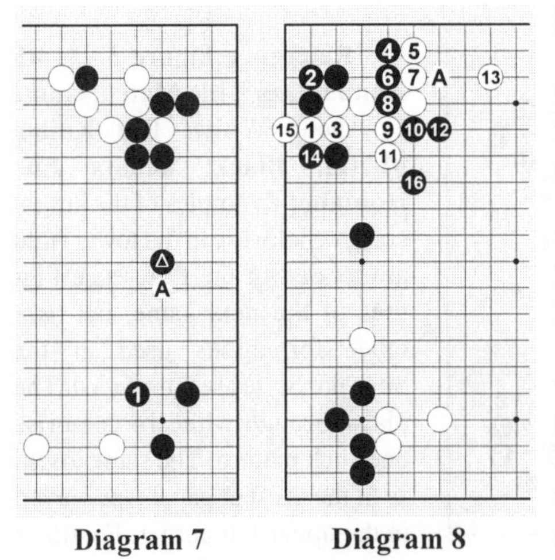

Diagram 7 **Diagram 8**

Figure 3 - Inviting a Knight's Play White took an ideal point with the checking extension of 28. There was a big difference between this and a black checking extension at **A**.

Black took pains over the placement of the extension at 29. This play made equivalent options of 30 and 31.

Diagram 7 - When black ▲is played here, building up at black 1 next becomes a splendid plan. If this extension is at **A**, 1 is not as good, so white will probably not make the knight's play at 30 in the figure.

Black's strategy was to entice white into playing at 30, then turn to 31 in the upper left corner.

Sakata's thought was that, "For 30, white should press at 38, and after black 30, invade at **B**."

Black ravaged the corner with 31, but white disposed of the matter naturally by letting black connect positions with 32 through 36, then white took sente. Instead of 34,

Diagram 8 - If white blocks at 1 and the following sequence is played, white would not like the position after the knight's play of black 4. If the attachment of 5 were effective it would be fine, but black would poke and cut with 8 and 10, leaving white in an excruciating situation. Black 12 and the block at 14 are severe, and if white descends at 15, the fencing-in tactic of black 16 annihilates white. White 5 as the diagonal play at **A** makes the breadth of the upper side too narrow.

Pressing at white 38 was a good point. While expanding the upper side, it aimed at the invasion of **B**.

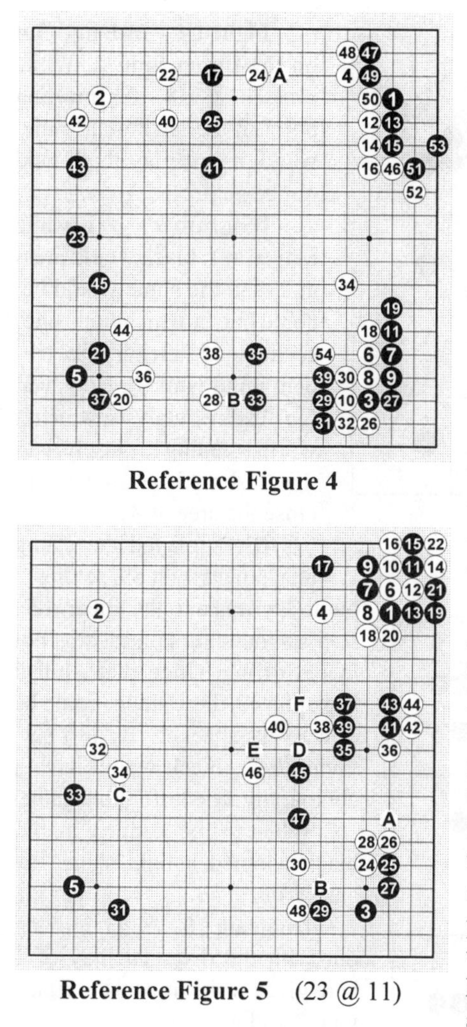

Reference Figure 4

Reference Figure 5 (23 @ 11)

Reference Figure 4 - [23rd Annual Honinbo Title Match, Game 5; 1968; White: Rin Kaiho, Meijin; Black: Sakata Eio, Honinbo] When black attached at 7, white played the avalanche plays of 8 and 10, then embarked on a strategy of forcing black into a low position on the right side with the fencing-in tactic of 12. Black split the upper side with 17. Black 23 was a dogged play. If this was played as the extension at **A**, white would develop the left side with 23. Using white 28 to advance as far as **B** would lead to a black fencing-in tactic at 36.

Reference Figure 5 - [24th Annual Honinbo Title Match, Game 2; 1969; White: Rin Kaiho, Honinbo; Black: Kato Masao 5 dan] Following the two point high attack on the corner with 4, white made thickness in the upper right with the plays up to 23. Black took profit with 25 and the following, but naturally a pincer at **A**, or else defending at **B** was also possible. White could have used 34 as the knight's play at **C**. Black 37 was questionable since it headed into white's thickness. Jumping at **D**, followed by white **E** and black **F** was better. With 48, white was playing in good form.

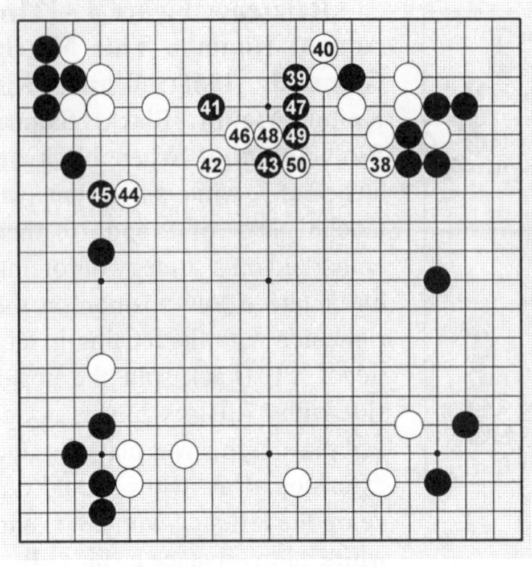

Figure 4 (38-50)

Figure 4 - Moving Out on the Upper Side White pressed at 38, the meeting point of the territorial frameworks and a play that could not be neglected. Here,

Diagram 9 - If white played at 1, black would press at 2, and the game would become one in which both sides surrounded territory in tandem up to white 7. However, Go Seigen's analysis, which is worth listening to closely, was that 1 should be used to enclose the area at **A**.

Black played the clamp attachment with 39, setting out to lay waste to the upper side, so a surrounding contest was not in the offing. Once that 41 had been played, these stones could be effectively attacked. By just surviving here, black would have a comparatively comfortable game.

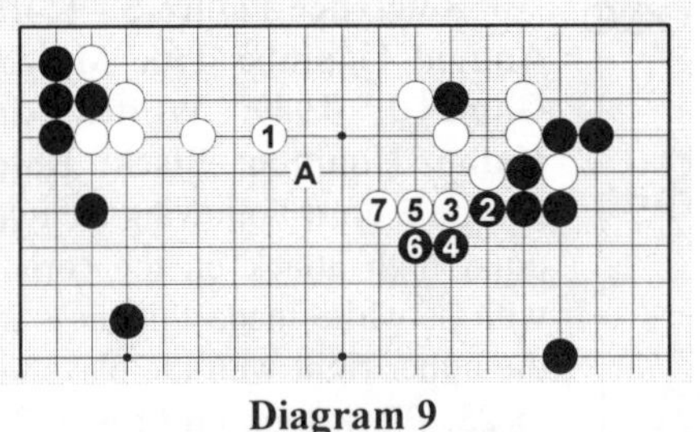

Diagram 9

When white capped at 42, black adopted a light stance by answering at 43.

Diagram 10 - At 43, moving out with the diagonal play of 1 here gives white impetus to attack with 2 and 4.

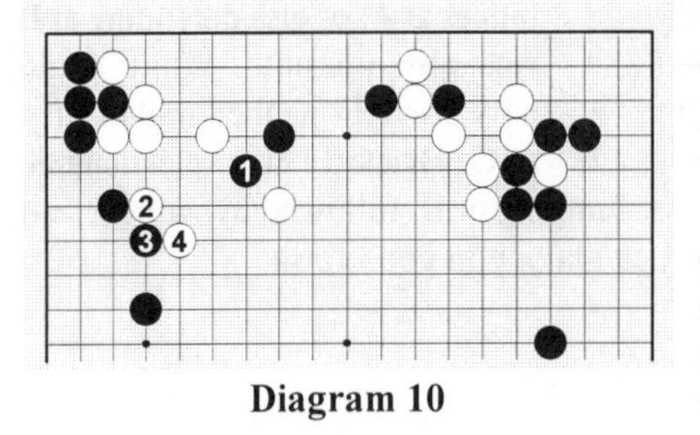

Diagram 10

At this point, white played 44 as a probe, but playing this in exchange for the diagonal attachment of black 45 erased potential weaknesses that might have been exploited. It was a questionable play and white had to simply make the diagonal play at 46.

In regards to white 46, once 44 has been played,

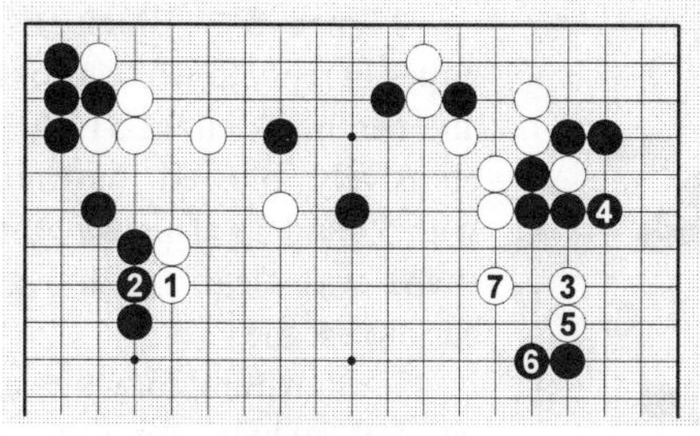

Diagram 11

Diagram 11 - It was perhaps better to extend at 1, maintaining a continuity of plays. This forces black to connect at 2, then white sets play in motion on the right side with 3 through 7. Black will put this group's shape in order with 8, and this can be thought of as a feasible game.

For 47,

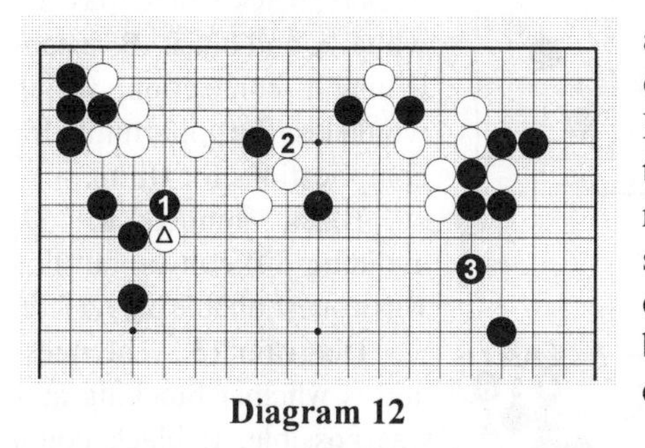

Diagram 12

Diagram 12 - Black could also hane at 1, with the intention of turning white Δ into a bad play. Blocking at white 2 is the norm in this situation, so black can surround profit at 3, and the game situation is one in which black can compete on territory. This would be more clear and simple than the course in the figure.

White pushed through at 48 and cut at 50 to attack, but black had no worries about dealing deftly with these stones.

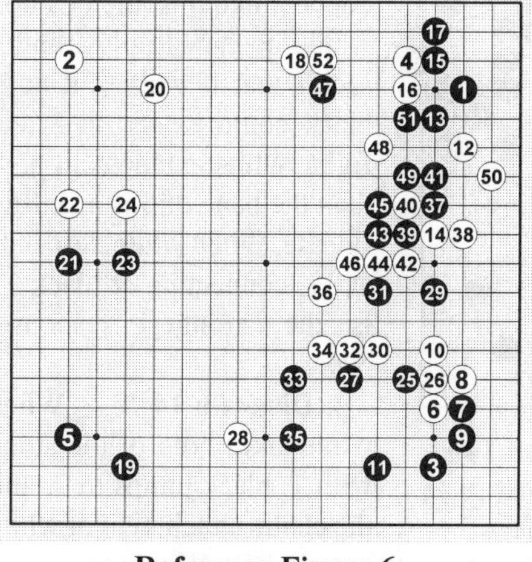

Reference Figure 6

Reference Figure 6 - [5th Annual Pro Best Ten Title Match, Game 2; 1968; White: Sakata Eio, Honinbo; Black: Fujisawa Shuko 9 dan] White made the tiger link at 10, then launched a scheme with 12 and 14. Instead of hurrying to play on the left side, white made the corner enclosure at 20, then when black played 21, white surrounded the upper left with 22 and the jump at 24. The attachment of black 37 was an overplay. It was better to play 43 with this, followed by white 49 and then the attachment of black 37. White 38 was a calm maneuver that prepared for the exquisite play of 48. White swallowed up black's two stones on the right side on a large scale with the plays through 50, achieving success.

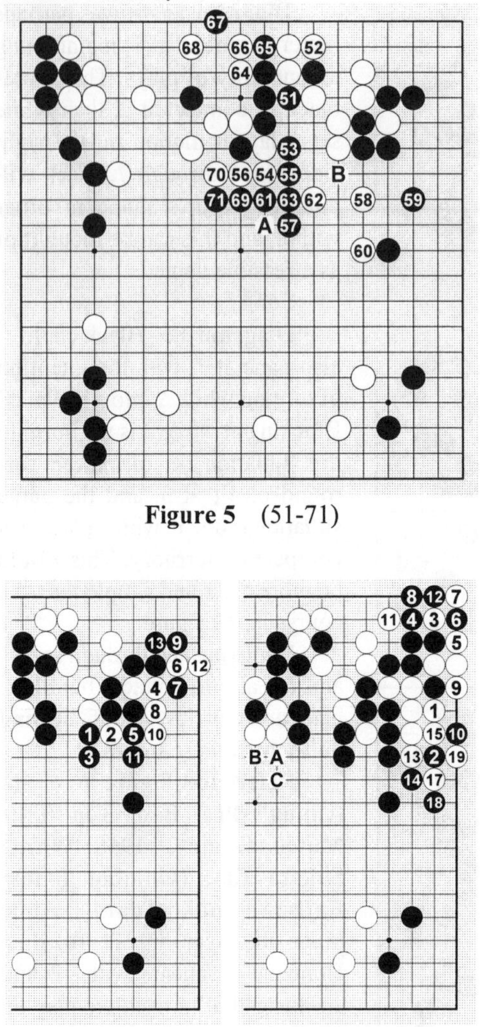

Figure 5 (51-71)

Diagram 13

Diagram 14 (15@6)

Figure 5 - Black Escapes In reply to white's poke and cut, black cut at 51, then abrasively plowed outward with 53 and 55. This way the shape was clear and it was easy to escape.

It was natural for white to take hold of black's stone with 56. If white had extended at 61 here, black would play 63, white **A** and black **B**, establishing a connection, which would lose the opportunity for complications for white.

Black jumped to 57, avoiding difficulties, but this was a questionable play. Here,

Diagram 13 - The question is whether blocking at 1 was possible. If black could connect like this, the position would be easy to play, and it seems that if white cut at 2, black could extend at 3 and fight. White extends out at 4, then the hane of 6 is a skillful finesse. When white descends at 12, connecting at black 13 is the strongest response. Next,

Diagram 14 - When white takes hold of the stone with 1, black jumps to 2, and the clamp attachment of white 3 leads to the sequence from black 4 through the atari of 12. Within this order of play, the diagonal play of 10 is good, then after both sides live with the continuation through 19, black can turn to hane at **A**, followed by white **B** and extend at black **C**. Even though white is permitted to live, gaining this kind of substantial position means that black has a playable game.

However, there are difficult points in this variation, so black played as in the figure in order to keep things clear and simple.

In answer to white 58 and 60, black played once at 59, then switched to 61, and when white took profit on the upper side with 64 through 68, with black 69 and the push at 71, black set out to make thickness in the center. At the present point of 71, the balance of territory is in black's favor and the lead may be seen to be so as well.

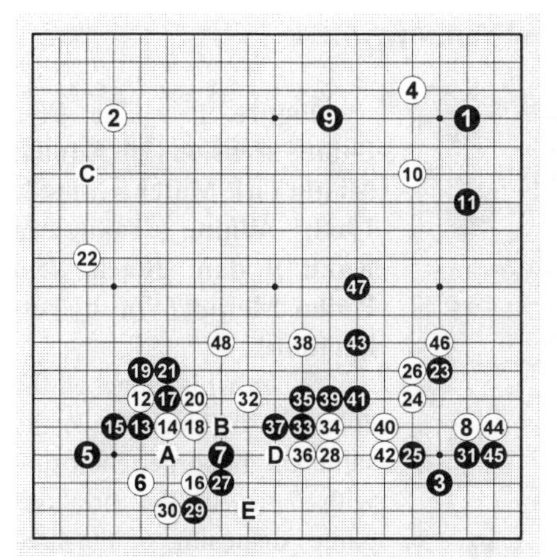

Reference Figure 7

Reference Figure 7 - [8th Annual Meijin Title Match, Game 1; 1969; White: Takagawa Kaku, Meijin; Black: Rin Kaiho, Honinbo] With 7 and 9, black made a pair of two point high pincers. If white used 16 to draw back at **A**, after black 17, white 20, black 21, white **B** and black 19, **C** and **D** would be equivalent options for black. Black 27 at 28, answered by white **E** would have been a mild maneuver.

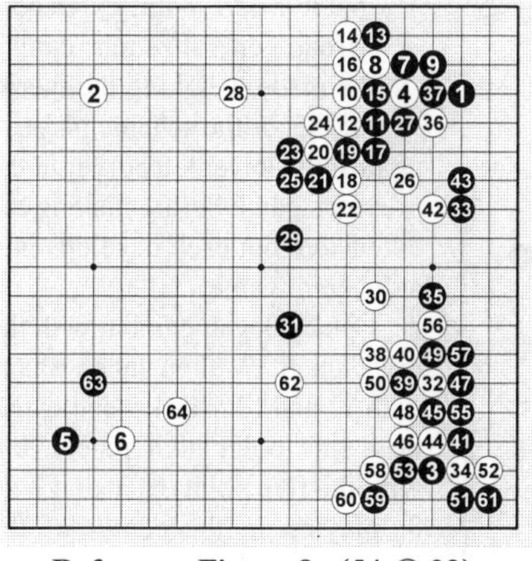

Reference Figure 8 (54 @ 32)

Reference Figure 8 - [5th Annual All Japan First Place Tournament, Game 2; 1975; White: Kudo Norio 8 dan; Black: Otake Hideo, First Place Titleholder] The fencing-in tactic of white 18 in the upper right initiated a pattern that is often played, and in this game the continuation with the jump of black 31 was played. Slicing through the knight's play with black 39 followed by 41 were severe plays typical of Otake, and skillfully took territory.

SHUSAKU STYLE - GAME 8

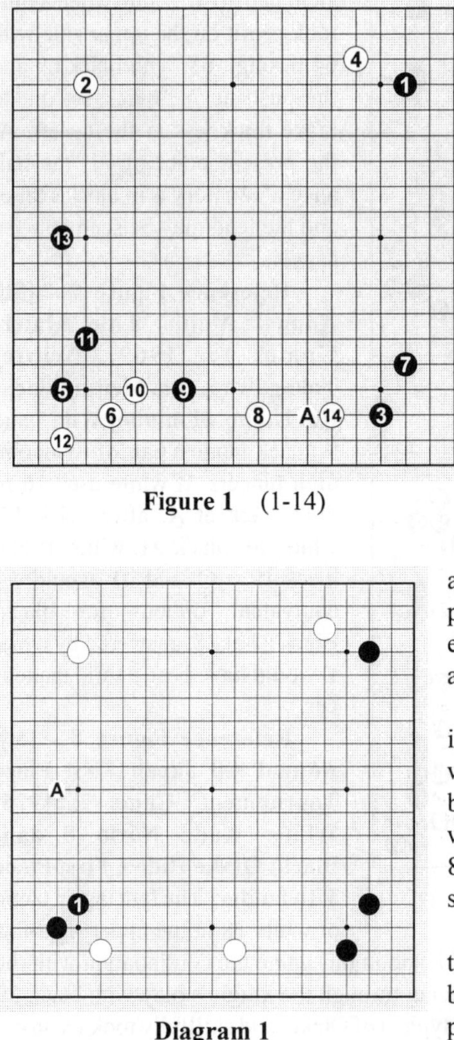

Figure 1 (1-14)

Diagram 1

Figure 1 - The Five Point Extension [7th Annual Meijin Title Match, Game 2; 1968; White: Takagawa Kaku 9 dan; Black: Rin Kaiho, Meijin; Wins by resignation]

When white attacked the corner at 6, black made the same knight corner enclosure with 7 as in the previous game, disposing of the area with one play.

With 8, white simply made a five point extension. Broad generalizations cannot be made weighing the merits of this or the scheme played against the lower left corner in the previous game before making the extension, but each develops into a different game.

Black began combat with the invasion of 9, then made shape with 11 and 13. Black 9 could also be a one point high pincer, but with the five point extension with 8, playing in the center of the stones is more precise.

Diagram 1 - In olden times, the diagonal play of 1 might have been made with the intention of playing solidly, but the big point of white **A** on the left side becomes ideal. An invasion on the lower side after that affords white scope to initiate a campaign.

As might be expected, it is desirable to initially invade and then play first on the left side. Particularly in this game, with white positioned on the upper left star point, black 13 played below the star point became a good play.

The extension of white 14 was a big point that could not be neglected. If it was not played, black would have immediately made the checking extension at **A**.

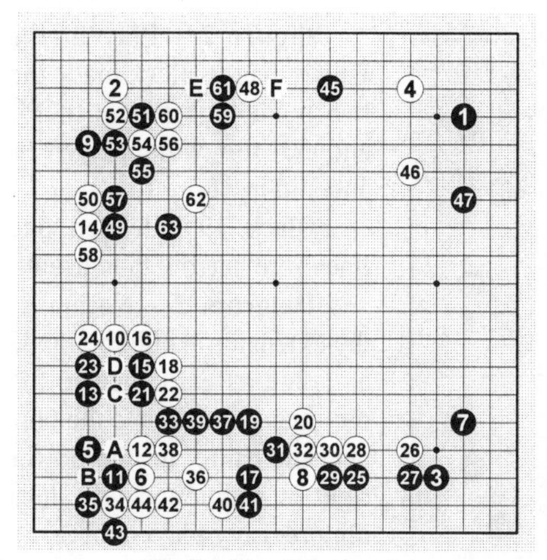

Reference Figure 1

Reference Figure 1 - [Jubango, Game 1; 1884; White: Murase Shuho 8 dan (18th hereditary Honinbo); Black: Hayashi Shuei 5 dan (Meijin, 17th and 19th hereditary Honinbo)] Up to white 8, the same pattern was played as in the present game, then after black 9, white initiated a scheme with 10. Black made the low checking extension at 13. For white 14, it would have been thick and strong to seal black in with **A**, black **B**, white **C**, black 23 and white **D**. Black played 15 and then invaded at 17 to fight. Black 45 was a dangerous play that led to a convoluted fight. Making a pincer at **E** followed by white 51 and black **F** was peaceful.

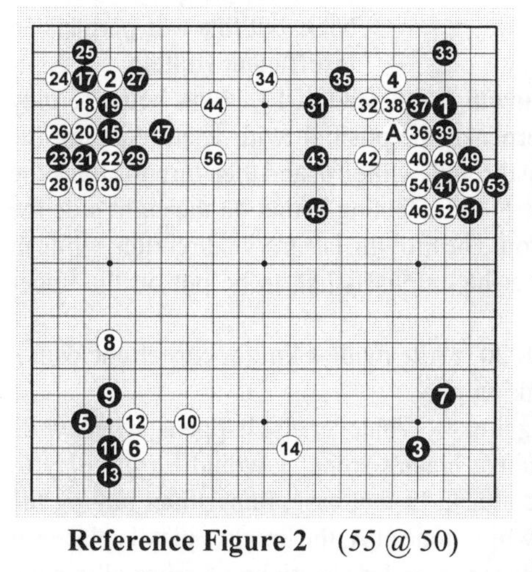

Reference Figure 2 (55 @ 50)

Reference Figure 2 - [14th Annual Nihon Ki-in Championship; 1966; White: Kano Yoshinori 8 dan; Black: Otake Hideo 7 dan] The plays through white 14 were the same pattern as in the previous game's joseki. Black set a scheme in motion by jumping at 33, but playing at the corner of white's stone at **A** could have also been considered. White provoked a reaction with 34, then played a skillful sequence starting with 36. Through 54, white built a thick and strong formation, and by jumping out at 56, white's play can be viewed as a success.

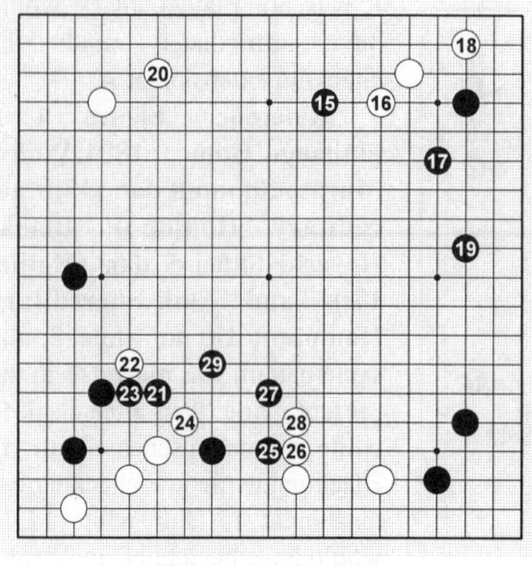

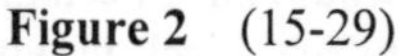

Figure 2 (15-29)

Figure 2 - Play in the Upper Right Black made the two point high pincer at 15, and here too, white played 16 and slid to 18.

Black 19 extended one line more narrow than usual.

Diagram 2 - Normally, the extension would be made at 1, but as explained in the previous game, since the corner enclosure in the lower right is positioned low, it is not precisely played there.

Therefore, black played the reserved play one line back, but this was perhaps an insufficient strategy.

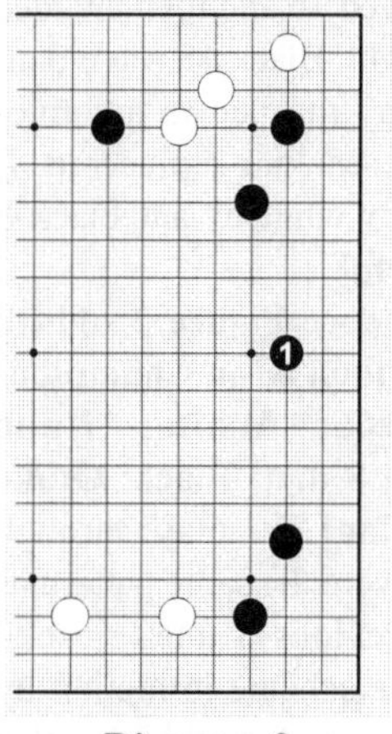

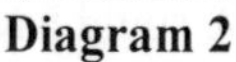

Diagram 2

Diagram 3 - Instead of 17, it was better to play at the corner of the position with 1, anticipating the sequence through white 10, and then turn to attack the corner at 11. The feeling is that on the right side the stones would be moving in a trivial direction, while in this game the emphasis had to be put on the upper side.

With 20, white made a knight corner enclosure, a painstaking play.

Diagram 4 - Whatever else happens, when white plays against black's stone, 1 would be the play to press the attack. In that case, rather than having the marked white stone at **A**, the knight's play is placed at a better distance, and is also tighter territorially in the corner.

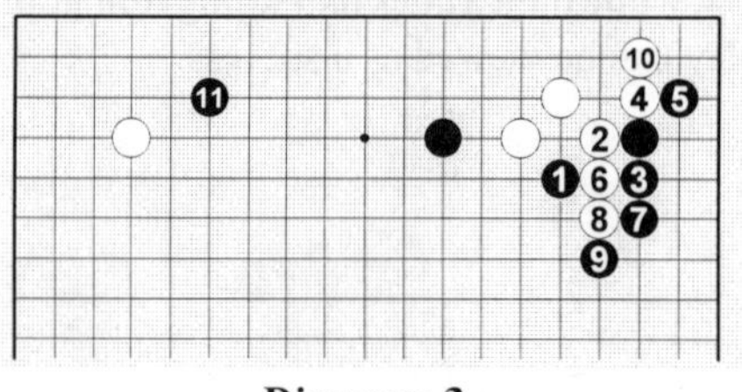

Diagram 3

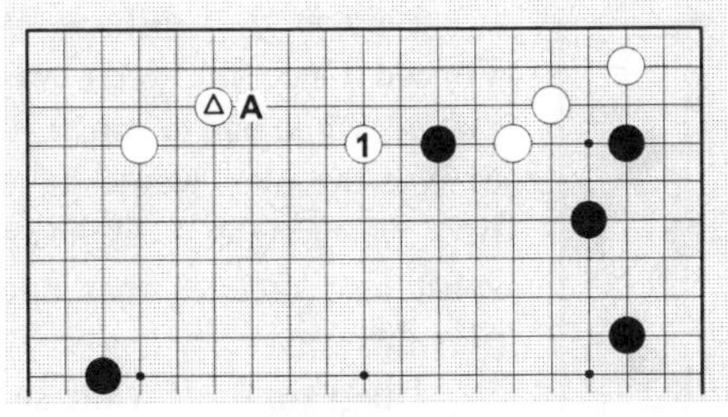

Diagram 4

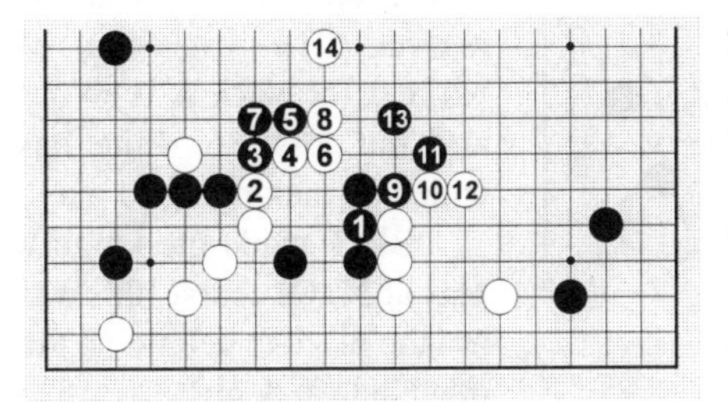

Diagram 5

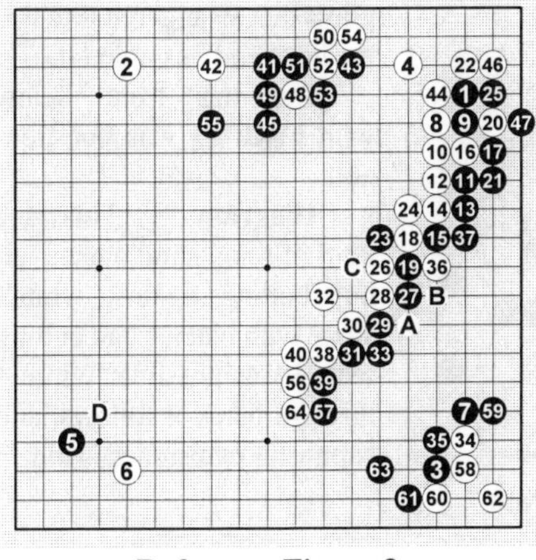

Reference Figure 3

This was a masterful play by Takagawa that must have given him great satisfaction.

Black jumped at 21 here, preparatory to moving out at 25.

White peeped at 22 in exchange for black 23, which prepared for activity on the left side.

Black waited for white to play out with the diagonal play at 24, then played 25 and played out at 27. Black then made the knight's play at 29, in general blocking white's exit route and building influence in the center.

However, the play at 29 was a half-measure that did not make secure shape.

Diagram 5 - It was better to connect solidly with black 1. White would play 2 and 4, getting out into the open, but black can turn at 9 and not worry about a nasty fight. Through 13, the stones are tautly played and this way follows true form.

Reference Figure 3 - [22nd Annual Honinbo Title Match, Game 3; 1967; White: Sakata Eio, Honinbo; Black: Rin Kaiho, Meijin] Considering the knight's play of black 7 placed low, white made the fencing-in tactic of 8 and pushed vigorously. Using white 28 to cut at 36 first was the proper order of plays. Cutting with white 32 at **A** leads to black 33, white 36, black **B**, white 37 and black **C** with a capture in a ladder. Black 57 was a bad play that should have been played as the diagonal play at **D**. The maneuver in the figure left plays in the corner.

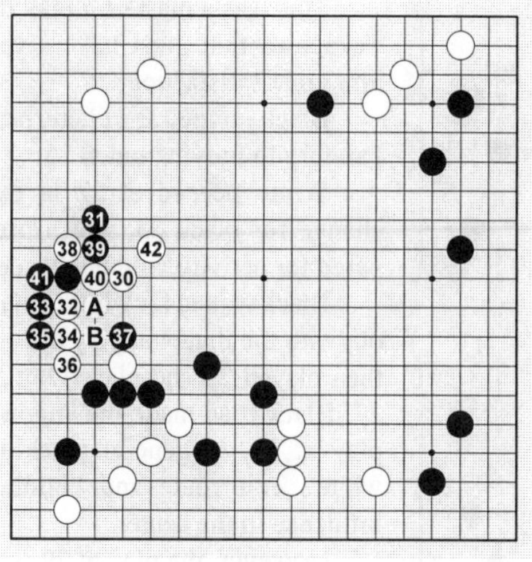

Figure 3 (30-42)

Figure 3 - Black is Forced Once the peep was played, white had to cap at 30 or else the play would have been meaningless. Fighting spirit also dictates that one play this way.

Diagram 6 - If white secured the upper left corner with 1, the jump of black 2 is perfect. The exchange of white Δ for black ▲ is an out and out loss, so white has ended up making a bad play.

Black made the knight's play at 31. Of course, this was not the place to defend on the other side at **A** or **B**.

Here, white attached at 32 and extended at 34, strong plays that swaggered into this territory and despoiled it.

Replying from below with black 33 was questionable.

Diagram 7 - This is a kind of roughshod maneuver, but butting against white's stone with black 1 and cutting with 3 was possible. White 4 through black 9 follows, and capturing two stones is big.

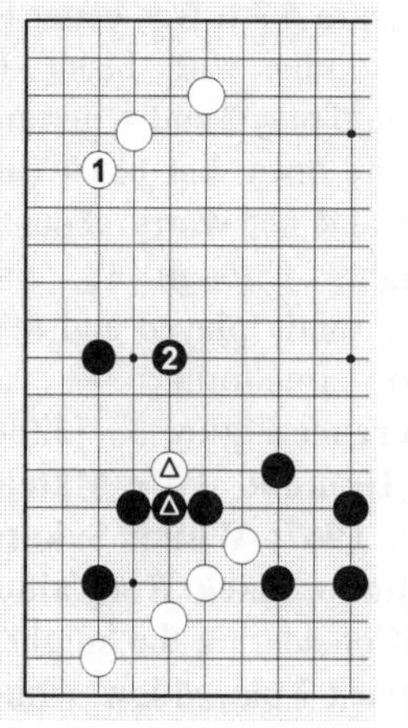

Diagram 6

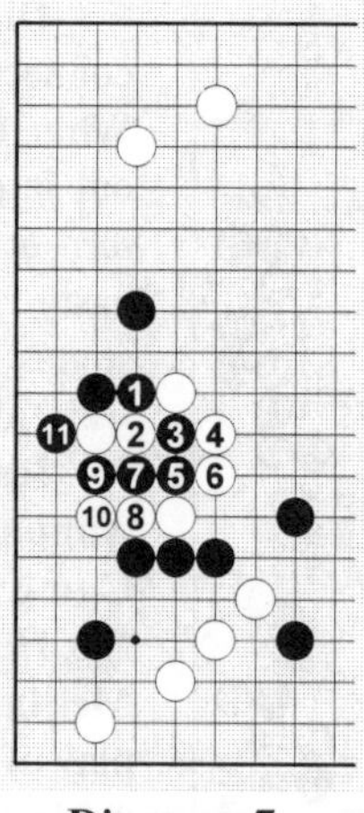

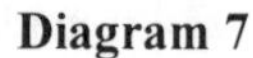

Diagram 7

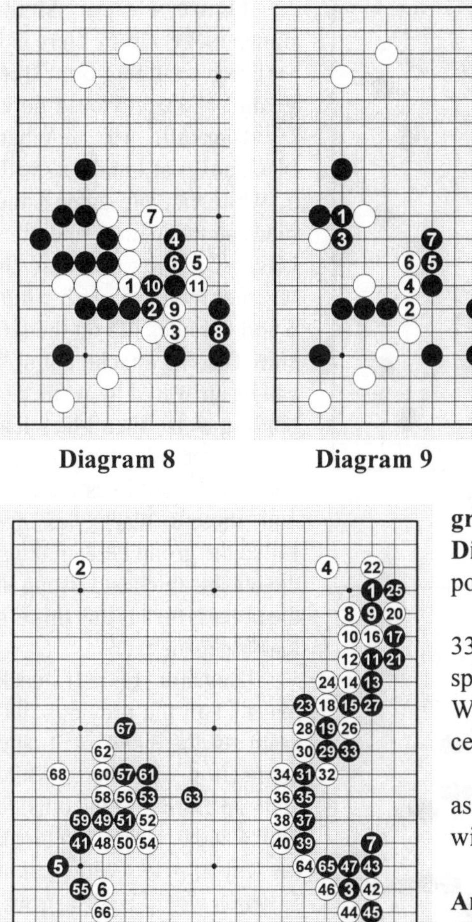

Diagram 8

Diagram 9

Reference Figure 4

Diagram 8 - Next, white runs away with 1 through 7, and the course of play through black 12 is conceivable. This position is no doubt playable for black.

Diagram 9 - In response to black 1, white can also push out at 2 as a probe. Black pushes through at 3, and after white 4 and 6, black 7 can be expected, and this is also playable for black. If black uses 3 to block at 4, following white 4 through black 11 in **Diagram 7**, the connection of 1 in **Diagram 8** cuts black, leaving the position in shambles.

Defending from below with 33 showed a lack of fighting spirit, with black being forced. White played 42, scoring a success here.

There are still other variations associated with **Diagram 7** which will be shown on the next page.

Reference Figure 4 - [22nd Annual Honinbo Title Match, Game 5; 1967; White: Sakata Eio, Honinbo; Black: Rin Kaiho, Meijin] In this game, too, white made the fencing-in tactic and pushed. Since there was a large territory to be made, this formation was not distasteful. This time, white threw in the cut at 26 and pressed at 40. This was a clash between profit and thickness in the center. However, instead of playing at 40, white had a chance to make the forcing plays from 42 through 47, and then play the Taisha fencing-in tactic at 59. By making the diagonal play at 41, black adopted a higher stance.

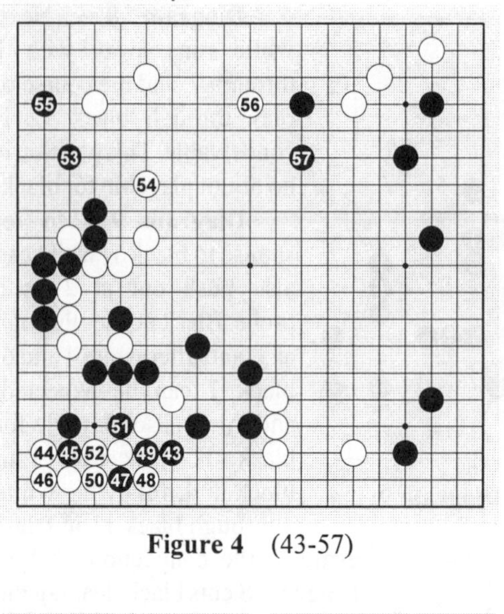

Figure 4 (43-57)

Figure 4 - An Abundance of Territory Here is a variation springing from **Diagram 7** of the previous figure.

Diagram 10 - When black pokes at 1 and cuts with 3, white can rub against the black stones with 4, and after black 5, the question is whether the tactic with white 6 and 8 makes life on the left side. Black's attachment at 9 can be answered by white extending at 10, then black has to turn at 11. Now white hanes at 12 and lives with 14, and though black has not killed the group here, making the outside thick and strong in the process means that this is a feasible maneuver.

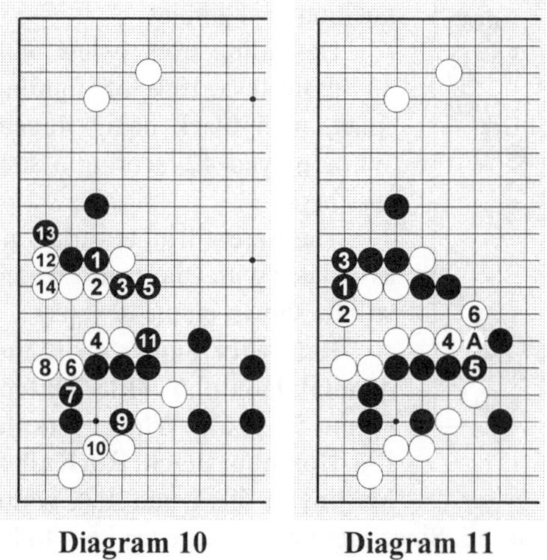

Diagram 10 **Diagram 11**

Diagram 11 - If black plays 11 in the previous diagram as the hane of 1 and connection of 3 here, white ends up exiting to the outside with 4 and 6. Using 5 to block the way at **A** lets white cut at 5, which would be disastrous.

At this point black played 43 and the following plays in order to torment white. Attaching below the stone with black 47 was the vital point of this position, and when white haned over the stone with 48, black cut off and captured the two stones inside in sente with 49 and 51. For 48,

Diagram 12 - If white makes the diagonal attachment at 1, black connects underneath with 2 and 4. With 3, white is able to capture a stone, but at the same time, the stones on the left side become thin. White skillfully jumps at 5, giving support to the left side, since cutting with black **A**, white **B** and black **C** can be met with white **D**, which is white's tactic for survival. However, black makes the extension at 6 and has a playable game.

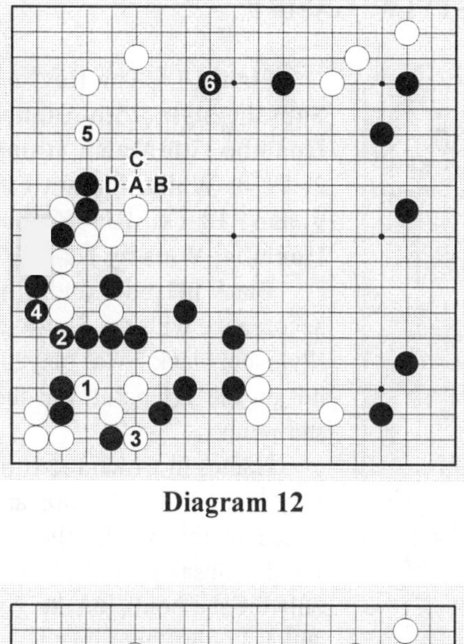

Diagram 12

The opinion was voiced that 48 was the losing play, but Takagawa denied that, stating that it was white 54 that went off track. According to Takagawa, for this play,

Diagram 13 - The diagonal attachment of white 1 in exchange for black 2 should have been played, followed by white 3 and the block of 5. Playing this way would have maintained contact with the corner so that black could not omit descending at 6, and white could then turn to play the checking extension at 7.

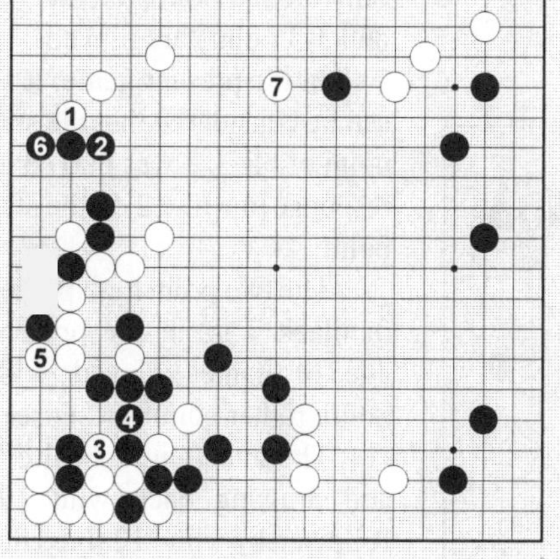

Diagram 13

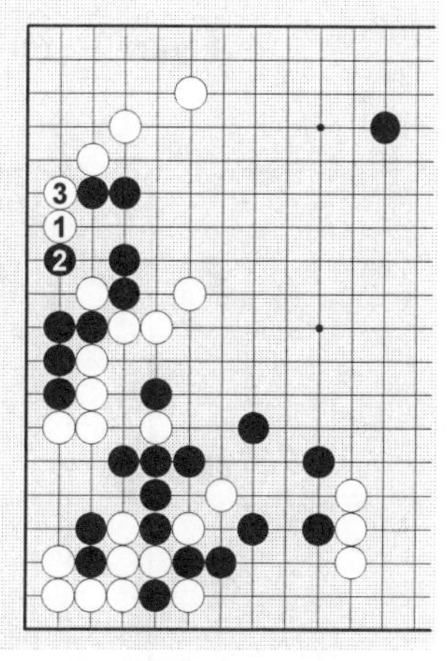

Diagram 14

Diagram 14 - If black neglects to play 6 in the previous diagram, white can make the sharp placement at 1. Since white must be allowed to connect underneath at 3, black ends up practically paralyzed.

Being able to slide to 55 made things easy for black.

When white played 56, black ran away with 57, but at this stage black has plenty of profit and an easy board position to play.

SHUSAKU STYLE - GAME 9

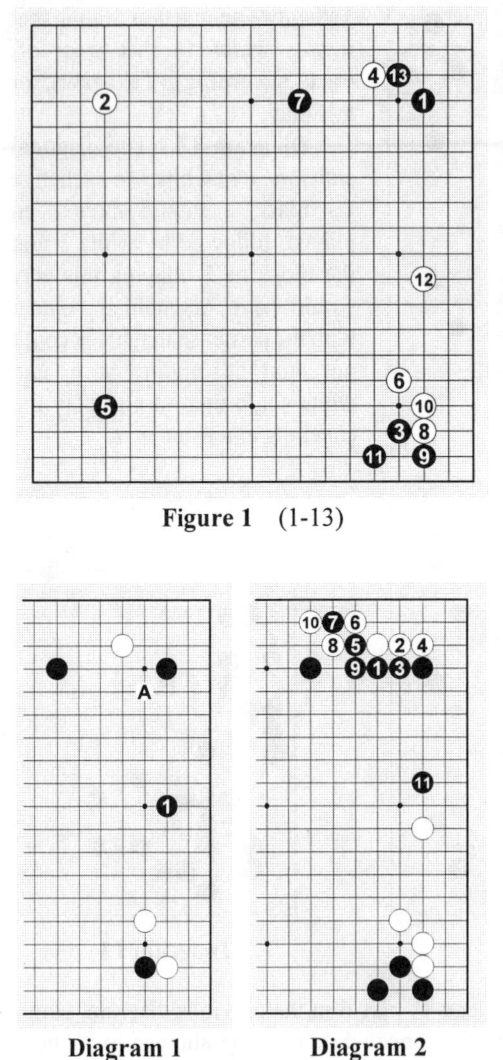

Figure 1 (1-13)

Diagram 1

Diagram 2

Figure 1 - The Revised Shusaku Style [25th Annual Honinbo Title Match, Game 2; 1970; White: Sakata Eio 9 dan; Black: Rin Kaiho, Honinbo; Wins by 1/2 pt.]

Black played 1 and 3 in accordance with the Shusaku Style, but black 5 was played, not on the 3-4 point, but the star point.

Games in which the fifth play is modified like this are called in this work "the revised Shusaku Style." Not only the star point, but the 5-4 and 5-3 points are played.

In the present game, it can be considered that the star point of black 5 was played in response to white 2 on the star point.

The two point high pincer of black 7 is, in the present age of games played with komi, rather common sense.

The attaching at white 8 and drawing back with 10, followed by white 12 fixed the shape. Answering with black 9 was also natural.

Diagram 1 - When the diagonal play at **A** is not in place, it is a bit odd to make the pincer of black 1 on the right side. Amidst this breadth there is no telling where white might start a fight.

Since white left the upper right as it was to play elsewhere, if black is to play there, the diagonal attachment of black 13 is the only play.

Diagram 2 - Attaching at 1 here lets white take profit with 2 through 10, and then the extension of black 11 is a narrow one.

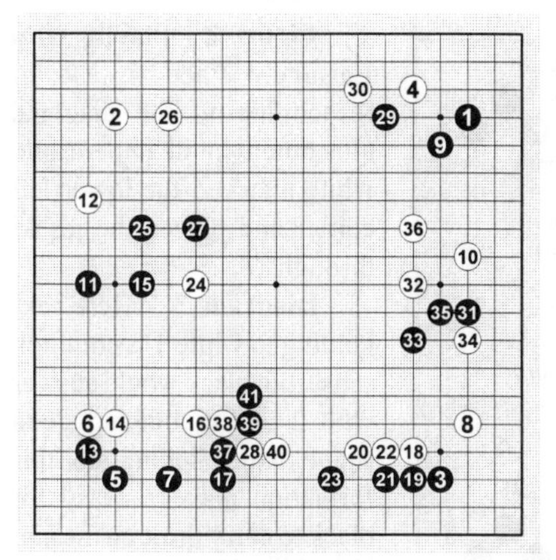

Reference Figure 1

Reference Figure 1 - [Hoensha Tournament; 1884; White: Murase Shuho 2 kyu (18th hereditary Honinbo); Black: Takahashi Kinesaburo 5 kyu] Black played at the star point with 5, conscious of white's star point play at 2. During this era, this was not a maneuver that was often adopted. White attacked the corner once with 6, then left it at that to develop the right side with 8 and 10. Black attacked with 11 and the following plays, expanding the field of battle.

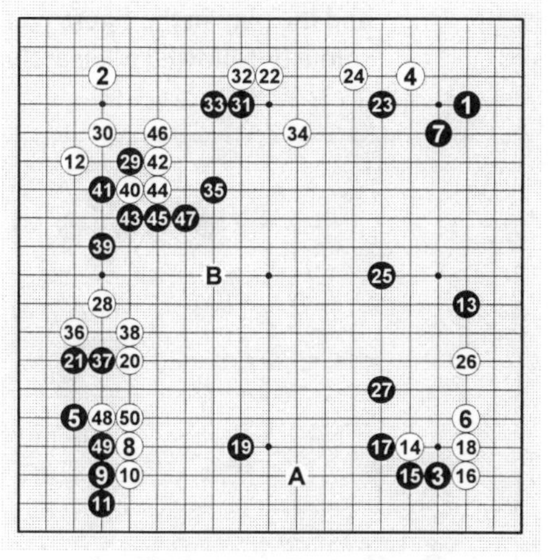

Reference Figure 2

Reference Figure 2 - [3rd Annual Honinbo Title Match, Game 6; 1945; White: Hashimoto Shou, Honinbo; Black: Iwamoto Kaoru 8 dan] This is a game where black played 5 on the 5-3 point. Iwamoto: "For black 19, **A** is usual, but that was insufficient." Hashimoto: "I didn't expect 25. For white 26, I should have jumped at 29 after all." Hashimoto: "36 and 38 had little effect on black. Perhaps it was better to attack with a play in the vicinity of **B**.

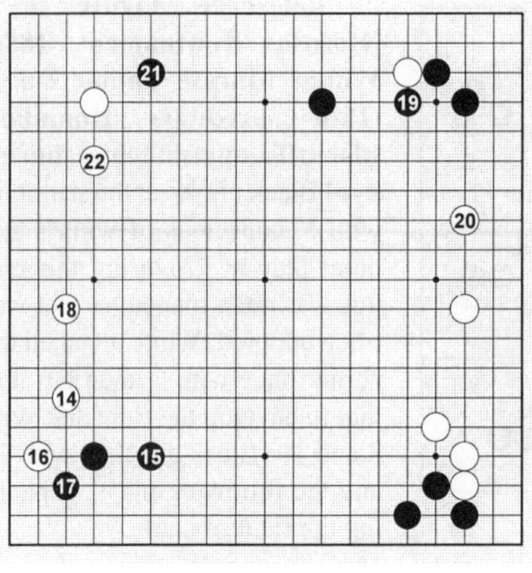

Figure 2 (14-22)

Figure 2 - Playing at a Leisurely Pace Instead of responding to the diagonal attachment in the upper right, white attacked the lower left corner and played the joseki through 18.

Diagram 3 - Here, extending to white 1 is common sense, but black would answer with 2 and 4, making good shape while setting up this formation makes it easy for black to carry through the aim of initiating sudden fighting. This is not to white's liking, and the play in the figure consciously followed a leisurely course with the komi in mind.

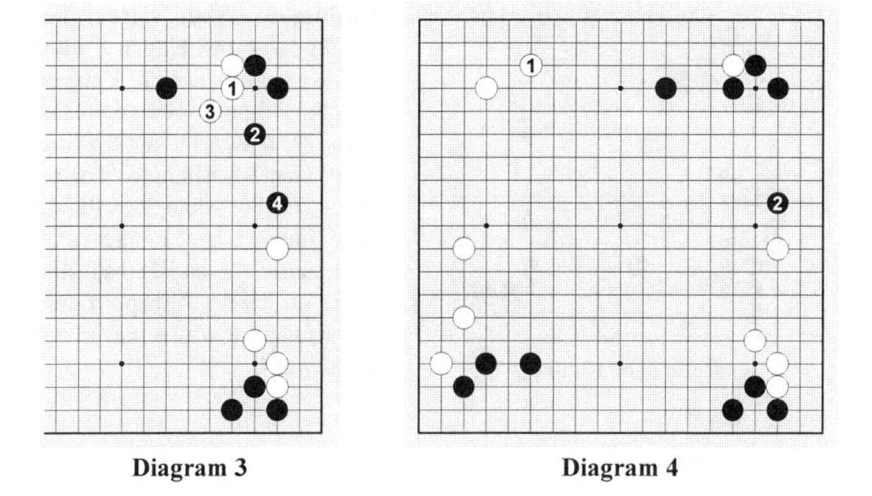

Diagram 3 **Diagram 4**

Here one sees how with the komi in go the positions of black and white are different. Black initiates fighting in order to quickly establish the superiority that playing first gives, while white seeks to avoid that and guide the game into leisurely channels in order to establish the win in the later stages of the game. That is the particular characteristic of contemporary go and the differences in strategy, with the give and take being interesting.

When black took control of the upper right with 19, the two point extension of white 20 was a big point that all attention had been focused on. Without putting the stone in the corner into motion but playing on the side, white's intention of aiming at a long, drawn out fight can be seen.

Diagram 4 - Here, the corner enclosure of 1 is also a good point, but the extension of black 2 is bigger, an ideal point. It is hoped that the reader can see how great a difference there is between this and **Figure 2**.

Black then attacked the corner at 21.

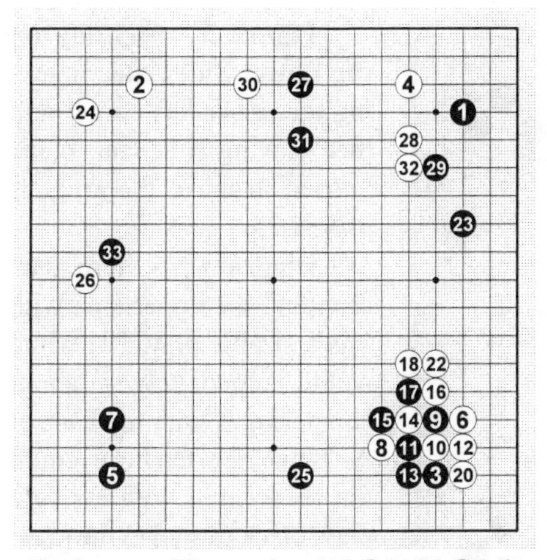

Reference Figure 3 (19@9, 21@14)

Reference Figure 3 - [Jubango, Game 9; 1870; White: Ito Matsukazu 7 dan; Black: Hayashi Shuei 4 dan (Meijin, 17th and 19th Honinbo)] The position of black 5 in parallel with 3 on the 3-4 point was truly an unusual play. This is a novel Shusaku Style variation. After the joseki through 22, black hurried to make the extension to 23. Then white made the corner enclosure at 24 and black the extension at 25 that he had been aiming at.

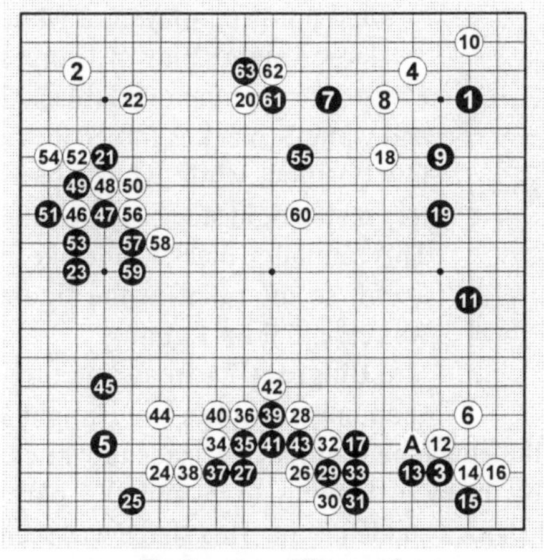

Reference Figure 4

Reference Figure 4 - [17th Annual Honinbo League; 1962: White: Magari Reiki 8 dan; Black: Honda Dogen 9 dan] Black played 5 on the star point. The wide extension of black 11 was a play that combined a pincer with it. On the other hand, black had to expend another play defending at 19. If 17 was used to make the extension at 29, white would have pressed at **A** as a forcing play, then invaded at 19. Through 45, black made considerable profit, but with 46 and the following plays, white also took territory on the upper side.

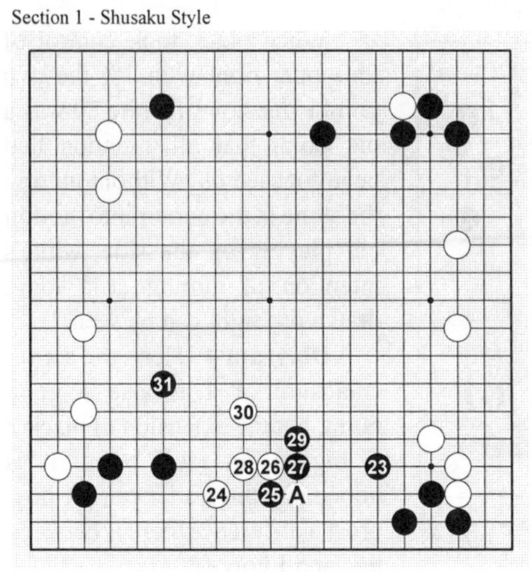

Figure 3 (23-31)

Figure 3 - Fighting on the Lower Side After attacking the upper left corner and then leaving it at that, black hurried to make the knight's play at 23.

Diagram 5 - Here, surrounding the upper side with 1 is a sizable play, but white would immediately set about countering it with the hane at **A**. Since the territory could not be secured with a single play, black turned to the good point in the lower right.

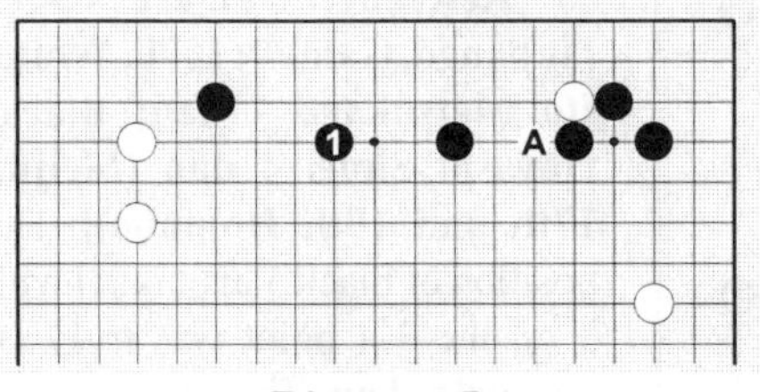

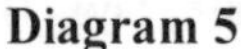

Diagram 5

Diagram 6 - If black 23 had not been played, a white large knight's play of 1 forces a response, and then with black 2 and white 3, black is forced into a low position, while white's territory on the right side becomes big. This formation black would like to avoid, so the point in the figure was essential for fighting.

Diagram 7 - In addition, responding to white's large knight's play with the attachment of black 1 leads to white 2 followed by black extending to 5 and the plays through 11, with a sudden fight. This shape was seen in **Game 6** (page 60), but after this white **A**, black **B** and white **C** will be played and I did not have confidence in how it would turn out. Also, white might use **A** to develop at **D**, probably followed by black **A** and white **E**. with an unclear result.

So after the black knight's play at 23,

Diagram 8 - The fencing-in tactic of black 1 forces white to answer, then developing with black 3 makes truly good shape. White will be a bit hard pressed to deal with the lower side. Had white played on the upper side, I planned to surround the territory in this way.

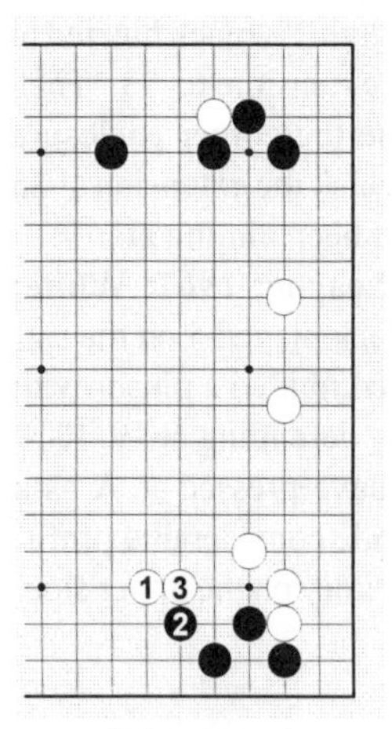

Diagram 6

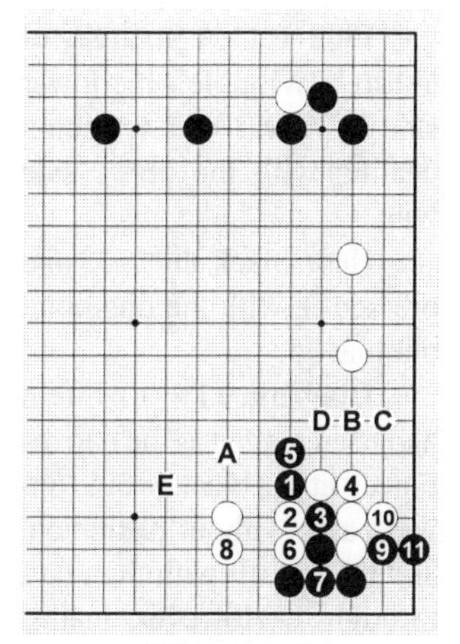

Diagram 7

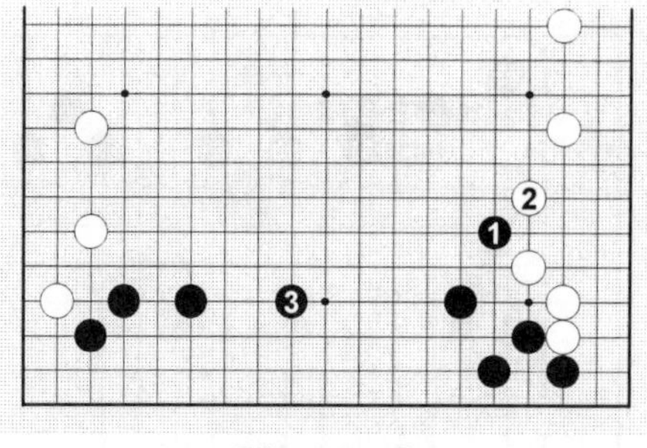

Diagram 8

Consequently, white played with the checking tactic at 24, a natural way to start a fight, and black's pincer at 25 was also natural.

The attachment of white 26 was a scheme typical of Sakata.

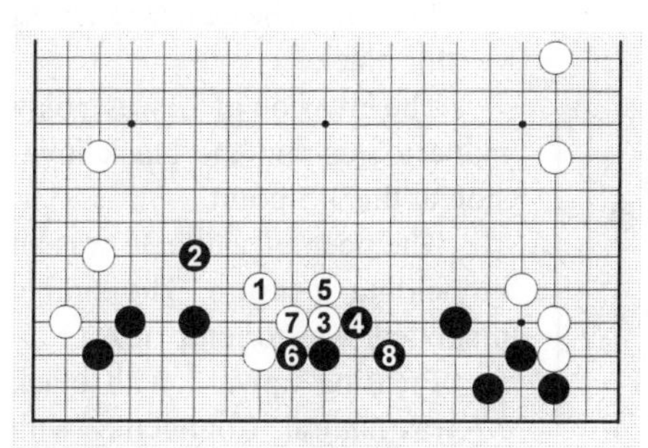

Diagram 9

Diagram 9 - Here, it is usual to jump at 1, and when black plays 2, attach at white 3 and extend at 5. Up to 8, black's shape is overconcentrated, a somewhat unsatisfactory result.

Diagram 10 - If black answers white's attachment of white 1 by drawing back at 2, white will jump to 3. If black **A** and white **B** follow, white has generally settled the group.

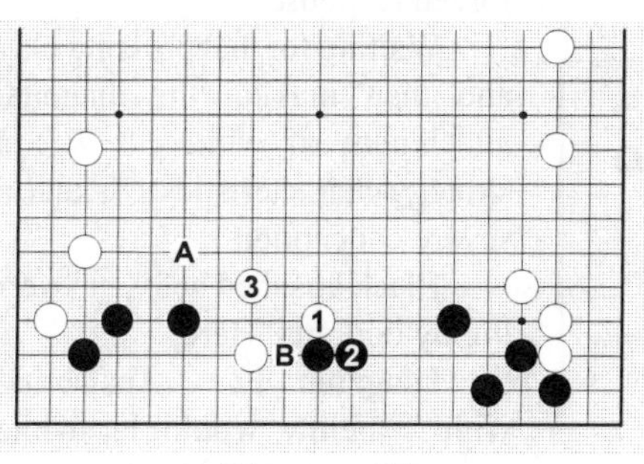

Diagram 10

After white made the attachment and black haned at 27, white pulled back at 28. Black was forced to extend at 29, and then white exchanged 30 for black 31, with the intention of leaving the position at that and turning to the upper side. Since there was a cutting point at **A**, there was no suitable attack, and black was distressed.

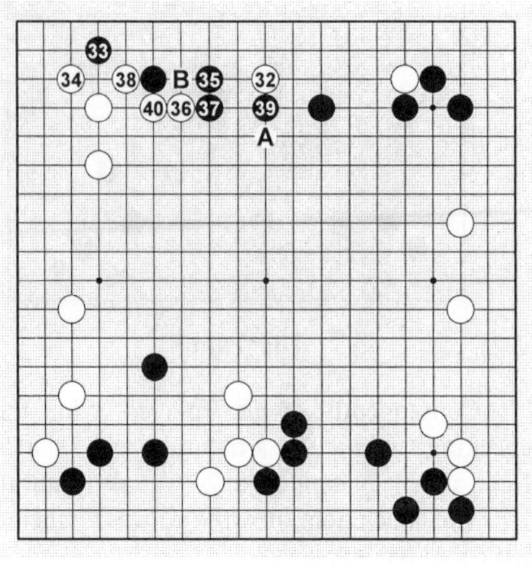

Figure 4 (32-40)

Figure 4 - A Strategy of White's White left the lower side as it was and set about dealing with the upper side with 32.

Here, black slid to 33 and pressed in with the one point jump at 35.

Diagram 11 - If white Δ had been played as the narrow pincer at **A**, black would invade at 1 without hesitation, and take profit with the plays through 7. However, in this case, white's jump at 8 makes a wide breadth of territory, so this cannot be called a success for black.

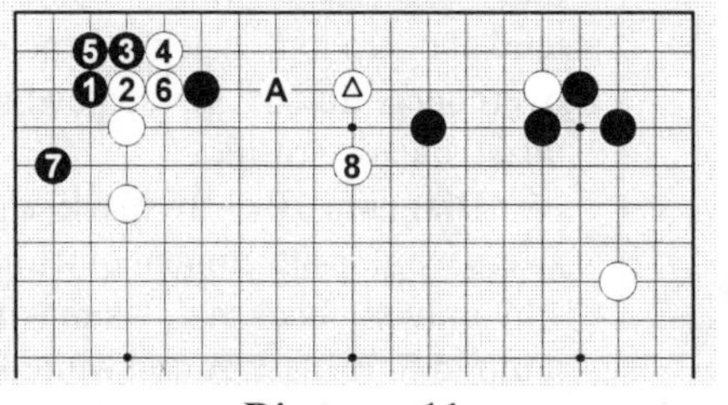

Diagram 11

The invasion of 32 was a play made to restrain the black invasion at the 3-3 point.

The peep of white 36 was an unyielding measure. The simple maneuver was to jump at **A**.

Pressing upward with black 37 was natural. Connecting with black **B** here would clearly be a forced response.

Waiting for that pressing play and then making the diagonal attachment of white 38 was a strategy characteristic of Sakata, a severe conception.

Black attached at 39, answering by dodging. Here,

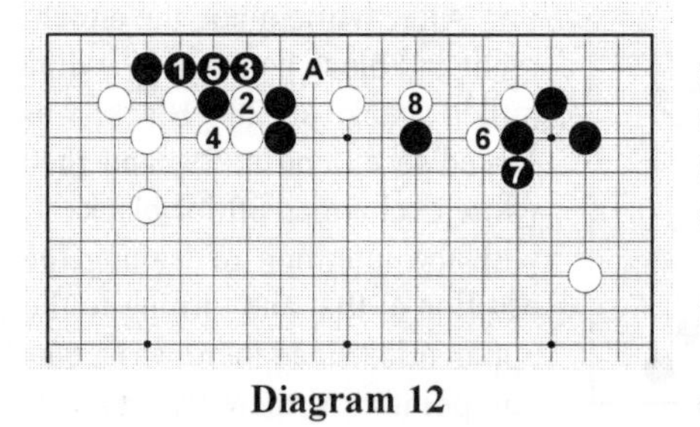

Diagram 12

Diagram 12 - Answering with 1 below would let white force with 2 and 4, then deal deftly with the situation with the hane at 6 and attachment at 8. White **A** is also a forcing play, so there is absolutely no way for black to successfully attack these stones here.

Therefore, impetus led black to play 39, then white's block at 40 next was

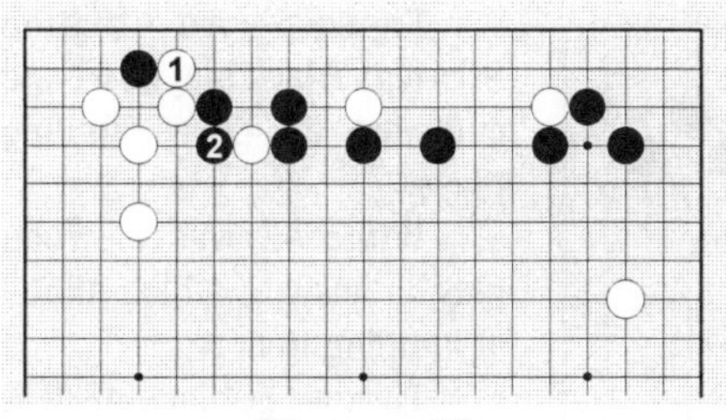

Diagram 13

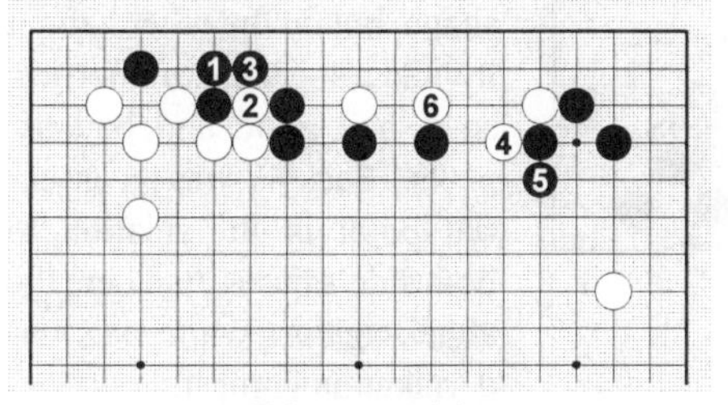

Diagram 14

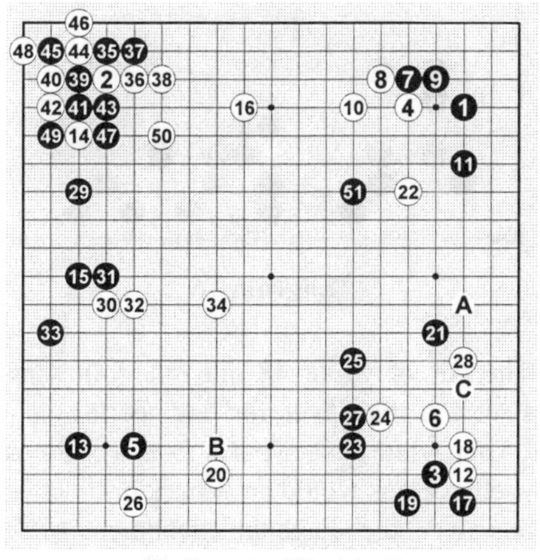

Reference Figure 5

a thick and strong play, quite interesting.

Diagram 13 - Here, taking the stone in the corner with 1 is small, while letting black play out at 2 ends up erasing white's thickness on the left side. The play in the figure was not geared to the local area, but dealt with the game on a large scale. Here,

Diagram 14 - Descending at black 1 is no good. On the contrary, this makes it easy for white to deal deftly with the situation with the tactic of 2 through 6. Black changed the object of attack to the lower side.

Reference Figure 5 - [4th Annual Meijin Title Match, Game 6; 1965; White: Sakata Eio, Meijin; Black: Rin Kaiho 8 dan] Black played 5 on the 5-4 point, and answered white 12 by making the corner enclosure at 13. White 20 and 22 were a resourceful maneuver. If white used 20 to make the extension at **A**, developing with black **B** would have been ideal. Playing in such a way as to invite an attack on the lower right was a typical scheme of Sakata's who excelled at devising ways of survival. Black 27 was questionable. It should have been used to press in at **C**.

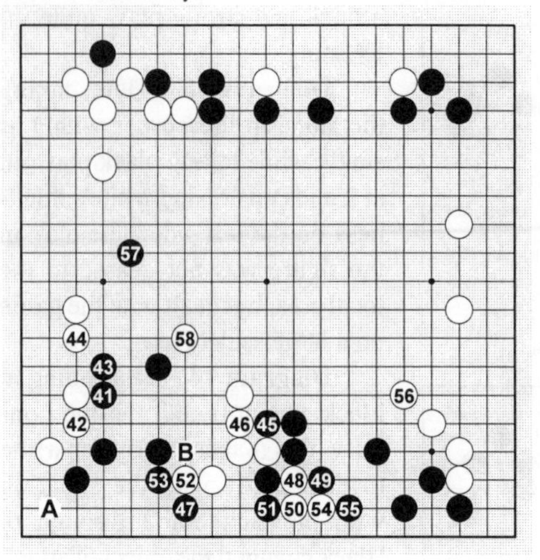

Figure 5 (41-58)

Figure 5 - An Attrition Strategy Black played 41 and extended at 43 as forcing plays.

White 42 was a strong play in answer, which aimed at jumping in at **A**.

Turning at black 45 was the first step towards attacking, taking away white's eye shape, but on the other hand it invited a shortage of liberties, so it had good and bad aspects. Black 47 was an essential point in the relation to both side's bases, and here the attack against white was undertaken in earnest.

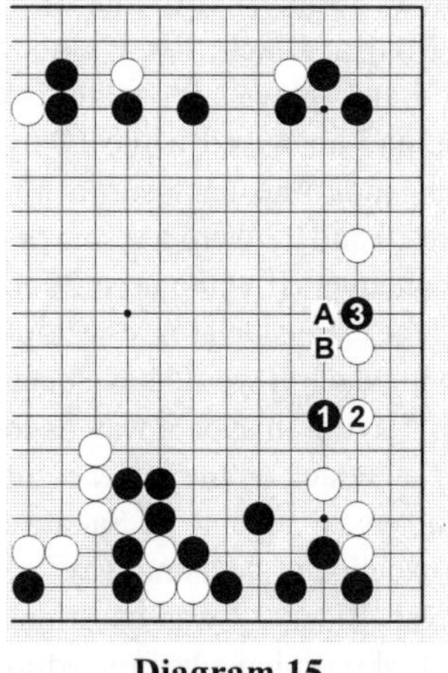

Diagram 15

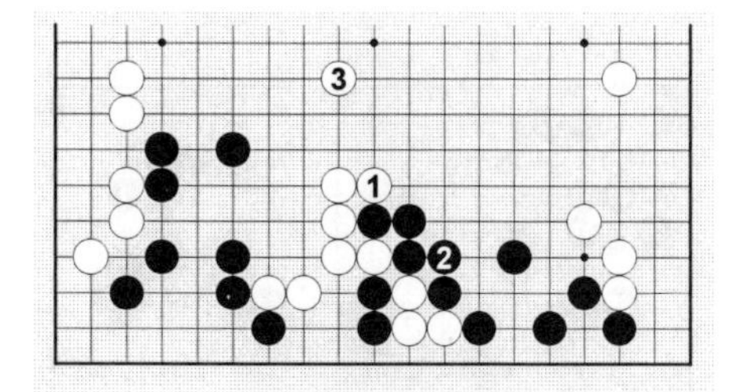

Diagram 16

The cut of white 48 and the following plays were a maneuver for engineering survival. Then white pushed out at 52 as a probe to see whether black would draw back or block at 53, but since the diagonal attachment of **B** could be played, this could be held in reserve. Here, the diagonal play of white was an attrition strategy, again indicative of Sakata's confidence is being able to survive.

Diagram 15 - On the right side, black 1 forces white 2, with black aiming at the attachment of 3. In reply to white **A**, black would cut at **B**, and according to the situation, the implication is that black would play to destroy white's territory. White played to counter this.

Around this point, the difference in the way of thinking was predicated on the styles of the players. Since it is unlikely that this aim would immediately be acted upon, the calm and collected maneuver in the next diagram was also possible.

Diagram 16 - White turns at 1 as a forcing play, then jumps at 3 to gain ground first in escaping. This is another method.

Black made the erasure play at 57, and white responded at 58, creating a difficult fight. The game would be decided from this stage on.

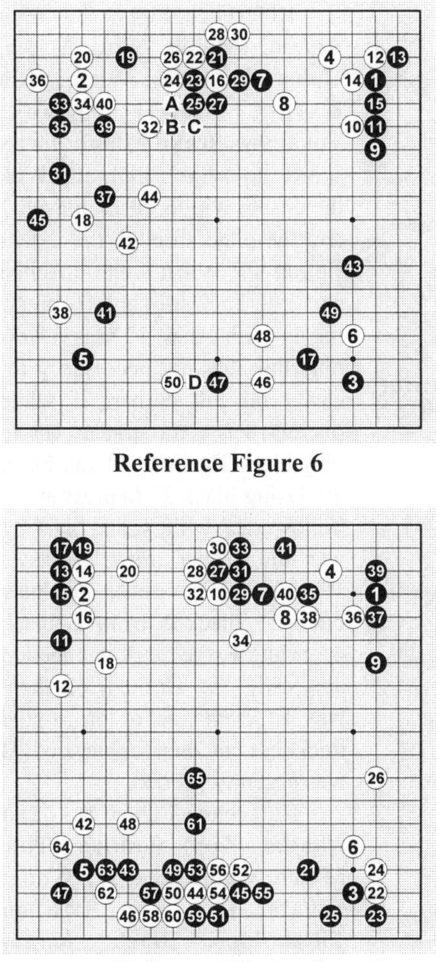

Reference Figure 6

Reference Figure 7

Reference Figure 6 - [26th Annual Honinbo Title Match, Game 1; 1971; White: Ishida Yoshio 7 dan; Black: Rin Kaiho, Honinbo] Since the extension of black 9 was in place, the feeling was to play the knight's play at 17. Black 21 through white 30 was a reasonable division of the position. If black played 31 as the knight's play of 32, white **A**, black **B** and white **C** would produce a fierce fight. Black playing the forcing play of 39 and made acceptable shape through 45. Splitting into the side with white 46 at **D** would have been peaceful.

Reference Figure 7 - [8th Annual Pro Best Ten Title Match, Game 5; 1971; White: Kajiwara Takeo 9 dan; Black: Ishida Yoshio, Honinbo] White played the narrow extension of 26 conscious of the black position above. Black played 27 and the following plays focused on the local area. Here, developing at 49 was an essential point in terms of the whole board. After playing at 42 and 44, the game was promising for white. For 50, white should have butted against black at 54, quickly making life. Black jumped at 65, making inroads into white's grand design in the center.

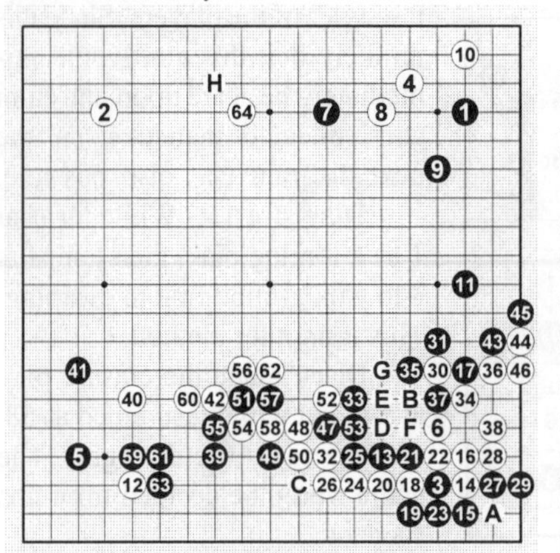

Reference Figure 8

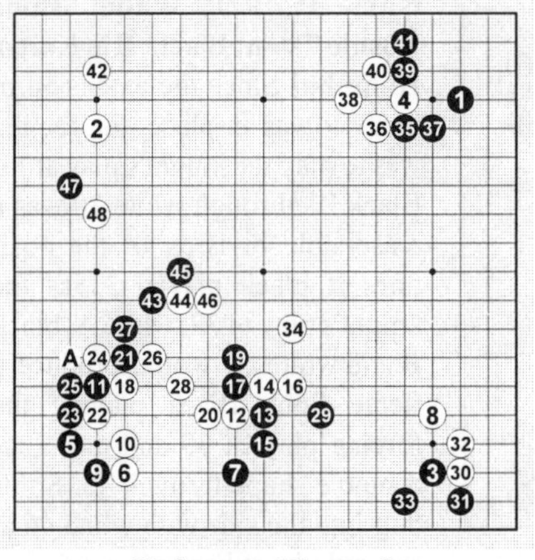

Reference Figure 9

Reference Figure 8 - [7th Annual Meijin Title Match, Game 1; 1968; White: Rin Kaiho, Meijin; Black: Takagawa Kaku 9 dan] In response to white's high attack on the corner with 6, black played 7 and the plays through the extension at 11. When white attached and drew back at 14 and 16, pressing in with black 17 was a new play that was not necessarily focused on the corner. If white played 18 at **A**, the strategy was to play black **B**, white 18 and black 39. Using black 31 to press at 32, followed by white **C** and black 31 was the proper order of plays. White should have used 36 to play out at 53, black **D**, white **E**, black 47, white **F**, the black connection and white **G**. Through 62 there was an exchange of profit and thickness, but then for black 63, **H** was urgently needed.

Reference Figure 9 - [2nd Annual Top Position Title Match, Game 4; 1957; White: Sakata Eio, Top Position Titleholder; Black: Kitani Minoru 9 dan] With 4 and the following, white made high attacks on two corners. For 8, it was also possible to exchange white 18 for black **A**, then play 8. White 16 was played out of fighting spirit. If this was used to connect at 17, black would have haned at 16 and extended. If white used 18 to draw back at 20, the extension of black 18 would become the vital point. This game was one of fierce competition.

SECTION 2
CORNER ENCLOSURES AND DIAGONAL MODELS

CORNER ENCLOSURES AND DIAGONAL MODELS

In this section, corner enclosures and diagonal models are treated, and these are two related positions. That is to say that openings with corner enclosures are often followed by a play placed in the diagonally opposite corner and the opening also has things in common with 3-4 points played first in diagonally opposite corners and then a corner enclosure made on the fifth play. Of course, the purposes of these initial plays are not the same, but the result is that it is possible that they revert to the same pattern. This is the reason that they have been put into this section together.

Corner enclosures can be knight enclosures, large knight enclosures, or one point jump enclosures. These are the representative ways of occupying the corner. Occasionally two point high enclosures are played, although there are not many examples in actual games.

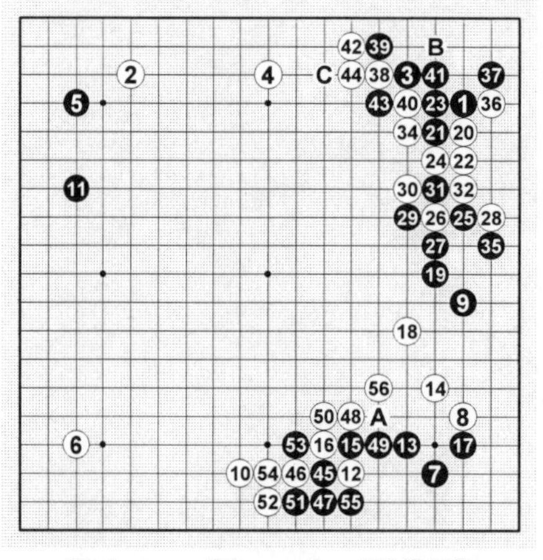

Reference Figure 1 (33@26)

Reference Figure 1 - [1678; White: Honinbo Dosaku (Meijin, 4th hereditary Honinbo); Black: Inoue Inseki (3rd hereditary Inoue, Dosa)] Here is an early example of black making a knight enclosure with 1 and 3. Already in Dosaku's era this maneuver had appeared, but up to that time black would play at the 3-4 point, white would attack the corner and black would make a two point (or else another kind of) pincer, starting the game with fighting right out of the opening. This maneuver drew criticism in time. At the least, games played in the early years of the Edo Period had nothing that resembled a real opening, while Dosaku painstakingly worked out maneuvers such as the three point pincer and other plays, opening up new vistas of ways of playing rationally that were dubbed the Dosaku Style. Both sides attacking corners in tandem to start a melee was abandoned, and it is interesting that this was the era in which corner enclosures made their appearance.

Black attached once at 15 to avoid being sealed in by a white play at **A**. The connection of black 41 was a terrible play. Black should have made the tiger link of **B**, and after white 44, black 42 and white **C**, taken sente. Through 56, white played skillfully around the board and the board position can be considered promising for white.

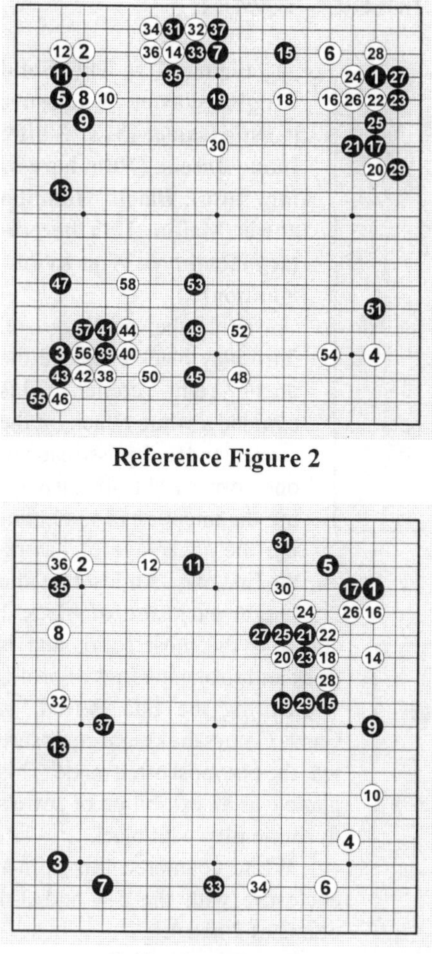

Reference Figure 2

Reference Figure 3

Diagonal models are a maneuver in which 3-4 points are occupied, and appeared at practically the same time in even games.

Games starting with black and white occupying diagonal corners on the star point, a kind of handicap system, was abandoned during some era, and perhaps that is what led to the form of go in place at present. The diagonal 3-4 points has a history that is rather old.

Reference Figure 2 - [Game at Suruga Castle; White: Honinbo Sansa, Meijin (First hereditary Honinbo); Black: Kashio Rigen] Here is a game played at the castle in Suru Province where black played diagonal 3-4 points. Attaching at white 8 and extending to 10 and again at black 39 and 41 were a joseki played in this era. Although this received much criticism, it is interesting that in certain circumstances it lives on to the present day. In the upper right, white played in a resourceful way with 20 through 28.

Reference Figure 3 - [Castle Game: 1692; White: Yasui Chitetsu (3rd hereditary Yasui); Black: Honinbo Sakugen (Successor of Dosaku)] After the diagonal 3-4 points of 1 and 3, here is an example where black made double corner enclosures with 5 and 7. White also occupied two corners so the game became one with all enclosures, but the knight enclosure with white 6 was often played in the early 19th century, and the large knight enclosure with white 8 was already a maneuver in the late 17th and early 18th centuries. Please examine this in conjunction with **Reference Figure 1** on page 103.

CORNER ENCLOSURE - GAME 1

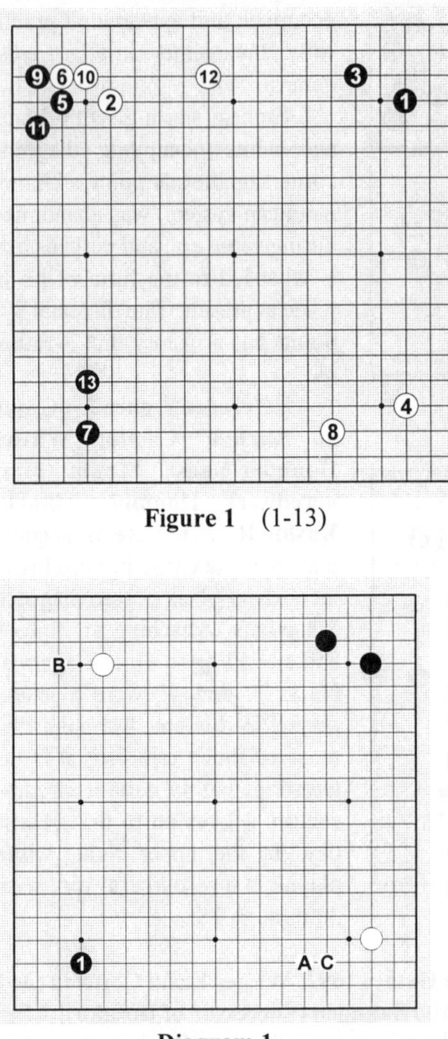

Figure 1 (1-13)

Diagram 1

Figure 1 - The Solid Knight corner Enclosure [Castle Game; 1822; White: Inoue Inseki (10th hereditary Insa); Black: Honinbo Jowa (Meijin, 12th hereditary Honinbo); Wins by resignation]

With the opening and third play black enclosed the upper right corner. This avoided a white attack on the corner, and took possession of one corner right off, displaying the intention of maintaining the advantage of having the first play. Amidst that, the knight enclosure of black 1 and 3 is the most solid, and is thick and strong in terms of profit.

During the Edo Period, in Castle Games the knight enclosure was the one most often made. This game was an exhibition of Jowa's dynamic play with black.

White countered this corner enclosure with the 5-4 and 3-4 points of 2 and 4.

Black 5 entered this corner.

Diagram 1 - Of course, it was also possible for black to occupy the empty corner in the lower left with 1. If white encloses a corner at **A**, black can invade at **B**, while if white uses **A** to enclose the corner at **B**, black will attack the corner at **C**. Those two attacks on the corner are equivalent options.

When white attached at the 3-3 point with 6, black left the position as it was in order to turn to play 7 in the lower left corner.

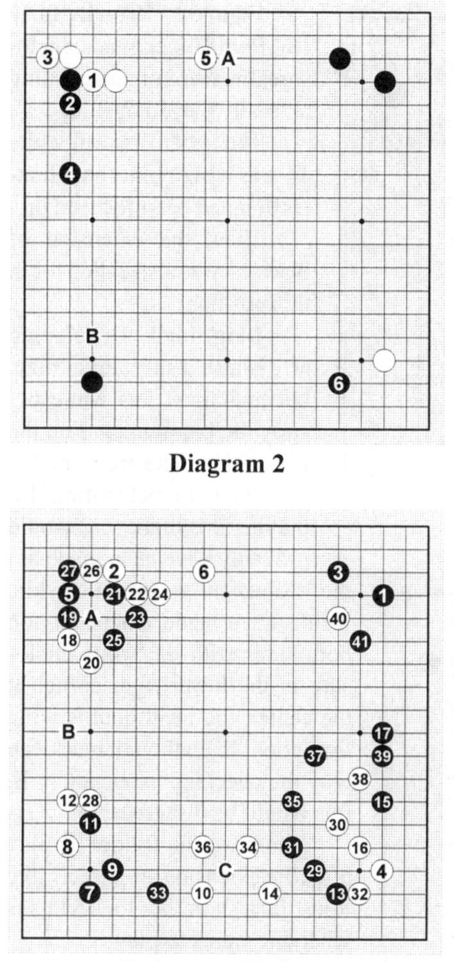

Diagram 2

Reference Figure 1

Here, white did not continue to play in the upper left corner, but made the large knight enclosure at 8 to counter black's corner enclosure in the upper right.

Diagram 2 - For 8, fixing the shape in the corner with 1 and 3, then developing with 5, or else at **A** lets black attack the corner with 6, or enclose the corner at **B**. This would be a feasible game.

For the first time black returned to play 9 and 11 in this corner, and white made the extension to 12.

Black then enclosed the corner at 13. There is no argument that this is an ideal play, and in order to gain a higher stance in this corner, black made the high one point enclosure.

Reference Figure 1 - [Castle Game; 1715; White: Hayashi Monnyu (4th hereditary Bokunyu); Inoue Insetsu (5th hereditary Sakuun)] This is recorded as a Castle Game, and is an example of a corner enclosure played in an early era. Up to then, most games were played with attacks in tandem on corners. The play order of black 15 as the diagonal play at **A**, white **B** and black 15 would have been more clear cut. Black 23 was an efficient play. White 36 was played out of distaste of the strong attacking play of black **C**, but by being able to turn to 37, black got a simple game.

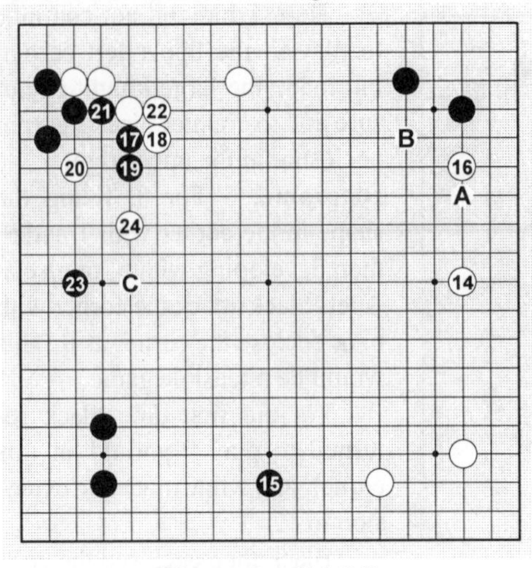

Figure 2 (14-24)

Figure 2 - Priority for a Big Point Black made enclosures in two corners, getting an easily played opening.

The extension of white 14 was a big point that all attention had been focused on.

Then, the extension of black 15 was also called for in this position.

Diagram 3 - Developing at 1 is also a substantial play, but making it lets white occupy the big point at 2 on the lower side. The trend of the time had no perception for playing this high, so 2 would probably have been made as the extension at **A**, but white would have made extensions on both sides with the white enclosure in the lower right corner at the center, the ideal double wing formation. Even though black can play the checking extension at **B**, this would be disagreeable.

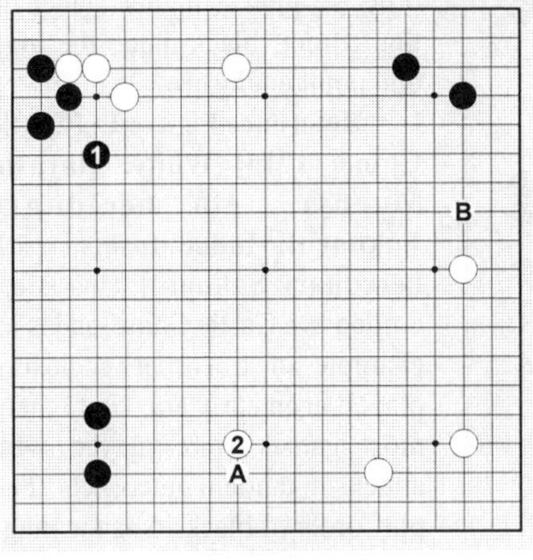

Diagram 3

There was no follow-up play after the extension, so it feels like it just falls short, but for 15 this is what one wants to play.

White made the checking extension all the way with 16. Since the knight enclosure is solid, white could also have considered making the more restrained two point extension at **A**, but during this era of playing without komi, white could not afford to play that kind of drawn out game. White 16 aimed at next making the knight's play at **B**, so advancing this far was in order here.

Then black attached at 17 and extended to 19. Of course, it goes without saying that this was planned to expand the left side. Attention should be paid to the fact that this was not made as the knight's play at 1 in **Diagram 3**.

White 20 provoked black 21 so white could connect at 22. This is joseki.

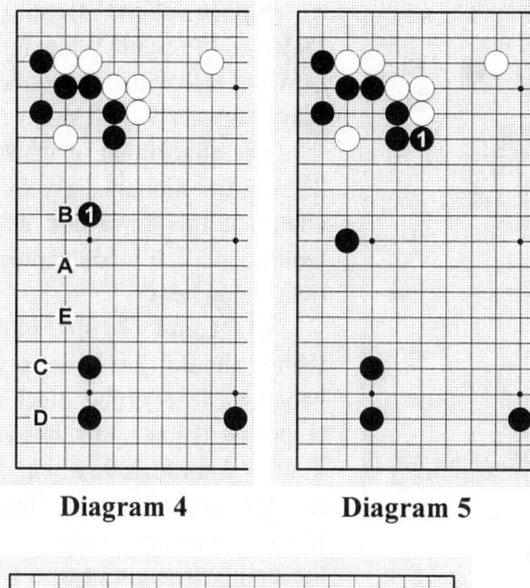

Diagram 4 Diagram 5

Next, the extension of black 23 underneath the star point was interesting.

Diagram 4 - If conforming to joseki, black 1 is the play. However, that leaves white scope to play **A**, black **B**, white **C**, black **D** and white **E**, establishing a comfortable position. While not permitting that,

Diagram 5 - Black's turn at 1 becomes good if white left things as they were. The aim was to make the game wide open.

White quickly made the probe of 24, but how is this to be evaluated? White could have made the light capping play at **C**, no?

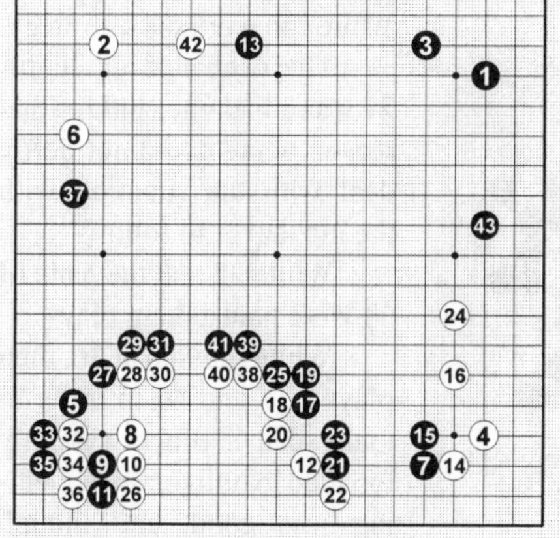

Reference Figure 2

Reference Figure 2 - [Castle Game; 1750; White: Yasui Senkaku (5th hereditary Shuntetsu); Black: Inoue Shuntatsu (7th hereditary Inseki)] For black 7, the corner enclosure at 9 was also possible, making the game one of all corner enclosures. The give and take through 41 on the lower side was interesting, with a textbook example of a division of profit for white and influence for black.

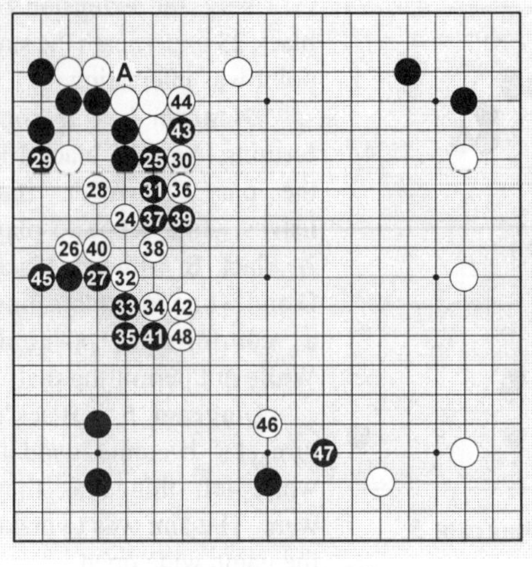

Figure 3 (24-48)

Figure 3 - Dealing Deftly not Possible White fell in with black's intentions and played out on the left side.

The attachment of white 26 was questionable. By exchanging this for black extending at 27, it made white's own shape heavy.

Diagram 6 - At this point white should have simply haned at 1 to probe black's response. If black attaches at 2, after 3 through 9, white Δ still has some life in it. Here black is expected to play 2 as the empty triangle at 3, then white can work out a strategy.

The exchange of 26 for 27 was a bad one, and for that reason white could not deftly deal with the situation with the maneuver to follow.

White 32 and the hane of 34 were painstaking plays.

White pressed at 36, then played 38 and 40 in order to make shape. Black was only too glad to oblige, since yielding was good, and though white made good shape somehow through 42, black solidified the lower left on a large scale, so the loss was obvious.

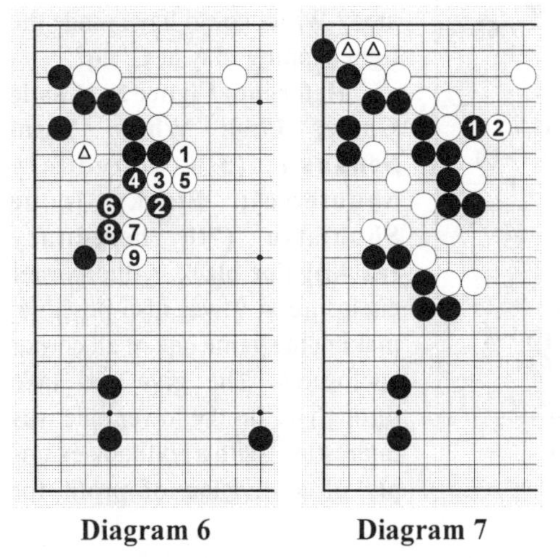

Diagram 6 **Diagram 7**

The cut of black 43 involved a subtle tactic, but whether this should have been immediately played or not is difficult to say.

Diagram 7 - If the cut is made after white has haned and connected in the corner with Δ, black 1 will be answered by the atari of white 2.

At this point, when the cut of black **A** was possible, white had no choice but to play defensively at 44.

Descending at black 45 was quite a play, not only because it eliminated potential problems, but also gave support to the black group in the upper left.

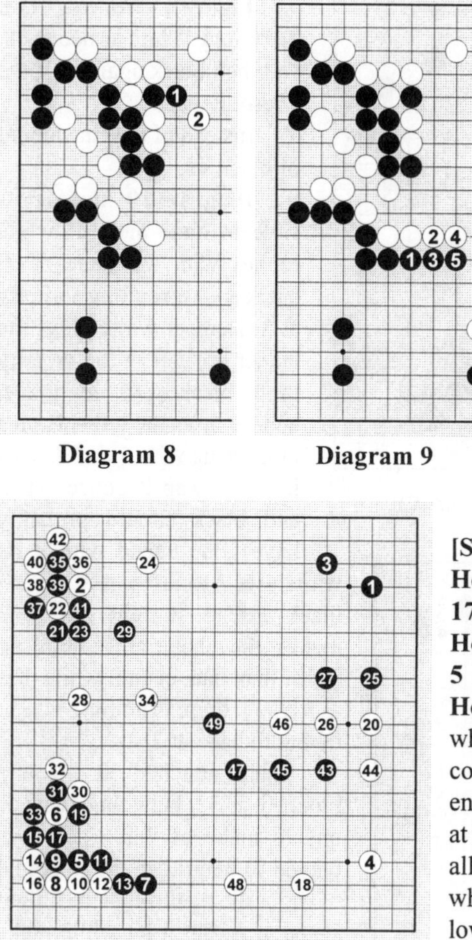

Diagram 8

Diagram 9

Reference Figure 3

Diagram 8 - Here, even if black tried to play out immediately at 1, having white play the fencing-in tactic of 2 is irksome. There is no necessity to deliberately look for trouble.

After white capped at 46, 48 was an essential turn.

Diagram 9 - If this was not played, black will vigorously push at 1 and the following plays, swallowing up the single capping stone, so this would have been dangerous.

Reference Figure 3 - [Shizokai Game; 1897; White: Honinbo Shuei 7 dan (Meijin, 17th and 19th hereditary Honinbo); Black: Tamura Hoju 5 dan (Meijin, 21st hereditary Honinbo)] The star point play of white 2 was Shuei's forte. The combination of the knight corner enclosure and the star point play at black 5 is a formation occasionally used. The early invasion of white 8 was the Shuei style, followed by the occupation of big points at 18 and 20. However, black had a thick and strong position with the plays through 47.

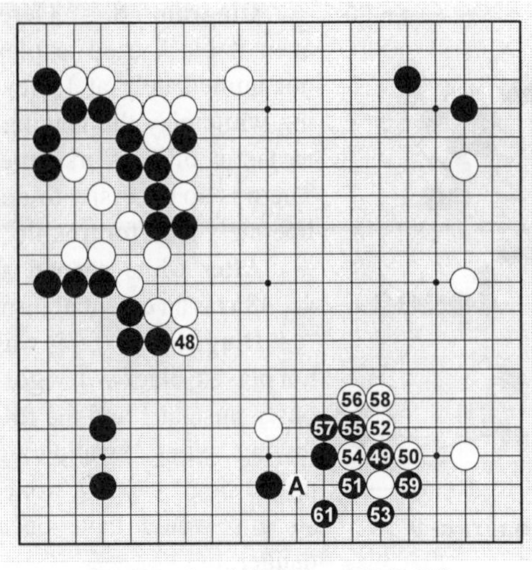

Figure 4 (48-61) (60@49)

Figure 4 - Making It on Territory White turned at 48, and then black again adopted a resolute tactic.

Instead of the attachment of black 49,

Diagram 10 - It was possible to hane at 1. If white replies with the hane of 2, black ends up cutting abruptly at 3. Here, if white plays the ladder breaker in the vicinity of 4, black pays no notice, and captures the left side on a large scale with 5 and 7. This kind of swap is conceivable, and black should probably have gone ahead with it. If white uses 2 to jump at **A**, letting black extend straight out at 2 makes the shape miserable, so rather than that, even if white dies as a result, there is nothing else to do but to hane at 2.

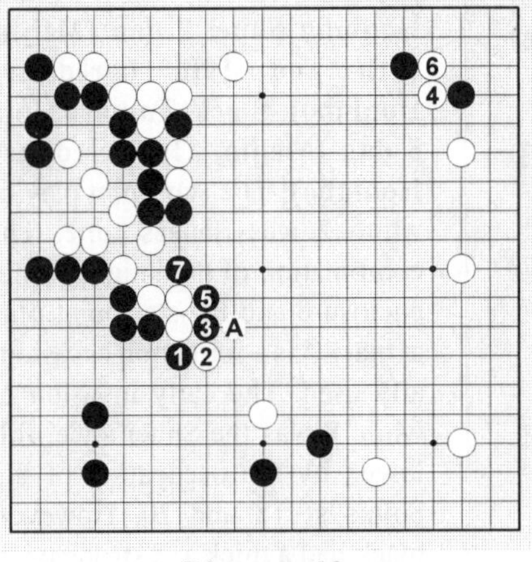

Diagram 10

Black attached at 49 and blocked at 51 here, but what is one to make of that? This was played to neutralize the potential of white slicing through the knight shape at **A**, but it let white make the punishing play at 52, giving black painful shape.

After the hane from below of black 53, the atari of 55 was a skillful finesse, but there was the undesirable factor of this being an overplay.

White missed an opportunity by playing the atari of 56.

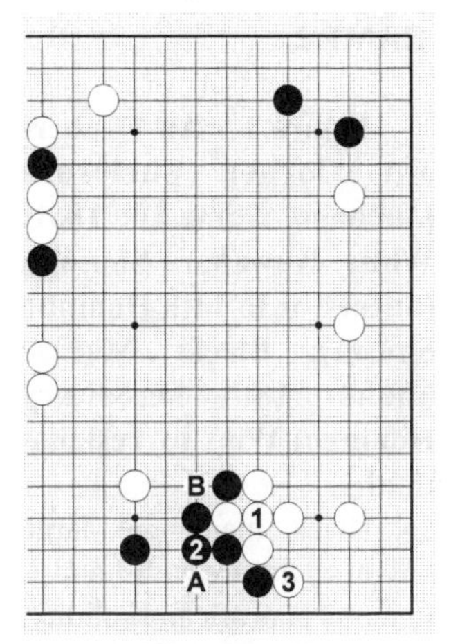

Diagram 11

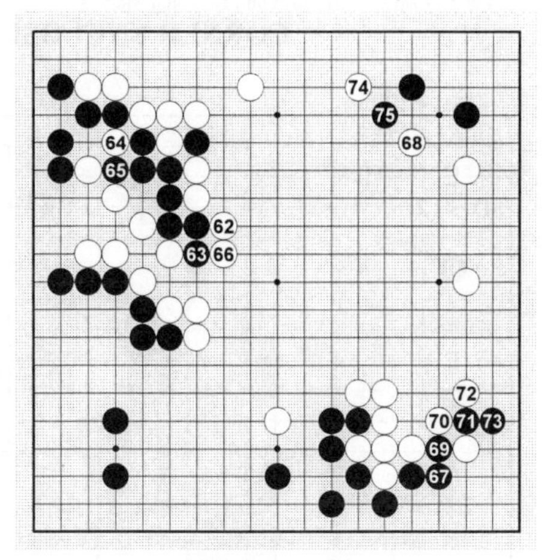

Diagram 12

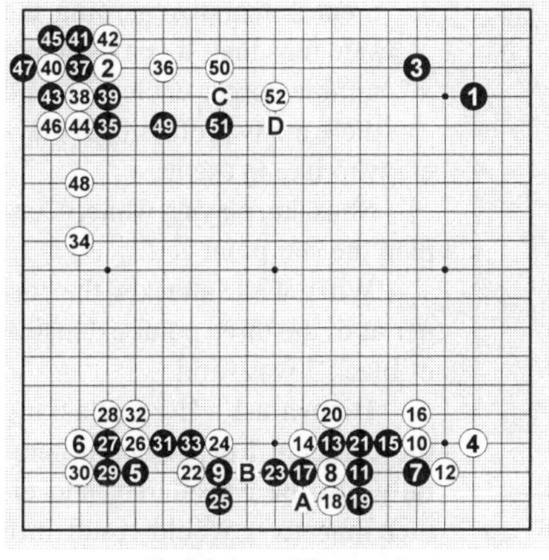

Reference Figure 4

Diagram 11 - Connecting at 1 is better, and if black 2, white blocks at 3, and this cannot be a successful shape for black. If black 2 is a tiger link at **A**, it would allow white to cut at **B**, putting black in trouble.

Diagram 12 - This shows the game's progress after **Figure 4**. White played 62 through 66, which, whatever else, sealed this black group in at the top.

When black extended at 67, white took a good point at 68, but the cut of black 71 and descent at 73 were big territorially.

White further made the checking extension at 74, but black played out with 75 and that stone could not be stopped. With a large amount of territory, the board position was an easy one for black to play.

Reference Figure 4 - [Oteai Ranking Tournament, Spring Session; 1932; White: Go Seigen 4 dan; Black: Kitani Minoru 5 dan] White's tactics of overconcentrating black on the lower side were skillful, and for that reason this game is famous. If black used 23 to hane at 33, considering the tactic of **A**, white could aim at making the clamp attachment at **B**, etc. Go: "White 50 should have been the knight's play at **C**. That would make the conditions in regard to surrounding the left side different." Black attached at **D** and pressed.

CORNER ENCLOSURE - GAME 2

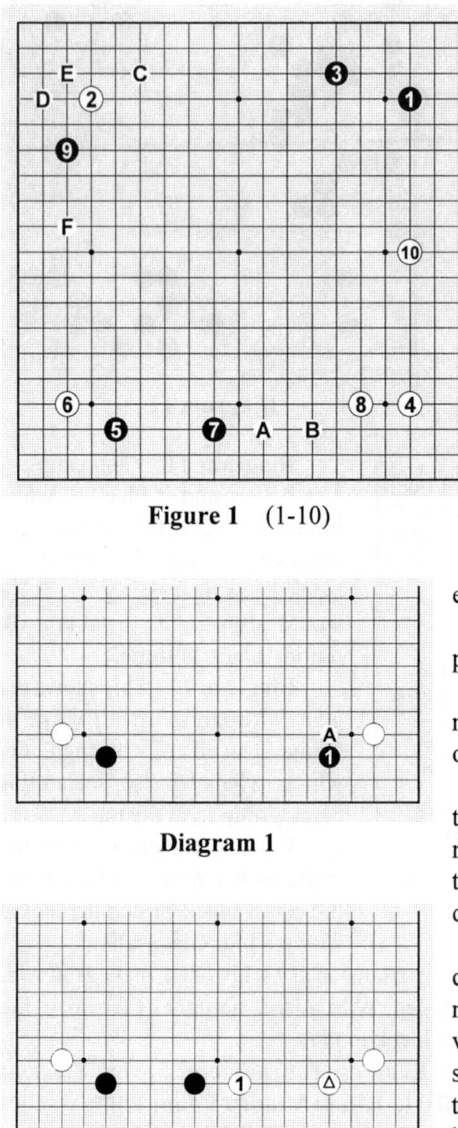

Figure 1 (1-10)

Diagram 1

Diagram 2

Figure 1 - An Exuberant Corner Enclosure [Jubango, Game 10; 1861; White: Kuwahara Shusaku (Successor to 14th Honinbo Shuwa); Black: Murase Shuho (18th hereditary Honinbo) Wins by resignation]

Black made the large knight enclosure with 1 and 3. In terms of profit and solidity, this is inferior to the knight enclosure, but its development potential regarding the side tops that. It is a light and nimble corner enclosure, and there many professional players who like to use it.

Shusaku, playing white, occupied the star point at 2.

When white attacked the corner at 6, the three point extension of black 7 was solid.

Diagram 1 - Here, attacking the corner at 1 or **A** could naturally also be considered, and either maneuver would result in a different game.

White's painstaking strategy can be seen in the one point corner enclosure of white 8. The development potential on the right side is apparent, while at the same time the checking extension of **A** became pressing. Conversely, the weak point of the checking extension of black **B** was created.

Diagram 2 - When white makes the knight enclosure with Δ, the maneuver in the corner is finished with one play, and because of that, the checking

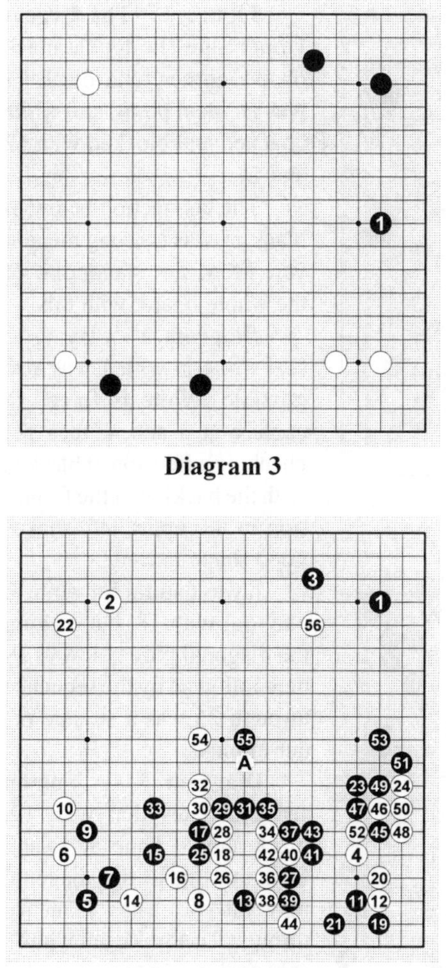

Diagram 3

Reference Figure 1

extension of white 1 becomes a play that is not urgent. It is hoped that attention is paid to the difference between this and the high corner enclosure.

Here, Shuho rushed to attack the corner with 9, giving white the big point on the right side.

Diagram 3 - There is naturally a case to be made for leaving the attack on the star point for later, and here the extension of black 1 on the right side is a splendid play. This would probably be the more usual maneuver.

White made the extension at 10, but today this play would be used to defend at **C**, and after black **D**, white **E** and black **F**, white turns to the play at 10. The intention is to mitigate the severity of a double attack on the corner by black.

Reference Figure 1 - [Jubango, Game 3; 1706; White: Inoue Inseki (Meijin, 4th hereditary Dosetsu); Black: Honinbo Dochi (Meijin, 5th hereditary Honinbo)] The large knight enclosure of 3 was already being played in this era. Meijin Inseki's go style manifested itself with the 5-4 point plays of white 2 and 4. Black 35 was an inferior play, the jump at **A** being desirable. Through 44, white obtained a good result.

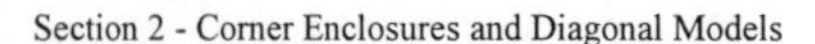

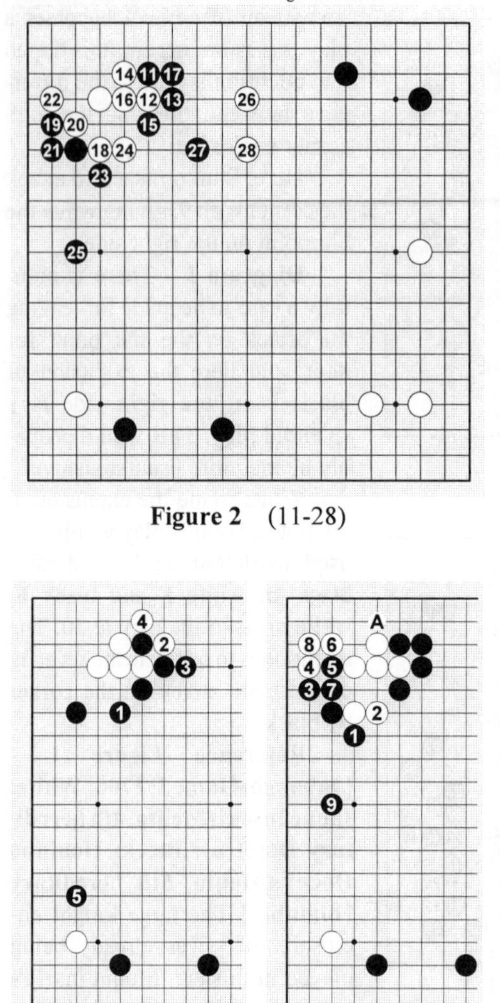

Figure 2 (11-28)

Diagram 4 **Diagram 5**

Figure 2 - The Urgent Upper Side The double attack on the corner with black 11 was an ideal point, and white attached and blocked with 12 and 14.

The connection below of black 17 was a strong maneuver. From the standpoint of the whole board, with this,

Diagram 4 - Playing to seal white in with 1 was also possible. White is forced to capture at 2 and 4, then the checking extension of black 5, with the backing of the formation in the upper left, makes good shape indeed.

It was natural for white to play out with 18, but making the diagonal play below at 19 here followed by the sequence through 25 was a strange order of plays.

Diagram 5 - Common sense dictates that with 19, black should hane at 1, and after that make the diagonal play at 3. The sequence through 9 is joseki, but white's submissive plays at 6 and 8 highlight the difference from the figure. In this position, in the case where white's access to the outside is barred, the hane of black **A** followed by connecting is a forcing play that white would find unbearable.

When black made the diagonal play at 19, in response to the wedging-in play of white 20,

Diagram 6 - The variation with white extending at 1 was also possible. When black plays 2, white's stones at 3 and 5 head for the side, and this is also feasible for white. There is considerable risk that white will dodge like this.

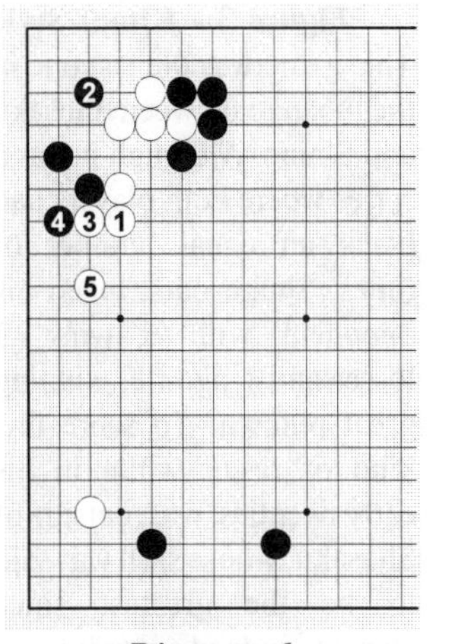

Diagram 6

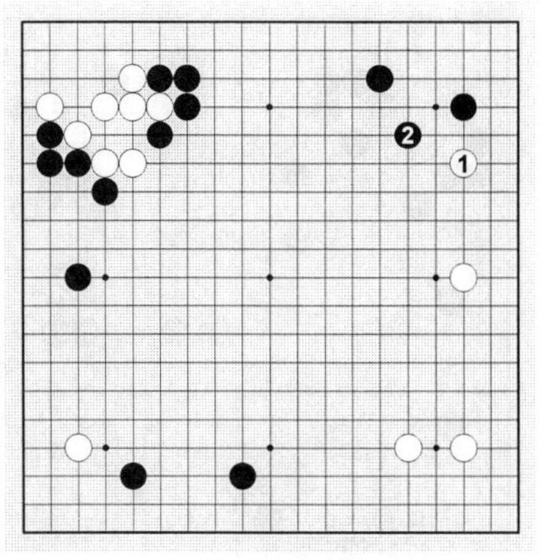

Diagram 7

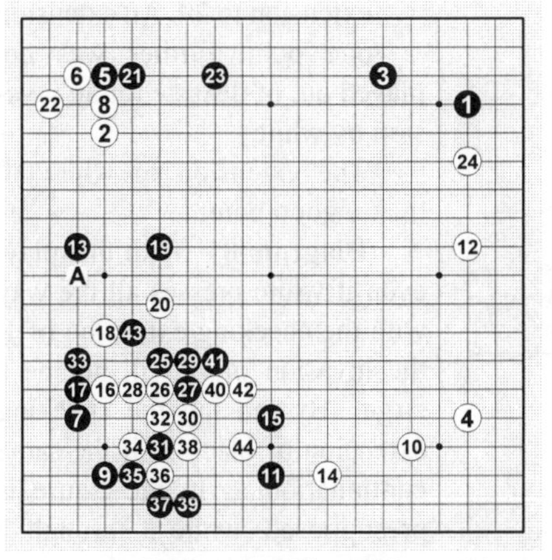

Reference Figure 2

Regardless of this, letting black play the double attack on the corner was responsible for white's plight. As a consequence, white had to rush to invade at 26.

Diagram 7 - Here, if white played the checking extension at 1, black would defend at 2, and the large knight enclosure comes to be working efficiently.

The knight's play of black 27 was what the position demanded.

Then white jumped to 28.

Reference Figure 2 - [Castle Game; 1820; White: Hattori Inshuku; Black: Honinbo Jowa (Meijin, 12th hereditary Honinbo)] Here is a large knight enclosure of Jowa's. In order to prevent the double wing formation by black, for white 12, making the extension of **A** or the atari of 21 was desirable. The two point jump of black 19 was a typical play of Jowa's. Black 25 and the following plays placed the importance on attacking, but through 44 the feeling is that black's forces are concentrated to no purpose.

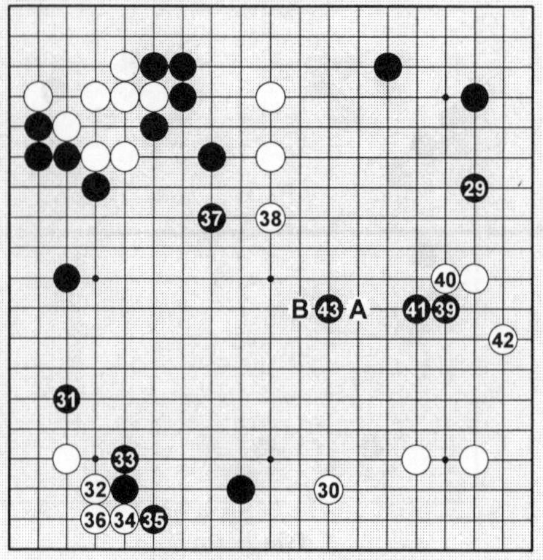

Figure 3 (29-43)

Figure 3 - Kitani Style

This game was the last one in the jubango between Shusaku and Shuho. Although it was a series where both players had black an equal number of times, Shuho outstripped his opponent with 6 wins, 3 losses and 1 jigo tie, winning great renown. To score this kind of result while in his early twenties, was, outside of Shusaku, whose skill was said to be the greatest since Dosaku, judged splendid.

Black made the two point extension to 29. An extension one point further was not played out of distaste for an invasion by white.

The extension of white 30 took a good point.

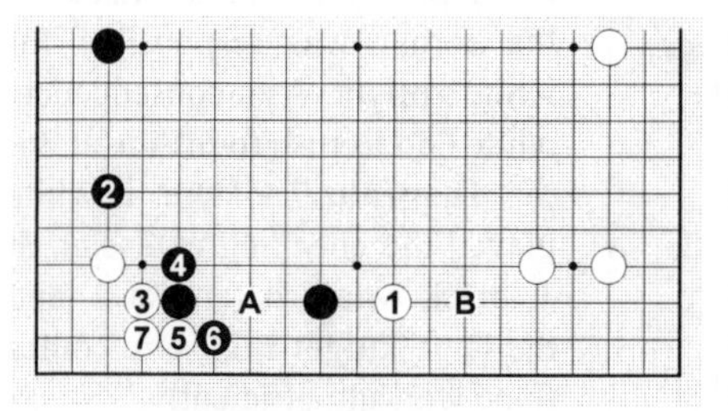

Diagram 8

Diagram 8 - With this play, even if white presses all the way with the checking extension of 1, the invasion of **A** will not be a target. By making the checking extension of black 2, if the same continuation as in the figure is presupposed, white 3 through 7 would allow black to aim at the invasion at **B**, and the over extension is obvious. That is the reason that white played the more restrained play a line to the right.

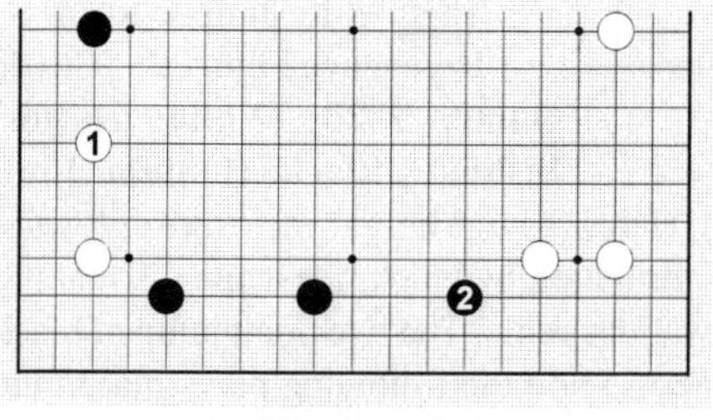

Diagram 9

Diagram 9 - At 30, playing 1 in the lower left would be splendid, but it does not compare to permitting black to play the checking extension of 2.

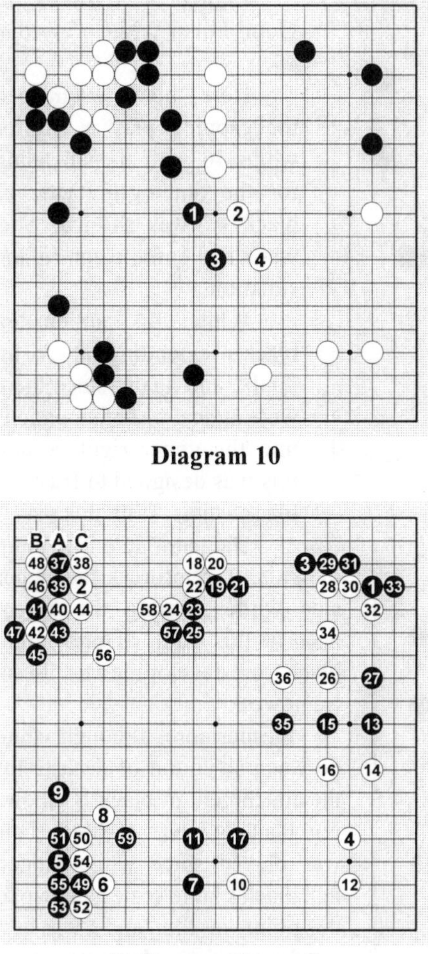

Diagram 10

Reference Figure 3

In response to the checking extension of black 31, the diagonal attachment of white 32 followed by the connection of white 36 would be viewed today as "Kitani style." This was a painful submission, but a diagonal play to get out into the open would be undirected, and quickly settling the group was, on this occasion, a simple and clear strategy.

After exchanging the jumps at black 37 and white 38, black made the shoulder hit at 39. Playing the one line restrained play at 29 was predicated upon this play, and this point in the game was the best chance to carry through with it. Here,

Diagram 10- Swooping from above with black 1, followed by the tandem plays of white 2 and 4, lead to white building the bigger territorial framework. Black has gaps in the position above and below, so the left area cannot become a big territory, while black has lost the chance to strike into white with an erasure play.

White pushed at 40, then slid to 42, the common shape.

Here, the two point jump of black 43 was typical of the energetic Shuho style. Making the one point jump of **A** was slow-footed, inviting the capping play of white **B**.

Reference Figure 3 - [Jubango, Game 3; 1953; White: Ishii Senji 5 dan; Black: Tamura Hoju 4 dan (Meijin, 21st hereditary Honinbo)] Here is Shusai's large knight enclosure. White responded with the star point play at 2 and the 5-4 point play at 4. This provoked controversy. "Using white 16 to jump at 17 was superior. Black 19 could not be described as a good scheme. Giving up the corner with 43 was usual. For white 40, **A**, black **B** and the connection of white **C** was best."

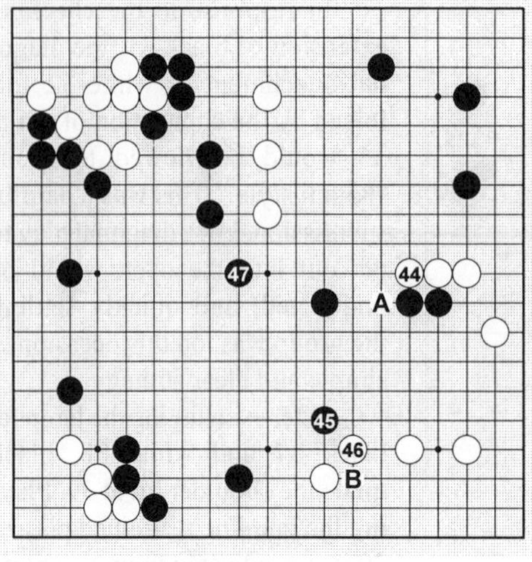

Figure 4 (44-47)

Figure 4 - Black in Good Form White pressed at 44.

Here, black exchanged the capping play at 45 for white 46, and then heading for the fencing-in tactic of black 47 was shrewd. This was a key point to control the situation.

White 44 anticipated black's extending at **A** no doubt, and again, since there were indications of incursions into the upper right corner, this was designed to frustrate black's aims. With this play,

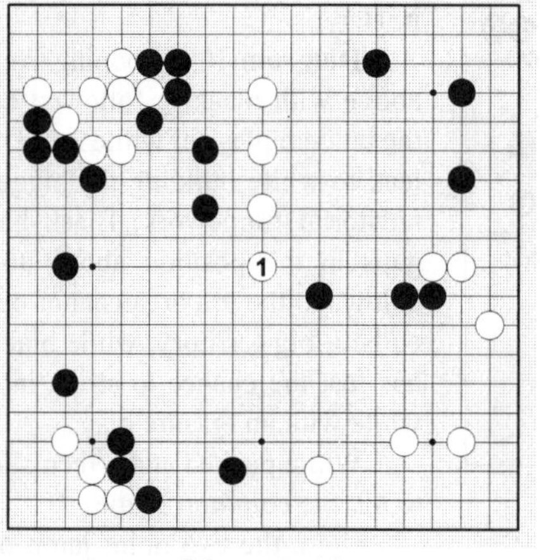

Diagram 11

Diagram 11 - The jump of white 1 reinforces the upper side while meeting the urgent need at this point of preventing black from developing a territorial framework.

Furthermore, although white 46 was played out of distaste for the attachment of black **B**, allowing black 47 was terrible. This was played since white judged that black's large scale game up to this point was thin, and it was best to take territory. However, occupying the key point of 47 was an essential plus for black.

Diagram 12 - After this was played, white haned at 1 and played out at 3, however, even doing so, there was nothing to be gained there. Black took control of the stone with 6, and on the contrary, black was relieved.

In these few plays, black secured the positional advantage.

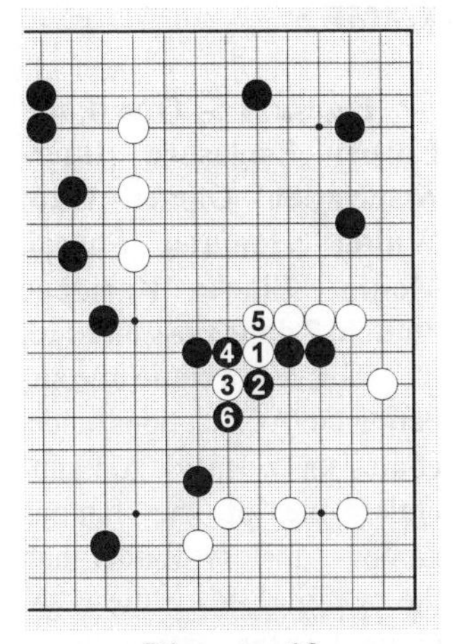

Diagram 12

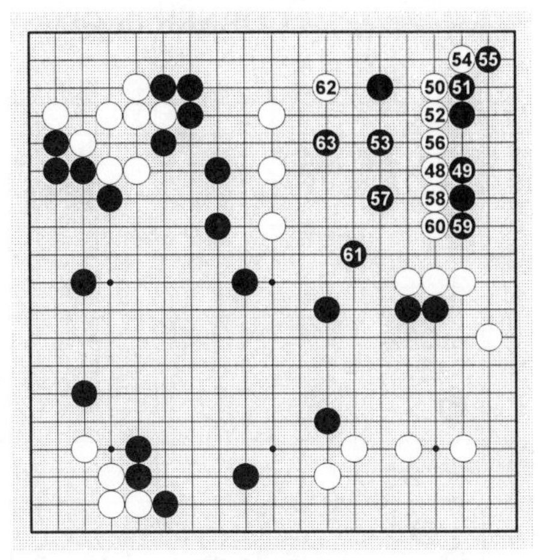

Diagram 13

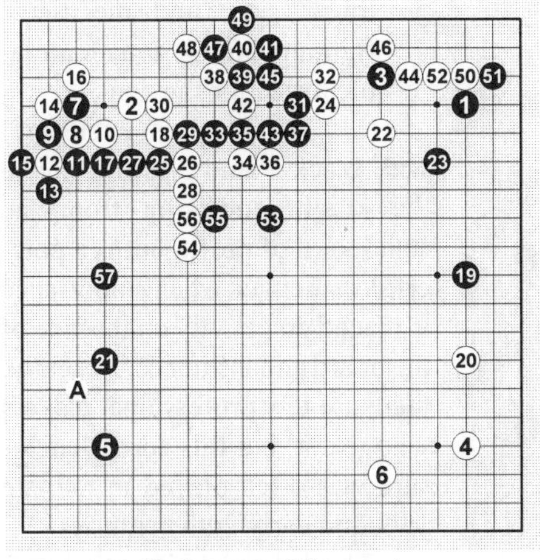

Reference Figure 4

White's mistaken plays are here analyzed simply as an addendum.

Diagram 13 - This shows the game's progress after **Figure 4**.

White played 48 and invaded at 50, a usual tactic in this kind of position, and with black inviting white to spoil the territory, 53 and 57 were played to separate white's three stones on the upper side on a large scale and attack them.

Within this play order, the single hane of white 54 was shrewd. Simply connecting at black 54 gave no continuation.

With black 63 and the following plays, the attack and defense continued, centering around the status of white's group.

Reference Figure 4 - [Oteai Ranking Tournament, Spring Session; 1928; White: Segoe Kensaku 7 dan; Black: Maeda Nobuaki 4 dan] This is a combination with a large knight corner enclosure and the star point at black 5. Segoe: "I also questioned whether to use white 20 to attack the corner at **A**. Black 21 was perfect." With 31 and the following, black was in charge. Maeda: "The cut of black 47 was reckless. A placement at 48 was in order."

CORNER ENCLOSURE - GAME 3

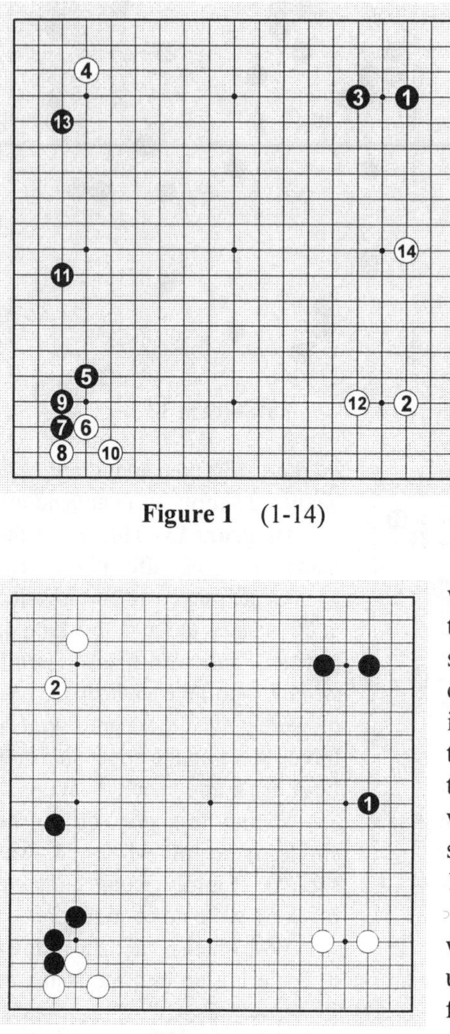

Figure 1 (1-14)

Diagram 1

Figure 1 - One Point Corner Enclosure [Inter-Association Game; 1926; White: Honinbo Shusai, Meijin; Black: Karigane Junichi 7 dan; Loss on time]

This was a battle of competing Go Associations, and a contest between the top generals, one of the famous games of history. Rather than the opening, this game is famous for the extraordinary battle that developed on the lower side, and the fierce fighting left this as a memorable tussle for the ages.

The one point enclosure with black 1 and 3 is inferior to the knight enclosure from the standpoint of profit, but is a powerful maneuver when importance is placed on activity on the side of the board and influence. Recently, there are few professional players who use it, but this corner enclosure was often played in the late 19th and early 20th centuries.

The 3-4 point play of white 2 was a maneuver that Shusai often used at times when he felt that it fit the situation best.

The 5-4 point play of black 5 is an opening method that has come to be often seen in combination with the one point enclosure.

When white attacked the corner with 6, black played the joseki from 7 through 11, making equivalent options of attacks on either open corner.

It was natural for white to make an enclosure in this corner. It has the implication of next making the extension at 14, so playing the enclosure in this corner was the biggest play.

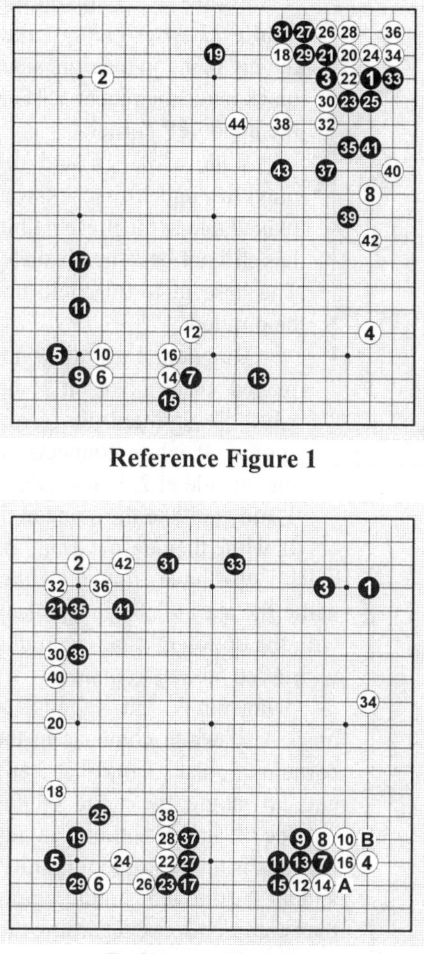

Reference Figure 1

Reference Figure 2

The attack on the corner with black 13 was also the only play.

Diagram 1 - Here, if black takes the big point of 1 first, it lets white make double corner enclosures with 2.

Reference Figure 1 - [Castle Game; 1789; White: Honinbo Retsugen (10th hereditary Honinbo); Black: Kono Motohara] The high corner enclosure of black 1 and 3 was an unusual maneuver at the time. Up to then, the large knight enclosure was played, but the knight enclosure was mainly used. This was perhaps also due to the influence of Sakaguchi Sentoku and others who like to develop high positions, and from this time forward, the one point enclosure gradually began to be seen.

Reference Figure 2 - [Castle Game; 1804; White: Yasui Chitoku (8th hereditary Yasui, Sanchi); Black: Honinbo Genjo (11th hereditary Honinbo)]Here is an example of Genjo playing the high corner enclosure against Chitoku. The plays at 4 and 5 were the fighting 3-4 points, and initiating a variation with the high attack on the corner with black 7 was in today's style. White 12 was an overplay. Had black played 15 at 16, followed by white **A** and black **B**, white would have been in trouble.

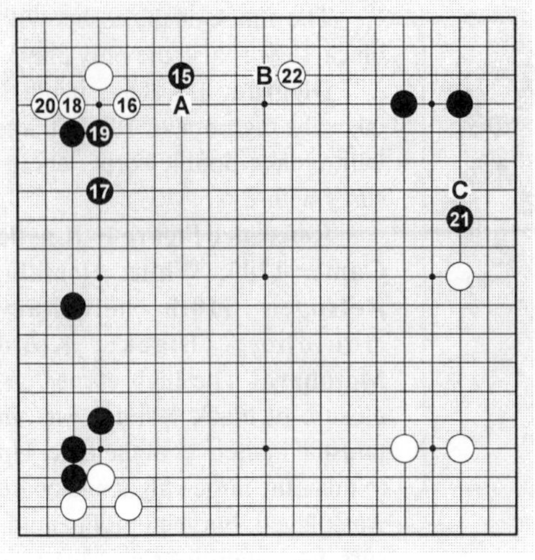

Figure 2 (15-22)

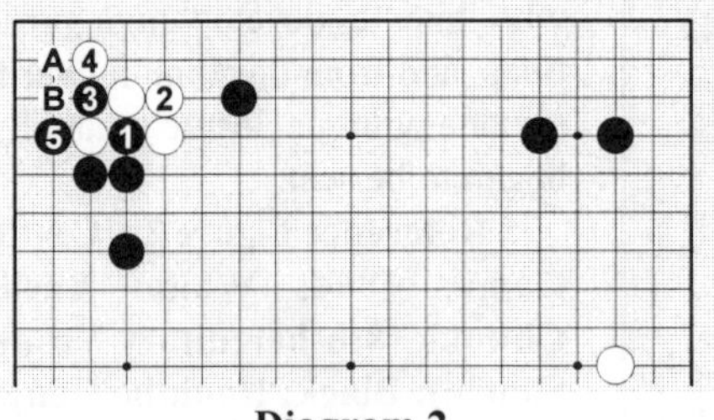

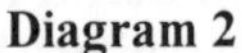
Diagram 2

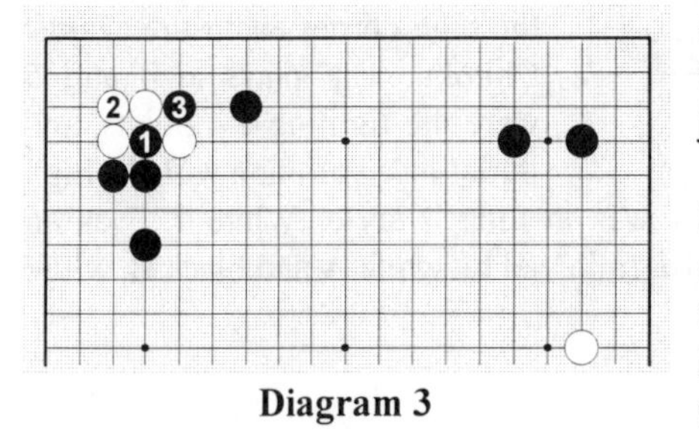

Diagram 3

Figure 2 - Painstaking White 22 After giving white the big point on the right side, black made the pincer at 15 in the upper left corner.

With white 16 and the plays through 20, a joseki was played that to the present time has still not become obsolete. The descent to 20 could not be omitted.

Diagram 2 - If this is not played, black pokes at 1 and white is stymied for a response. If white connects on the outside at 2, black cuts at 3 and can take the stone at 5. If white then descends at **A**, black will have forced white, while the atari of **B** leaves black with the option of challenging ko with **A**, so anxiety remains.

Diagram 3 - In response to black 1, if white connects in the corner at 2, black can cut at 3 and end up taking the stone on the outside. It goes without saying that this is unfavorable for white, and all the above is nothing more than common sense regarding this joseki.

In present day go, playing black 15 as the high pincer at **A** can also be considered, and at one time in response to this the knight's play of white 20 was often made.

The checking extension of black 21 was a good point. If this was played as the extension on the upper side at **B**, white would play the extension at **C**.

Splitting the upper side with white 22 was a painstaking play by Shusai.

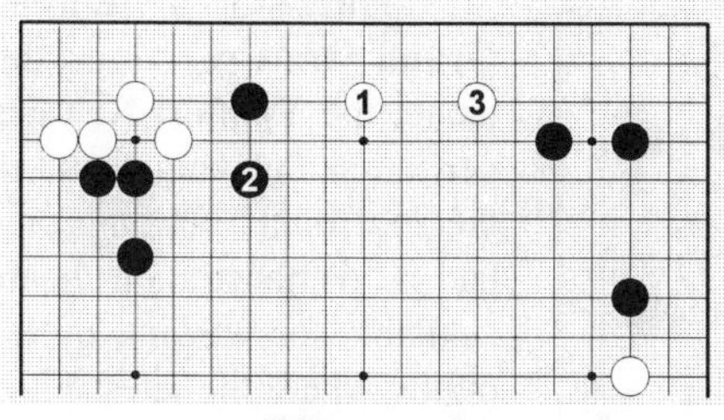

Diagram 4

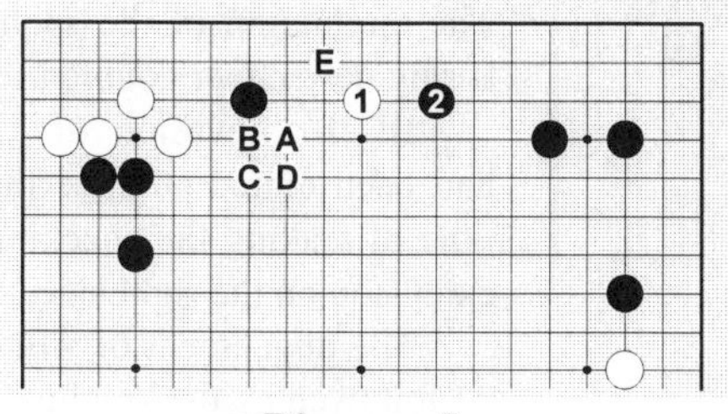

Diagram 5

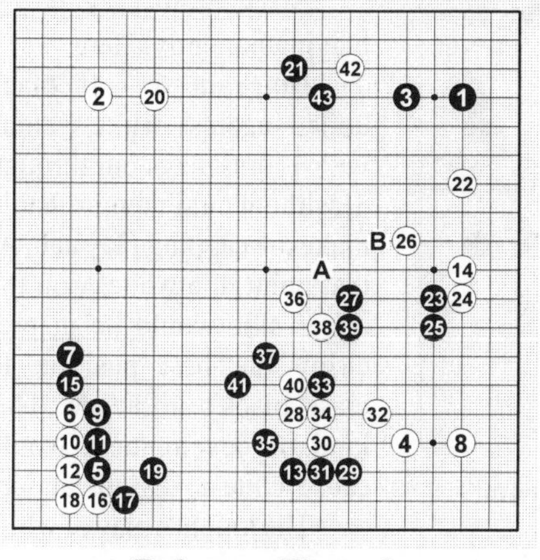

Reference Figure 3

Diagram 4 - If the effect on black's single stone is considered, white should approach closer, one line to the left at 1. Should black jump at 2, white makes the extension at 3, and this is satisfying shape for white. However, it does not seem like this can be expected.

Diagram 5 - When white plays 1, the checking extension of black 2 is conceivable. If this is played, even if white makes the fencing-in tactic at **A**, black's single stone cannot be captured with that one play. Black **B**, white **C** and then the cut of black **D** is hard to handle. For **D**, sliding to black **E** is also possible, and white would struggle to come up with a counter strategy.

White played one line wider than this waiting for black to play out, and making it a wide open game.

Reference Figure 3 - [Jubango, Game 1; 1895; White: Ishii Senchi 5 dan; Black: Tamura Hoju 4 dan (Meijin, 21st hereditary Honinbo)] White made the corner enclosure at 8 to counter black's high corner enclosure in the upper right. White 34 made bad shape, but the capping play of 36 was a good point. Black 41 was the strongest play here, and then white played 42, judging that after **A** the attachment of black **B** would make it impossible to capture. White played on the upper side to enliven the position on the board.

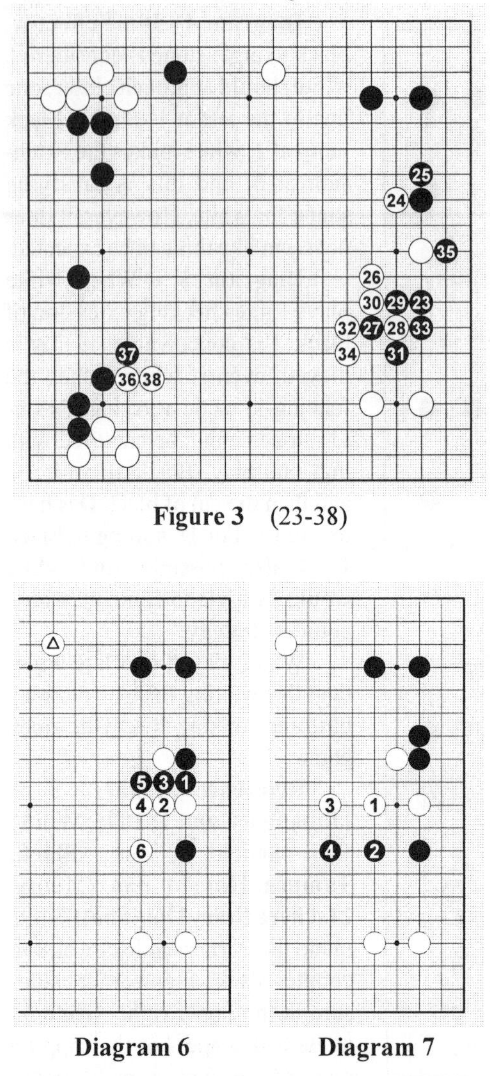

Figure 3 (23-38)

Diagram 6

Diagram 7

Figure 3 - White's Grand Strategy For this game, the Yomiuri Newspaper set up a playing venue on the roof of its building, and had a demonstration board available for viewing by the public where the latest plays were displayed. It excited the go world of the middle 1920s. The circulation of the sponsoring newspaper doubled.

Black's invasion of 23 had been aimed at since the time of making the checking extension on the right side.

The attachment of white 24 followed by the knight's play of 26 were ambitious plays typical of Shusai.

Black drew back at 25, playing patiently. Here,

Diagram 6 - If black butted against white's stone with 1, and plays out through 5, white would then probably make the capping play at 6. At that point, the white Δ on the upper side would be in precisely the best position to erase black's influence. This kind of development would cause white no dissatisfaction.

The knight's play of white 26 was also what the position called for.

Diagram 7 - If white simply jumps to 1 and 3, black is permitted to play out with 4, and from white's standpoint, this would be less than having no strategy at all.

After slicing through the knight's play with 28, white played 30 through 34, letting black capture a stone but making thickness directed at the center, an interesting maneuver.

Black was forced to connect underneath with 35, and then white attached at 36 and extended at 38 in order to expand the lower side to the greatest extent, a grand strategy. This was a vivid example of Shusai's strength in playing in the center.

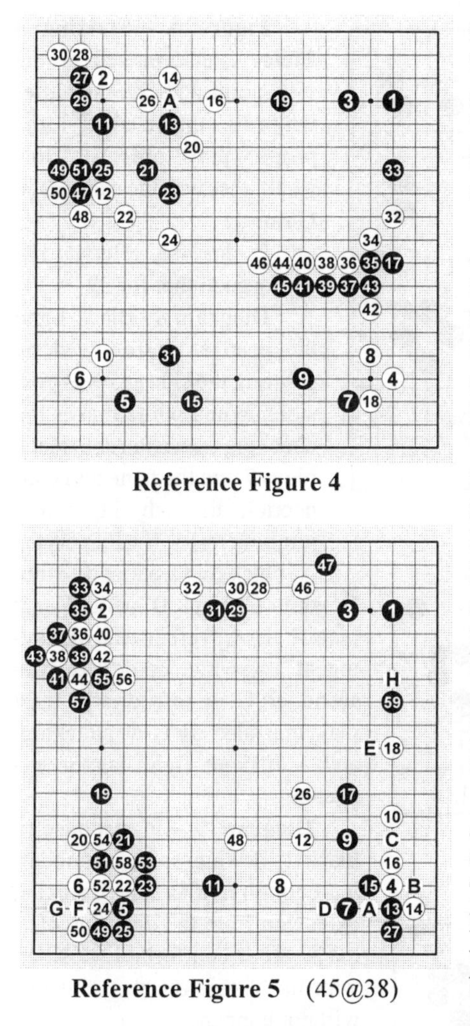

Reference Figure 4

Reference Figure 5 (45@38)

Reference Figure 4 - [1st Annual Honinbo Title Match, Game 6; 1941; White: Kato Shin 7 dan; Black: Sekiyama Riichi 6 dan] This was the game that gave Sekiyama Riichi the first Honinbo title. White 12 and black 13 are a maneuver that is still seen in contemporary go. Afterward, the maneuver with 13 as the large knight's play at **A** was developed. Following the two point extension, black 31, building up the lower side while keeping watch over white's territorial framework on the left side, was interesting. Black gained the lead in the opening.

Reference Figure 5 - [7th Annual Honinbo Title Match, Game 2; 1952; White: Takagawa Kaku 7 dan; Black: Hashimoto Shou, Honinbo] If white used 16 to hane at 27, after black 16, white **A**, black **B**, white 13 black **C**, white **D**, black **E** would be ideal. Black 21 was questionable. With this play, black **F**, white **G** and black 52 was strong. For white 58, the extension at **H** was better. Instead, black made the checking extension at 59, rallying.

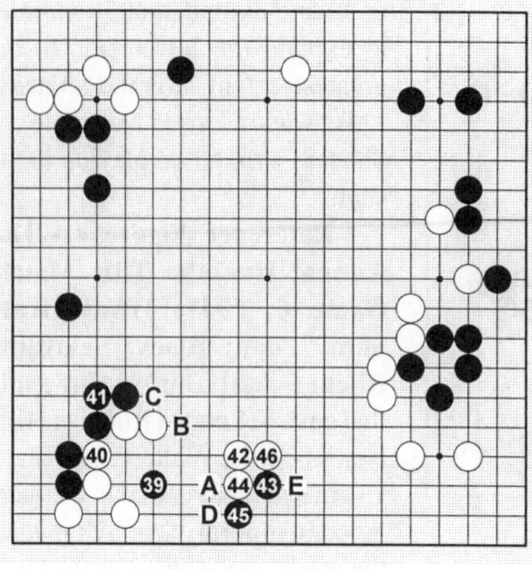

Figure 4 (39-46)

Figure 4 - Starting a Melee Black played at the vital point with 39, then after white 40, connected at 41, the proper play order in this joseki that was the same as in **Game 1**.

In analysis afterward it was argued that for 39,

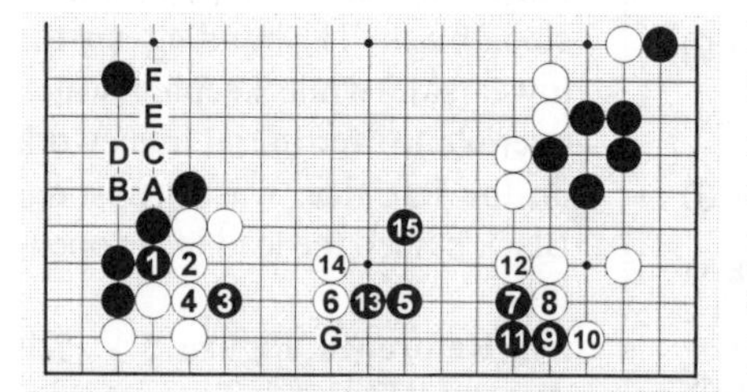

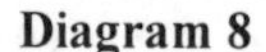

Diagram 8

Diagram 8 - Black 1 and the peep at 3, followed by splitting the side at 5 was possible. When white makes the checking extension at 6, black plays 7 and the hane and connection through 11 before jumping to 15. If white cuts at **A**, black plays patiently with **B**, white **C**, black **D**, white **E** and black **F**. However, instead of playing at 14, white could also descend at **G**, a territorially tight play that also aims at attacking, and a difficult fight can be expected.

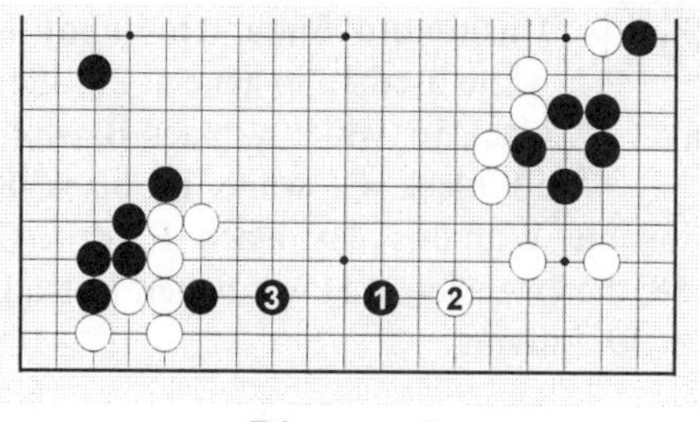

Diagram 9

Diagram 9 - In response to black 1, if white is accommodating enough to make the checking extension from the direction of 2, black gets a comfortable position with the extension at 3, but this will not happen.

White 42 was a skillful play that expanded the position.

Diagram 10 - Here, playing below the star point at 1 invites the shoulder hit of black 2 followed by the plays through 8, giving black an easy position to play.

Black played at the corner of the stone with 43, seeking a foothold to destroy the territory here. With this play, the attachment of 44 allows white to play out with 43, black **A**, white 46, black **B** and white **C**, leaving black badly off. This would fall in line with white's desires.

When white blocked at 44, the hane of black 45 was an obstinate play, and was the spark that ignited the melee that came after this.

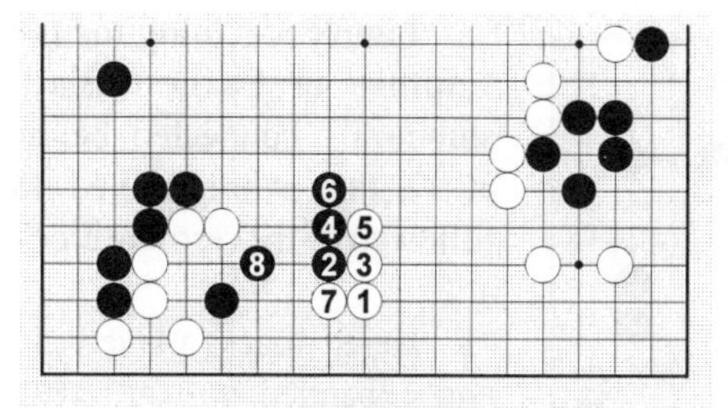

Diagram 10

Diagram 11 - Here, if black pushes up at 1, white descends at 2, and through 5, black has a comfortable position, but the hane of 45 was played in order to make use of 39. Since black did not choose the seemingly safe course in this diagram, the board position became complex.

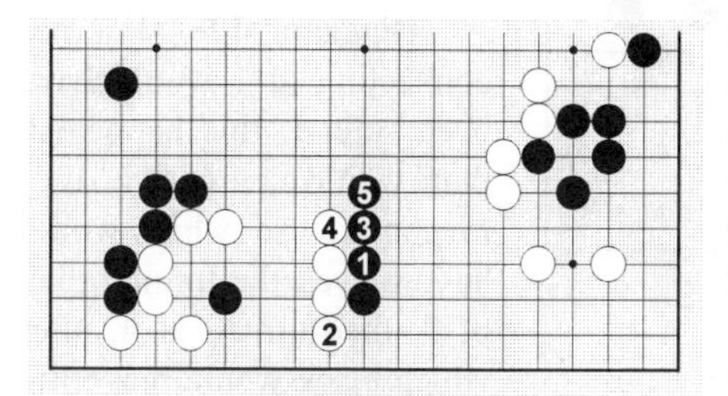

Diagram 11

For white, too, blocking at **D** would mean being forced after black connects which would be wretched. White blocked from above with 46, trying to coerce black into extending at **E**. This was fighting spirit.

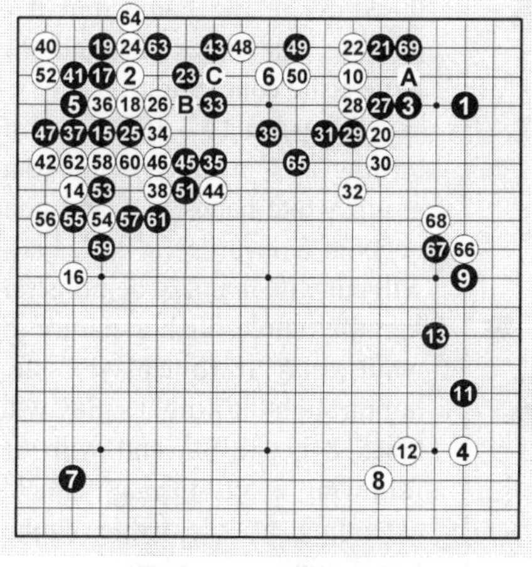

Reference Figure 6

Reference Figure 6 - [Jubango, Game 2; 1953; White: Sakata Eio 8 dan; Black: Go Seigen 9 dan] It was twenty years before Go had played the first play anywhere other than on the star point. The combination of the high corner enclosure with the play at the 3-3 point at 7 is rare. Instead of white 22, one wants to play up against black's stone with 27 or slicing through the knight's play at **A**. White 24 was heavy. Here was where white should have dealt deftly with the situation with **B**, black 33 and white **C**. The swap through 65 was greatly in black's favor.

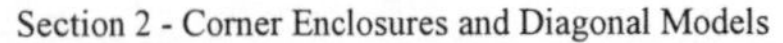

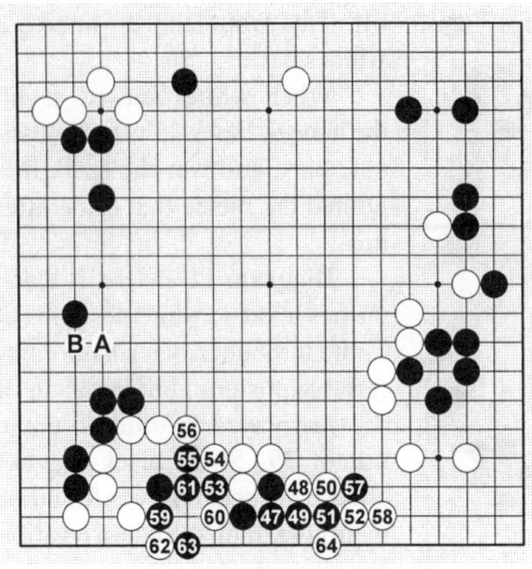

Figure 5 (47-64)

Figure 5 - Going for the Capture in Earnest Black stubbornly connected below at 47, then white played 48 followed by the resolute block at 52.

Here, black played 53 and expanded outward with 55, showing an all-out determination to resist.

Diagram 12 - For 55, connecting at 1 would have been safe. If this happened, there would have been no way to capture, so white would have played the forcing play of 2, then turned at 4, after which black would make life with 5. With the jump at 6, white would play to utilize the central thickness in the game, but it is obvious that black disliked this large scale conception.

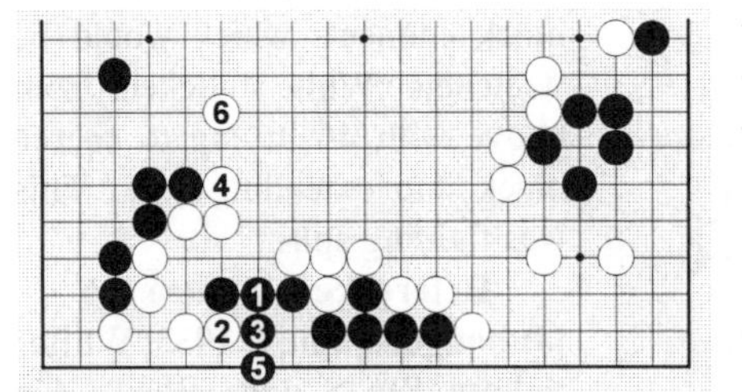

Diagram 12

Diagram 13 - If, instead of turning at 4 in the previous diagram, white hanes at 1 and connects at 3 in order to kill, black will cut with 4 and 6, demonstrating the unreasonable nature of white's play. If white plays 7, slicing through the knight's play with black 8 is skillful, and with the following plays through black's extending at 14, white cannot avoid ruin.

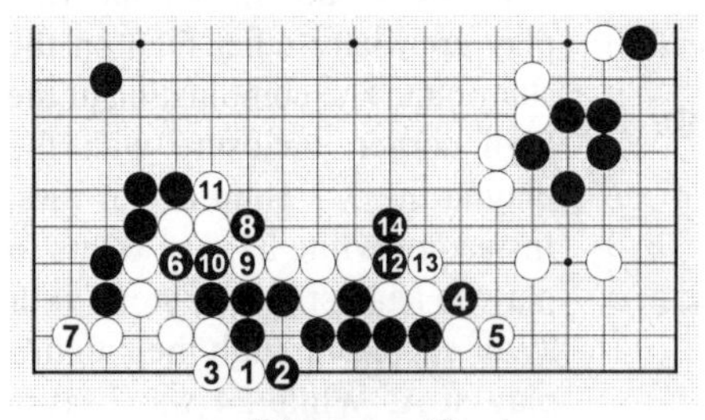

Diagram 13

Since black did not adopt the peaceful course of **Diagram 12**, instead playing 55 through 59, white cut with 60 and through 64, made a concerted effort to capture. One can sense the indomitable spirit of both players in this no holds barred struggle.

In his analysis after the game, Shusai suggested that before going for the kill with 64, perhaps white should have exchanged **A** for black **B**, but this would have required extraordinary reading.

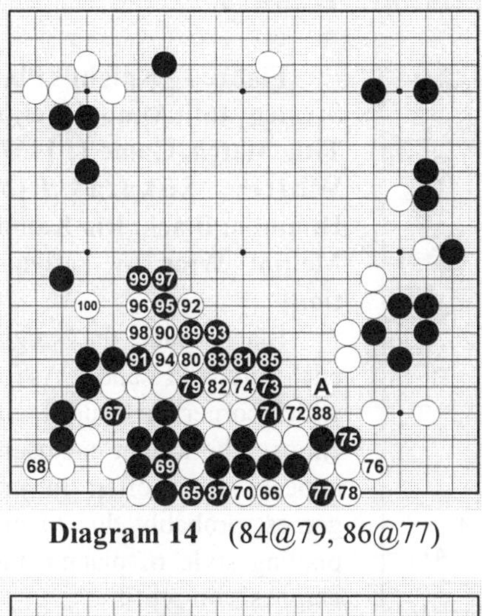

Diagram 14 (84@79, 86@77)

Diagram 14 -

Since the opening stage had already passed, the play order leading to the climax of black's death that followed, along with brief comments, is appended here.

Following the cut of black 67 up to 99, the progress of plays from the point where white first went after the capture was practically an unforked road. White could not avoid pressing up against black's stone with 74. When white jumped to 100, an impenetrably difficult capturing race resulted.

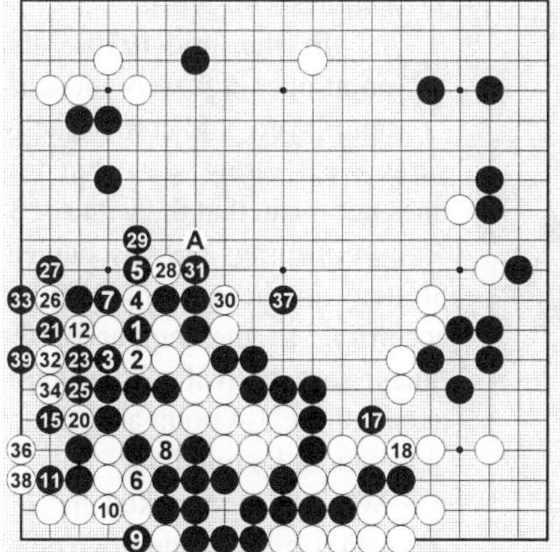

Diagram 15 (13, 19, 24@1, 14 above 6, 16, 22@4, 35@20)

Diagram 15 - Black 1 through 7 were maneuvers to give white a shortage of liberties. Through 10, white connected the stones above and below, and then black had no choice but to fill the liberty of white's at 11. There are an abundance of variations, such as using 5 to play atari at 6, but a winning theme for black does not emerge. With both players standing on the edge of a precipice play by play, this was a thrilling series of plays.

For 15, black could also have connected at 20.

Ko broke out at the point of 1, but it was clear that white would win it, so black fought it through to find the best way to squeeze white while giving up the stones on the lower side.

The placement of white 36 was an exquisite play. White captured 15 black stones, and after 39, white haned at **A** and fighting developed in the center. At play 255, black lost on time.

CORNER ENCLOSURE - GAME 4

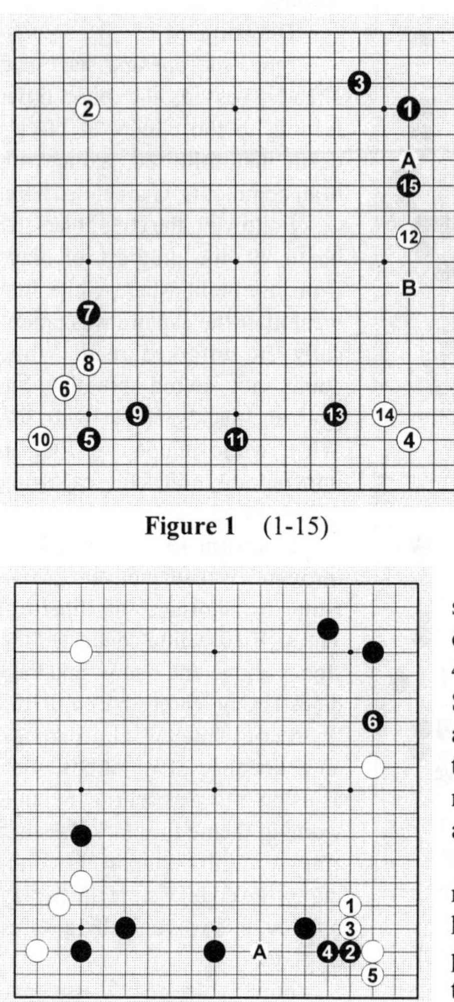

Figure 1 (1-15)

Diagram 1

Figure 1 - Knight's Play Strategy [6th Annual Meijin Title Match, Game 1; 1967; White: Sakata Eio, Honinbo; Black: Rin Kaiho, Meijin; Wins by resignation]

Black made the knight enclosure with 1 and 3. As for which corner enclosure I will choose, the knight enclosure appears most often in my games, probably due to my playing style of placing the emphasis on profit.

In the mid-1970s, star point openings were most often played, and corner enclosures were rarely seen, but this does not mean that the value of 3-4 point openings was discounted. Strategy in the opening changes according to the temper of the times, so a revival of the dominance of the 3-4 point as fashionable cannot be ruled out.

When white attacked the corner with 6, black made a two point high pincer at 7, and with the plays through 11, a joseki resulted that was often played at the time. With the 3-3 point play of white 4 made as Sakata's forte, the feeling is that this is how it should go.

The extension of white 12 played one line beyond the point below the star point, naturally stressed the follow-up checking extension to be pressed in all the way at **A**.

Black attacked the corner with the large knight's play at 13 and white answered with the diagonal play at 14, which is one pattern for defending. It may look like an unusual play, but in the past it appeared in one of Go Seigen's

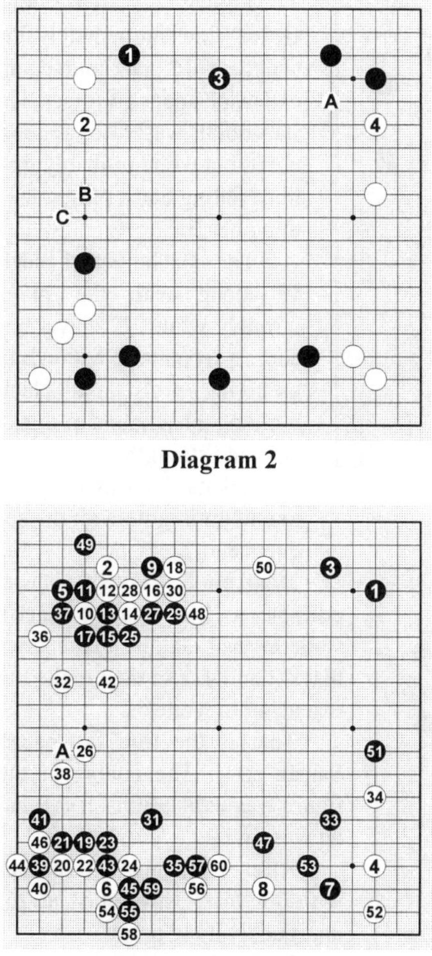

Diagram 2

Reference Figure 1

games. With it, a higher stance is developed, with the significance that black's stone that attacked the corner is not permitted to deal deftly with the situation. It is a maneuver with depth to it.

Diagram 1 - Here, if white defends with the knight's play at 1, black can play the joseki of 2 and 4 to fix the shape, and the aim of invading at **A** is lost.

As shown in the next figure, white put great importance on that aim, and the diagonal play of 14 was designed to make it pack a punch.

Here, black extended at 15, denying white the checking extension at **A**. Of course, it also looks toward invading at **B** next.

Diagram 2 - If black used 15 to play 1 and 3 on the upper side, white would play the checking extension at 4, making the vital point of **A** an urgent one. If black defends at **A**, the game would probably develop with white playing at either **B** or **C** on the left side.

Reference Figure 1 - [Oteai Ranking Tournament, Spring Session; 1928; White: Suzuki Tamejiro 7 dan; Black: Segoe Kensaku 7 dan] After making a corner enclosure, black attacked the corner at 5. The one point pincer of black 9 was often played at the time. If black used 25 to make the extension at **A**, white would press at 25. However, according to Segoe, black's attitude about this lacked objectivity.

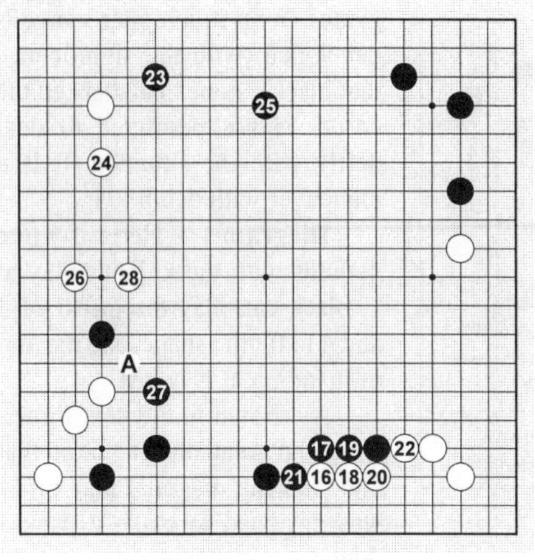

Figure 2 (16-28)

Figure 2 - Sente and Gote White immediately invaded at 16. Of course, an extension under the upper side star point was also a good point, but white probably disliked letting black play something here.

The attachment of black 17 along with the plays through white 22 have become a set pattern, with white garnering profit and black building a backbone of thickness and strength.

Sakata: "It was no good to end up in gote with the sequence to 22.

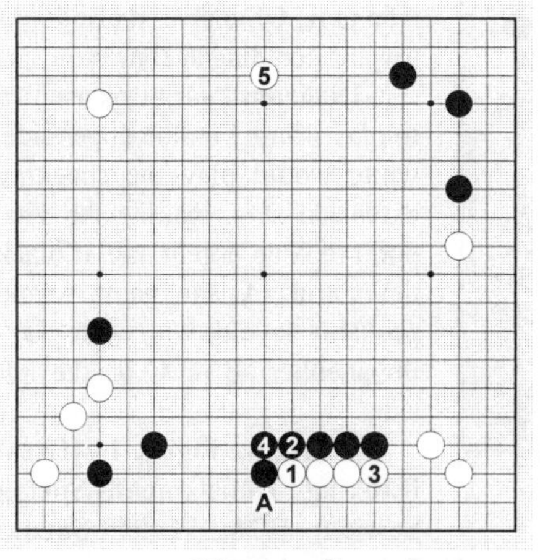

Diagram 3

Diagram 3 - For 20, it was possible to butt against black's stone with 1, taking sente after black 2 and 4, and then make the extension to white 5."

That is the true fast-paced Sakata style. The course in the figure was unlike himself is what he was saying.

After attacking the corner with 23, black developed at 25, unarguably a big point.

Here, white pressed in all the way with the checking extension of 26, a painstaking play.

Diagram 4 - If white had made the two point high pincer at 1, it would be easy for black to enter the corner immediately at 2. Should white respond with 3 and 5, black takes profit through 8, and it is difficult for white to next make the attachment **A**, since after black **B**, white **C**, black **D** and white **E**, black will cut at **F**. The position of white 1 has become unfocused.

Black 27 expanded the territorial framework on the lower side, while extending support to black's stone on the left side.

The jump of white 28 was a good play.

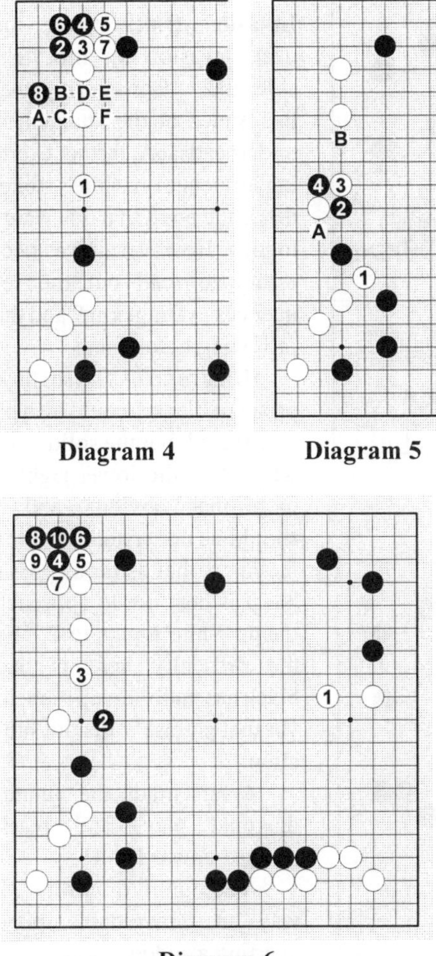

Diagram 4

Diagram 5

Diagram 6

Diagram 5 - Here, moving out with the diagonal play of white 1 would be senseless since it would let black put things into motion by attaching at 2 and cutting at 4. If white then extends at **A**, black will attach at **B**, and one way or another deal deftly with the situation. Black's jump becomes a forcing play when white replies with the diagonal play, and this is worthless for white.

Diagram 6 - In addition, for 28, jumping to 1 on the right side also takes an ideal point. If that was played, black would make the knight's play at 2, and when white plays 3, black will probably invade the 3-3 point at 4. This time, white answers with 5 through 9, taking sente after black 10 to turn elsewhere, but black gains the profit in the corner, and would not be dissatisfied with this result. The exchange of 2 for 3 comes to be an efficient one.

It was to avoid this kind of development that white played 26 and 28, and these two plays also served to expand white's territory. Next, white aimed to capture black's stone with a play at **A**.

After having white play on the left side, black turned to play on the right side.

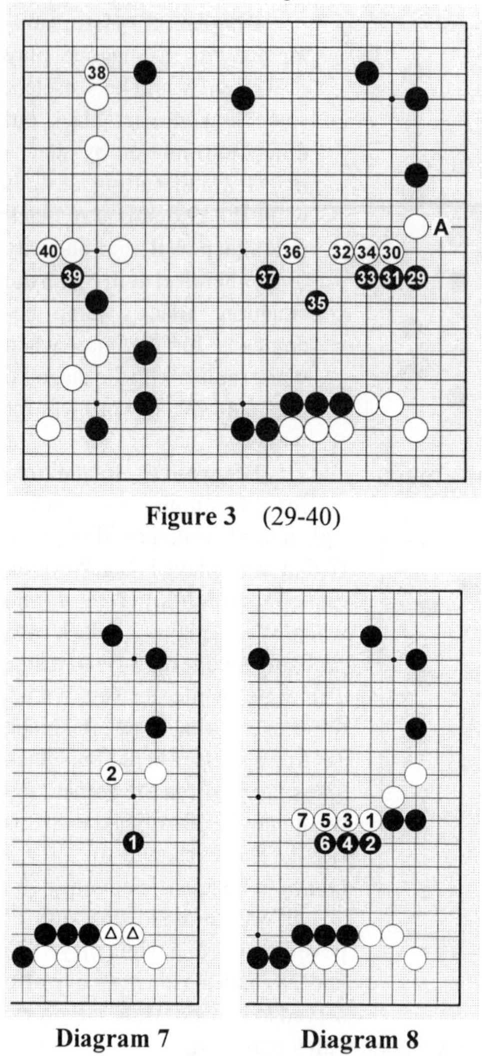

Figure 3 (29-40)

Diagram 7

Diagram 8

Figure 3 - Following the Invasion Black made the deep invasion on the right side at 29. Considering that this aimed at the attachment underneath at **A**, further exerting influence on white's stone, this is the point that one wants to play. However, it was necessary to read out the sequences in **Diagram 9** and the following beforehand.

Diagram 7 - The shallow probe of black 1 could also be considered, but the solidity of white Δ in the lower right is more than obvious, and it should be understood that the feeling is that as far as possible it is best not to approach them. White jumps to 2, and the difficulty here is that black has no followup maneuver that precisely fits the situation.

White made the natural diagonal play, and black pressed upward at 31.

The jump of white 32 was an unavoidable play, averting a sudden battle.

Diagram 8 - Should white use this to hane at 1 and black hanes at 2, if the sequence through white 7 follows, white would be greatly satisfied to make thickness that operates in the center. However, instead,

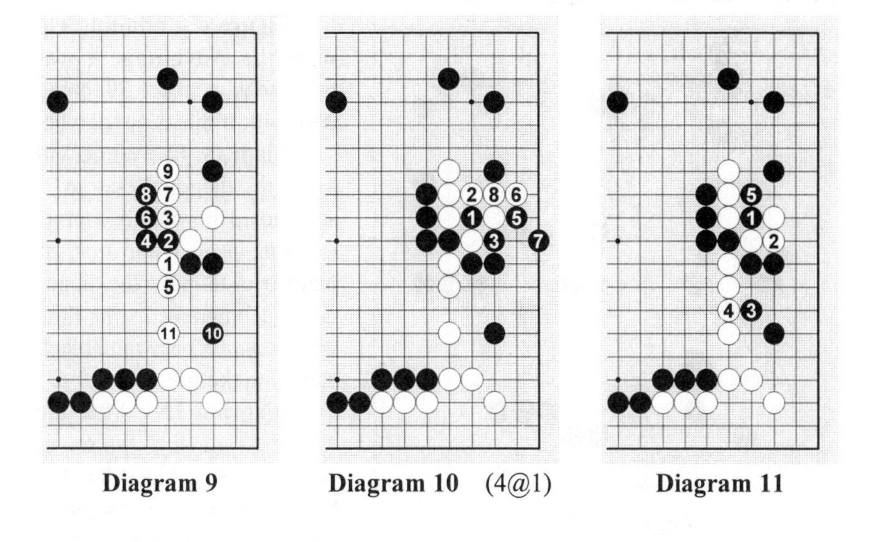

Diagram 9 **Diagram 10** (4@1) **Diagram 11**

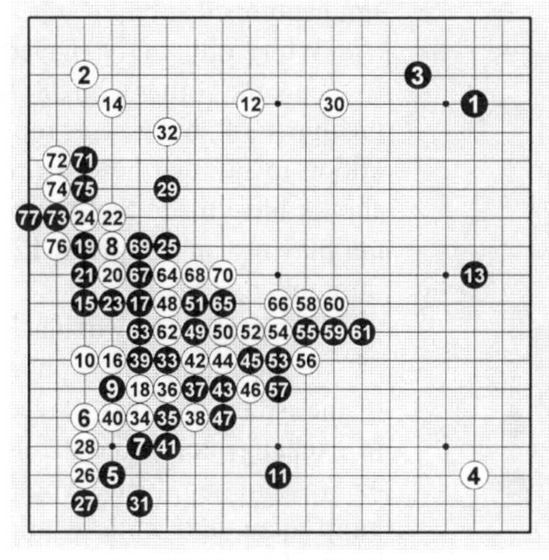

Reference Figure 2

Diagram 9 - It is possible that black will cut with the play at 2 and counterattack. After the continuation through 11,

Diagram 10 - The throw-in of black 1 is a stylish tactic. If white captures at 2, black makes good shape with 3 through 7.

Diagram 11 - In response to black 1, if white connects at 2, black makes the forcing play at 3, then extends out at 5 and fights. A capturing race on the right side would be a nuisance for white, while the three stones in the center are also in danger, so white could not carry this out successfully. The above is what black read out.

For that reason, the plays through black 35 and white 36 were unavoidable. At 37, black should first fix the shape with the exchange of 39 for 40.

Reference Figure 2 - [Jubango, Game 1; 1946; White: Go Seigen 8 dan; Black: Hashimoto Utaro 8 dan] Instead of black 13, one would like to make the erasure at 14. The diagonal play of white 14 was an ideal point. Black 15 could also be the knight's play at 63. Using 37 to draw back at 38 would have been safe, but black made the strong block, starting a fierce fight. After 77, black squeezed white's four stones and then captured them.

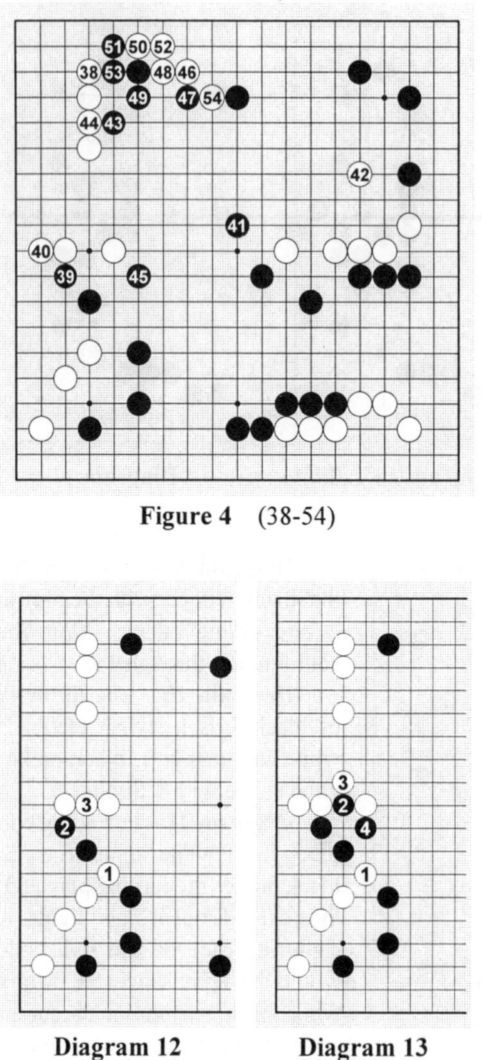

Figure 4 (38-54)

Diagram 12 **Diagram 13**

Figure 4 - Winding Up with the Advantage I was relieved when black 39 forced white 40. If this is not played,

Diagram 12 - White will make the diagonal play at 1, and end up thoroughly capturing the side. After that, if black tries to make the diagonal attachment at 2, this time white connects at 3, and black cannot make life.

Diagram 13 - After the exchange in the figure, if white plays 1, black has the tenacious tactic of creating a ko with 2 and 4, so white cannot capture cleanly.

White obligingly played to secure the corner with 38 in the upper left, but it bears repetition to say that here white should have made the diagonal play at 1 in **Diagram 12**, immobilizing black.

The knight's play of black 41 was the climactic key point of the game, and was played in exchange for white 42. If 42 was omitted, black would jump there, and white would suddenly be in dire straits.

When black peeped at 43, the connection of white 44 was a slack play.

Sakata: "The connection of 44 was close to being the losing play.

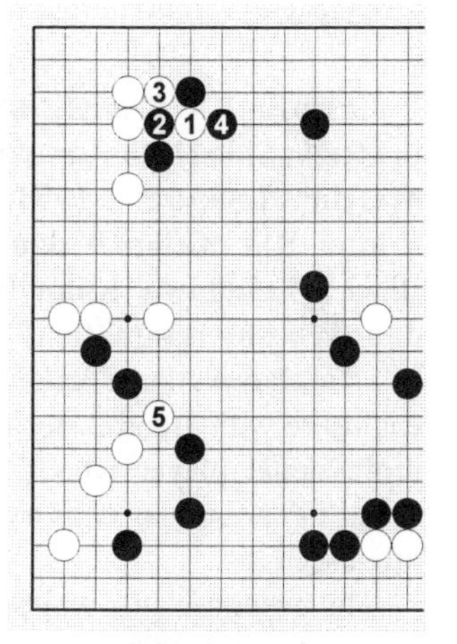

Diagram 14

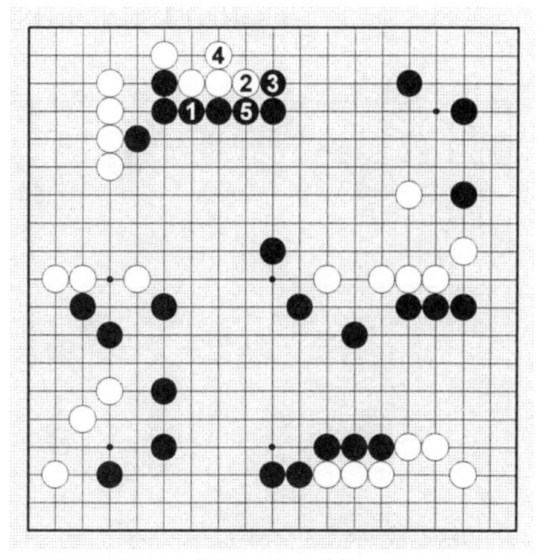

Diagram 15

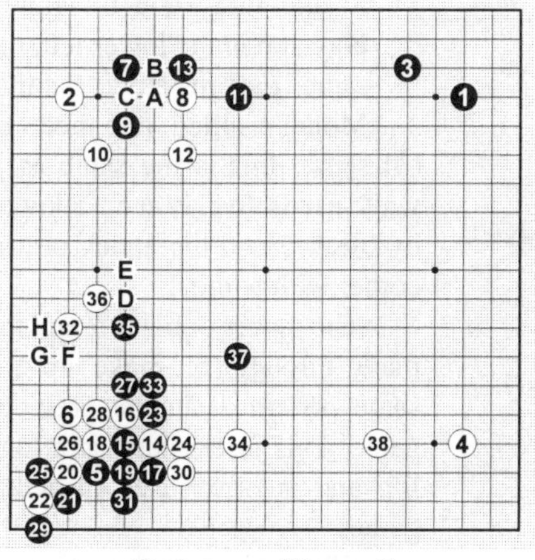

Reference Figure 3

Diagram 14 - White should have played 1 followed by the plays through 4, then counterattacked with 5."

I am also of the same opinion.

White 44 let black make the perfect knight's play at 45, leaving black clearly ahead on the board.

With the invasion of 46 and the following plays, white opened up hostilities on the upper side, but black 51 was an overplay. Here,

Diagram 15 - Connecting at 1, letting white connect underneath, and then connecting at 5 was sufficient. This maneuver would have preserved black's positional advantage.

White counterattacked with 54, with fierce fighting to follow here.

Reference Figure 3 - [2nd Annual Japan's Strongest League; 1958; White: Go Seigen 9 dan; Black: Sakata Eio 9 dan] Black played 15 and the following plays to avoid the main Taisha joseki variations because white could make the forcing plays in the area above with white **A**, black **B** and white **C**, so the position was thick and strong for white. The maneuver with white 20 and the rest was invented by Go. After 37, black **D**, white **E**, black **F**, white **G** and black **H** was sharp, initiating a fierce fight.

CORNER ENCLOSURE - GAME 5

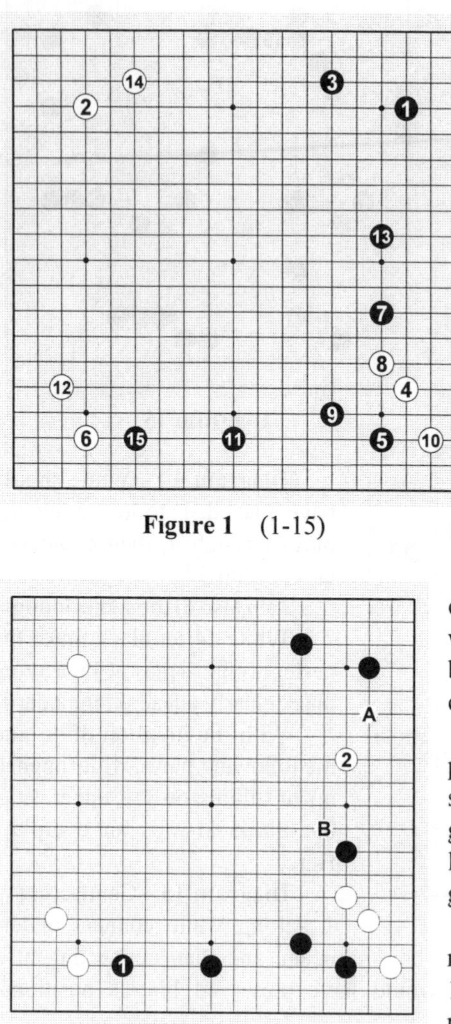

Figure 1 (1-15)

Diagram 1

Figure 1 - Priority of the Right Side [10th Annual Meijin League; 1971; White: Rin Kaiho 9 dan; Black: Takagawa Kaku 9 dan; Wins by resignation]

Takagawa's large knight enclosure with 1 and 3, for a professional player who favored star point play, was not often seen.

In response to white's play at the 5-3 point with 4, black attacked the corner with 5, and then, due to white's play at 6 in the lower left, the same pattern as a Parallel Model resulted. In a theoretical sense, this is the same as if white used 4 to play at 6, followed by black 5 and the attack on the corner with white 4.

The pincer of black 7 and the plays through 11 make up the same pattern as in the previous game. This joseki has had a long life and is often used in actual games.

When white played 12, black made the two point extension at 13, putting the emphasis on the right side.

Diagram 1 - Here, the checking extension of black 1 was also a good point. After doing so, white would split the right side at 2, with the checking extension at **A** or a play **B** being the next aim. This would also be a feasible game.

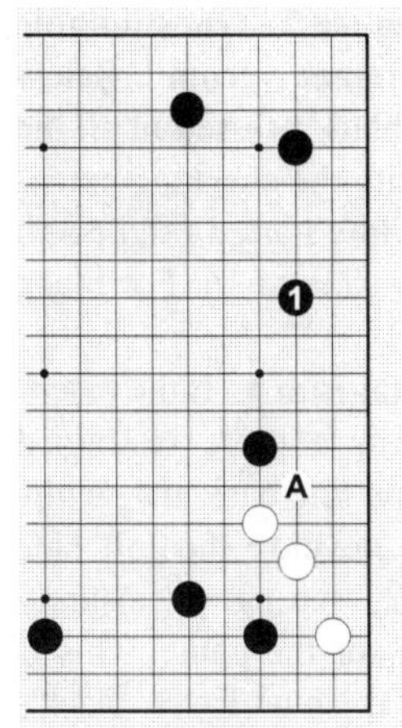

Diagram 2

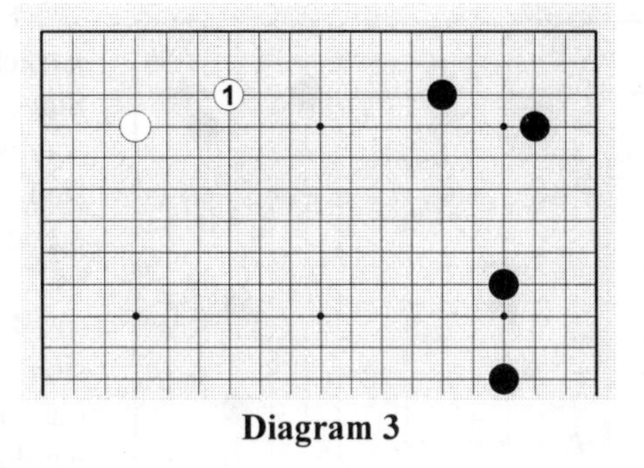

Diagram 3

Diagram 2 - For 13, black could also consider developing with 1. However, it is easy for white to effectively play against a large knight corner enclosure, and in that case, it is not clear whether the position of 1 will be good or not. After 1, the diagonal play at **A** becomes good, but the feeling is that it does not match the large knight enclosure well.

When envisioning the cases where white disrupts the upper right corner in the figure, this positioning is better than that of **Diagram 2**, and it should also be understood that if the object is advantage in central fighting, playing the high play is best.

White made the solid corner enclosure at 14.

Diagram 3 - If white made the large knight's play at 1, it would be inferior to black's shape in the upper right. Here, the feeling is for the knight's play.

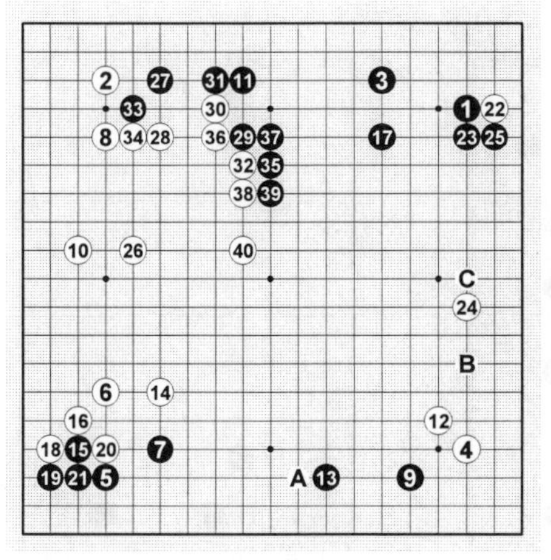

Reference Figure 1

The checking extension of black 15 was an ideal point.

Reference Figure 1 - [Oteai Ranking Tournament, Autumn Session; 1930; White: Hasegawa Akira 4 dan; Black: Sekiyama Riichi 4 dan] White made the extension at 10 as had been planned. Hasegawa: "If white used 12 to make a pincer at **A**, black **B**, white 12 and then black **C** would give black an easy game." Sekiyama: "For 17, the extension at **C** was also a substantial play, but that would let white cap at 17, and black's position would be low all over."

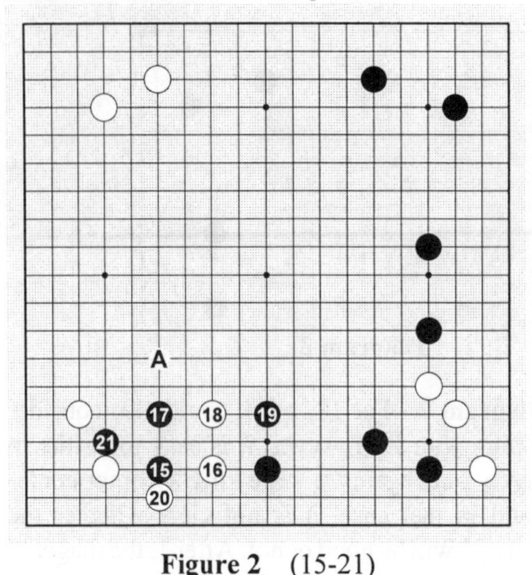

Figure 2 (15-21)

Figure 2 - Questionable Attachment from Below Since black pressed in all the way with the checking extension, white started a fight with the invasion at 16. For black 15,

Diagram 4 - If the extension was a more restrained play one line back at 1, white would develop the left side with 2, setting a leisurely course for the game. This is peaceful, but from black's standpoint, the burden of the komi means that it is impossible to just play solidly.

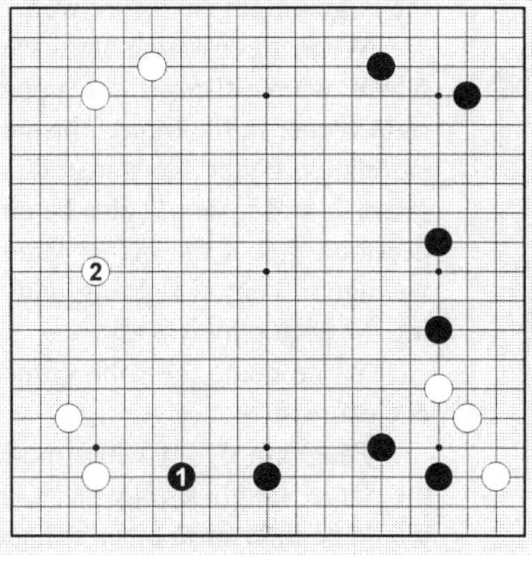

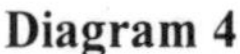

Diagram 4

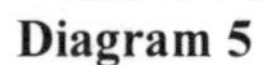

Diagram 5

Instead of white 16,

Diagram 5 - Hurrying to play 1 on the left side lets black make the knight's play at 2, ideal since it expands the lower side.

If one is to play here, one wants to forestall that by entering at 16.

Black jumped at 17, with white 18 and black 19 doing so as well in tandem. If 19 was used to jump to **A**, white would turn at 19, and these stones would have an easy time of it.

Here, the attachment from below of white 20 was a makeshift tactic that let

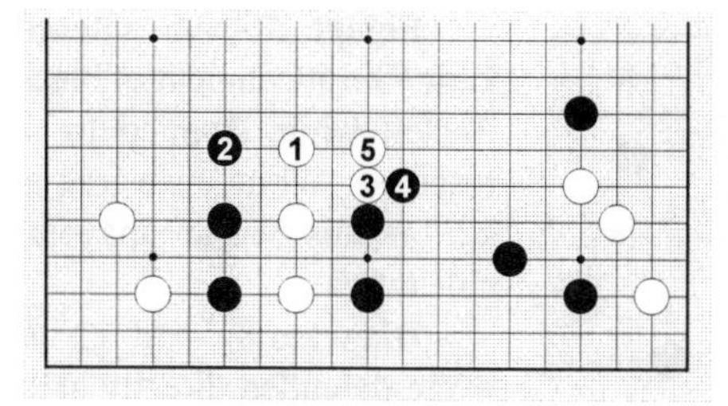

Diagram 6

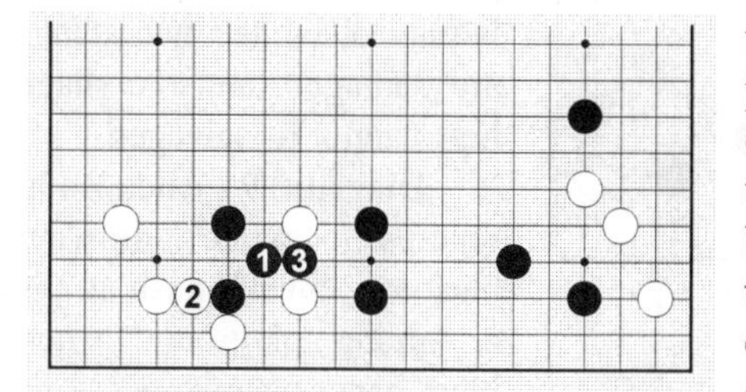

Diagram 7

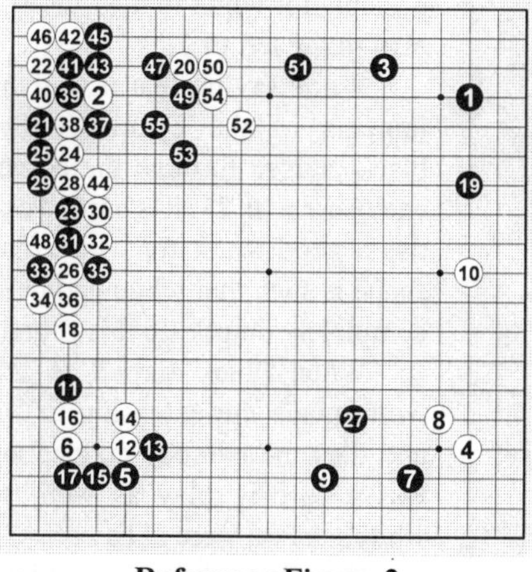

Reference Figure 2

black seize the initiative in the opening fighting.

Diagram 6 - White had to jump out in a composed manner with 1, and after black 2, attach at white 3 and extend at 5. In this kind of position, the main front cannot be abandoned to avoid fighting.

Diagram 7 - White played the attachment from below expecting black to next make the diagonal play at 1, then connect underneath with white 2, allowing black 3 in order to take sente and turn elsewhere. However, this was complacent of white, who did not even dream that a black counterattack was possible.

The attachment of black 21 was a sharp play, and this one play eliminated white's connection underneath.

Reference Figure 2 - [Oteai Ranking Tournament, Spring Session; 1941; White: Handa Hayami 4 dan; Black: Koizumi Shigeo 4 dan] Here is Handa Dogen's large knight corner enclosure. For white 22, one is inclined to make the extension at 39. When white attacked at 26, black left the area to build up here at 27, reading out completely the sequence from white's sealing black in with the plays through 32, then the continuation from black 37 to 47. Black discarded the left side, but with the plays up to 55, brought about conditions so as to attack white. This was playable for black.

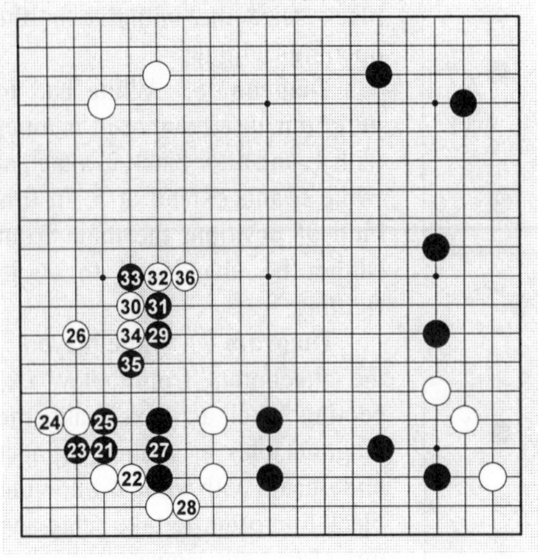

Figure 3 (21-36)

Figure 3 - An Altered Line The attachment of black 21 left white stymied for a response. White answered at 22, but this was an unavoidable retreat.

Diagram 8 - At 22, if white defended directly at 1, black 2 through the hane of 6 put white in trouble. When 8 is played, white's two stones are damaged, and the shape here cannot be salvaged.

Diagram 9 - And also in regards to white's drawing back at 1, black's push at 2 is a forcing play, and when black hanes over white's stone with 4, white cannot cut. After white 5 through black 8, it is impossible for white to next insert a play to the left of 7.

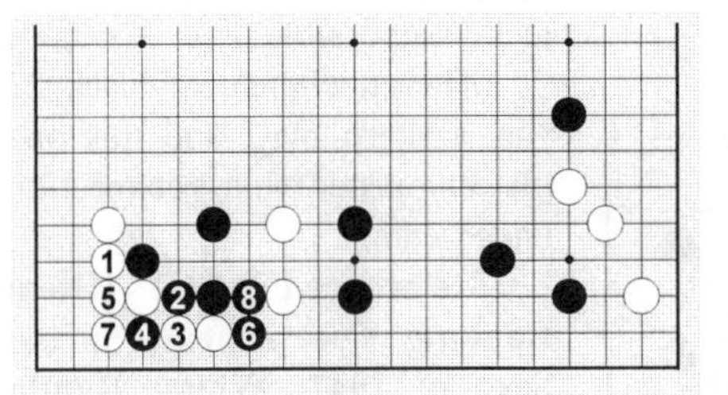

Diagram 8

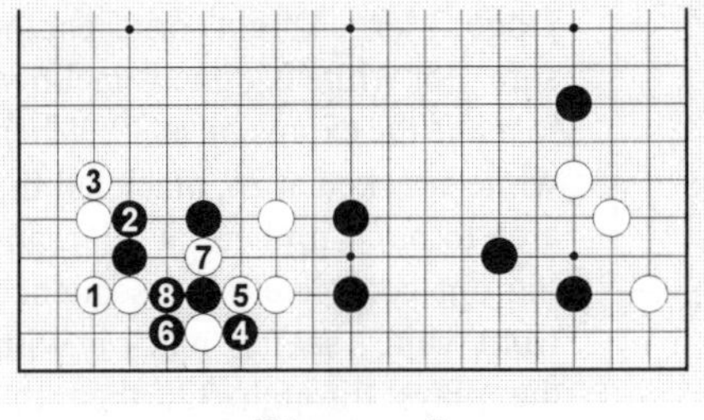

Diagram 9

While saying that it was the impetus of the position, after black pierced through the corner enclosure with 21, it is hard to call this a good result for white. The shape is such that white had been completely outplayed this round.

When black turned at 25, white made the extension to 26, and then the bamboo connection was a forcing play as well, so white's spirits were at an ebb.

In reply to the jump of black 29, white played 30 and then doggedly haned at 32.

The cut of black 33 was natural in terms of fighting spirit, and then white 34 and black 35 followed.

White extended at 36, but this was a change of plans.

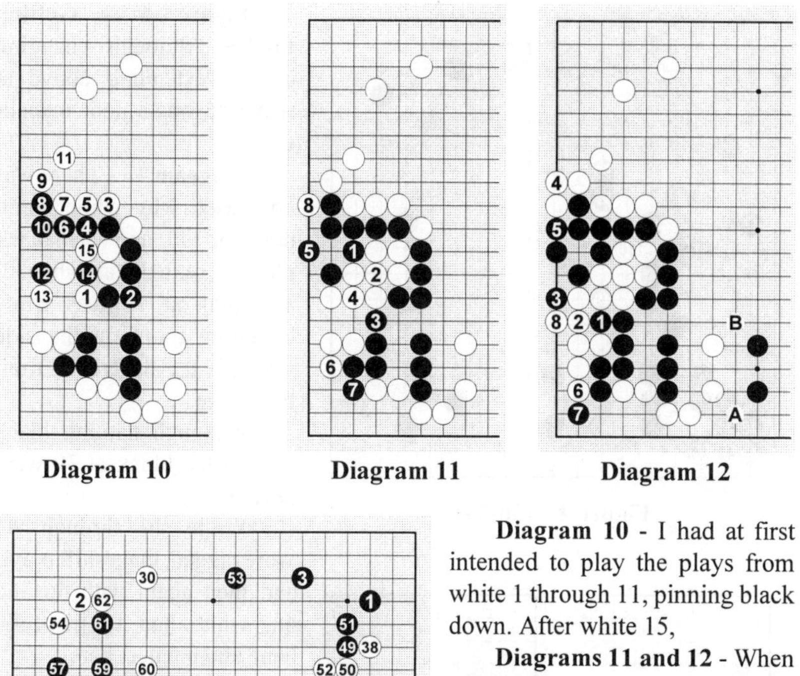

Diagram 10 **Diagram 11** **Diagram 12**

Reference Figure 3

Diagram 10 - I had at first intended to play the plays from white 1 through 11, pinning black down. After white 15,

Diagrams 11 and 12 - When black plays 7 and white goes for the capture with 8, a one play approach play ko results. However, when I was thinking it over, in reference to the ko, black could make the diagonal play at **A**, and it seemed to me that the lower side would not survive. But over and above all, this was an approach play ko, and white could run out at **B**, making a fine showing. There was probably no need for the change of plans.

Reference Figure 3 - [7th Annual Honinbo Title Match, Game 4; 1952; White: Takagawa Kaku 7 dan; Black: Hashimoto Shou, Honinbo] In the lower left, a joseki of that period was played. For white 10, the pattern with the attachment of **A** was also possible. After 33, black expected white **B**, black **C** and white 37, but white dodged. Hashimoto: "Instead of 35, 36 was better." White 56, 60 and 66 were Takagawa's patented capping plays.

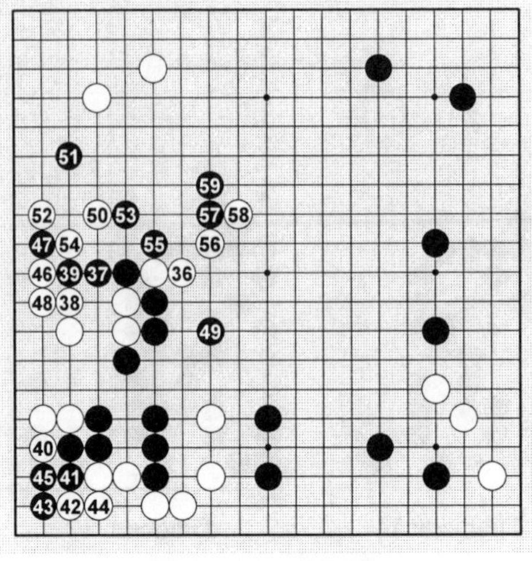

Figure 4 (36-59)

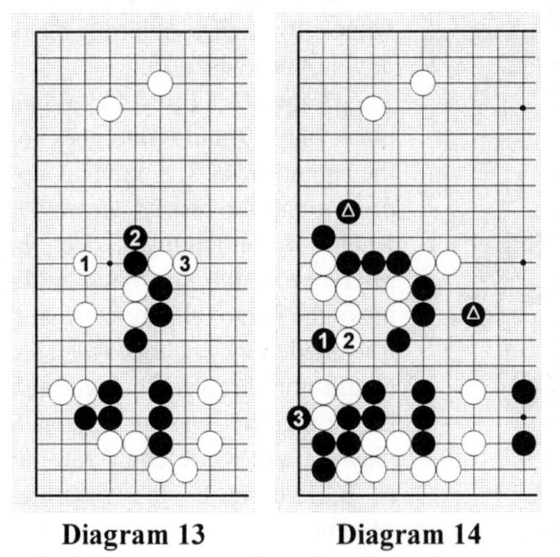

Diagram 13 **Diagram 14**

Figure 4 - Getting Fooled Although changing course, extending above at white 36 was a poor maneuver.

Diagram 13 - There was no reason why white could not jump to 1, and when black plays 2, extend at white 3. The play at 1 gives white breathing room on the side which is the difference from the figure.

Although natural, black 37 and the block at 39 were severe plays.

White 40 through 44 were ragged, makeshift plays, and then again with 46 and 48, white had to painfully hane and connect here.

Diagram 14 - Once this is played, in addition, if black is strengthened on the outside with black ▲, the placement of 1 followed by the hane of 3 leave this group without eyes. It should be noted what an excruciating shape this is for white.

When black jumped out at 49, white closed in at the vital point of 50. This black group had to be besieged, since the left side was still not alive.

Dodging at black 51 was an interesting play. Here,

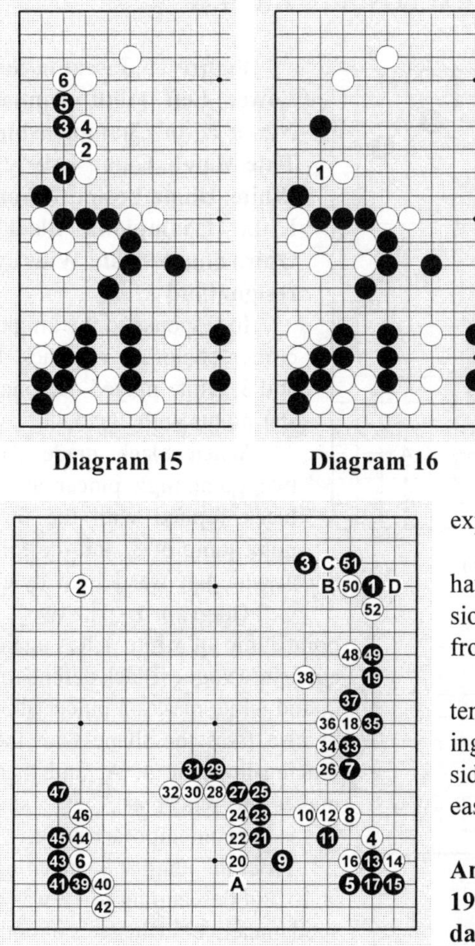

Diagram 15 Diagram 16

Reference Figure 4

Diagram 15 - If black makes the tiger link at 1, white plays 2 and the plays through the block of 6, put black's group into considerable danger. The play at 51 avoided that.

Since black dodged like this, I thought that the intention was to definitely discard the three stones, so I blithely made the clamp attachment of white 52. However, black made a U-turn by moving out with 53 and 55, shocking me. My expectations were frustrated.

Diagram 16 - White should have used 52 to make the extension at 1 in order to suppress black from moving out.

Black attached at 57 and extended at 59, spreading the fighting from the center to the upper side. This may be said to be an easy position for black to play.

Reference Figure 4 - [1st Annual Top Position League; 1956; White: Kajiwara Takeo 7 dan; Black: Maeda Nobuaki 7 dan] Today, white 8 and 10 are an unusual maneuver.

Maeda: "For black 13, I had planned to make the extension at 37, but letting white attack the corner at **A** was distasteful. White should have played 18 at **B**, black **C**, white 50, black 51, white 52, black **D** and white 37."

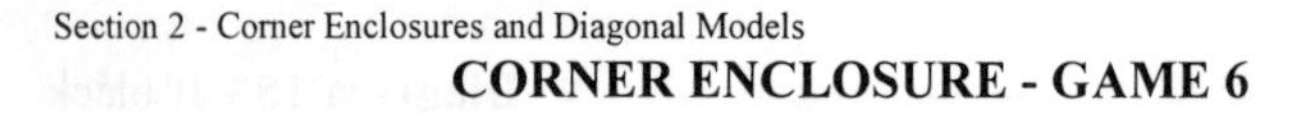

CORNER ENCLOSURE - GAME 6

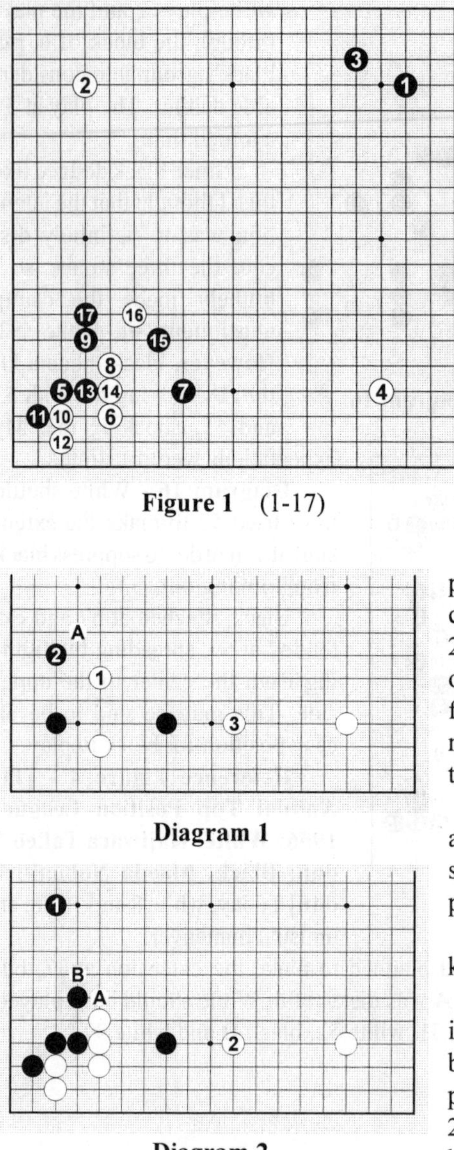

Figure 1 (1-17)

Diagram 1

Diagram 2

Figure 1 - Joseki in the Lower Left [19th Annual Nihon Ki-in Championship Title Match, Game 4; 1972; White: Ishida Yoshio, Nihon Ki-in Champion; Black: Ohira Shuzo 9 dan; Wins by resignation]

In response to the knight corner enclosure of black 1 and 3, white played diagonal star points with 2 and 4.

When black made the two point high pincer at 7, black replied with the one point jump of 8, and the following play was Kitani style.

Diagram 1 - The two point jump of white 1 has again come into vogue. Black defends at 2, and white makes a pincer at 3, or else fixes the shape with the fencing-in tactic at **A**, and then makes the pincer at 3, etc., and this is the contemporary style.

After the jump at 8, attaching at 10 and descending to 12 was a staid maneuver in the style of both player's teacher, Kitani.

Black initiated action with the knight's play of 15. However,

Diagram 2 - With this play, it is desirable to simply extend to 1 below the star point. White will probably answer with the pincer at 2, but according to circumstances black might find it expedient to push at **A**, discarding the stone on the lower side. This kind of flexibility is to be hoped for. If white presses at **A**, black will gratefully extend at **B**.

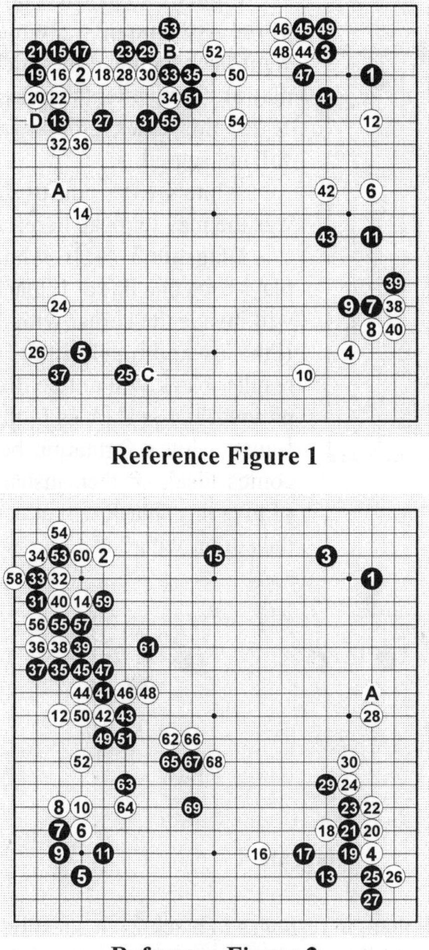

Reference Figure 1

Reference Figure 2

In the figure, black provoked white into making the knight's play at 16, seeking to gain impetus to extend at 17, but as far as my own taste is concerned, I do not much care for the joseki that results through 21 in the next figure.

Reference Figure 1 - [11th Annual Honinbo League; 1956; White: Shimamura Toshihiro 8 dan; Black: Fujisawa Shuko 7 dan] Here is a knight corner enclosure and star point combination. Shimamura: "If white used 14 to defend at 28, after black 19, white 15 and black **A**, **B** and **C** become equivalent options." Black 27 and the following were severe. Using white 32 to extend at 33 would let black attack the whole group with **D**. By playing thickly at 55, black had no cause for dissatisfaction with this shape.

Reference Figure 2 - [9th Annual All Japan Women's Championship, Game 1; 1961; White: Ito Tomoe, Champion; Black: Kitani Reiko 2 dan] Instead of white 28, at the very least one wants to advance as far as **A**. White let loose with a strong play at 36, starting the fighting here. Black played efficiently with 53 through 59. With white 68 and black 69, contesting for the game continued.

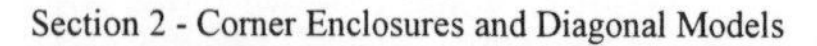

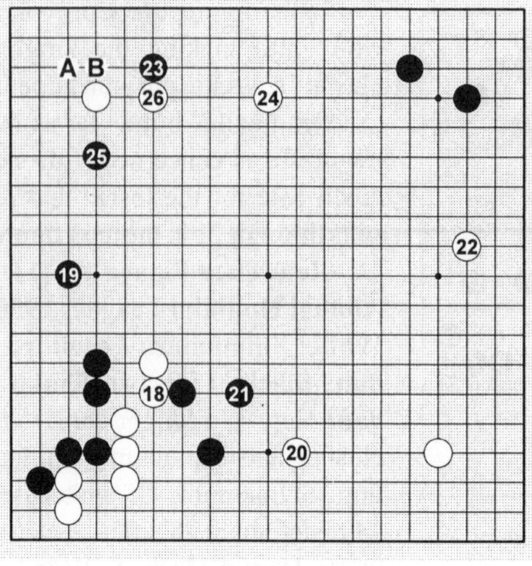

Figure 2 (18-26)

Figure 2 - The Direction of the Attachment White went back to make the thick play at 18 and after the pincer at 20, this black group was still not settled.

White's extension of 22 was the play to make here.

Diagram 3 - If white plays back one line at 1, black will invade the corner with 2. If the joseki through white 13 results, black will not be displeased. If 1 is at **A** as in the figure, white's formation becomes ideal, so then instead of invading, black will attack the corner with 2 at 13.

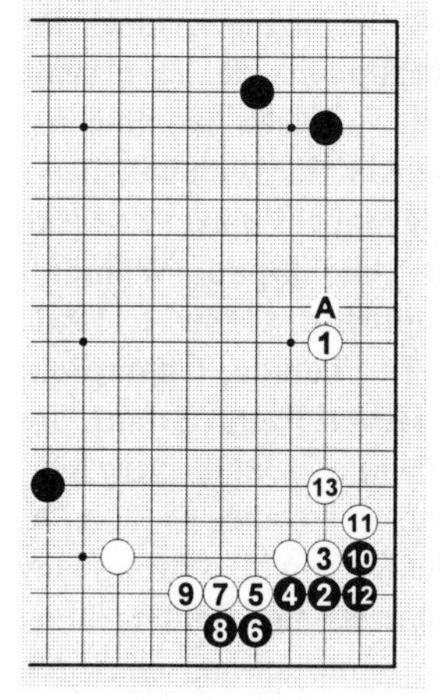

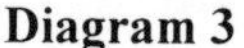
Diagram 3

Diagram 4

Well then, in response to black 23, a questionable point in the opening emerged concerning the pincer of white 24.

For the pincer of 24,

Diagram 4 - One is not inclined to defend at 1. Black is allowed, after 2, to extend to 4, and since in this game the upper side is the main front, to have black play there is not agreeable. With black ▲ in place, the value of the left side is diminished, so aiming the stone of white 1 in that direction is no good.

With black 25, too, one wants to make this kind of double attack on the corner. Entering at **A** here would let white block at **B**, while directing black's own stones to the side with the diminished value. Black would not be inclined to do that.

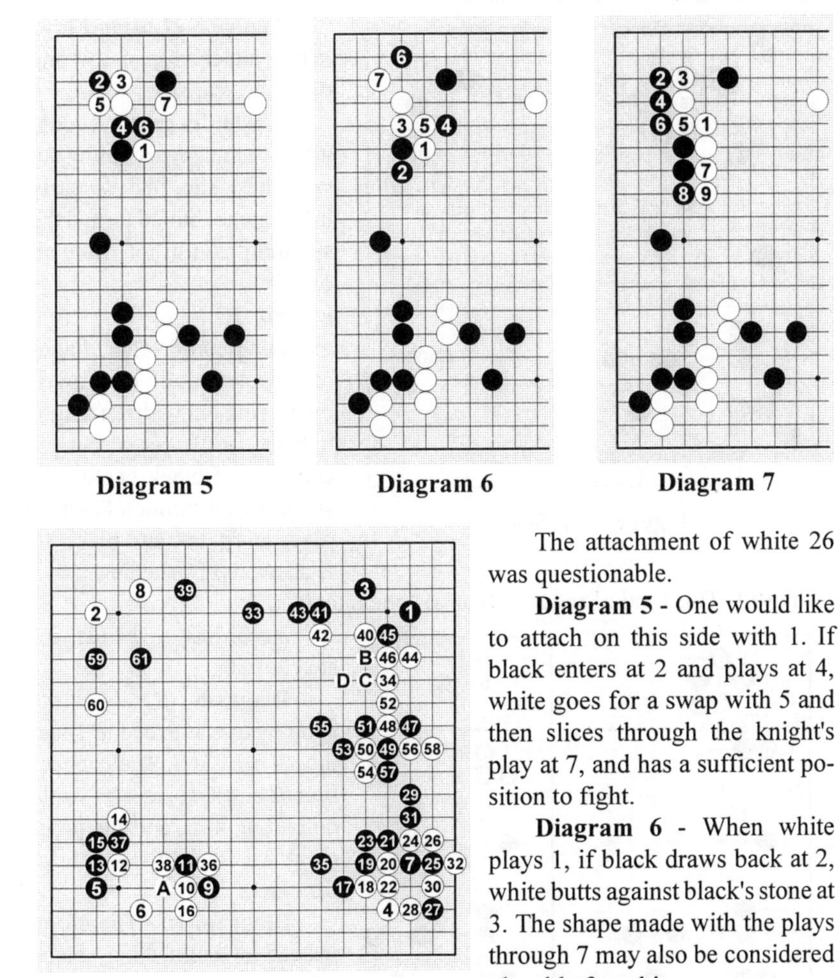

Diagram 5

Diagram 6

Diagram 7

Reference Figure 3

The attachment of white 26 was questionable.

Diagram 5 - One would like to attach on this side with 1. If black enters at 2 and plays at 4, white goes for a swap with 5 and then slices through the knight's play at 7, and has a sufficient position to fight.

Diagram 6 - When white plays 1, if black draws back at 2, white butts against black's stone at 3. The shape made with the plays through 7 may also be considered playable for white.

Diagram 7 - White can also draw back at 1. Should black play 2, white presses through 9, and with this backbone of thickness, has a playable position.

Reference Figure 3 - [6th Annual Meijin Title Match, Game 3; 1967; White: Sakata Eio, Honinbo; Black: Rin Kaiho, Meijin] New patterns were created in the lower left and lower right. White 12 at **A** is part of the old pattern. White 18 and 20 were played Kitani style. Later on, playing black 27 at 29, followed by white 30 became the established plays. Black 35 was slack. This should have been played as **B**, white **C** and black **D**.

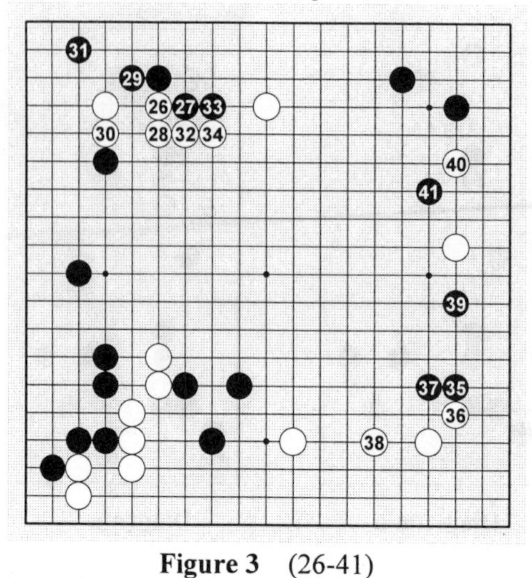

Figure 3 (26-41)

Figure 3 - Losing Play? White attached in the wrong direction with 26.

Ishida: "Honestly, I could not have imagined coming out with the losing play so early in the game, but 26 turned the situation painful for white all over."

For 26,

Diagram 8 - The diagonal attachment of 1 followed by moving out with the diagonal play at 3 was also conceivable. If black captures a stone with 4 through 8, white plays atari at 9, and black 10 is answered by the push at white 11. This kind of sequence can also be imagined.

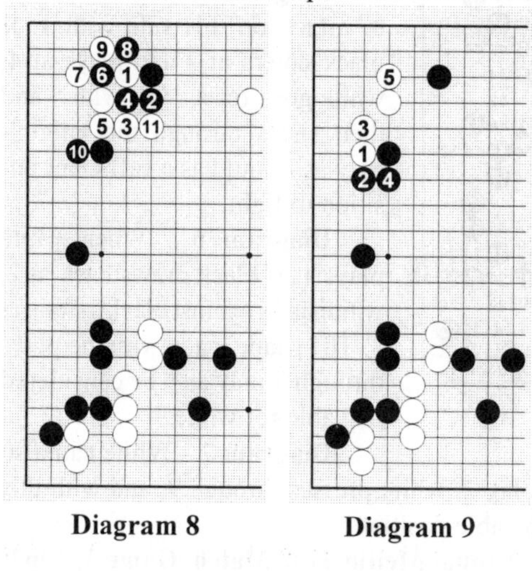

Diagram 8 **Diagram 9**

According to Ishida, instead of 26,

Diagram 9 - White should have attached at 1 and drawn back at 3. The connection of black 4 is met by white defending at 5, and his judgment was that this is painful for black.

Diagram 10 - Therefore, instead of connecting, black slides to 1, and white cuts at 2 followed by the atari of 4. When black makes the diagonal play at 5, white attaches at 6 and jumps to 8. This can be thought of as a promising plan.

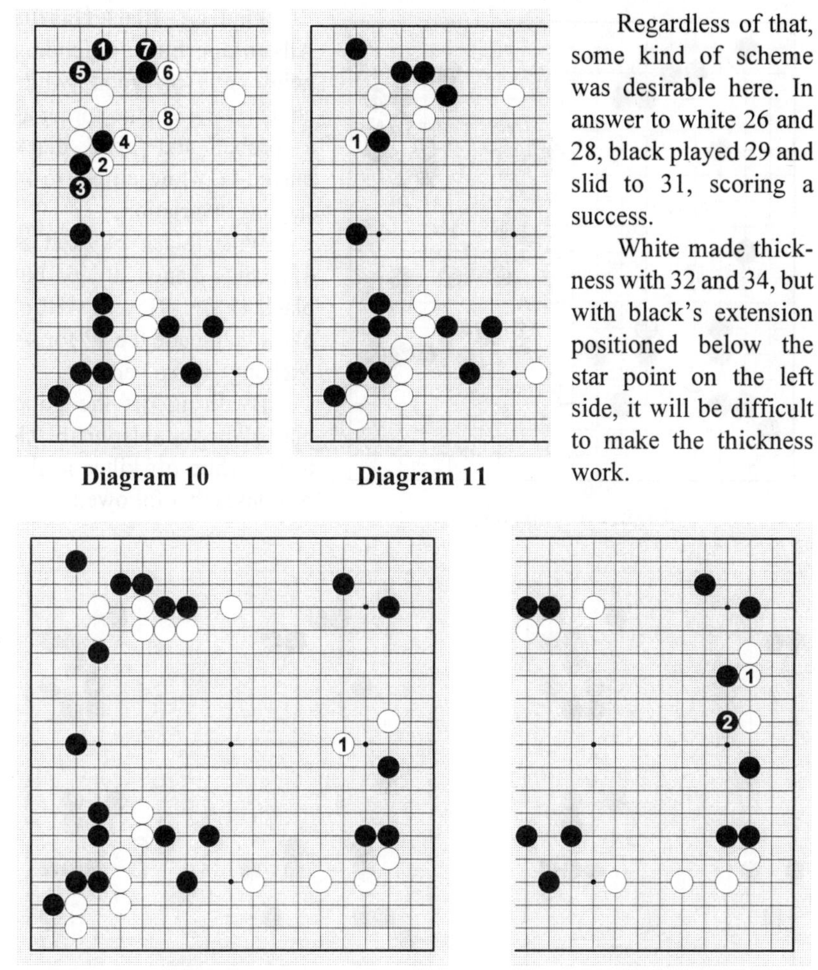

Diagram 10

Diagram 11

Regardless of that, some kind of scheme was desirable here. In answer to white 26 and 28, black played 29 and slid to 31, scoring a success.

White made thickness with 32 and 34, but with black's extension positioned below the star point on the left side, it will be difficult to make the thickness work.

Diagram 12

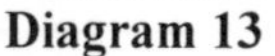

Diagram 13

For white 32,

Diagram 11 - Playing hane at 1 was no good either.

Black played 35 through 39, then white made the extension to 40.

Ishida went on to say that instead of 40,

Diagram 12 - White had to play 1 and attack black. That would put the thickness in the upper left to use, and make the game wide open.

The shoulder hit of black 41 was perfect.

Diagram 13 - If white defends in the usual way with 1, black slaps the position down with the attachment of 2, preventing white from moving out. Sustaining this blow put white into a painful position.

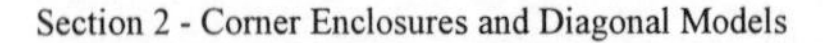

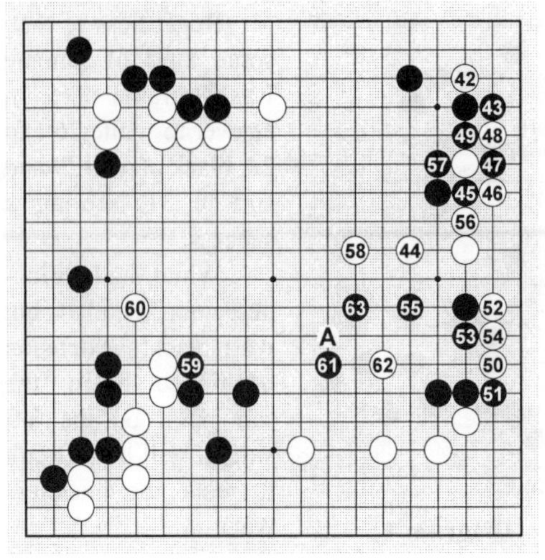

Figure 4 (46-63)

Figure 4 - Black Has the Advantage Since defending below was no good, white attached at 42 in the corner as a probe, and after black played 43, white jumped to 44 seeking a variation.

When black blocked at 45, white haned at 46, but black 47 and 49 were skillful plays that made the 42 for 43 exchange into a bad one.

By firing off the good play of the shoulder hit, black threw white off kilter in the responses that followed.

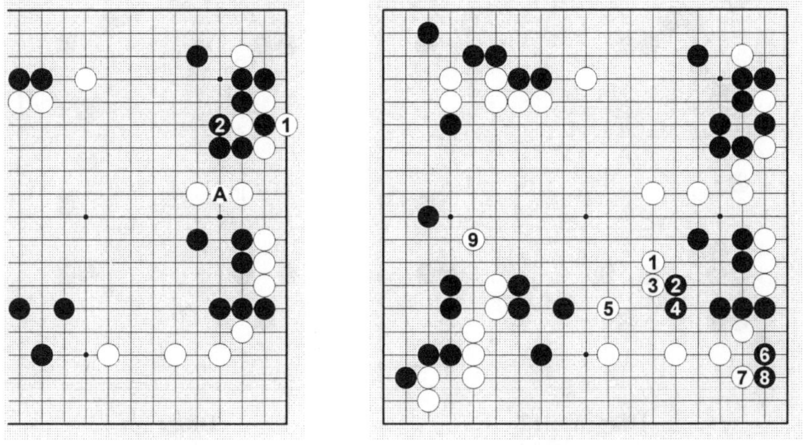

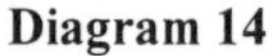
Diagram 14

Diagram 15

White 50 through 54 were a common skillful finesse for attacking. However, a jump by black into the corner was left, and after black jumped to 55, white was not left with much of a result.

White 56 was followed by black's capture at 57, but after painstakingly playing up to here, white had comparatively little to show for it, and the outcome was failure.

Diagram 14 - At 56, even if white captures a stone with 1, once black captures after playing at 2, the wedging-in play at **A** can be aimed at, so there is no way that white can carry this off.

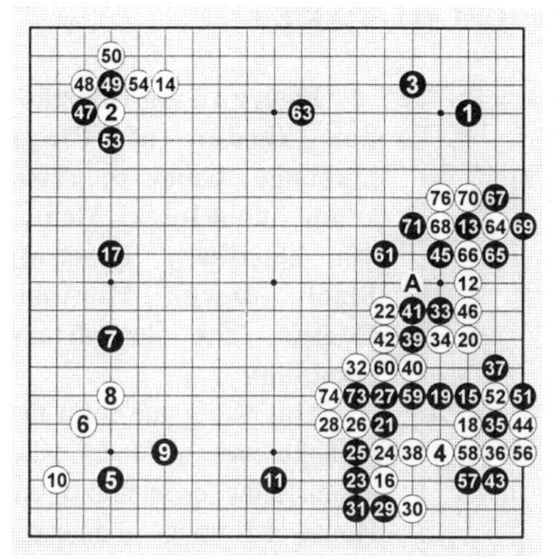

Reference Figure 4 (55@35, 62 @52, 72@64, 75 @13 ,77@64)

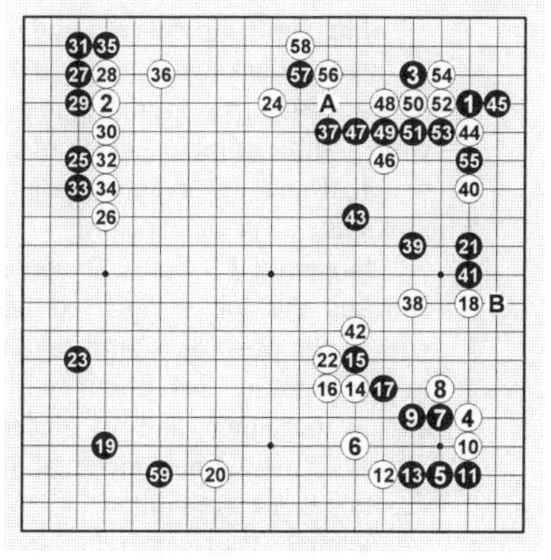

Reference Figure 5

In response to white 58, pressing up against white's stone with black 59 was slack. Simply playing 61 was best.

White 60 was also bad. Here, **Diagram 15** - White should first attack these stones with 1 and 3, then probe at 9.

After defending at 61 and 63, black's lead was clear. Following this, white started a fight with **A**, but the feeling is that white had fallen a step behind.

Reference Figure 4 - [23rd Annual Honinbo Title Match, Game 2; 1968; White: Sakata Eio, Honinbo; Black: Rin Kaiho, Meijin] For 17, black could also have capped at **A**. Black 31 at 32 would have been safe. When white resolutely played 32 and the following plays to capture, it was a painful battle for black. On 33, black spent a long 3 hours and 3 minutes thinking. After the failure in the lower right, black's hopes centered around 61 and the following plays, building a territorial framework in the upper right.

Reference Figure 5 - [29th Annual Honinbo Title Match, Game 5; 1974; White: Takemiya Masaki 7 dan; Black: Ishida Shuho, Honinbo] White 4 and 6 were a maneuver that Sakata often used. Black exchanged 19 for white 20, then hurried to make the checking extension at 21. Black had an interesting conception with 37. If this was played at **A**, white would probably attach at 37. At white 42, descending at **B** was desirable. Through 55, black had the advantage.

DIAGONAL MODEL (1) - GAME 1

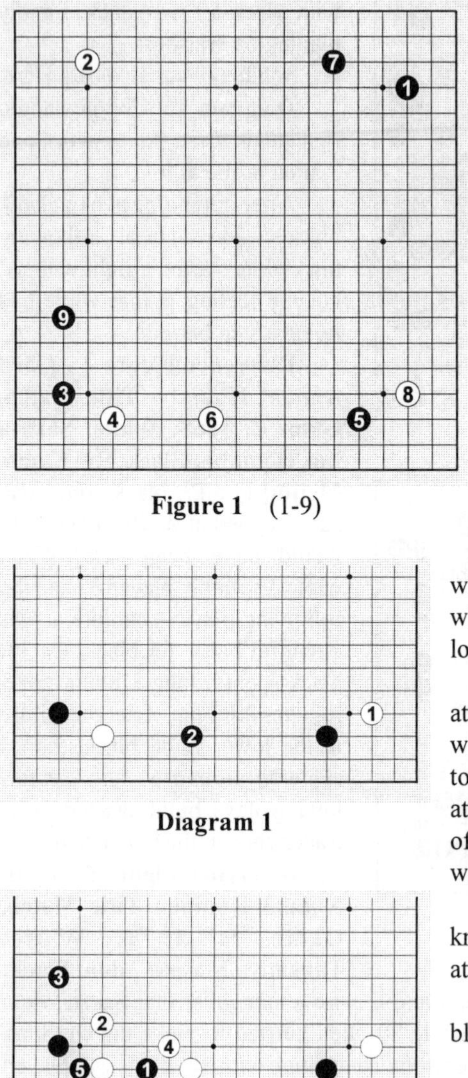

Figure 1 (1-9)

Diagram 1

Diagram 2

Figure 1 - An Unorthodox Order of Plays [Jubango, Game 6; 1706; White: Inoue Inseki (Meijin, 4th hereditary Dosetsu); Black: Dochi, Honinbo (Meijin, 5th hereditary Honinbo)]

This is a game form the jubango between Dochi, who assumed the leadership of the House of Honinbo at an early age, and Inseki, who later became Meijin.

In response to black's diagonal 3-4 points at 1 and 3, white attacked the corner at 4.

Black 5 was answered by white's three point extension of 6, which, from today's vantage point, looks like a curious opening.

Diagram 1 - For 6, if white attacked the lower right corner with 1, the position would revert to the fighting 3-4 points with attacks in tandem, and the pincer of black 2 would become ideal. It was this that was avoided.

With 7, black made the large knight corner enclosure, and white attacked the corner at 8.

The two point extension of black 9 was a solid maneuver.

Diagram 2 - In the present age, since white's extension is narrow, black would probably think of invading at 1, and through white 6, take sente. Of course, this maneuver was unknown in that age.

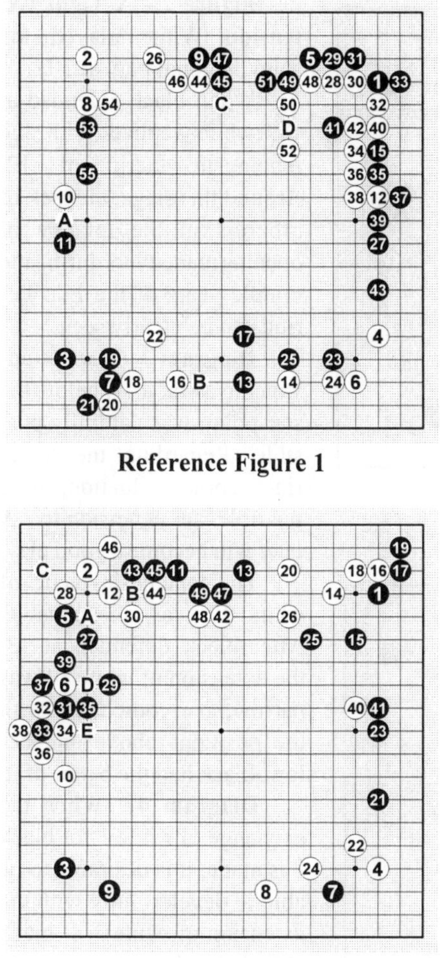

Reference Figure 1

Reference Figure 2

Reference Figure 1 - [Castle Game; 1696; White: Inoue Dosetsu (4th hereditary Inseki); Black: Honinbo Sakugen (Successor to Dosaku)] Rather than the play of simply making the large knight corner enclosure with the third play, the maneuver with diagonal 3-4 points followed by a corner enclosure appeared early. Here is an example of all corner enclosures after white 8. White 10 at **A** is usual. For 16, this was the place to invade at **B**. Instead of connecting at black 47, one wants to extend at **C**, aiming at **D**.

Reference Figure 2 - [Castle Game; 1684; White: Yasui Shunchi (3rd hereditary Yasui); Black: Honinbo Doteki (Successor to Dosaku)] Several examples of the diagonal 3-4 points will be shown here. Instead of white 10, today 28, black **A** and white **B** would probably be played. Black 27 and 29 made up a pattern that was played at the time. For 27, sliding to **C** to get settled quickly was best. Black 31 and 33 were strong plays. Instead of 34, if white 35, black's strategy would be to play 34, and then white **D** is answered by black **E**.

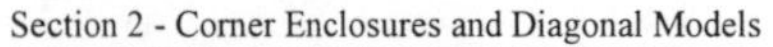

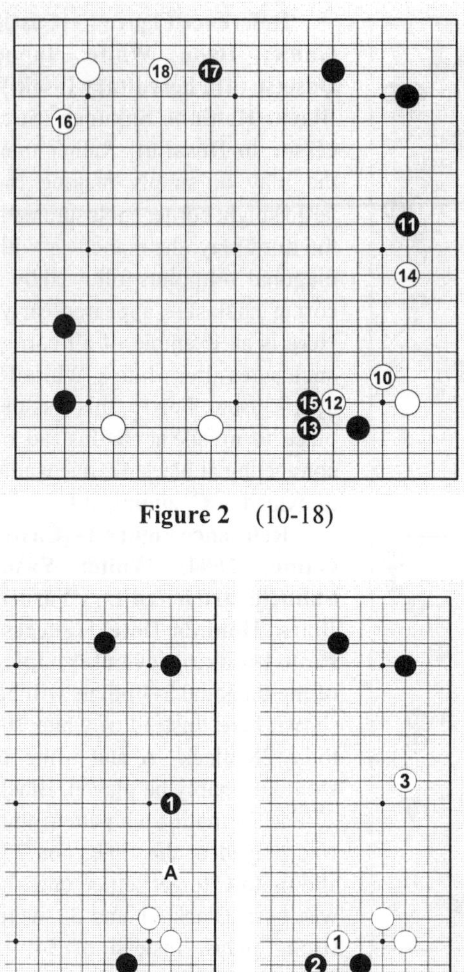

Figure 2 (10-18)

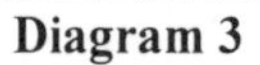

Diagram 3

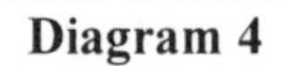

Diagram 4

Figure 2 - A Tight Extension White played the solid diagonal play at 10.

When black extended at 11, white replied with the fencing-in tactic of 12. Around this stage, the lack of progress in the infancy of opening maneuvers during the middle years of the Edo Period can be clearly seen.

Diagram 3 - For 11, advancing as far as 1, below the star point, was naturally possible. Regarding the lower right corner situation, it is possible an extension to **A** later will become a good play.

The fencing-in tactic of white 12 was questionable. After black defended at 13, the extension of white 14 was narrow, so in comparison with the positions above and below, black had the better of it.

Diagram 4 - When the exchange of white 1 for black 2 is made, it is desirable to be able to develop fully with the extension of white 3. If black already has an extension as in this game, this exchange made with the fencing-in tactic should rather be called a loss.

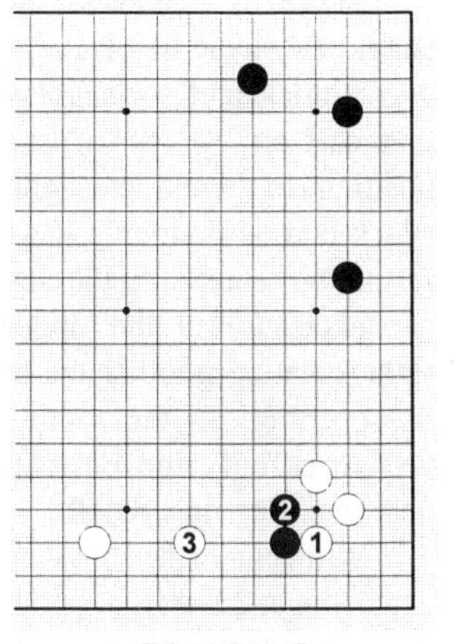

Diagram 5

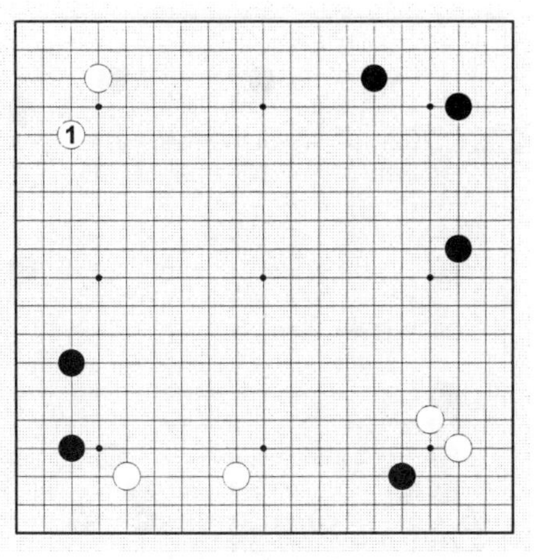

Diagram 6

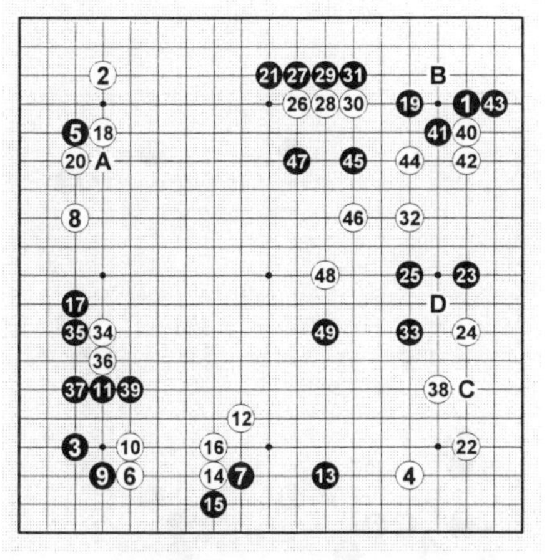

Reference Figure 3

Diagram 5 - If playing here, the diagonal attachment of 1 is the follow-up to the purpose behind the diagonal play at 10. Should black extend upward at 2, white pincers at 3, chasing black out while attacking.

After the 12 and 13 exchange, it is difficult to attack black here.

In addition, for white 12,

Diagram 6 - Instead of hurrying to play in the lower right area, it was also possible to enclose the corner at white 1 in the upper left. One's inclination is to take this big point first.

When white extended at 14, black pushed at 15. From the standpoint of separating white left and right on a large scale, this was powerful, but attacking the corner at 16 was also splendid, and this is the correct choice in direction.

Black extended to 17, and white replies with the checking extension of 18.

Reference Figure 3 - [1857; White: Ito Matsukazu; Black: Murase Yakichi (18th hereditary Honinbo Shuho)] This is a game from Shuho's youth. With 19, black could also have immediately played out at **A**. The extension of 23 gave black the ideal "crane's wings" formation. White 26 was a difficult point; playing at **B**, or else simply 32 was also possible. For 38, defending at **C** would have left **D** to aim at.

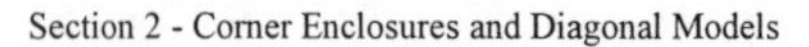

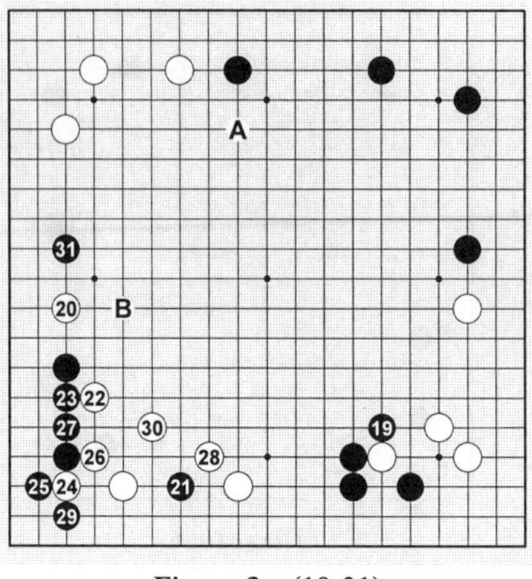

Figure 3 (19-31)

Figure 3 - Success for Black The hane of black 19 was a thick and strong play that cast an eye on white's positions to the left and right. Black laid out a double wing formation centered on the corner enclosure in the upper right, creating good shape in the opening, so the motive was to solidify the position here, building up strength.

White made the checking extension at 20. At that point, black invaded at 21, detonating the power of the thickness of 19.

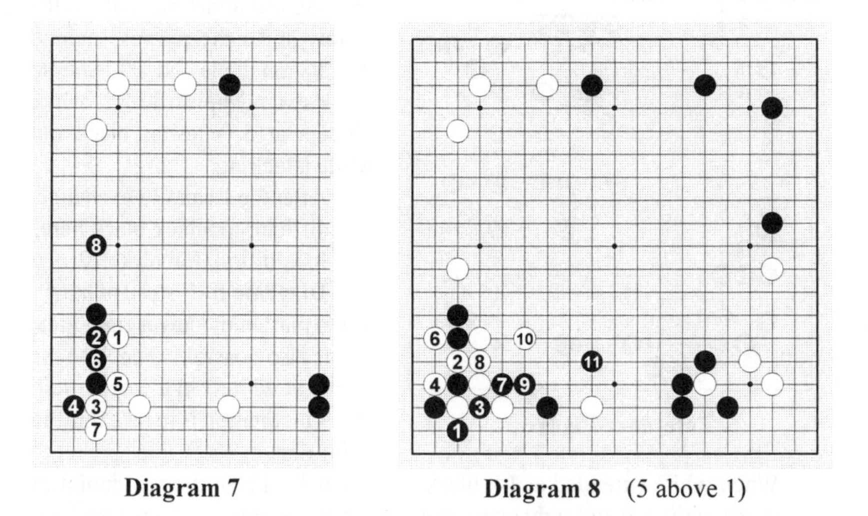

Diagram 7 **Diagram 8** (5 above 1)

Diagram 7 - For white 20, in order to forestall this storming in, making the preparatory plays of white 1 through 7 would have been peaceful, but the reasoning was probably that letting black extend to 8 would have offered no subtle opportunities.

Following the shoulder hit of white 22, 24 and the play expanding outward at 26 were related skillful finesse that even today are often played.

Black answered with the connection of 27.

Diagram 8 - Here, the return hane of 1 could also have been considered.

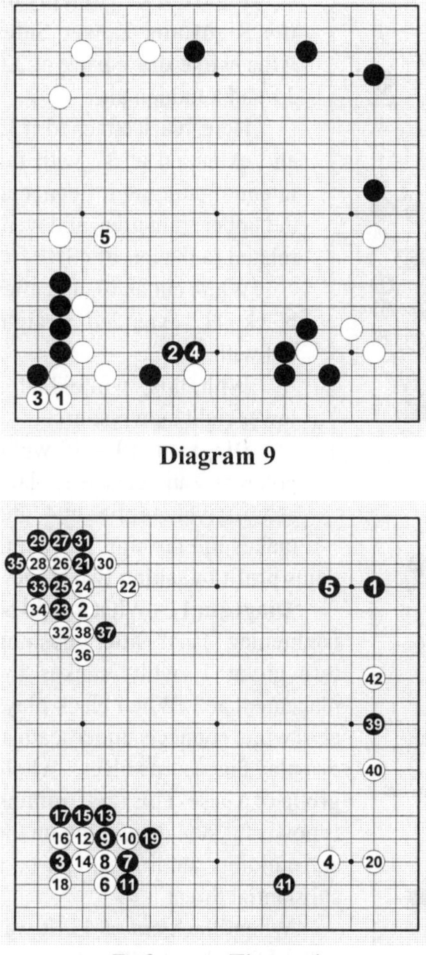
Diagram 9

Reference Figure 4

When white plays 6, black cuts at 7 and extends at 9, and then white 10 and the cap of black 11 will probably be played. Black makes more than thirty points of secure territory on the lower side, while white will play to use the influence on the left side, but this division is perhaps a little painful for white. In response to the diagonal play of white 28, the hane of black 29 was truly satisfying. With the result through white 30, capturing in the corner is a forcing play as well, so black has no cause for dissatisfaction. Instead of 28,

Diagram 9 - The desire to descend at 1 is enormous. When black plays 2, white turns at 3, followed by black 4 and white 5, and the breadth of the left side gives life to the rationale behind white's plays.

The jubango was played with Dochi set to always hold black, with the understanding that it was a test of his strength. The result was that Inseki won six games and lost three, with one jigo tie, but Dochi, who was 17 years old at the time, fought valiantly. Inseki was 61 years old.

Black made a pincer at 31, but here one would like to jump to **A**. If white jumps at **B**, black is not badly off.

Reference Figure 4 - [Nihon Ki-in Insei League; 1939; White: Fujisawa Tamotsu - [Shuko]; Black: Suzuki Keizo] This is a game between Suzuki, who suffered an early death, and Fujisawa. Following the diagonal 3-4 points, black made a one point corner enclosure with 5. Black 7 and the following was a maneuver that was much analyzed among insei. Before the war, Suzuki Keizo, Fujisawa Shuko and Yamabe Toshiro were called the "Three Crows" - (an illusion to three famous counselors of olden times).

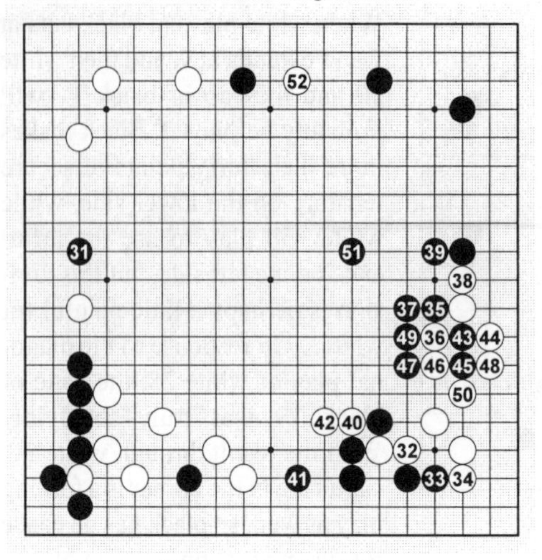

Figure 4 (31-52)

Figure 4 - Problems on the Right and Lower Sides After white drew back at 32, 34 had a hidden aim.

Here, black attached at 35 and extended at 37 with the intent of building influence in the upper right area, and were related to the cut of 43.

White cut at 40, and after black 41, extended straight out with 42.

With this, white had a lower right side resource.

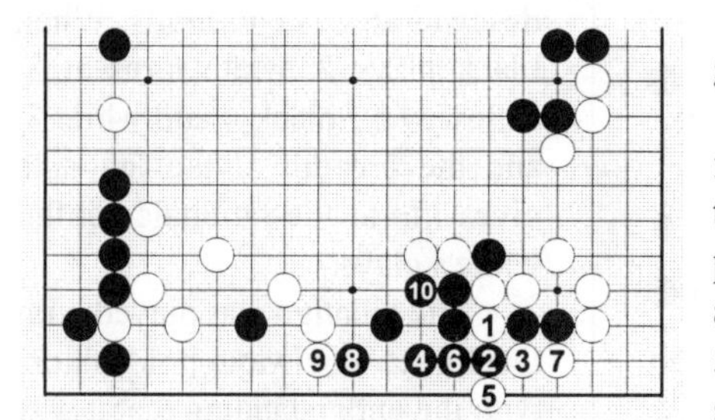

Diagram 10

Diagram 10 - If white pokes at 1 and cuts at 3, black submissively replies at 4, and makes life through 10. White gains profit by taking two stones.

Diagram 11 - What would be frightening is if after pushing through at 1, white makes the placement at 3. When black plays at 4, white connects underneath at 5, a play that usurps black's whole group of a base. This undermining is powerful, and depending on the surrounding conditions, can be a substantial threat.

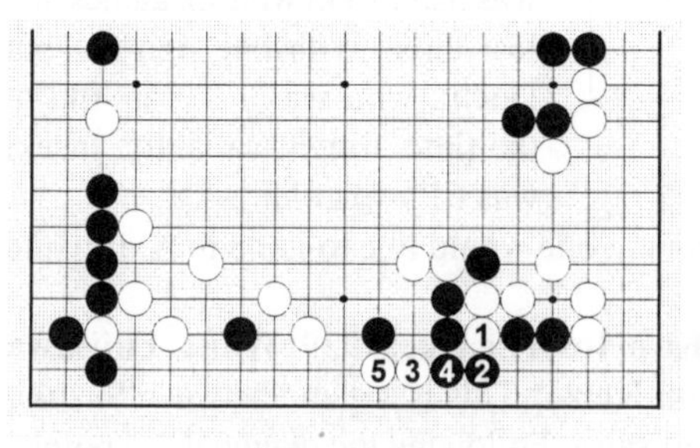

Diagram 11

When black cut at 43, it was natural for white to play atari from below with 44.

Diagram 12 - Here, taking hold of black's stone from above with 1 and 3 is no good. Black cuts at **A**, and after white **B**, black **C**, white **D**, black **E** and white **F**, black separates white in sente with **G**, and white's two stones in the center end up floating. Even without that, it is miserable for white to get wrapped up with the forcing plays of black **H**, white **I**, black **J** and ending with white **K**. Black is poised to consolidate the upper right area on a large scale.

White played atari at 44 and pressed at 46.

The jumping attachment of black 47 followed by the atari of 49 were standard.

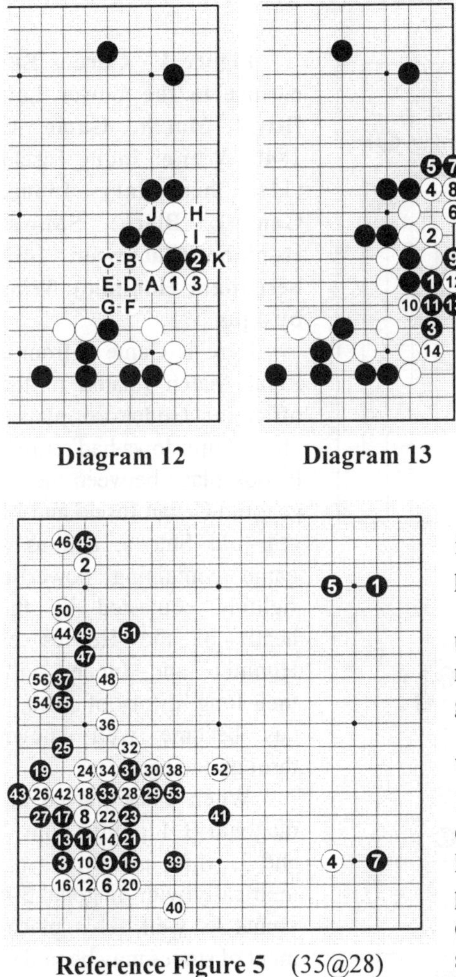

Diagram 12 Diagram 13

Reference Figure 5 (35@28)

Diagram 13 - If black tries to create a capturing race here by blocking at 1 and jumping to 3, white frustrates that plan by making eyes with 6 and 8. With the plays through white 12 and 14, it is a case of white having an eye and black not. And cuts are produced on the outside that are dangerous for black.

Black jumped to 51, developing on a large scale, and at that point white invaded at 52.

The fighting switched to the upper side, and with problems remaining on the lower side, the game was yet to be decided.

Reference Figure 5 - [East-West Knock-Out Tournament; 1950; White: Kajiwara Takeo 6 dan; Black: Hashimoto Shou, Honinbo] After the diagonal 3-4 points, black made the high corner enclosure at 5 in this game. The sequence through 37 has become an established Taisha variation, but at this time it was unusual. By connecting underneath at 56, white pressed black hard here.

DIAGONAL MODEL (1) - GAME 2

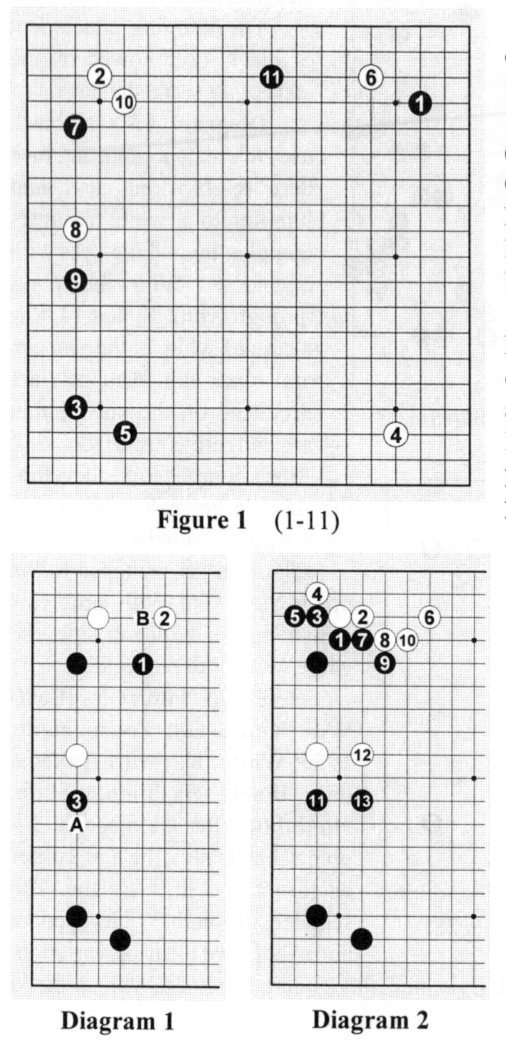

Figure 1 (1-11)

Diagram 1

Diagram 2

Figure 1 - Corner Enclosure in the Lower Left [Rival Match, Game 1; 1840; White: Inoue Inseki (11th hereditary Inoue; Genan); Black: Shuwa, Honinbo (Successor, 14th hereditary Honinbo); Wins by 4 pts.]

Here is Game 1 from a Rival Match related to the office of Godokoro played after Meijin Jowa had retired. It took place between the 41 year old Genan Inseki and 21 year old Shuwa, and as a game containing powerful fighting contested by the heads of the Houses of Honinbo and Inoue, with their long history of strife, it has become well known through the ages.

When black played the diagonal 3-4 points with 1 and 3, white answered symmetrically with diagonal 3-4 points as well. This placement of stones may be said to constitute an orthodox opening.

Black made a knight corner enclosure with 5 in the lower left. In reply to white 6, black attacked white in the upper left with 7.

When white made the three point pincer at 8, instead of taking action in the corner, black simply made the checking extension at 9. At that time, this kind of playing strategy was often used.

Diagram 1 - Jumping out at black 1 in exchange for the defense of white 2, followed by the checking extension of black 3 is the contemporary method. If white finds the checking extension distasteful and uses 2 to extend to **A**,

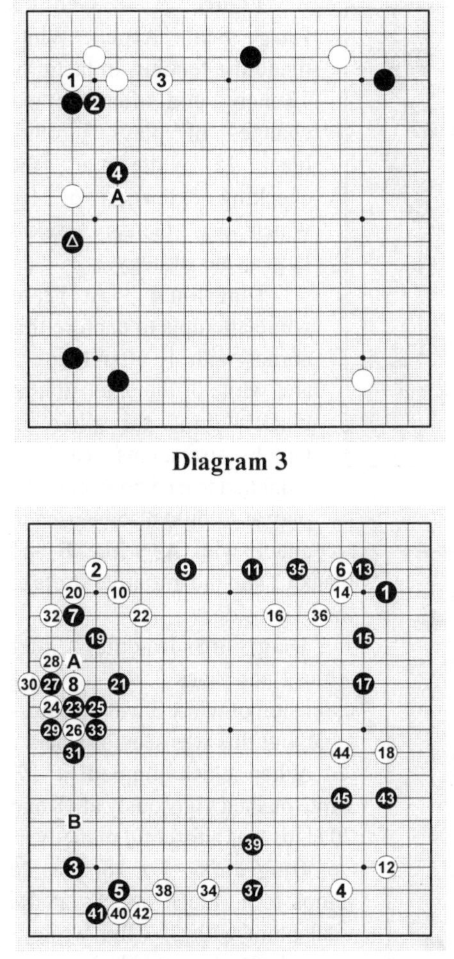

Diagram 3

Reference Figure 1

black **B** becomes an ideal point.

Diagram 2 - Instead of black 9, playing joseki from 1 through 5, and if white extends at 6, fixing the shape with 7 and the following plays, and then attacking with 11 and 13 was also possible.

White's diagonal play of 10, is a leisurely maneuver.

Diagram 3 - Here, if 1 and 3 are played, black 4, or else the capping play at **A**, results in a sudden battle. Since the checking extension of black ▲is in place in this opening, provoking a fight here is not white's intention.

Black made another three point pincer here at 11.

Reference Figure 1 - [Castle Game: 1715; White: Yasui Sankaku (4th hereditary Yasui); Black: Honinbo Dochi (Meijin, 5th hereditary Honinbo)] Black made a knight corner enclosure with 3 and 5. In response to white 8, black played 9 and made the extension to 11. If white played 22 as the extension at 31, the fencing-in tactic of black 22 would not be precisely suitable. From black 23 through the capture of 33, the distancing with the lower left was ideal. For white 28, 29, black **A** and the extension of white **B** was better.

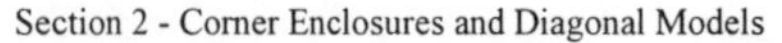

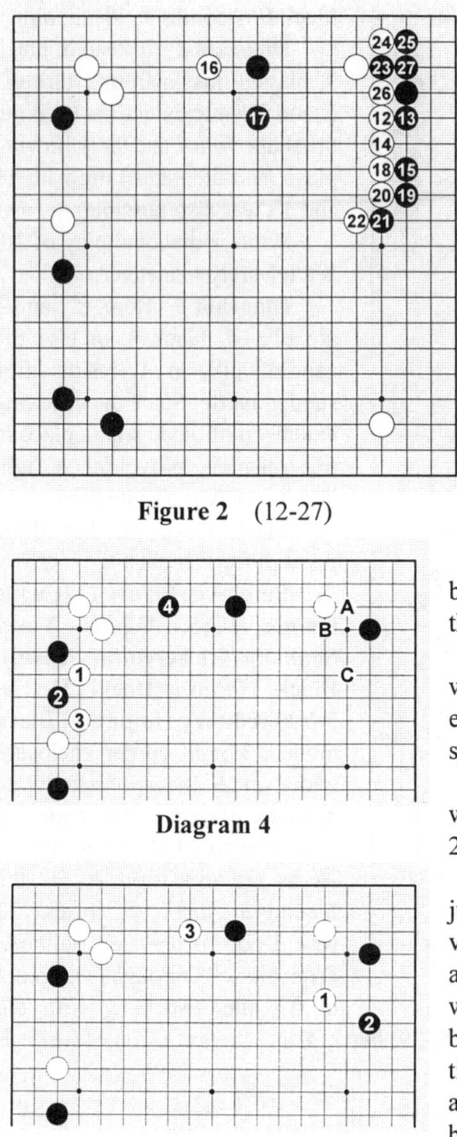

Figure 2 (12-27)

Diagram 4

Diagram 5

Figure 2 - Genan's Large Scale Attack White made the fencing-in tactic of 12 here, and after the exchanges of plays through black 15, white made the checking extension of 16, which was Genan Inseki's large scale strategy.

Diagram 4 - At 12, if white attempts to capture this corner with 1, after black 2 and white 3, the extension of black 4 limits the sphere in which stratagems can be launched to a narrow one. The play at 4 could also be used to attack with **A**, white **B** and black **C**, and the initiative shifts to the black side.

Diagram 5 - In addition, after white 1 and black 2, the checking extension of white 3 was also possible, but this was seen as slack.

When black jumped at 17, white pushed vigorously at 18 and 20. This was a forceful maneuver.

Diagram 6 - For 18, if white jumps to 1, black attacks at the vital point with 2. After white 3 and black 4, considering that white **A** forces black **B**, it is possible to deal deftly with the situation by playing white **C**, black **D** and white **E**, but there is a possibility that black would be allowed to get settled in the process.

Black 21 and white 22 haned, with black's attack coming into focus.

Here, black made the diagonal attachment of 23, extending support to the two stones on the upper side, a composed play typical of Shuwa. Alternately,

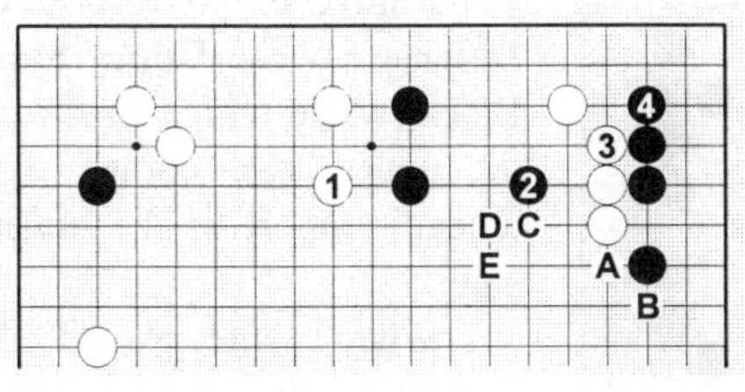

Diagram 6

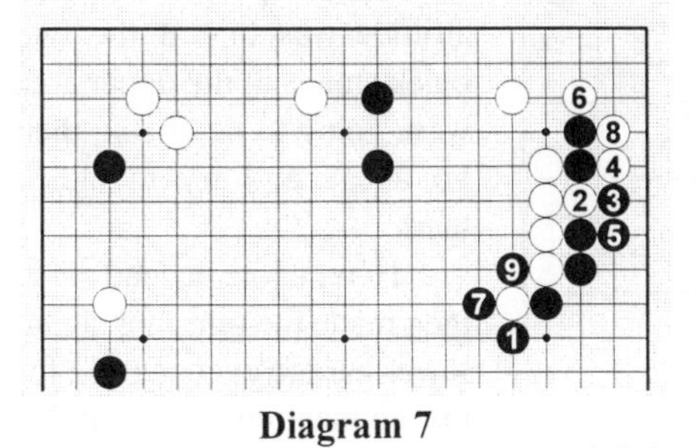

Diagram 7

Diagram 7 - What about playing the contemporary fighting method of the two-step hane at 1? One's first impression is that the division resulting from white 2 through the one stone capture of black 9 is playable for black.

Diagram 8 - When black raps white on the head with 1, connecting with white 2 shows a lack of fighting spirit, and after white 8, the game continues with the attachment of black **A**.

Diagram 9 - The actual game example of white 1 through 19 (**Reference Figure 4** , page 77) results in a completely different game if there is no black position to attack on the upper side.

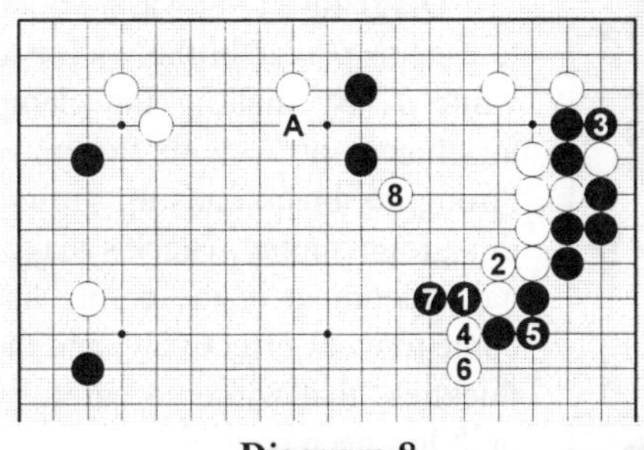

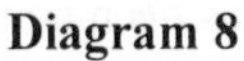

Diagram 8

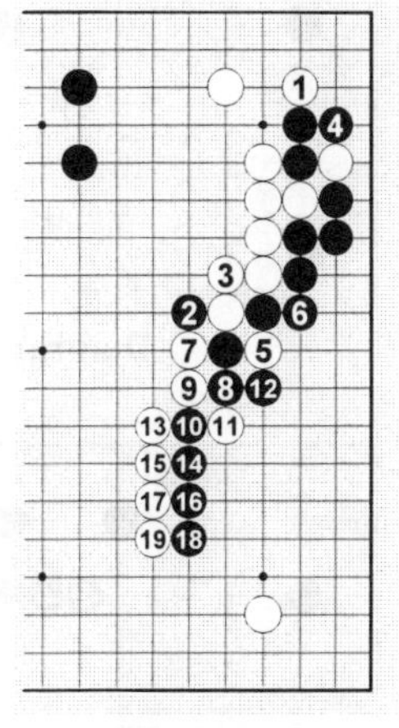

Diagram 9

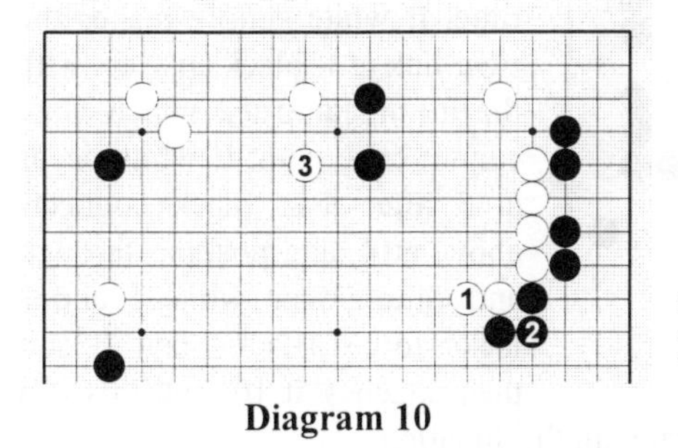

Diagram 10

Diagram 10 - White can also simply extend at 1, and after black 2, attack with white 3.

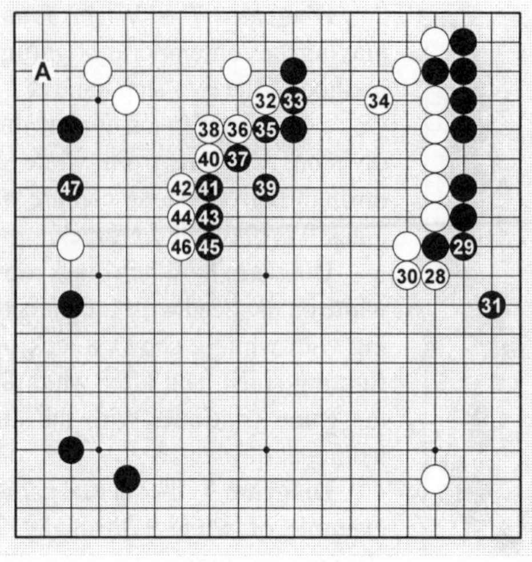

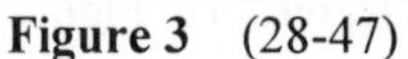

Figure 3 (28-47)

Figure 3 - Attack and Defense on the Upper Side Black, while taking profit in the upper right corner, extended support to the upper side.

When white played 28 and 30, black patiently made the knight's play at 31. The attitude was that if the two black stones in the upper area were going to be attack, then go ahead and try to attack them.

Here, white peeped at 32, then made the tiger link at 34. It was hard to exchange 32 for the connection of black 33, but it was a makeshift strategy in an emergency.

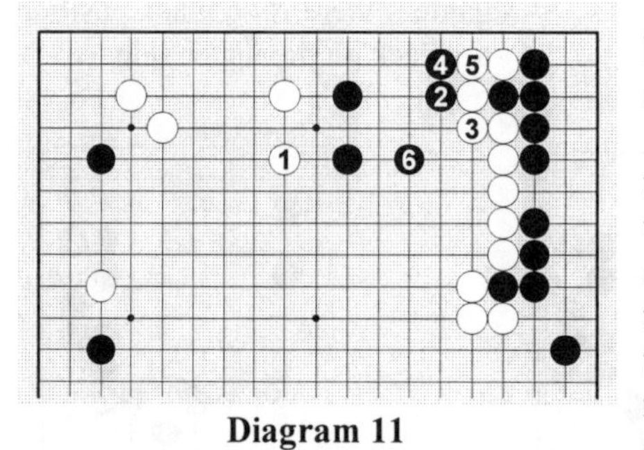

Diagram 11

Diagram 11 - It was no good to use this play to blithely jump to white 1. By making the clamp attachment at 2, with the plays through 6, black ends up settling this group simply. Black's diagonal attachment in the corner has come to work effectively, and the thickness that white so carefully built has been neutralized.

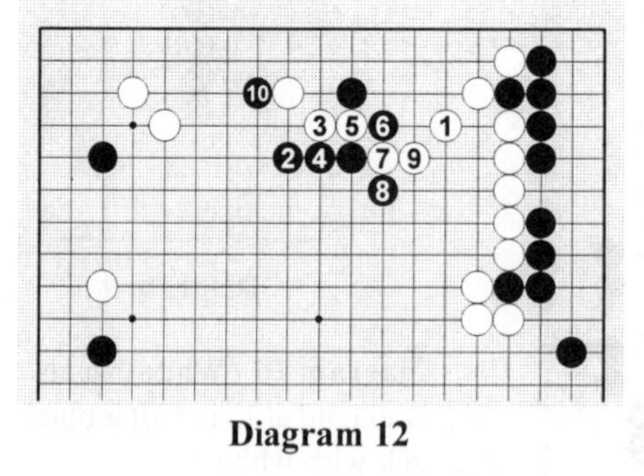

Diagram 12

Diagram 12 - At the same time, if white simply makes the tiger link at 1, black answers with the turning jump at 2, which white cannot cope with. If white peeps at 3 after that, black connects above at 4, and pushing through and cutting with white 5 and 7 lacks force. Black plays 8 and then attaches at 10, and this is a skillful way for black to deftly deal with the situation.

The peep once of white 32 was a forcing play, and then black could not use

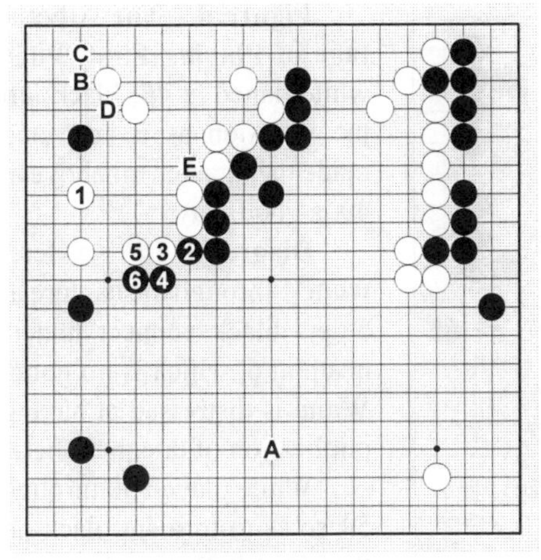

Diagram 13

35 to advance as far as 36. That would invite complications after white pokes at 35.

Black made thick and strong shape with the connection at 33, so playing 35 and the hane at 37 built a sufficient position. With the tiger link of 39, black was playing as far as possible for thickness.

Turning at white 40 was an unyielding play. Here, making the knight's play at 42 would have no effect on black, and would let black turn to play the play at **A** in the corner.

White pushed bluntly with 42 through 46.

Diagram 13 - For 46, it was also possible to make the checking extension at 1, and in the past there was much debate over this. After white 3 and 5, black presses thickly with 6, followed by white occupying the lower side first at **A**. However, the upper left area cannot be called white's territory, since there is the potential of black starting a ko fight with **B**, white **C** and black **D**, and wrapped up with the cut at **E**, this would be aggravating. If white expends a play here, black develops on the lower side.

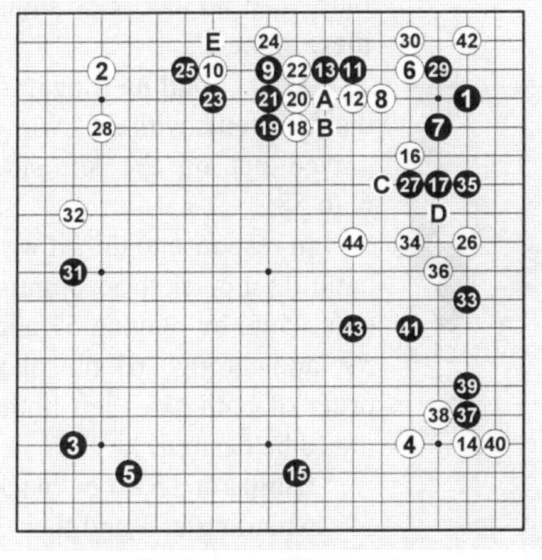

Reference Figure 2

Black made the one point jump at 47.

Reference Figure 2 - [Rival Game 3; 1766; White: Honinbo Satsugen (Meijin, 9th hereditary Honinbo); Black: Inoue Inseki (6th hereditary Shunseki)] Without black playing 13 as the hane at **A**, followed by white **B** and black 20, there was no attack here. For 15, black 18, white **C** and black **D** was better. White 18 was a key point for attack and defense, and white's thrusting through with the plays up to 24 represented failure for black. With the attack at **E** on the upper side available, the position was promising for white.

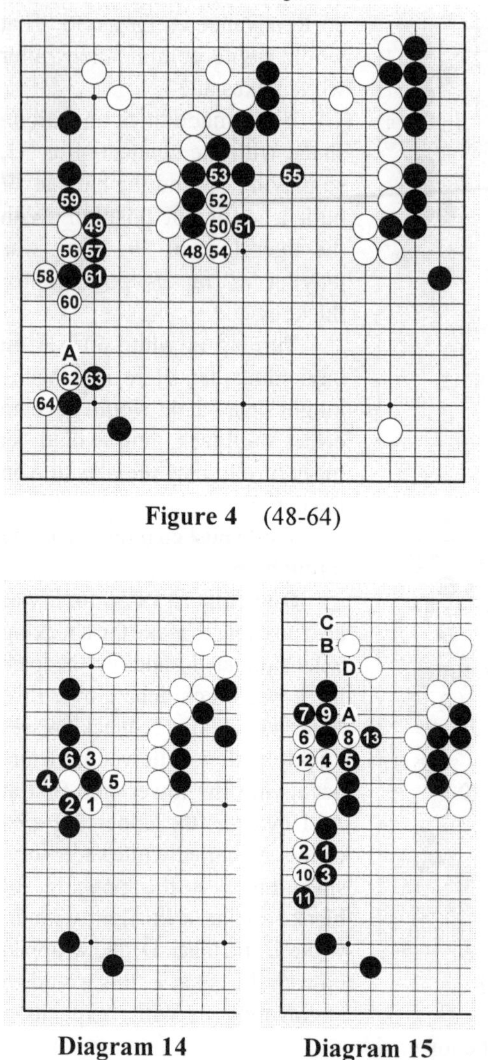

Figure 4 (48-64)

Diagram 14

Diagram 15

Figure 4 - The Advantage of Playing First When white haned at 48, black left the situation as it was, and made the attachment above at 49, a good play.

Diagram 14 - Here, white 1 through the capture at 5 lets black connect underneath at 6, which is no good. White is distressed at having duplication of thickness here.

White played 50 through 54 so as to torment black on the upper side, but after putting the shape in order with 55, black had no anxieties about these stones.

After butting against black's stone with 56, white played out on the left side with 58.

In response to this, it was natural for black to accommodate white by playing 57 and 59, and through 61 the play order of both sides left nothing to be desired.

Diagram 15 - For black 59, extending at 1 and then 3 would have been slack. White lives smugly with 12, while black ends in gote with 13. If white tries to run away at **A**, black is all right since after **B** and white **C**, black **D** is a forcing play, but having the territory scooped out is a loss.

White attached at 62, and then the hane of 64 was a skillful finesse. At 64, drawing back at **A** has a heavy feeling. Here,

Diagram 16 - If black connects at 1, white will settle the group with 2 and 4. After living with fully expanded shape, white has no cause for dissatisfaction.

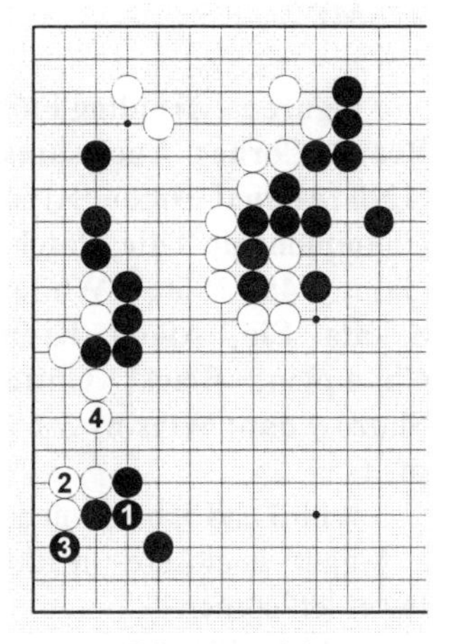

Diagram 16

Diagram 17

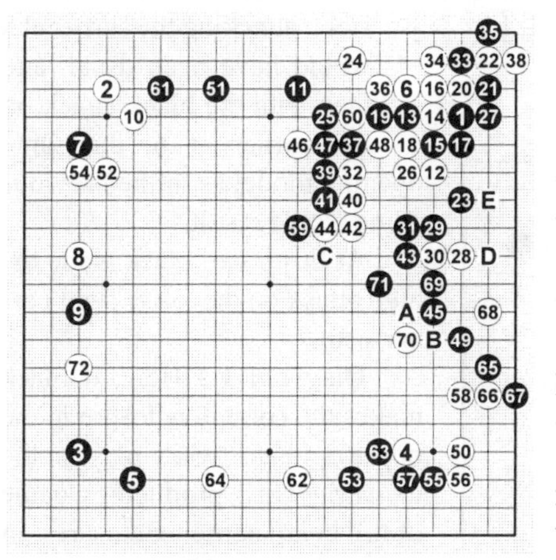

Reference Figure 3

Diagram 17 - This shows the later course of the actual game.

Black counterattacked strongly with 65 and 67, and a natural swap resulted through white 72.

Black 73 through 77 were characteristic of Shuwa's outstanding whole board vision, and the plays splendidly maintained the advantage of playing first.

After losing this game, Genan resigned the Rival Match and withdrew his application for Godokoro.

Reference Figure 3 - [The House of Matsudaira Go Tournament; 1835; White: Honinbo Jowa, Meijin (12th hereditary Honinbo); Black: Akaboshi Intetsu] This is the game during which Intetsu vomited blood. After playing the diagonal pattern, black made the corner enclosure at 5. In the upper right, a variation of the Taisha joseki was played that was being analyzed at the time. Black 33 was a secret play of the House of Inoue. White 44 at 45 is no good, since black replies with **A**, white **B** and black **C**. Shuwa pointed out that playing 44 at **D** was a saving play that would have been followed by black **E**, white 44, black 45 and white 49. White 68 and 70 were exquisite plays.

DIAGONAL MODEL (1) - GAME 3

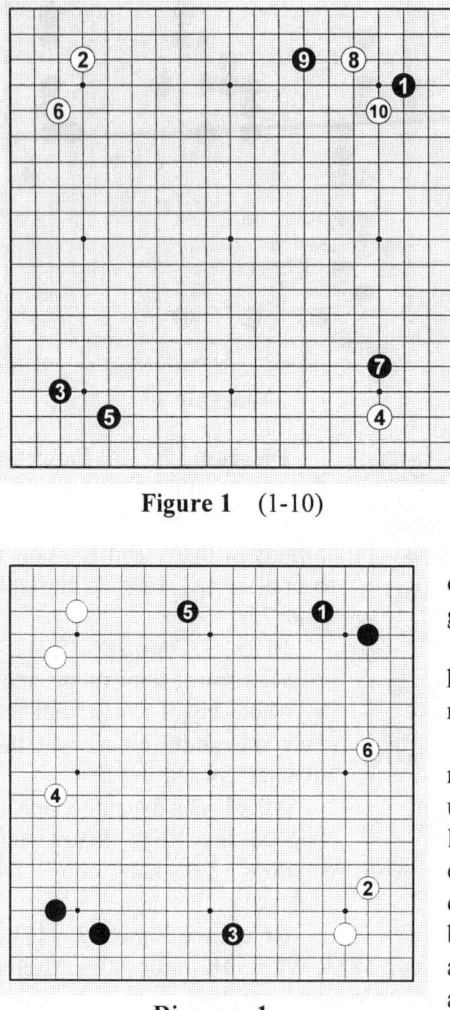

Figure 1 (1-10)

Diagram 1

Figure 1 - Avoiding Full Board Corner Enclosures [13th Annual Nihon Ki-in Championship Title Match, Game 4; 1966; White: Sakata Eio, Nihon Ki-in Champion; Black: Ohira Shuzo 9 dan; Wins by 3 1/2 pts.]

With 3 and 5, black made a knight enclosure in the lower left corner.

White played a scheme with the corner enclosure at 6. Here, attacking the corner at 8 would have been usual, and then with the black attack on the corner at 6, the same opening model as in the previous game would result.

At this point, black made the high attack on the lower right corner with 7.

Diagram 1 - Here, if black makes the corner enclosure in the upper right at 1, white plays in the lower right at 2, producing a game of full board corner enclosures. In diagonal 3-4 point games where black makes a corner enclosure and white does so as well (black 5 and white 6 in the figure), it is easy for a position with full board corner enclosures to develop. Following black 3, regardless of the variety of differences in high and low or positioning, up to white 6 both players occupy the sides in tandem, moving around the go board. Full board corner enclosure openings are powerfully effective for white in games with komi (see **Reference Figure 2**, page 179), and that intention can perhaps be surmised from white 6.

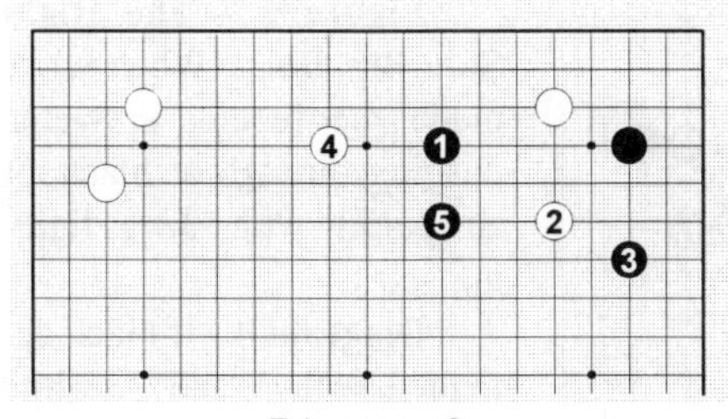

Diagram 2

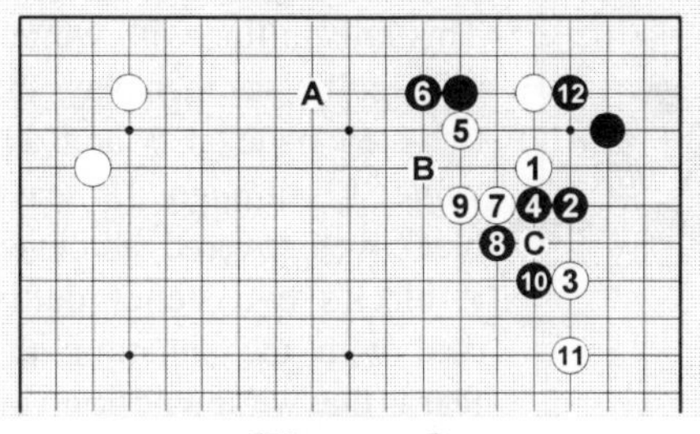

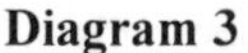

Diagram 3

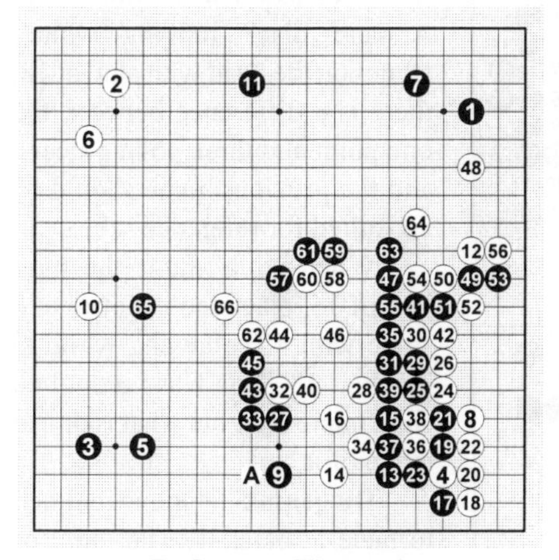

Reference Figure 1

Black disliked that, and so attacked the lower right corner.

Black made the one point pincer with 9, and white repled with the fencing-in tactic at 10.

Diagram 2 - In this game, the fencing-in tactic was good, so perhaps at 9, black should have made the two point high pincer at 1. White jumps at 2, and developing with black 3 and 5 could be considered, leading to another possible game.

Diagram 3 - For 10, if white had jumped to 1, black 2 through 12 was a joseki that was often played at the time. White 11 at **A** would be met by black contesting the position with **B**. However, afterward white 9 was played as the cut at **C** (reference Volume I, page 260 and the following).

Reference Figure 1 - [1st Go Championship Title Match, Game 1; 1957; White: Kitani Minoru 9 dan; Black: Hayashi Yutaro 7 dan] Here is a full board corner enclosure game with a one point high corner enclosure mixed in. When black played 13, white 14 initiates a fierce contest.

Kitani: "White 24 at 25, followed by black 26 and white **A** was probably better."

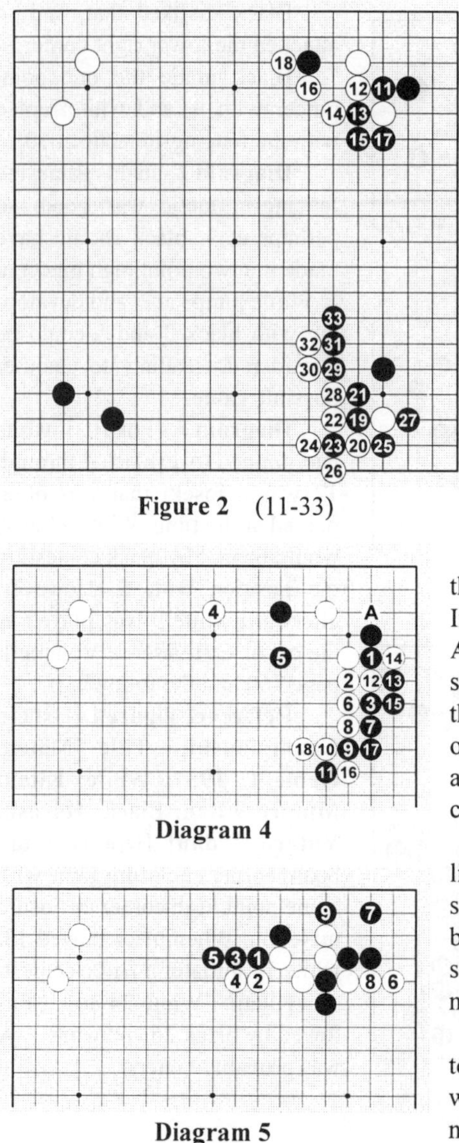

Figure 2 (11-33)

Diagram 4

Diagram 5

Figure 2 - The Right Side Big, But... When white made the fencing-in tactic, pushing through at black 11 and cutting with 13 was fighting spirit.

Diagram 4 - If black defended with 1 and 3, white would have played 4 and the plays through the push at 8. This falls in line with white's wishes. If black then plays the two-step hane at 9 and 11, white 12 through 18 leave black well covered, and even if black's two stones deftly deal with the situation, the fear is that white's position on the upper side will be solidified. In the variation with white 18 at **A**, and black rapping white's stones on the head with atari at 18, there is a difference between the one point and three point pincers, and the previous game should be consulted for reference sake.

When white made the tiger link of 16, black took control of a stone with 17, allowing white to block at 18. This was no doubt a solid maneuver, but what is one to make of it?

Diagram 5 - One is inclined to hane at black 1. The jump of white 6 is met by the skillful finesse of black's jumping to 7 and attaching at 9.

Diagram 6 - Next, black connects underneath with 15, and the sequence proceeds to white 26. Playing this kind of large scale joseki settles the character of the game, and is easy to play. The development on the upper side is not bad, while if the game becomes one in which black turns at **A**, the high position of the stone attacking the lower right will probably also become good.

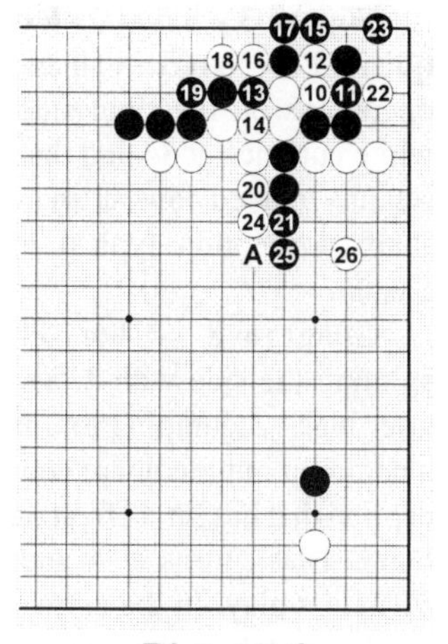

Diagram 6

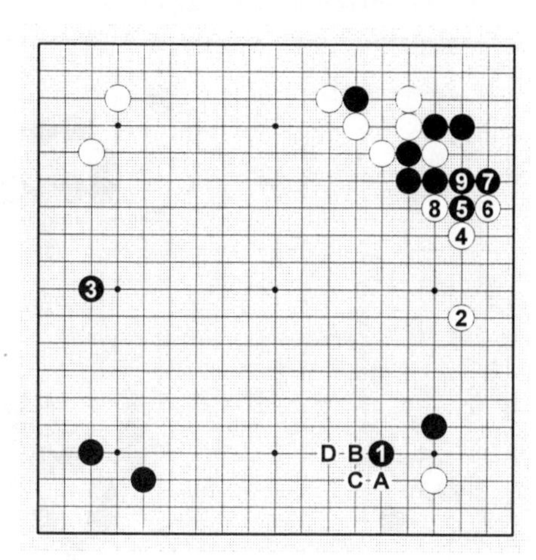

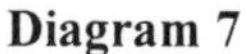

Diagram 7

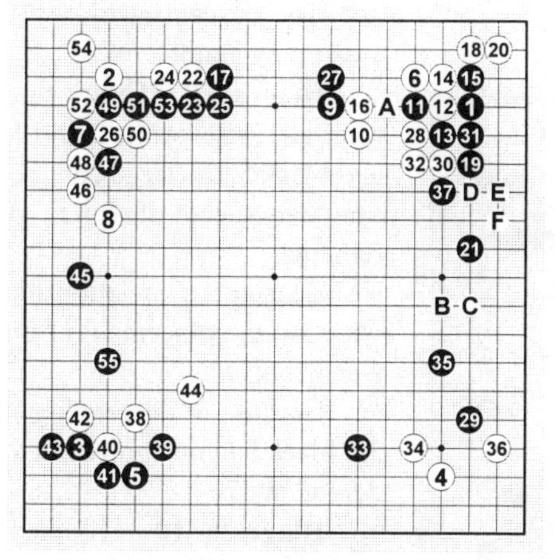

Reference Figure 2

The joseki with the attachment of black 19 and the plays through 33 is also played often.

Diagram 7 - However, in this board position, instead of 19, majority opinion was that the knight's play of 1 was better. If white splits the side at 2, black occupies the big point of 3, and after white 4 through black 9, or else white **A**, black **B**, white **C** and black's extending at **D**, black has thick and strong positions all over the board.

Black made the right side big through 33, but the territory cannot be consolidated just like that.

Reference Figure 2 - [5th Annual Meijin League; 1965; White: Kajiwara Takeo 9 dan; Black: Ohira Shuzo 9 dan] Black played 15, avoiding the Kajiwara joseki that starts by black extending at **A**. White 16 was unusual. Black played a fast paced opening with 17 and the following plays. Descending at 27 was a forcing play, and white 28 could not be omitted. If black neglected to play 37, the maneuver of white **B**, black **C**, white **D**, black **E** and white **F** would be possible.

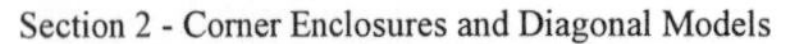

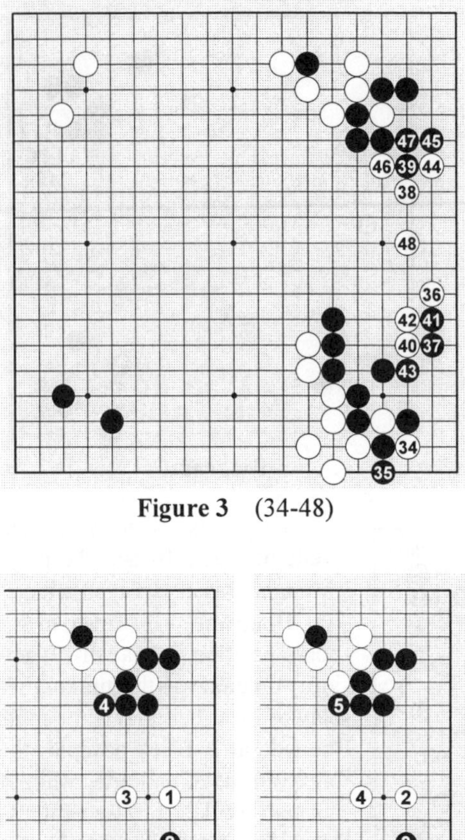

Figure 3 (34-48)

Diagram 8

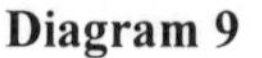

Diagram 9

Figure 3 - Sakata's Exquisite Play In order to begin operations on the right side, white cut once at 34 and then stealthy played low at 36, a sharp conception typical of Sakata.

Diagram 8 - For 34, splitting the side with 1, and after black 2, jumping to 3 is a common but mediocre conception that has little effect on black. Black turns at 4 with sufficient play. In the corner, all that is left is the hane of white **A** that forces black **B**.

The descent at black 35 was unavoidable.

Diagram 9 - If black captures at 1, after white 2 and 4, and black 5, the large connection underneath of white **A** remains.

Bearing a relationship with 34, the placement of 36 was exquisite.

Because of descending at 35, black had no choice but to defend at 37.

Diagram 10 - If black answers low from this side at 1, white ends up living with 2 through 6, bullying black in the corner in the process.

Forcing black to defend at 37 was the correct order of plays.

Diagram 11 - If white makes the placement at 1 first in exchange for black 2, when white cuts at 3, black captures at 4. Should black obligingly use 4 to descend at **A**, the position would revert to the previous diagram, but that would be too much to ask.

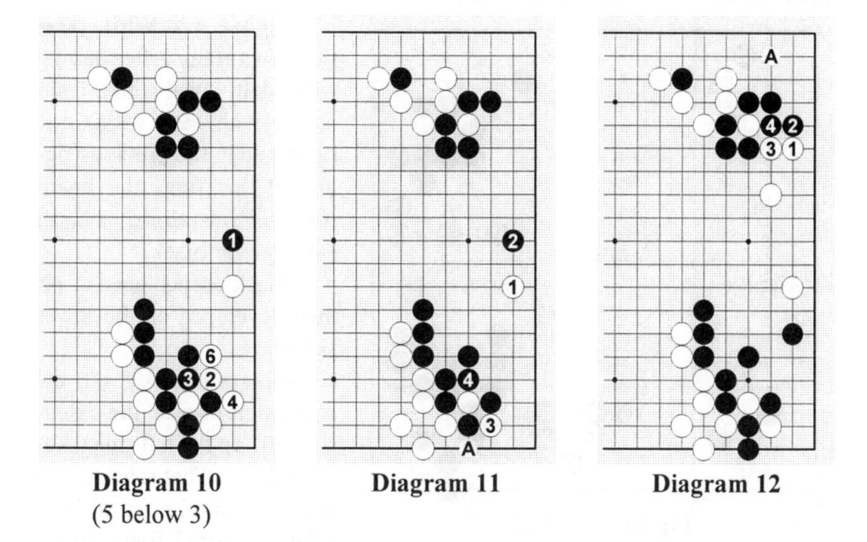

Diagram 10
(5 below 3)

Diagram 11

Diagram 12

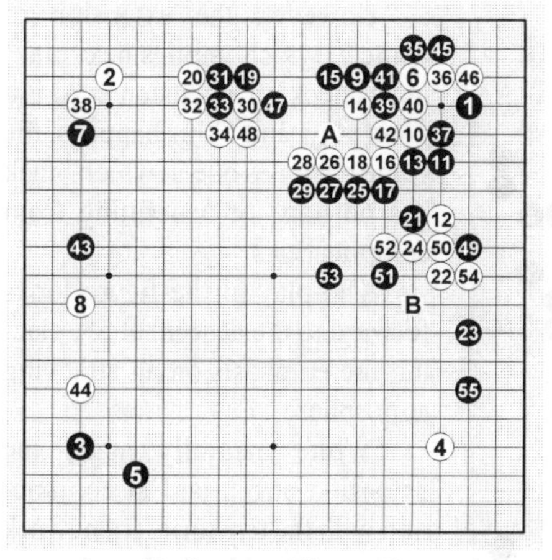

Reference Figure 3

It was something of an investment that turned bad, but the cut at 34 was the reason for the exquisite play that followed, and white made good shape with 38 and the following plays.

Black 39 was unavoidable.

Diagram 12 - If the position was left as it was, suffering white's slide at 1 would have been terrible. Black gets forced with the plays through 4, and if white further jumps to **A**, the whole group would be threatened.

White got settled with 48, and black's territorial framework had vanished like the morning dew.

Reference Figure 3 - [13th Annual Nihon Ki-in Championship; 1965; White: Otake Hideo 7 dan; Black: Ohira Shuzo 9 dan] A popular joseki was played through 22. With black 23 and the following, a sudden battle developed. Here, it was also possible for black to press with 36, white 41 and black **A**. Pushing at black 25 followed by the rest was the large and spirited Ohira style. White 30 was painful but unavoidable. Black could have also used 49 to attack at **B**.

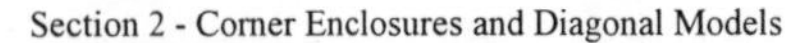

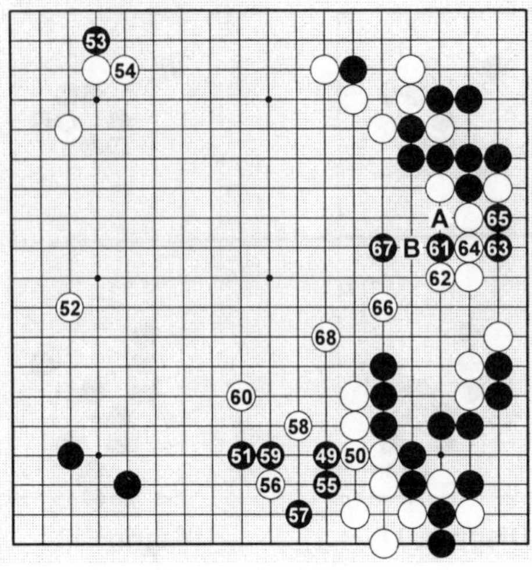

Figure 4 (49-68)

Figure 4 - White Has the Advantage After having white deftly deal with the situation with ease within the right side in the previous figure, at this stage the board situation was already not an easy one for black.

Black peeped once at 49, then developed on the lower side at 51.

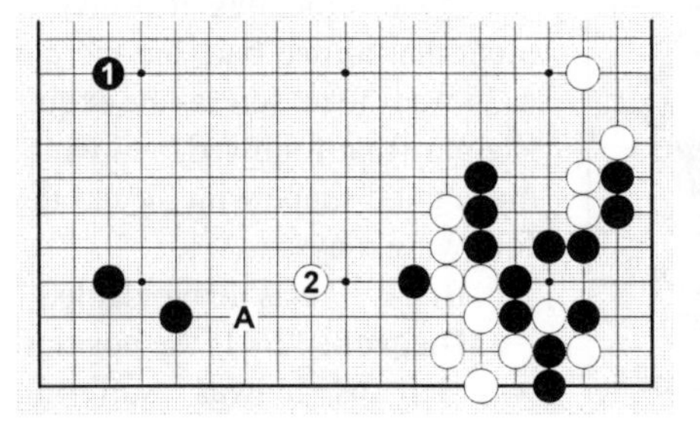

Diagram 13

Diagram 13 - From the standpoint of size, the extension of 1 on the left side takes precedence. That is because it is at the central point of both sides' territorial frameworks. However, the extension of white 2, which implies next making a checking extension at **A**, is a good play, and if this happens, the game becomes one in which black has no hope of benefitting from complications.

The play in the figure looks forward to the descent at 55, placing the emphasis on an attacking atmosphere.

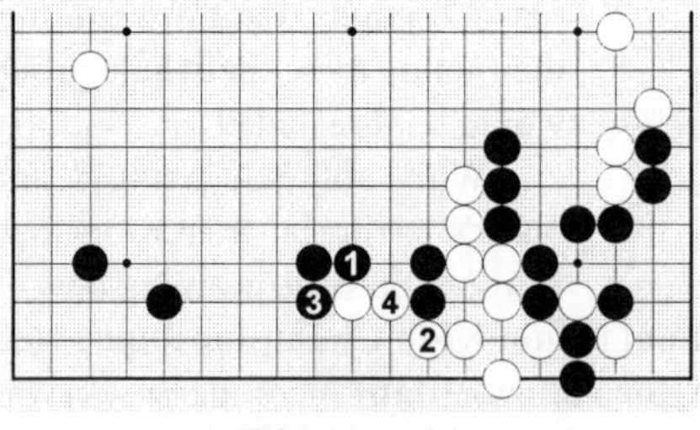

Diagram 14

White naturally made the extension at 52, and in conjunction with the territorial framework on the upper side, the board situation was promising for white.

Black attached once at 53 as a probe, then descended at 55 in order to attack the lower side. White still had weak points on the right side, and unless black could work up a two-pronged attack in this game, there was no way of winning it.

Here, white made the placement at 56 as a probe, which was a skillful play. The diagonal play of black 57 was natural.

Diagram 14 - If black blocks above at 1, white connects underneath with

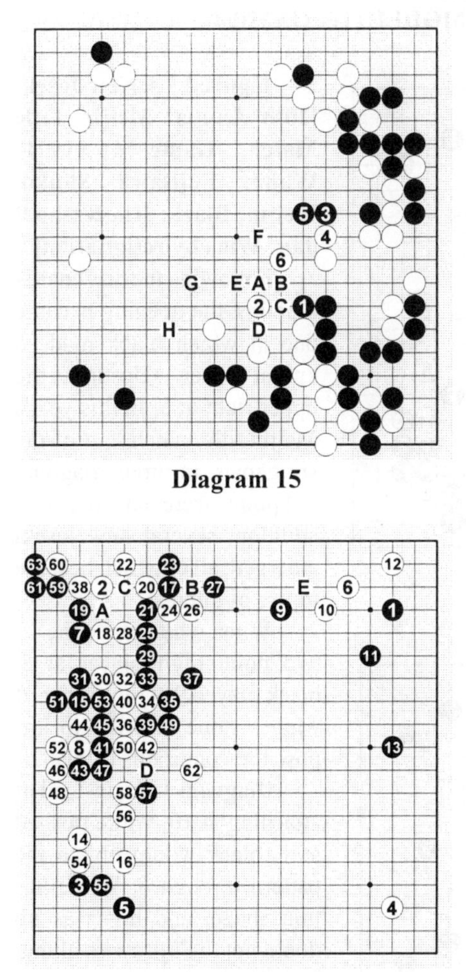

Diagram 15

Reference Figure 4

2 and 4, and obtains a base.

White played 58 and the knight's play at 60, and the stone at 56 would come into play later as well.

Black 61 this time brought the right side under sudden attack, with 63 and 65 depriving white of a base. If white used 62 to connect at **A** out of greed, black's drawing back at **B** would have left white's eye shape questionable.

After 66 and 68, white had made sufficient shape to survive, and black had no play to immediately play against it.

For black 67,

Diagram 15 - Even if 1 through 6 was played, after the sequence from black's slicing through the knight's play with **A**, in alphabetical order through white's running away at **H**, it does not seem likely that white will be caught.

At this stage white had the advantage, and it was only in the later half of the game that black managed an upset.

Reference Figure 4 - [9th Annual Meijin Title Match, Game 3; 1970; White: Fujisawa Shuko 9 dan; Black: Rin Kaiho, Meijin] White played leisurely with 8. White 14 and 16 were in keeping with Fujisawa's taste. For 27, black considered pushing through at **A**, but the profit to be gained with white **B** was big, and black could not go through with it. If white used 50 to cut at 53, black intended to play 51, white 52, black 50, white **C**, black **D** and white 59 to discard these stones, then go ahead with black **E**.

DIAGONAL MODEL (1) - GAME 4

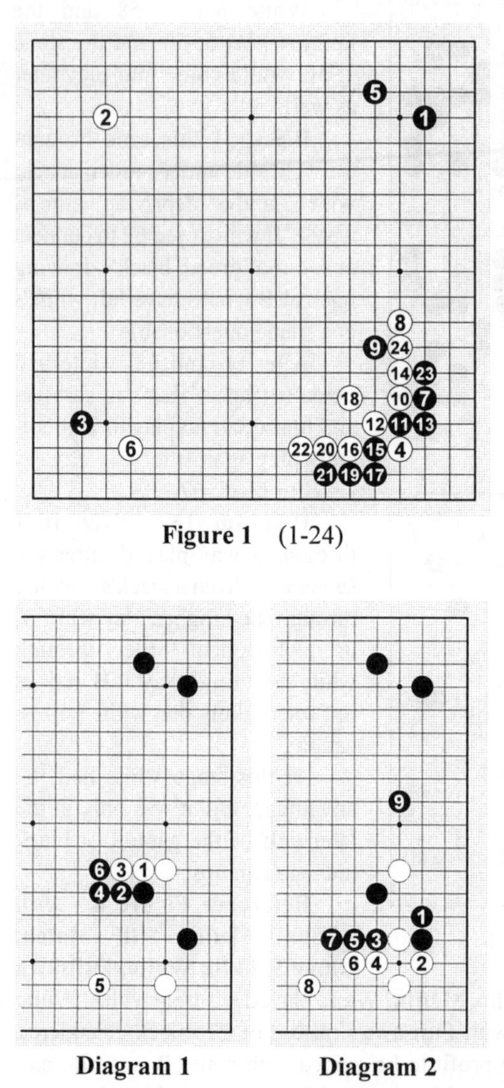

Figure 1 (1-24)

Diagram 1

Diagram 2

Figure 1 - A New Joseki [10th Annual Meijin Title Match, Game 6; 1971; White: Fujisawa Shuko, Meijin; Black: Rin Kaiho 9 dan; Wins by resignation]

Following the diagonal 3-4 points, the opening became one in which black made a knight corner enclosure in the upper right at 5. In this year's Meijin title match, out of the six games, in three, diagonal 3-4 points were played, and in addition, several new joseki emerged, all of which became topics of interest.

When white made the two point high pincer at 8, black played 9 at the corner of white's stone in order to impose the conditions of play.

Diagram 1 - If, instead of attaching at 10, white pushed at 1, black would obtain the pattern through 6. White has thin shape, and this was no doubt not to Fujisawa's liking.

Black haned between white's stones with 11, aiming to play the Kajiwara joseki.

Diagram 2 - With this play, the joseki that starts by drawing back to 1, followed by the sequence through black 7 and white 8, can also be considered. The checking extension of black 9, with the corner enclosure in the upper right as the backdrop, is perfectly matched to the position, and this was another strategy.

My intention was that for 16,

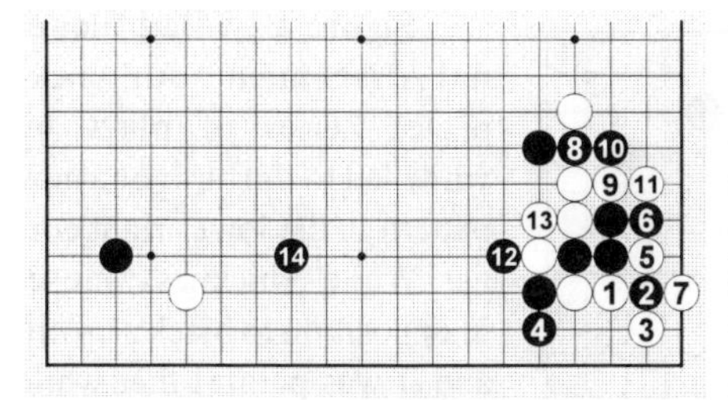

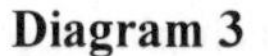

Diagram 3

Diagram 3 - The white block at 1, followed by black 2 through white 13 produce the Kajiwara joseki. This is a loss in terms of profit, but black gains good impetus to next make the pincer at 14, and this was black's plan.

However, Fujisawa frustrated my intentions by introducing new plays at white 16 and 18.

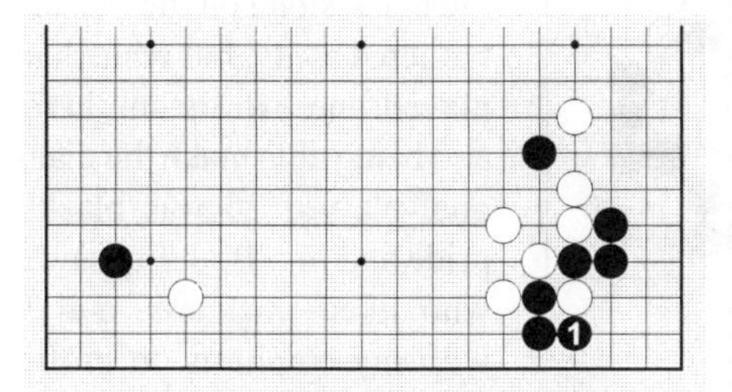

Diagram 4

Diagram 4 - For 19, I also thought about playing black 1, taking control of white's stone.

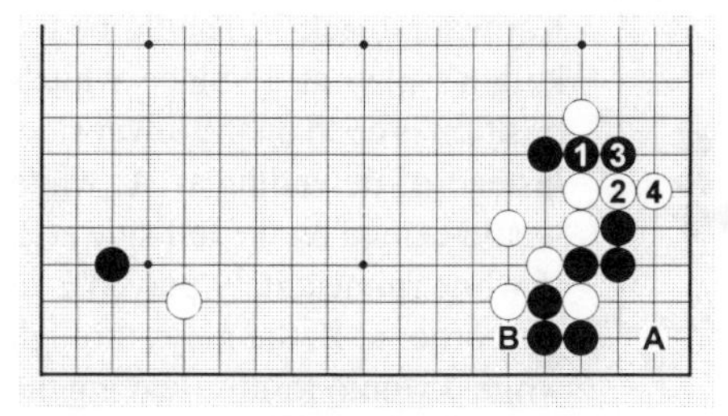

Diagram 5

Diagram 5 - However, this play is gote in the present board position, and it is difficult for black to aim at pushing through with 1 and 3. With implication of the placement of **A** to follow, white's block at **B** is a forcing play.

Without regret, black fixed the shape with 19 and 21, and also exchanged black 23 for white 24. Unexpectedly, a new joseki pattern was born.

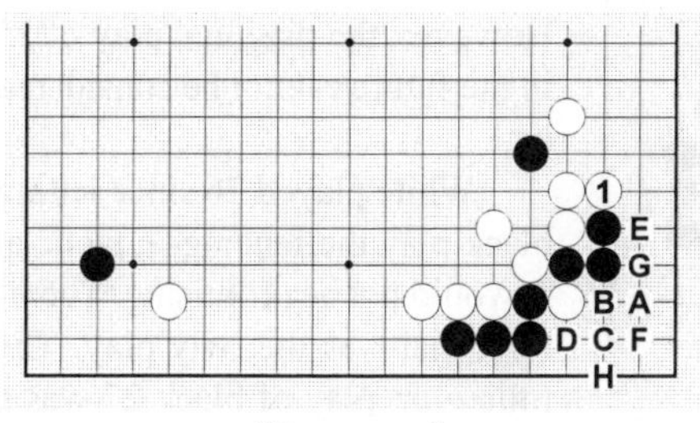

Diagram 6

Diagram 6 - If 23 was not played, blocking at white 1 is a good point that aims at the placement at **A**. Black would be dissatisfied after being forced with the sequence from black **B** through **H**.

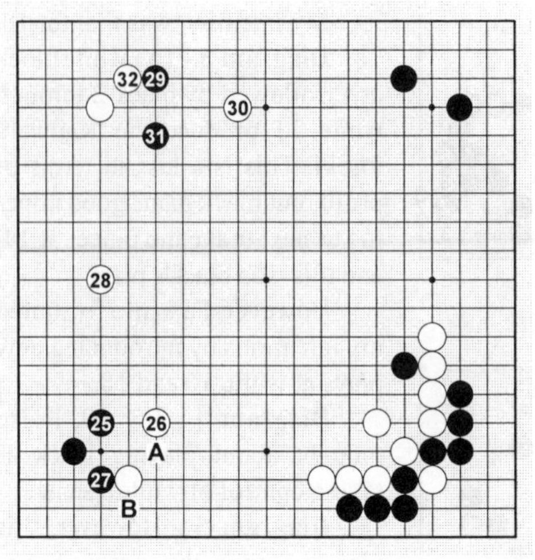

Figure 2 (25-32)

Figure 2 - A Bad Diagonal Attachment An unexpected series of plays by white led to the birth of a new pattern in the lower right corner. White's thickness was set in opposition to black's profit, and it was painful that while each play represented a loss, the black stone on the outside withered away, but white had played one extra stone here, and being able make the diagonal play of 25 was black's pride and joy. Both Fujisawa, who liked thickness, and I, with my emphasis on profit, were satisfied with the result.

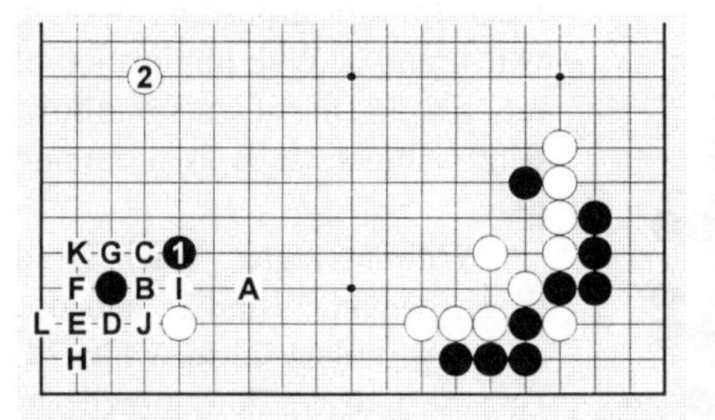

Diagram 7

Diagram 7 - According to Kajiwara, black 25 should be the knight's play at 1. Since white's position is open on the lower side, instead of defending at **A**, white would extend on the left side at 2. If white immediately played 2 in the corner at **B**, the plays through white **J** would follow, leaving the thickness in the lower right erased, which would be terrible. However, the diagonal play of 25 in the figure cannot be considered bad.

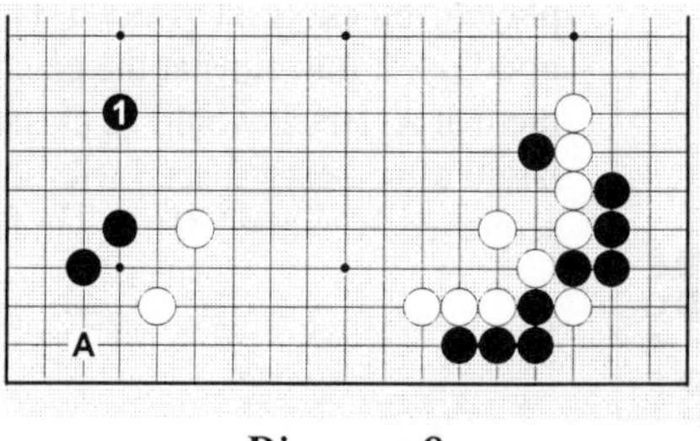

Diagram 8

White played 26 since letting black play the fencing-in tactic at **A** would not be promising. Therefore, that was the only play. The follow-up play of black 27 was a mistake. White could not have been expected to descend at **B**, so black should not have hurried to play here.

Diagram 8 - Black should have extended high at 1. It is hard for white to slide to **A** because it leaves the potential for problems, so the side takes precedence over the corner.

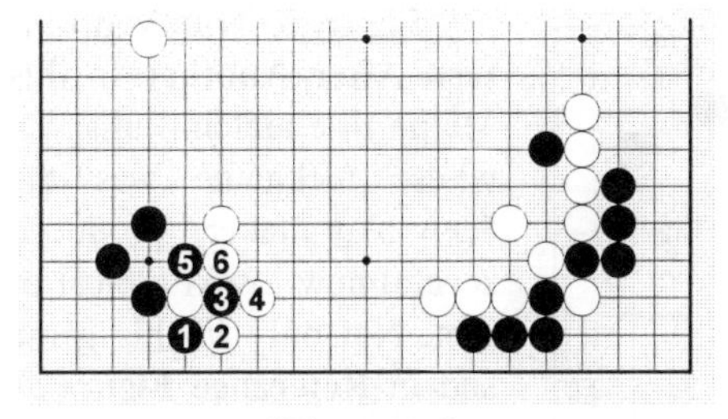

Diagram 9

Diagram 9 - Even after the diagonal attachment in the corner, black 1 through 5 is met by the atari of white 6, so this is practically worthless. Rather, white's shape is put in order instead.

White 28 was an ideal point.

Black turned to fight at 29, whereupon white made the pincer at 30.

When black jumped at 31, white made the diagonal attachment at 32 in order not to fall in with black's designs.

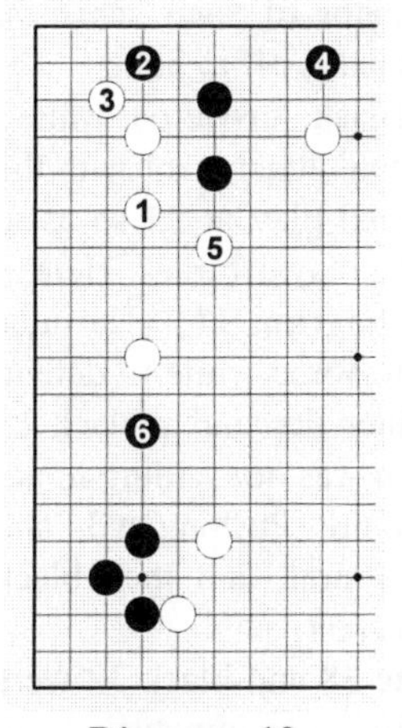

Diagram 10

Diagram 10 - Here, defending at white 1 lets black slide at 2 and 4, and after white 5, black is allowed to make the good checking extension at 6. White must have considered this too clear and simple. The give and take with the following plays here is a highlight of the game.

Reference Figure 1 - [9th Annual Meijin Title Match, Game 6; 1970; White: Rin Kaiho, Meijin; Black: Fujisawa Shuko 9 dan] Here is a diagonal model played the previous year. The jump of black 21 was a new play, with 25, white 26, black **A**, white 27, black 31 and white **B** the usual sequence here. For white 22, 24, black 22, white 34, black **C** and white **B** was better. At 30, white 34 was urgently needed, and had black played 33 at **D**, white **E** and black **F**, white would have been in trouble.

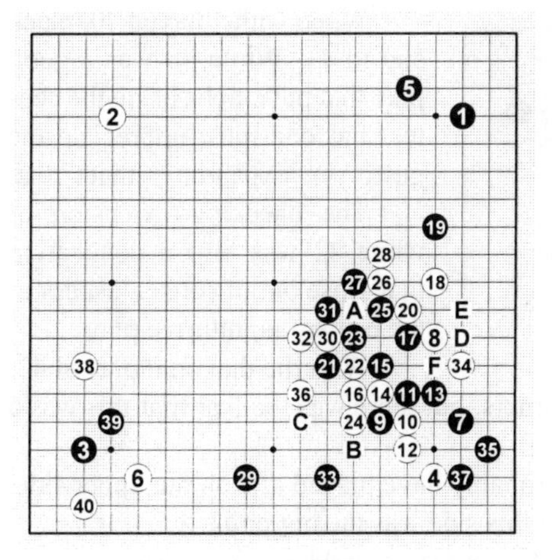

Reference Figure 1

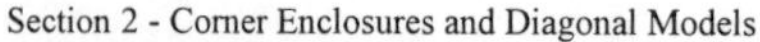

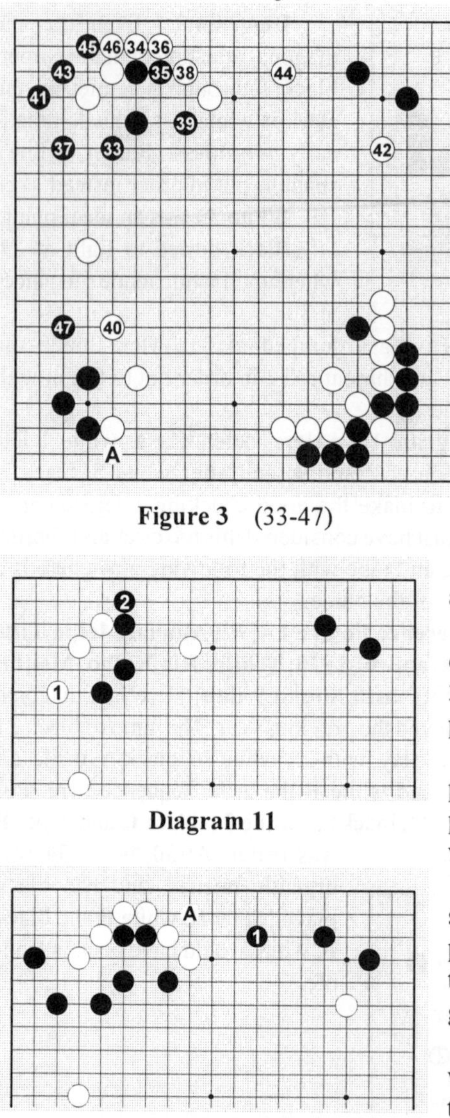

Figure 3 (33-47)

Diagram 11

Diagram 12

Figure 3 - One New Pattern After Another In this Meijin title match, Fujisawa, whose nickname was the "new play maker," produced several new joseki typical of him. Not only in this game and in **Reference Figure 3**, but also in the model on page 278 of Volume I, and as the originator of such schemes, one's hat is off to him.

Black answered white's diagonal attachment with the diagonal play at 33 so as to get the play off track. Here,

Diagram 11 - The idea was to force white to defend at 1 and then descend at black 2.

White was not willing to acquiesce to this. Pushing at 34 and 36 was natural, and then black played in at 37.

White 38 and black 39 were played from the impetus of the position, and another new pattern was born in this corner.

When white played 40, black slid to 41. White 40 was a good play that put emphasis on the center, and one must appreciate the gusto in expanding that area.

The checking extension of white 42 was also a conception that arose out of consciousness of the center, an intuitive play.

With the diagonal play at 43, black gained control of all four corners, but there was the fear that this was a little too biased towards profit.

Diagram 12 - Black should probably have played at 1 on the upper side. The peep at **A** is also possible, and this side was the big point.

White took a good point with the extension at 44.

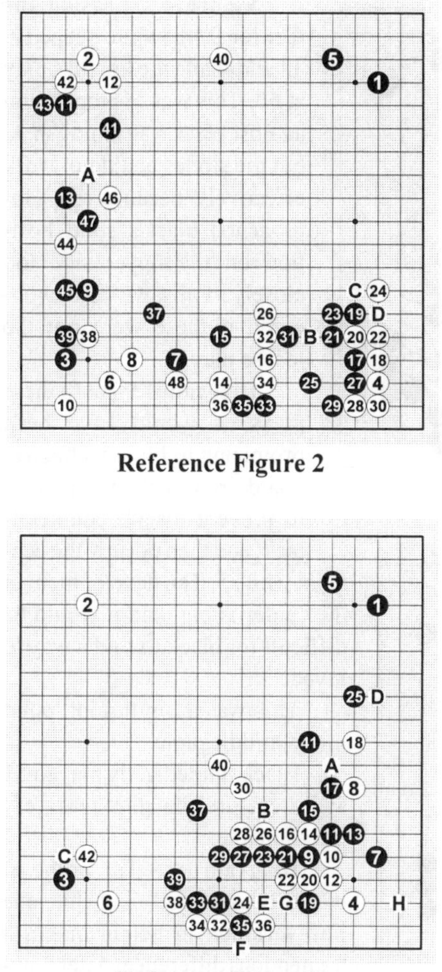

Reference Figure 2

Reference Figure 3

Black could not neglect defending at 47. If white was allowed to jump in here, descending at **A** would become a forcing play, giving white good shape.

Reference Figure 2 - [9th Annual 10 Dan Title Match, Game 5; 1971; White: Otake Hideo, 10 Dan; Black: Hashimoto Utaro 9 dan] Using white 12 to make the pincer at **A** was common sense, but white played leisurely in the figure. Black 15 and 17 were the rhythm of the stones. Black 23 was heavy. Here, the knight's play of black 25, followed by white 23, black **B**, white **C** and black 32 was better. White could have played 24 at 25, and then black **D** and white 26 was promising. Black dealt deftly with the situation with 27 and the following plays.

Reference Figure 3 - [10th Annual Meijin Title Match, Game 1; 1971; White: Rin Kaiho 9 dan; Black: Fujisawa Shuko, Meijin] Black played 25 with the idea that if white replied at **A**, black would play **B**. White's moving out with 26 and the following plays was premature and cannot be endorsed. Here, it was better to settle the group with 42, black 29, white **C**, black 41 and white **D**. Instead of 32, 35 was correct. Black 35 was exquisite. Considering the sequence of black **E**, white **F** and black **G**, black could play **H** in sente.

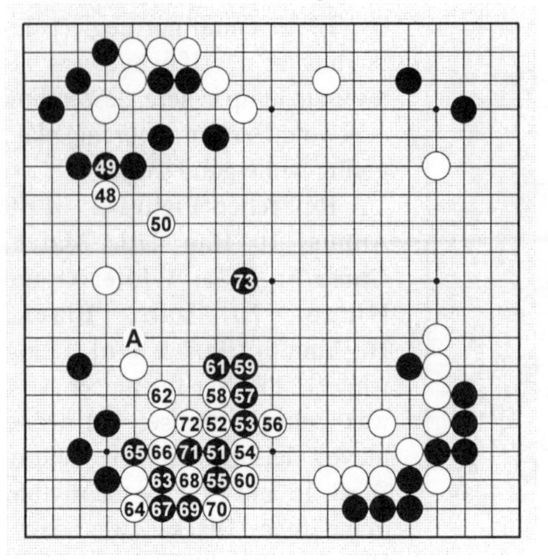

Figure 4 (48-73)

Figure 4 - Erasing the Center Here, white peeped at 48 and made the knight's play at 50. This was in preparation against black's attaching at **A**, but the stones could not work effectively because they approached black's solid position on the upper side too closely. Fujisawa also wondered if these were not the losing plays.

Diagram 13 - With these plays, it would have been promising to bluntly attach at 1 and draw back at 3 in order to prevent black's counterattack, and then occupy the center at white 5. The development in the center is big, and it would be difficult for black to find a way to invade.

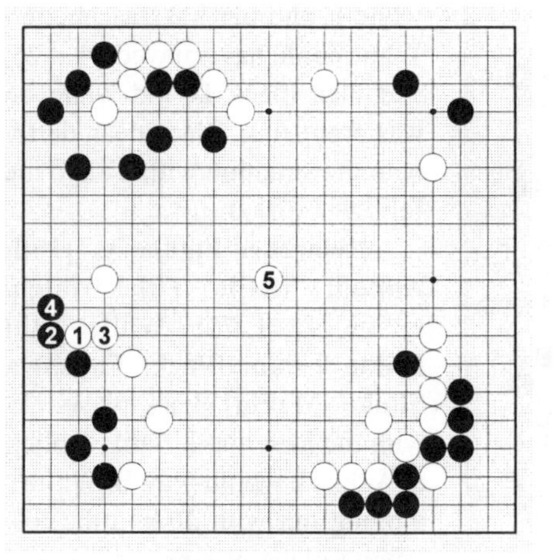

Diagram 13

This was a big turning point in the middlegame.

Black immediately played 51 as an erasure, but this was very questionable.

Diagram 14 - The probe of black 1 was good, and that one line variation in height makes a tremendous difference. After playing here, white would have to answer at 2 in order to defend against black's slicing through the knight's play, and then black would jump to 3, easily erasing white's territorial framework. If black can further jump to **A**, it would be also possible to aim at playing at the corner of white's stone at **B**. Black had to play this way.

Since black charged in one line deeper, white attached at 52 and cut at 54, leaving black painfully groping for a counter strategy.

Descending at black 55 put up the strongest resistance, and then white, seeing that the ladder was favorable, tenaciously played 56 and the following plays.

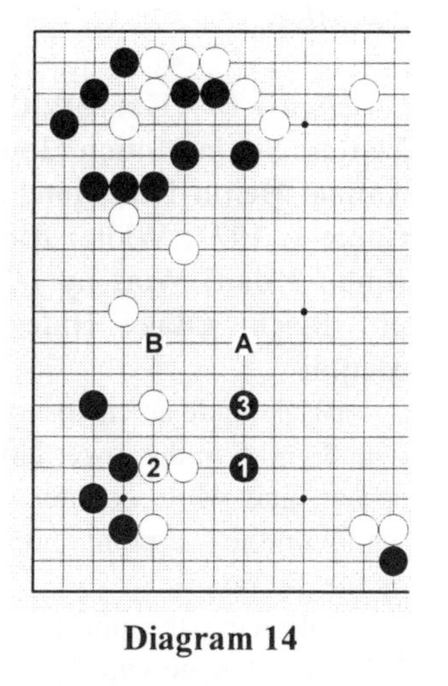

Diagram 14

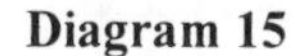

Diagram 15

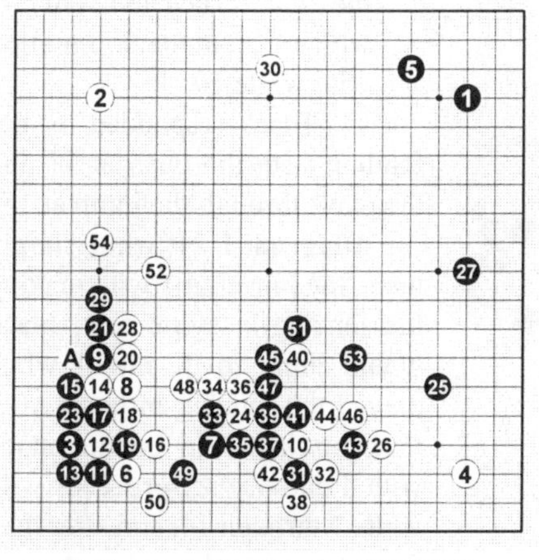

Reference Figure 4 (22@12)

Diagram 15 - For 56, playing atari at white 1 and blocking at 3 would have been sharp. In that case, black was prepared to hane at 4, and then use the method of playing atari with 6 and 8. When black plays the ladder breaker at 10, a swap results through 12, and since white's thickness has been erased, this is probably playable for black. On the lower side, black has the tactic of the diagonal play at **A** available to connect underneath.

Through 73, black had three stones taken, but the center was erased so this was an acceptable result.

Reference Figure 4 - [2nd Annual Kisei Tournament, All Dan Knock-Out Round; 1977; White: Rin Kaiho 9 dan; Black: Honda Kunihisa 9 dan] White dodged at 10 to see what would happen. The joseki in which 10 is used to push at 20 was not to my taste. At 17, black should have simply connected at **A**. In the lower left, a new pattern developed from 12 and the following plays, and through 54, white had a playable position.

DIAGONAL MODEL (1) - GAME 5

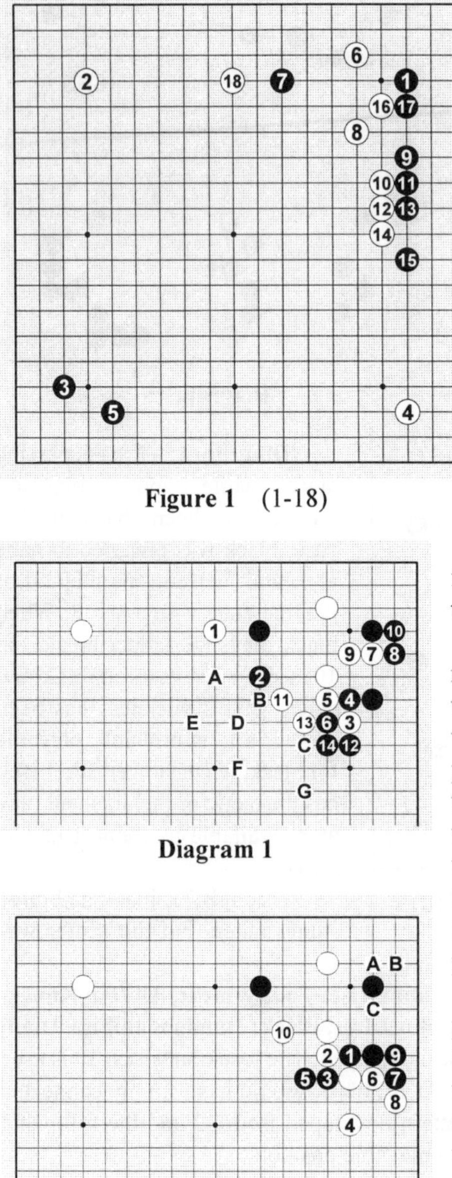

Figure 1 (1-18)

Diagram 1

Diagram 2

Figure 1 - A Game With Matters Set in Motion [2nd Annual Meijin Title Match, Game 1; 1977; White: Rin Kaiho 9 dan; Wins by 1/2 pt.; Black: Otake Hideo, Meijin]

Black made an enclosure with 3 and 5 in the lower left corner, and white countered with 2 on the star point and 4 on the 3-3 point.

Following the pincer of 7, black defended with 9, and the game became one in which I set matters in motion with white 10.

Black responded by defending with the push at 11 and the plays through the jump at 15.

Diagram 1 - If white simply made the pincer at 1 with making the fencing-in tactic first, black would jump to 2, and if white played the fencing-in tactic after that, black would counterattack with 4 and 6. Play proceeds with white 7 through 14, and after that, for reference sake the maneuver from white **A** to **G** can be compared with page 170 in Volume I.

Diagram 2 - At 11, if black pushed through at 1 and cut with 3, the sequence through white 10 would result. White can make the forcing plays at **A**, black **B** and white **C**, and therefore has a playable position.

It is common to exchange 16 for 17 before the pincer.

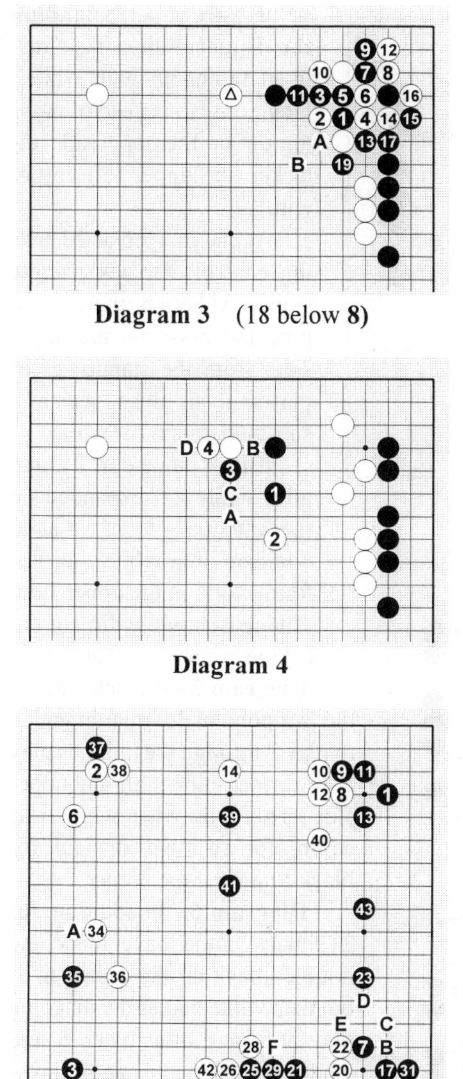

Diagram 3 (18 below 8)

Diagram 4

Reference Figure 1

Diagram 3 - If that was not played and white simply made the pincer with Δ, black would play for a variation with 1 followed by the outward hane at 3. White can capture the corner with 4 through 18, but black plays atari at 19 in the center, which does not end up as white had planned. If white now connects at **A**, black makes the fencing-in tactic at **B**, making it difficult for white to play out. Since white's three side stones are floating, this is no good.

White pressed in at 18, waiting for black to play out. Next,

Diagram 4 - If black jumps out at 1, white attacks with 2 and 4. After that, black can consider playing at **A** or **B**. If black uses 3 to turn at **C**, white makes shape by jumping to **D**.

Reference Figure 1 - [17th Annual Nihon Ki-in Championship Title Match, Game 4; 1970; White: Ishida Yoshio 6 dan; Black: Ohira Shuzo, Nihon Ki-in Champion] At 15, if black extended at **A**, white would immediately fix the shape by playing **B**, black **C**, white 17 and black **D**. With 19, black was seeking impetus to play on the right side. For 23, **D**, white **E** and black 23 was thick. If black played 25 at **F**, white would have connected underneath at **G**.

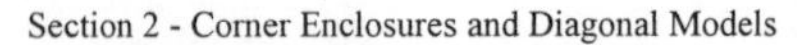

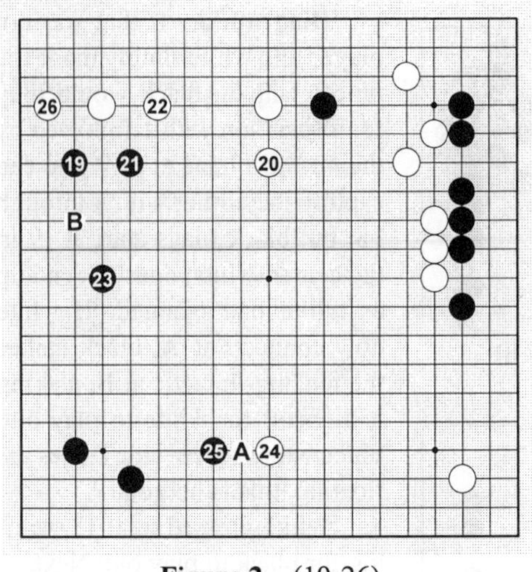

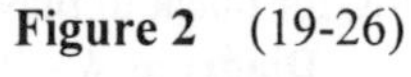
Figure 2 (19-26)

Figure 2 - Expanding the Upper Side Black disliked falling in with white's intentions, so instead of moving out on the upper side, attacked the upper left corner with 19.

White jumped at 20, taking control of black's single stone. Although there were potential plays on the upper side, from the standpoint of play analysis, this is seen as a substantial gain for white.

Black jumped at 21, and after white 22, expanded on the left side with 23 so as to compete with white's territorial framework on the upper side.

The reason white did not defended the corner was that for 21,

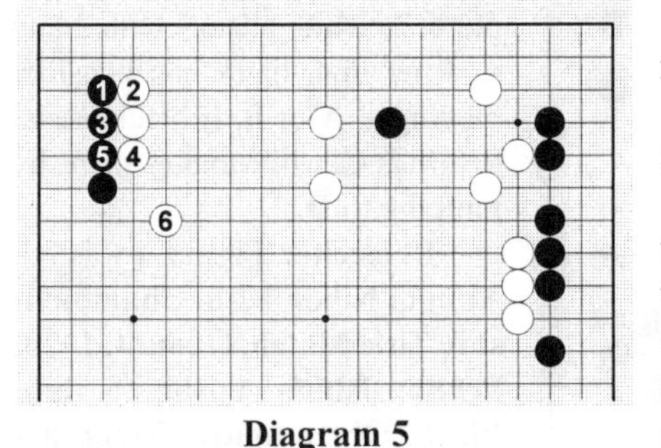

Diagram 5

Diagram 5 - If black entered the 3-3 point at 1, white intended to play 2 through the knight's play at 6, further expanding the upper side. This was what white was calling for, so it was difficult for black to invade the corner.

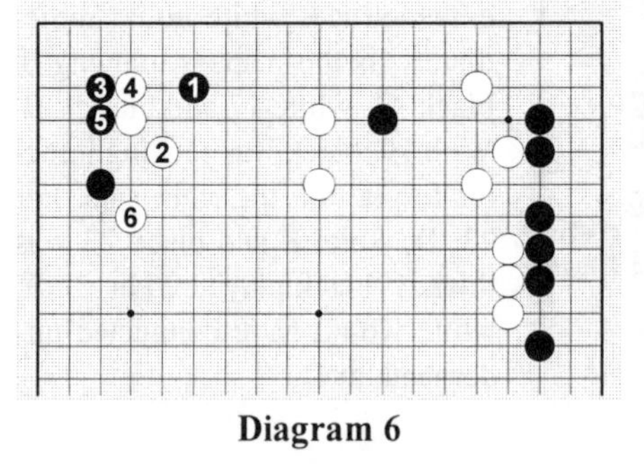

Diagram 6

Diagram 6 - In addition, for 21, black could have made the double attack on the corner at 1, but then white makes the diagonal play at 2, and after black 3 and white 4, I planned to apply pressure with the play at 6. On the upper side, black still had scope for initiating action. For instance,

Diagram 7 - Pushing once with black 1, and then making the plays at 3 and 5 to deftly deal with the situation, etc., could be considered. Here, white captures a stone with 6 and 8, and when black plays 11 and 13, white answers at 14. Next,

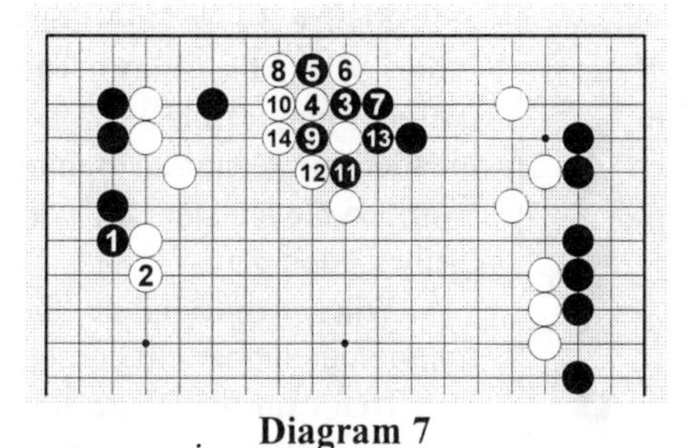
Diagram 7

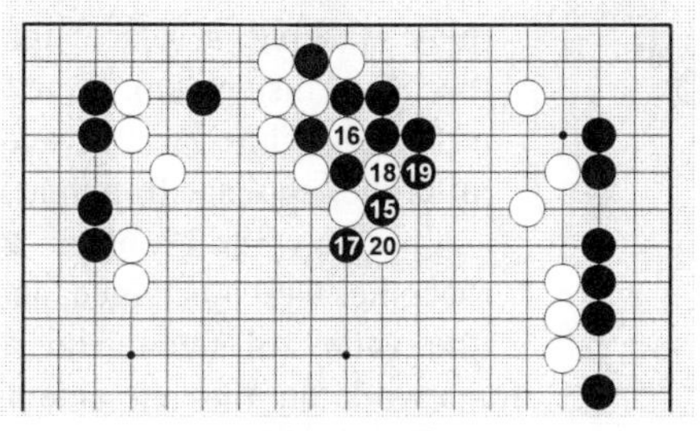
Diagram 8

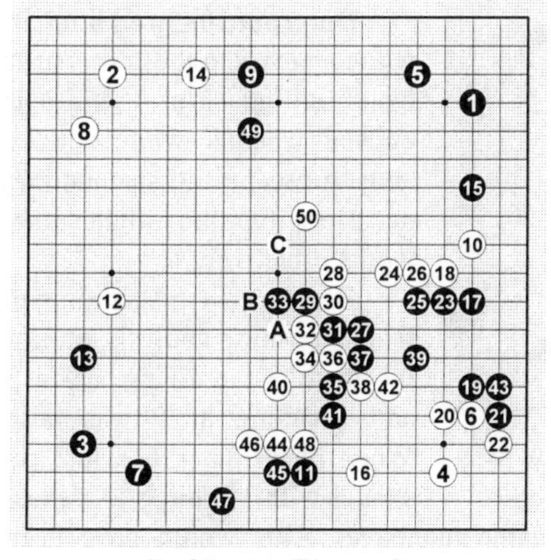
Reference Figure 2

Diagram 8 - When black hanes at 15, white plays 16 through the cut at 20, resulting in a difficult fight.

There were various maneuvers for black 21, but with actual game experience with this position (**Reference Figure 4**), black boldly adopted the strategy with 21 and 23. Up to here, the course of play was practically the same in both games, the only differences being the stone at the 3-3 point in the lower right, and the play order of 20 through 23.

White headed for the big point on the lower side at 24, but this was somewhat questionable. That is because the high checking extension of black 25 that followed was perfectly placed. Therefore, 24 had to be played one line further at **A**.

White jumped at 26, protecting the corner and aiming at the invasion of **B**.

Reference Figure 2 - [12th Annual Meijin Title Match, Game 1; 1973; White: Ishida Shuho, Honinbo; Black: Rin Kaiho, Meijin] Here is an all corner enclosure game. Only the extension at 12 was played high. If black played 29 at 32, white would reply with 33, black **A** and white **B**, and then invade the upper side. The invasion with black 41 and the following was questionable. One wanted to jump at **C**. After having two stones captured with 48, black had a difficult game.

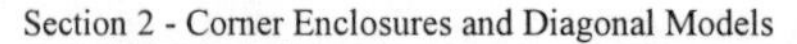

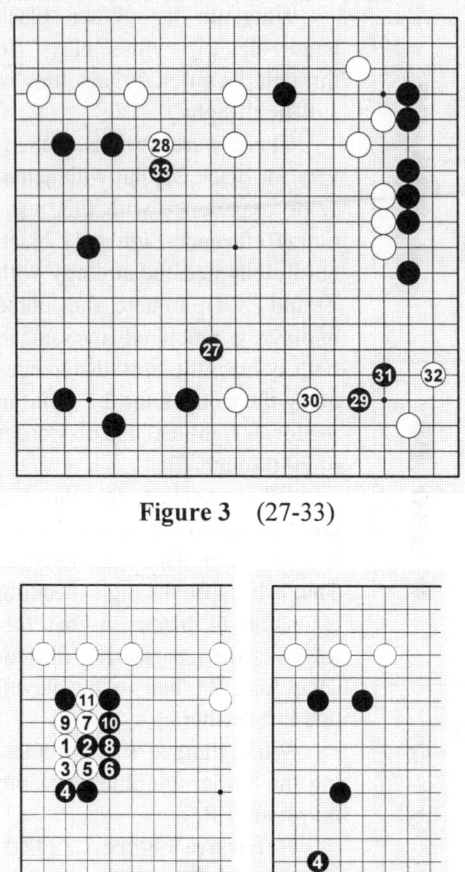

Figure 3 (27-33)

Diagram

Diagram 10

Figure 3 - A Questionable Knight's Play The knight's play of black 27 expanded the territorial framework on the left side, and was truly a good play.

When white made the jump in the upper left corner,

Diagram 9 - There was an implication of the invasion of 1, but when the knight's play was put in place, that became a distant aim. If, nevertheless, white does invade, after the sequence from black 2 through white 11, black ▲ becomes well positioned, and the valley of the territorial framework on the left side is deep. Immediately playing here is no good.

Diagram 10 - In addition, if white attaches in the corner at 1, black will attack at 4, and it is unclear whether white will be able to escape the surrounding net. Here, too, the knight's play works effectively.

Diagram 11 - According to Ishida Yoshio's analysis, attaching at white 1, drawing back at 3 and invading at 5 was best. When black plays 6, white responds with 7 through 13, devastating the territory in an actual game maneuver. This would have been powerful.

Without an obvious play to make, white made the knight's play at 28, but this was a questionable play. Since this was the meeting point of the two territorial frameworks, I thought that it was big. However, contrariwise, it made it easy for black to play on the upper side, and if black managed to make life there, white's play would end up being slack. This maneuver was dangerous.

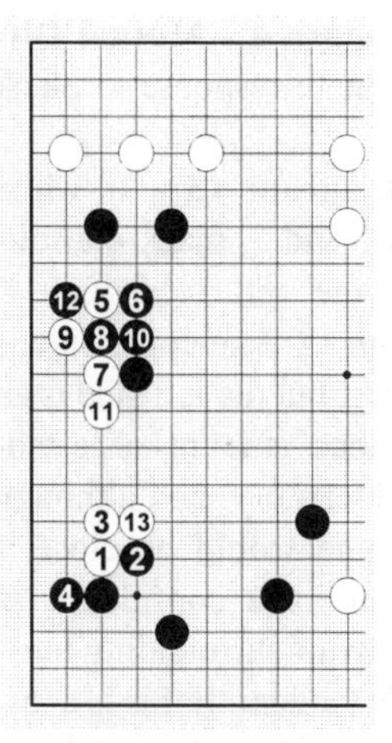

Diagram 11

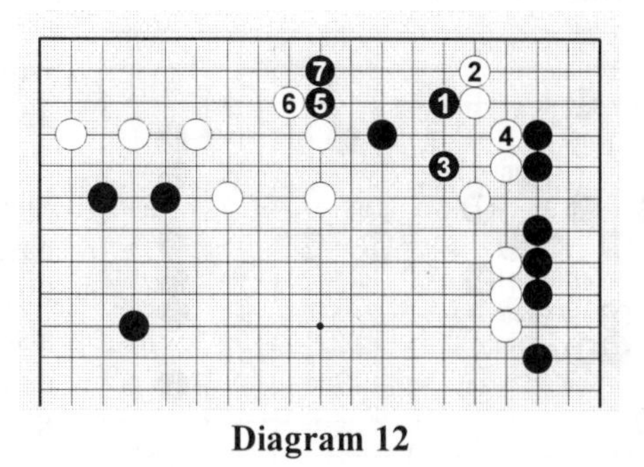

Diagram 12

Diagram 12 - For instance, there are various way to play the sequence from black 1 through 7, but the fact is that there are thin points that can be exploited on the upper side, so starting operations there would not be very difficult.

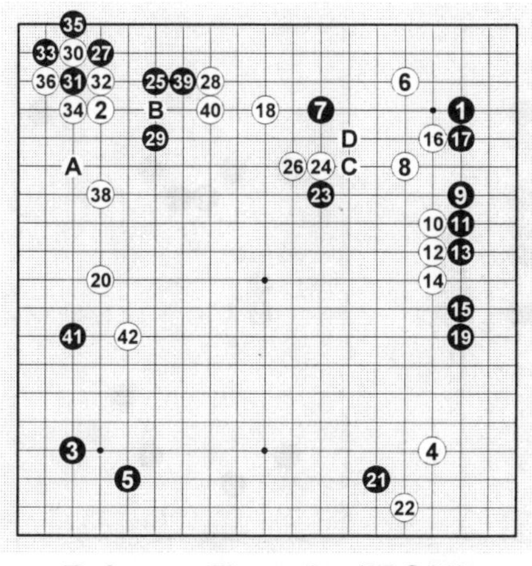

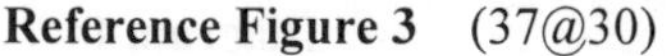

Reference Figure 3 (37@30)

From that standpoint, 28 was questionable, and white should have played as in **Diagram 11**.

Black attacked the corner with 29, and then white 30 and 32 were par for this situation. At that point, black attached at 33, vying to contest territorial frameworks.

Reference Figure 3 - [1st Annual Tengen Title Match, Game 1; 1975; White: Fujisawa Shuko 9 dan; Black: Ohira Shuzo 9 dan] Up to white 18, this bears close resemblance to the present game. The extension of black 19 was too restrained. Here, the attack on the corner with black **A**, followed by white **B** and black 20 would result in the same model as in **Reference Figure 4**. When white occupied the left side at 20, the game was wide open. The two point jump of black 23 was questionable. White let fly a strong play with 24. If black played 25 at **C**, white **D** would put black in trouble.

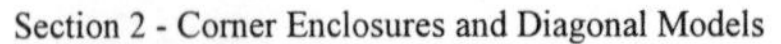

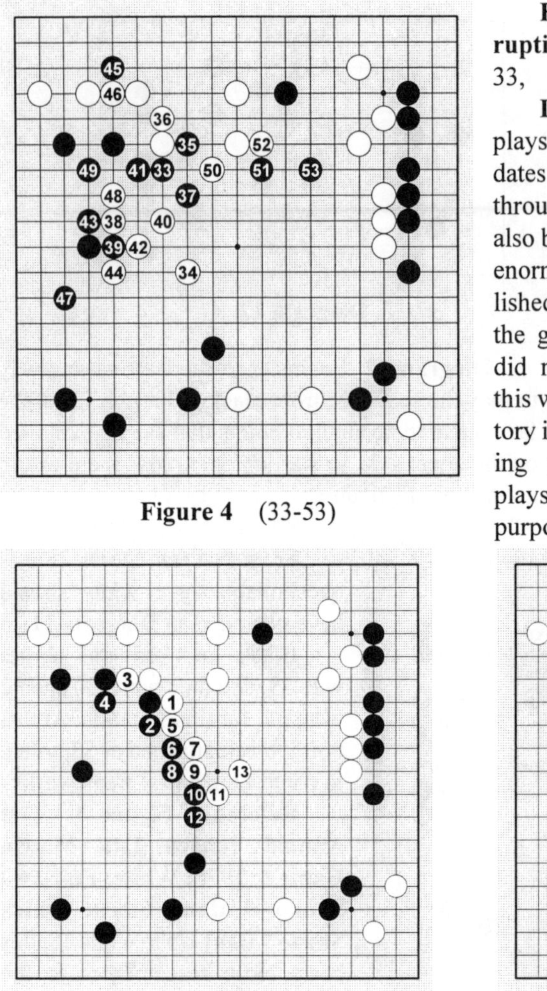

Figure 4 (33-53)

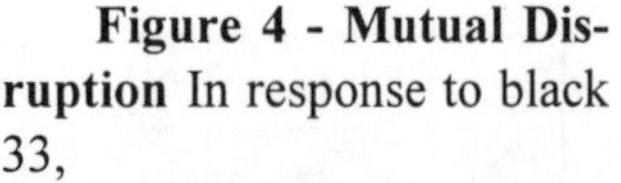

Figure 4 - Mutual Disruption In response to black 33,

Diagram 13 - If white plays 1 and 3, black consolidates the left side with 6 through 12. The upper side is also big, but the left side is an enormous amount of established territory, and although the game would be close, I did not have confidence in this way of surrounding territory in tandem. If this is a losing position, then white's plays have been played to no purpose.

Diagram 13

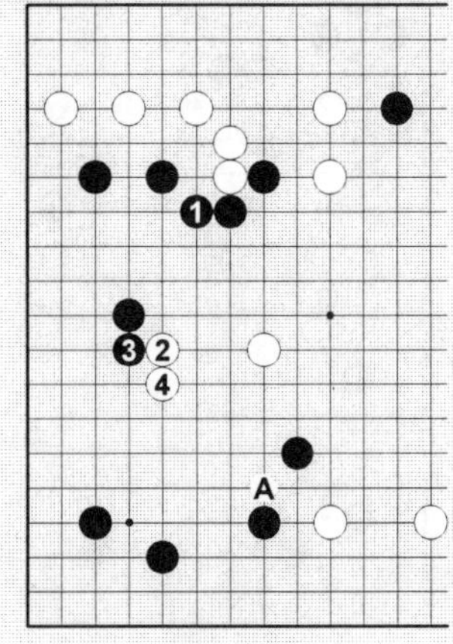

Diagram 14

White dodged at 34 in order to start erasing the territory that black was surrounding.

Black played tenaciously by making the tiger link of 35 and 37, seeking a foothold for disrupting the upper side. Play advanced here with both sides conscious of the other's territorial framework.

Diagram 14 - For 37, drawing back at black 1 was a safe strategy, but would have had little effect on white, who would be satisfied by making the erasure plays at 2 and 4. This produces the aim of striking through the knight's play at **A**. This would be a lack of fighting spirit by black.

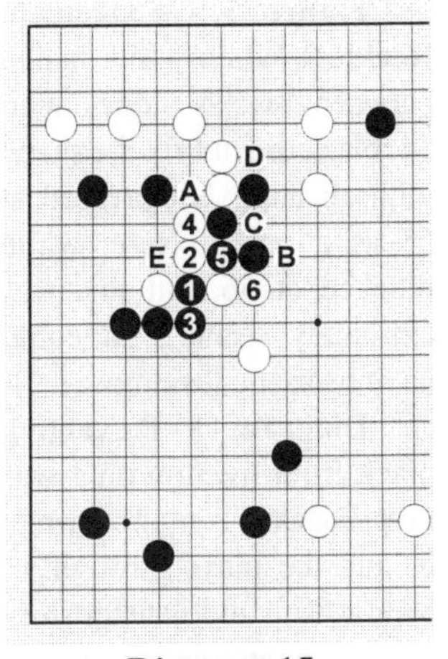

Diagram 15

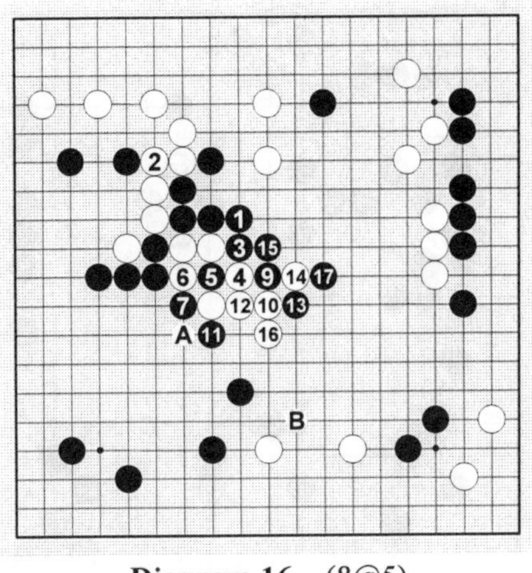

Diagram 16 (8@5)

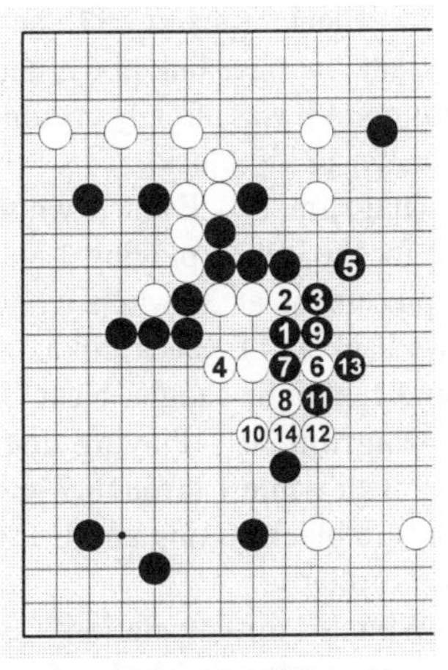

Diagram 17

The tiger link left cutting points, which white aimed at by closing in at 38 and 40.

Black pulled back at 41, but this was a slack play.

Diagram 15 - With this play, wedging in at 1 was possible. When white plays 4, black cuts at 5, and then white presses at 6. Here, if black cuts at **A**, white discards two stones with **B**, black **C**, white **D** and black **E**, but white wraps black up and squeezes, which is no good for black.

Diagram 16 - Following the previous diagram, instead of cutting at **A**, black extends at 1. In answer to white 2, black's turn at 3 is sharp, and after squeezing white, black makes two-step hanes on both sides with 7 through 13. The cut of white **A** remains, but in the present position black's fencing-in tactic of **B** is severe, and the fight is difficult for white. Using white 4 to make the bamboo link at 7 would let white make the sweeping play at 10 in good form.

Diagram 17 - If black jumps at 1, white escapes with 2 through 14, but the strong play of black 3 in the previous diagram would have put white in trouble.

After white 42 through black 49, the situation was calm for the moment. In the middle of this sequence, black peeped at 45 to create a resource for disrupting the upper side.

White peeped at 50 as a forcing play. No, that is not forcing, declared black by making the sparkling skillful finesse at 51 and 53.

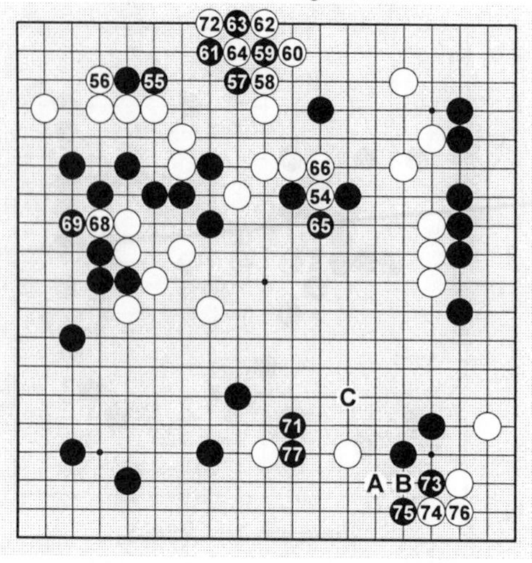

Figure 5 (54-77) (67@59, 70@64)

Figure 5 - Extremely Reckless When white haned between black's stones with 54, black did not fix the shape with an atari, but pressed at 55 as a probe. Here, white blocked at 56, but this was extremely reckless. It could have been the losing play.

Diagram 18 - Preventing black from living with 1 was best. Black 2 is met by white 3, and the plays through 11 follow. The inviolate territory on the upper side is big, giving white a promising game.

Black played 57 and made the tiger link at 61, and at this point it was already no simple matter to kill black.

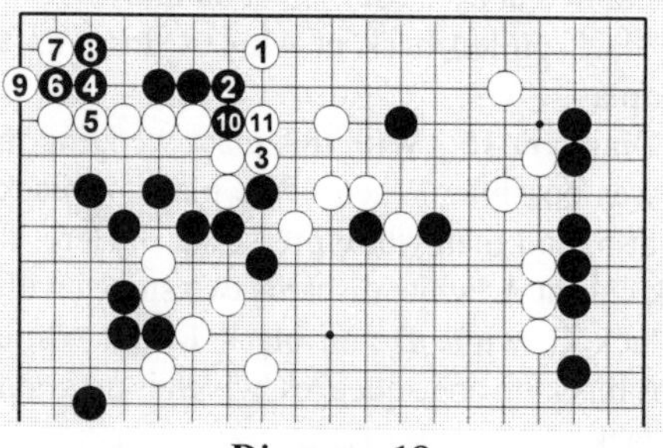

Diagram 18

Diagram 19 - Even if white went for the kill by playing 1 and the placement at 3, when white draws back at 11, black pokes at 12 and cannot be caught. Next,

Diagram 20 - Playing doggedly with white 1 through 7 and 9 leads to black cutting at 10, and white's collapse.

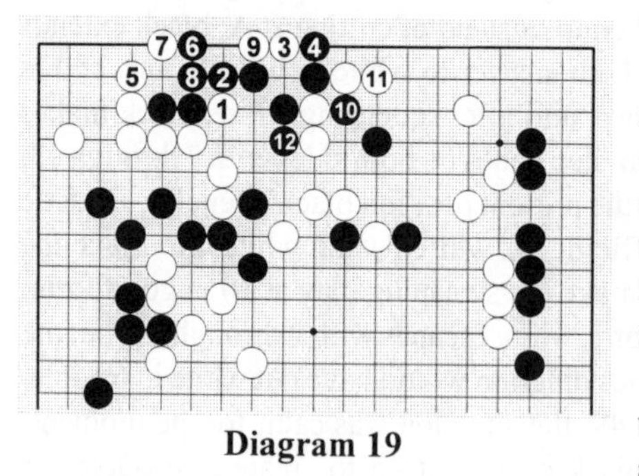

Diagram 19

White's miscalculation resulted in an inevitable ko fight with 62 and the following play, and it goes without saying that it was a disadvantageous situation for white. At this stage, I was resigned to losing.

Playing in good form, black used the atari at 65 as a ko threat, and after each side took the ko once, black made the knight's play on the lower side at 71.

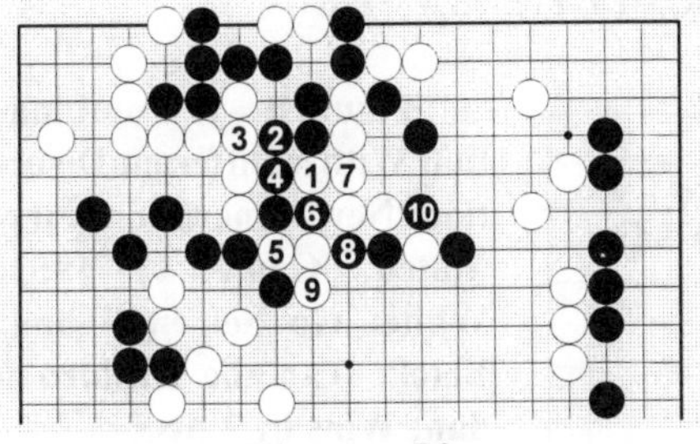
Diagram 20

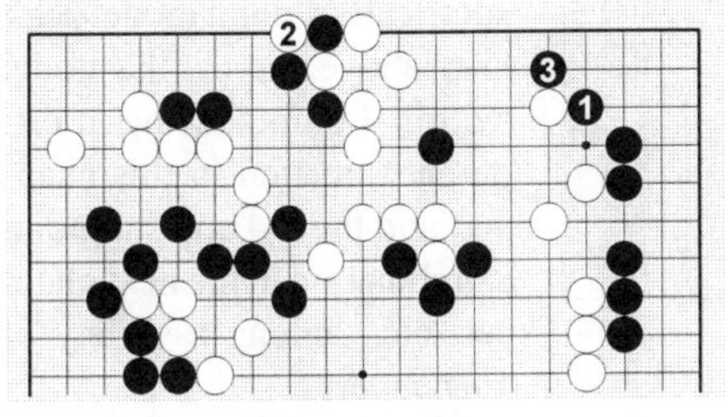
Diagram 21

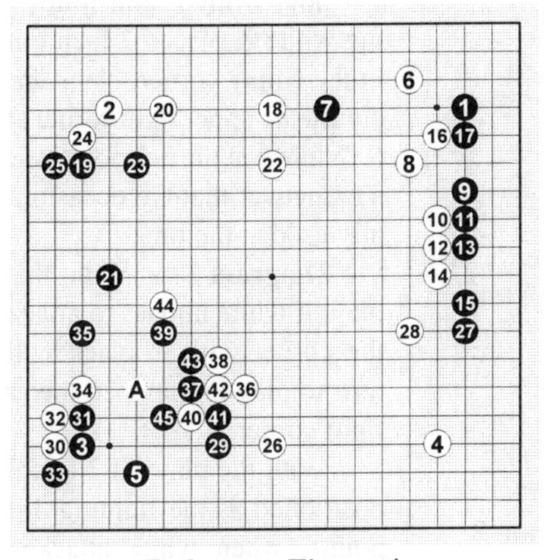
Reference Figure 4

Here, if white answered, there were no other ko threats available. Fully aware that black would block at 77, white dissolved the ko with 72. With this, black had the advantage, but in order to make the matter obvious, for 71,

Diagram 21 - It was better to play the diagonal attachment of black 1. If white plays 2 and black hanes at 3, the win is clear.

In the figure, white was left with **A**, black **B** and jumping out at white **C** to look forward to.

Black, after leading the whole game, played slackly in the latter half, and by turning the tables with the final endgame point, white won by half a point.

Reference Figure 4 - [14th Annual Meijin Title Match, Game 5; 1975; White: Otake Hideo, Meijin; Black: Ishida Yoshio 9 dan] In this game, white made the diagonal attachment of 24 in exchange for black 25. White could not neglect playing 28. White played out with 30 through 34, but not with the intention of living, in order to aid in the large territorial framework strategy of 36 and 38 from the inside. If white played 36 at **A**, the group would not die, but then black jumps to 42, and white's strategy collapses.

DIAGONAL MODEL (1) - GAME 6

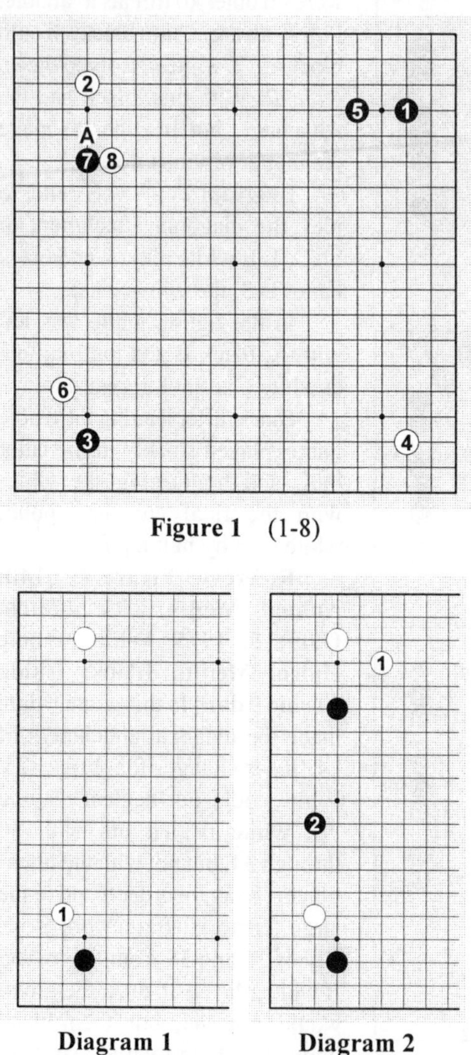

Figure 1 (1-8)

Diagram 1 **Diagram 2**

Figure 1 - A Combination With a Different Direction [New Generation, First Match, Game 1; 1953; White: Go Seigen 9 dan; Black: Yamabe Toshiro 6 dan; Wins by 2 pts.]

There are various diagonal models. Besides the symmetrical 3-4 point model dealt with above, there is the model with 3-4 points facing in different direction in this chapter, and the 3-4 and star point combination in the next chapter, etc., among a variety of maneuvers.

After black played at the 3-4 point with 1, and following white 2, placed 3 facing it in the empty corner, black enclosed the upper right corner at 5. White 4 at the 3-3 point was a maneuver that Go occasionally used at the time.

Diagram 1 - With this play, if white hurries to attack the corner with 1, black will turn to play in the open lower right corner.

With the plays at 2 and 3 positioned as the fighting 3-4 points, when white attacked the corner with 6, black made the two point high attack on the corner at 7. For this play, the high attack on the corner at **A** is also often played.

White's severe attachment at 8 set things in motion on the board.

Diagram 2 - Defending at white 1 is slack since it lets black make the ideal pincer at 2. This kind of play was not in keeping with Go's taste.

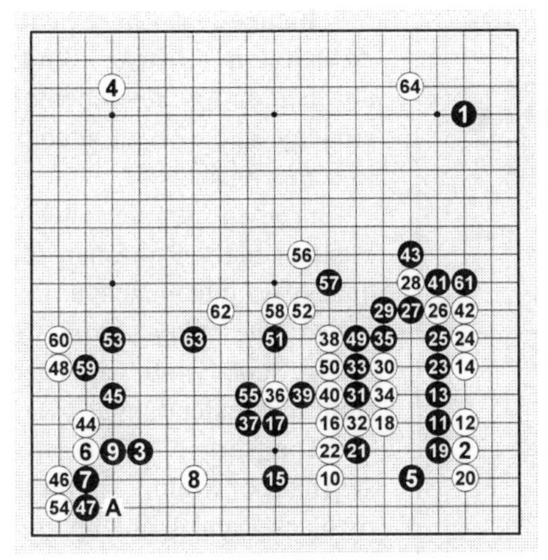

Reference Figure 1

Reference Figure 1 - [Castle Game, Jubango, Game 1; 1705; White: Yasui Sankaku (4th hereditary Yasui); Black: Honinbo Dochi (Meijin, 5th hereditary Honinbo)] Here is an example where, after black 1, instead of the 3-4 point play, the 5-4 point was played with 3. For 47, the tiger link of black **A** made shape, and it was this miss that was the cause of a painful and difficult fight for black. The play at 59 was a difficult one to play, and making it at 64 would have left the outlook unclear. This is a famous game in which the 16 year old Dochi, challenging Sankaku, played a series of exquisite plays in the endgame and won by 1 point.

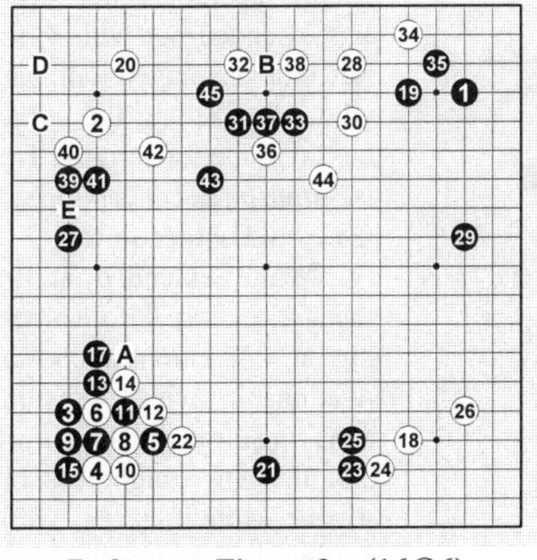

Reference Figure 2 (16@6)

Reference Figure 2 - [1846; White: Honinbo Jowa, Meijin (12th hereditary Honinbo); Black: Tsuchiya Shuwa (14th hereditary Honinbo)] Here is a 3-4 and 5-3 point play diagonal pattern. Jowa, who liked to play the Taisha joseki, adopted a simple strategy in this game. Even if black used 15 to play at **A**, after the joseki with white 6, black 15, white 11 and black 17, white would probably still play at 18. Black 27 was a sound and solid play, but it was also possible to play **B** here, followed by white 29, black **C**, white **D** and black **E**.

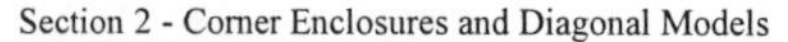

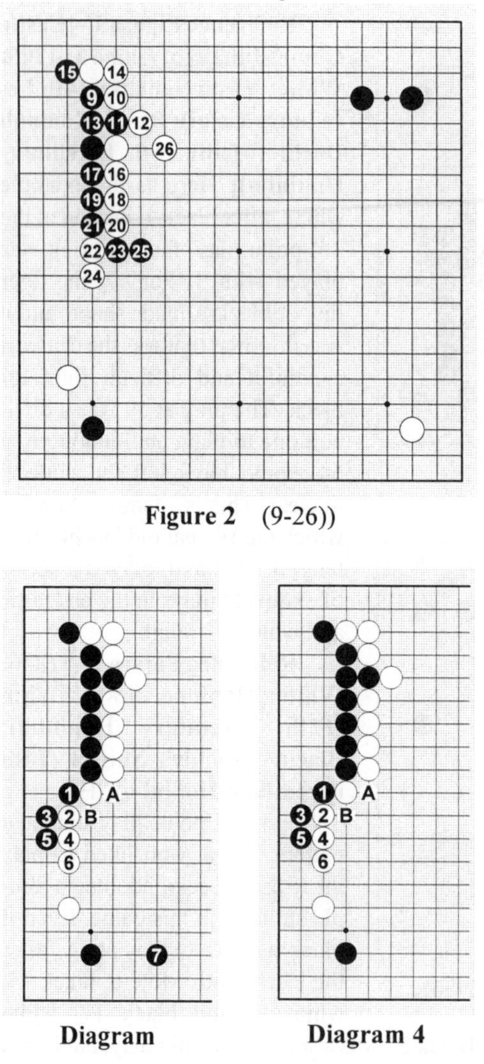

Figure 2 (9-26))

Diagram

Diagram 4

Figure 2 - A Large Scale Attachment Joseki White attached on top, one opening strategy, and also an attempt to coerce black.

From the jumping attachment of black 9 through the hane of 15, the maneuver followed the play order of joseki, but white deviated from it by extending at 16.

Diagram 3 - The two-step hane of white 1, followed by black 2 and 4, and up to 8, is a common sequence that anyone would play. However, in this position, once black has extended out with 4, the left side is played out, and white Δ attacking the corner has no scope for activity. This is a uninspired conception that Go would not resort to.

White extended at 16, then twice more before blocking at 22, emphasizing the relationship with the stone attacking the corner. Territorially, this was a slight loss, but it gave white thickness while putting the previously played stone to use. It is hoped that the difference between this and **Diagram 3** is apparent.

Black also found a hackneyed defensive play here unattractive, and so bluntly cut above at 23. One can feel young Yamabe's exuberance in this play.

Diagram 4 - With this play, instead of cutting, playing the hane from below at 1 could also be considered. When white replies with the two-step hane at 2, black plays 3 and pushes at 5, before making the two point extension at 7. Profit is pitted against outward influence here, and black will aim at the cut at **A**. If white uses 4 to connect at **B**, black makes good shape by extending straight out at 5.

According to Yamabe,

Diagram 5 - If he played this game today, he would probably make the territorially tight play of black 1. Should white answer with 2 and 4, black extends at 5, and this would be another pattern.

Diagram 6 - In response to black's descent, if white makes the atari at 1 and connects at 3, black extends at 4. Black sacrifices two stones and then turns to a good point elsewhere.

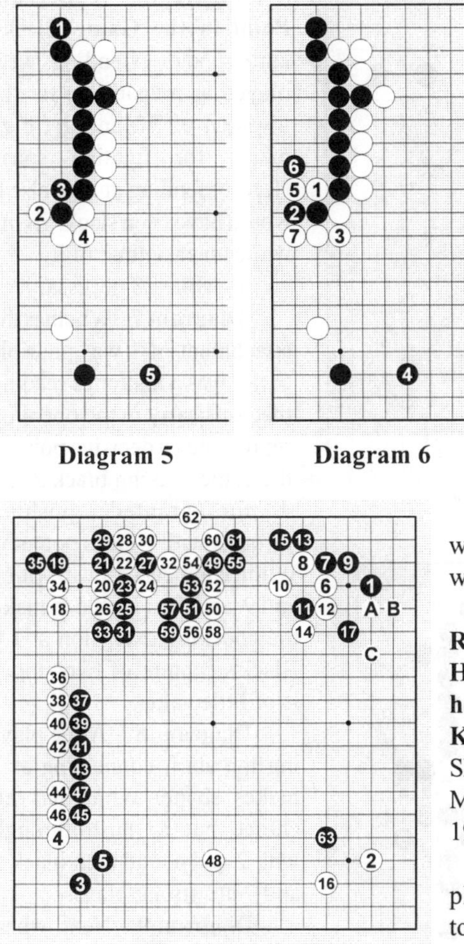

Diagram 5

Diagram 6

Reference Figure 3

Black extended to 25, and white put the formation in order with 26.

Reference Figure 3 - [Meijin Retirement Game; 1938; White: Honinbo Shusai, Meijin (21st hereditary Honinbo); Black: Kitani Minoru 7 dan] This is Shusai's retirement game as Meijin, and his opponent was the 19 year old Kitani.

In answer to white 2, black played 3 in this direction, leading to white 4 and the diagonal play of black 5. Black 17 prevented white from making good shape with **A**, black **B** and white **C**.

White 24 and 26 created a new pattern. Black 37 and the plays through 47 were a thick and strong maneuver. This permitted white 48, and black made the erasure play at 63.

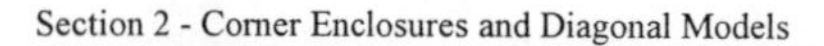

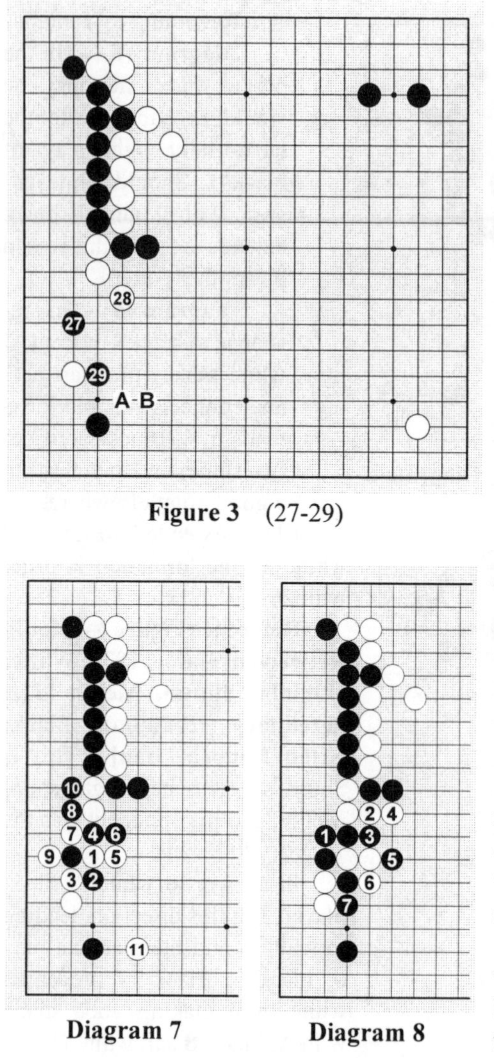

Figure 3 (27-29)

Diagram 7

Diagram 8

Figure 3 - A Decisive Point in the Game Black's cutting and extending were played as preparation for the invasion of 27, and get high marks for fighting spirit. Here, defending at **A** or else **B** would have been slack, giving white an easy time of it.

Is white 28 necessary?

Diagram 7 - Whether the attachment of 1 was possible or not was a matter of reading that, this early in the opening, represented a decisive point in the game. Taking black 2 and 4 for granted, pushing through with 6 lacks potency. White engineers a swap with 7 and 9, and then is able to make the checking extension at 11. Black's capture of two stones is of little value.

Diagram 8 - After playing the atari, connecting at 1 makes shape. White has no choice but to push through with 2 and 4, and then black 5 and 7 are strong plays.

Diagram 9 - Next, when white plays 8 through 12, black extends at 13, and since the thickness gained by capturing three stones was good, this is a sufficient position for black. If white uses 10 to play out at 11, black is well off after 10, white **A**, black **B** and white **C**.

Diagram 10 - If white responds by making the diagonal play at 1, black plays 2 and hanes out at 4, and then the tight connection of 6 is a good play.

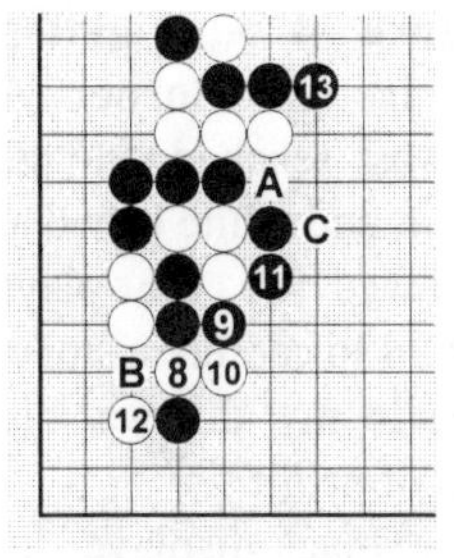

Diagram 9

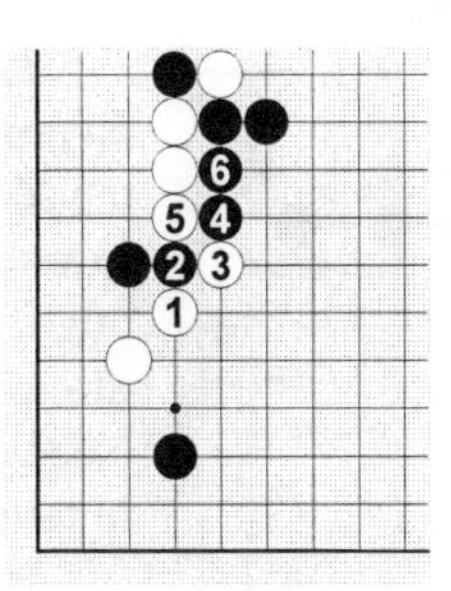

Diagram 10

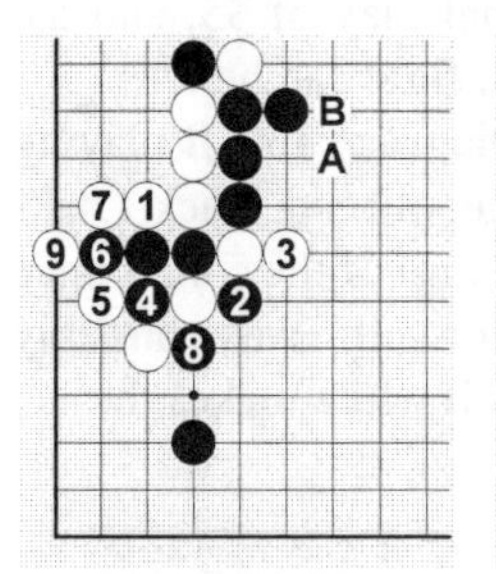

Diagram 11
(10 above 8)

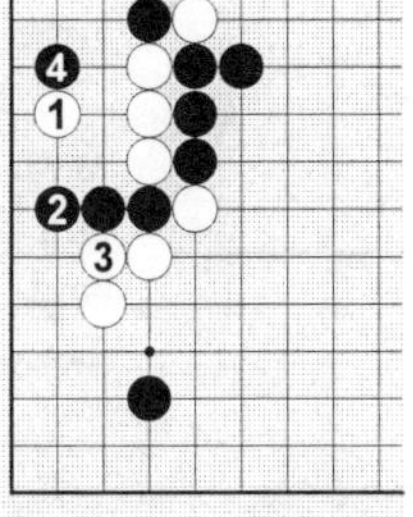

Diagram 12

Diagram 11 - Next, if white blocks at 1, black plays atari with 2 and 4. Even though white can squeeze with 5 through 9, it is ineffective, and it will be difficult for white to make life on the side. White **A** would be rendered useless by black **B**. If white 5 connects at 8, the black hane at 7 annihilates white.

Diagram 12 - At the same time, if white jumps to 1, descending to black 2 is a good play, and when white plays 3, black attaches at 4, and white's resources are exhausted.

It might seem as though white was overpowered by black's fighting spirit, but playing the diagonal play of 28 was unavoidable.

Black attached at 29, demonstrating the value of the invading stone.

Reference Figure 4

Reference Figure 4 - [Oteai Ranking Tournament, Spring Session; 1929; White: Miyasaka Shinji 6 dan; Black: Suzuki Hideko 3 dan] Black made a high corner enclosure with 3 and 5. Miyazaka: "If white played 20 at **A** under the star point, black would be left with the good point of the checking extension at **B**." Suzuki: "Perhaps black should have used 39 to make the fencing-in tactic at **C**. For 49, black should have defended at 53." White was able to make shape with the atari at 54.

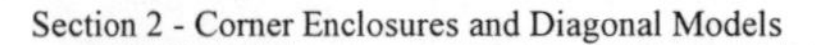

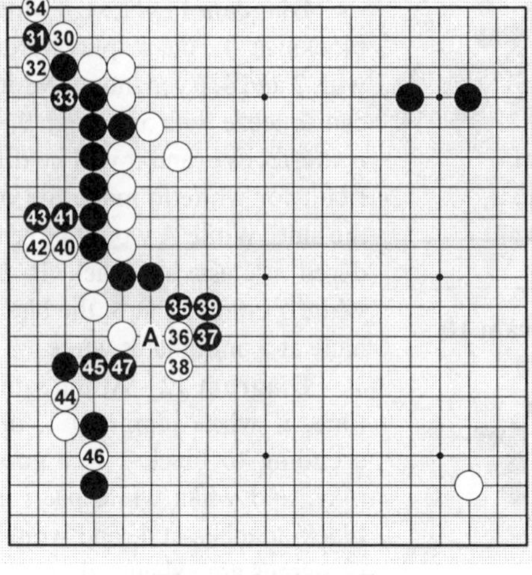

Figure 4 (30-47)

Figure 4 - Fighting Erupts in the Corner A pause was reached in the lower left, and white haned at 30 followed by the plays through 34 to capture a stone. Needless to say, this was big in terms of profit.

Here, black displayed an imposing manner with the diagonal play of 35, and the urge to fight can be felt.

Diagram 13 - If playing with a cool head, black 1, taking control of the corner once and for all, was possibly better. If white makes the

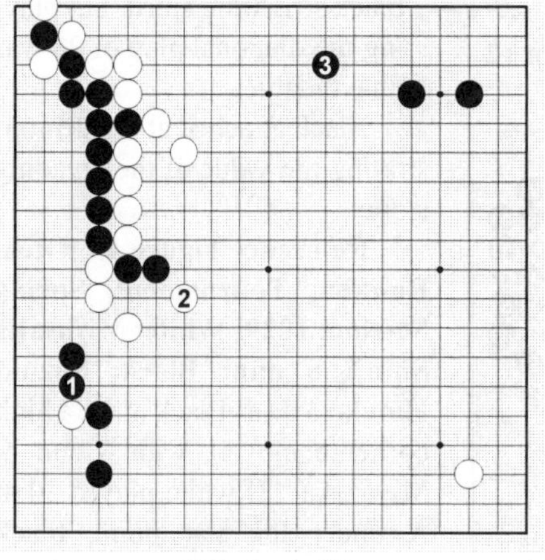

Diagram 13

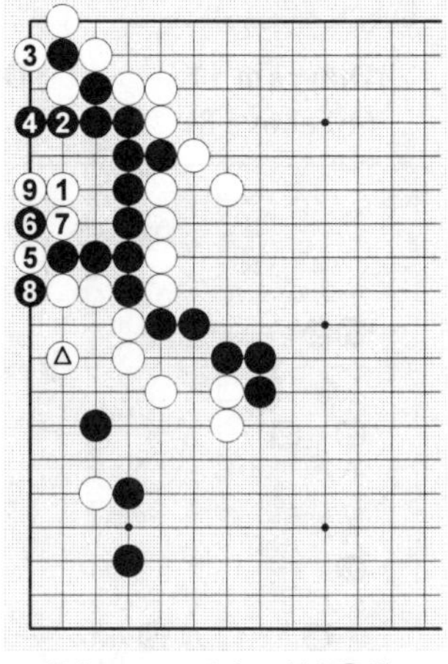

Diagram 14 (10@5)

fencing-in tactic at 2, black plays the ideal point at 3, and this would also be a fine game. The two stones in the center still reverberate with potential, and this is an easy game for black to play.

White played forcing plays with 40 and 42, but after black 43, white could hope for nothing further.

Diagram 14 -Even if white gets to strengthen the position with Δ, trying to capture with 1 does not work. After 10, black's group is alive.

When black played out in the center with 35,

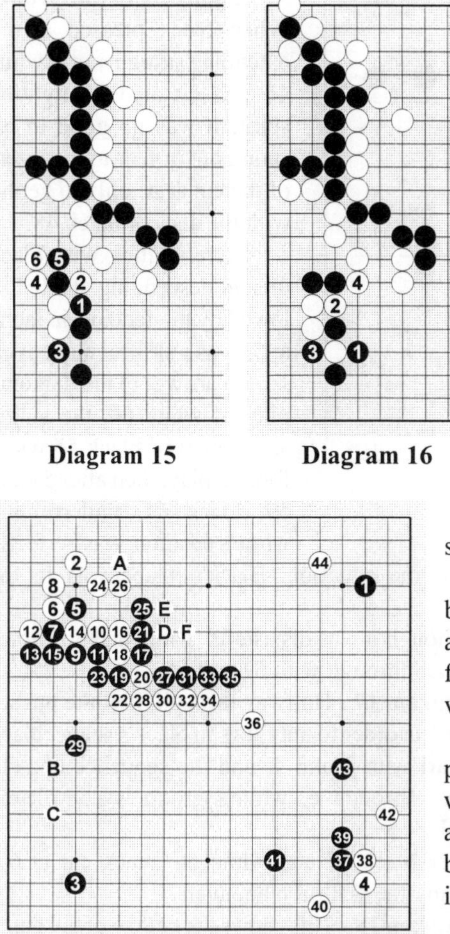

Diagram 15 Diagram 16

Reference Figure 5

white could not just sit still, and so put the stones in the lower left corner into motion to set up a decisive confrontation.

First, white attached at 36 and extended to 38, waited for black to connect at 39, then butted against black's stone with 44.

It was natural for black to extend at 45.

Diagram 15 - If black uses this play to block at 1, white gets settled simply with 2 through 6.

The hane between black's stones at 46 was a skillful finesse.

In response to this, pressing at black 47 was a fierce play that aimed at cutting at **A**, and with the following plays, an unexpected variation resulted.

Diagram 16 - At 47, if black plays atari at 1, a swap takes place with white 2 and 4. Black is thick and strong after capturing a stone, but white is also satisfied by taking two stones.

Reference Figure 5 - [20th Annual Prime Minister's Cup, Game 1; 1976; White: Kobayashi Koichi 7 dan; Black: Ishida Akira 7 dan] Recently, the high attack on the corner at black 5 is most often played. If white played 10 at **A**, the game would proceed with black **B**, or else **C**. Connecting with black 11 at 14 would be met by the diagonal play at 24, which would enhance the value of the attack on the corner at 44. Pushing through and cutting with white 20 was a new play. Before this, the pattern with 18 at 21, black **D**, white **E** and black **F** was played frequently.

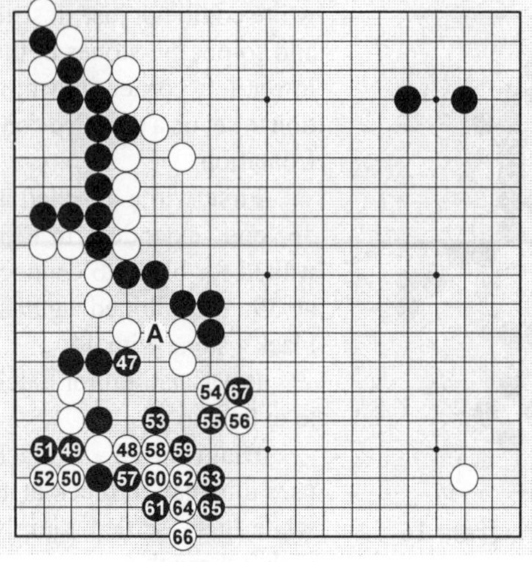

Figure 5 (47-67)

Figure 5 - In the Groove

When black pressed at 47, extending straight out at white 48 was dictated by fighting spirit. It was no good to respond out of fear to the threat of the cut at **A**, only to get hit with the atari of black 48.

Here, cutting with black 49 and descending at 51, followed by the fencing-in tactic at 53 was a skillful maneuver.

In answer to the diagonal play of white 54, the single attachment of black 55 was a forcing play, then after 57 and 59, black 61, undermining white's position, was perfectly suited to the situation. Black's shape was in the groove.

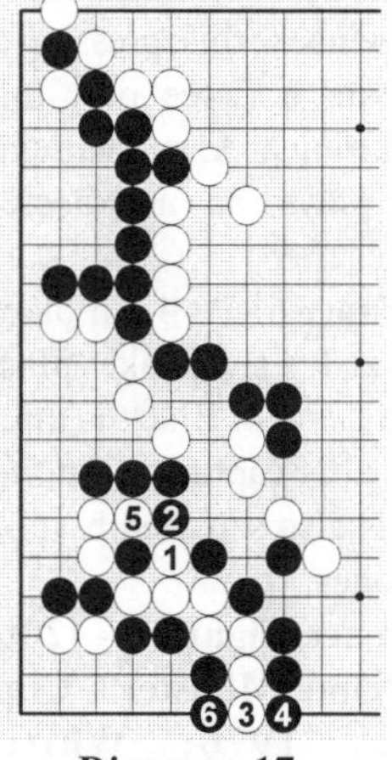

Diagram 17

Although it was distasteful, white had no choice but to push through with 62 and 64.

Diagram 17 - Halfway through, if white pushes out with 1 in order to put flaws in black's shape, black plays atari with 2 and 4, and the sequence ends in calamity. Through 6, white's group is completely captured.

After black 65 and white 66, black cut at 67, completing the skillful maneuver.

Diagram 18 - This shows the course of the game following Figure 5.

When white played to the outside with 70 and 72, black 73 forced white 74, and then black cut off the tail of white's group with 75. Through 80, a fine swap was orchestrated. White gained twenty-odd points of profit in the lower left, but black ripped away the five stones on the left side, and the thickness on the lower side was directed towards white's weak stones in the center. This was a good result for black.

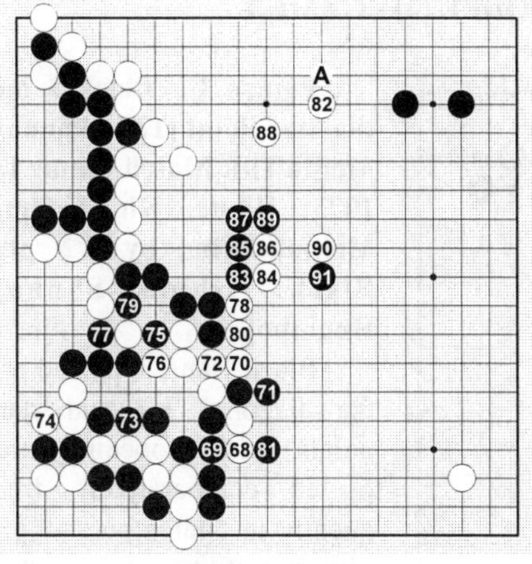

Diagram 18

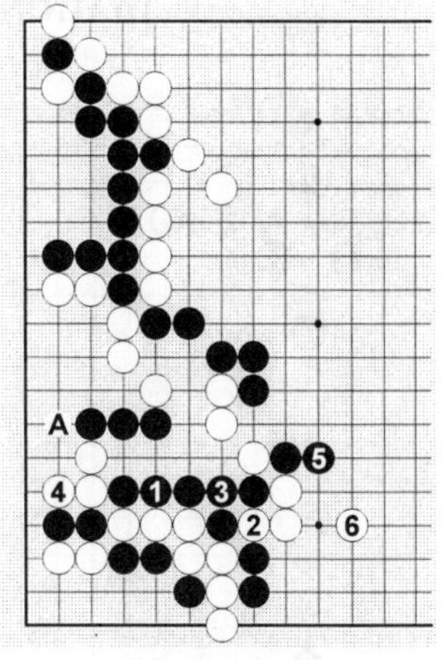

Diagram 19

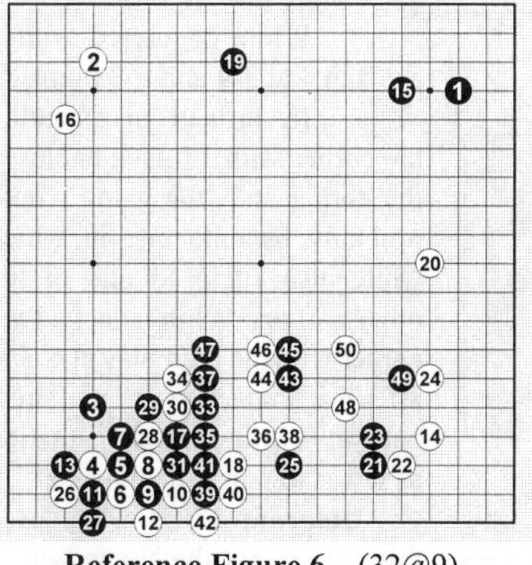

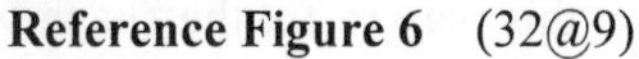

Reference Figure 6 (32@9)

Diagram 19 - Amidst this order of plays, black could have used the connection of 69 to connect at 1, and after white 2 and 4, extend at black 5, capturing a few more stones, but white also makes a big profit on the lower side with 6. White also has the potential of playing hane at **A**, so black could not choose this continuation.

The attachment of black 81 was slack. The extension at **A** on the upper side was the key point in the overall board position, and white could not play out with the two stones on the lower side.

White made the extension at 82, and black launched an attack against this white group with 83 through 89, and then 91, engineering a splendid struggle in the center.

Reference Figure 6 - [2nd Annual Meijin League; 1977; White: Kato Masao, 10 Dan; Black: Kubouchi Shuchi 9 dan] Black played the high play at 3, and then the joseki from 5 through 13 was Kubouchi's forte. Cutting with white 26 was questionable, but pushing through with 28, cutting with 30, and the writhing skirmishing that followed was tremendous. For 36, attaching at 38 was better. After black 49 and white 50, the melee spread to the center.

DIAGONAL MODEL (2) - GAME 1

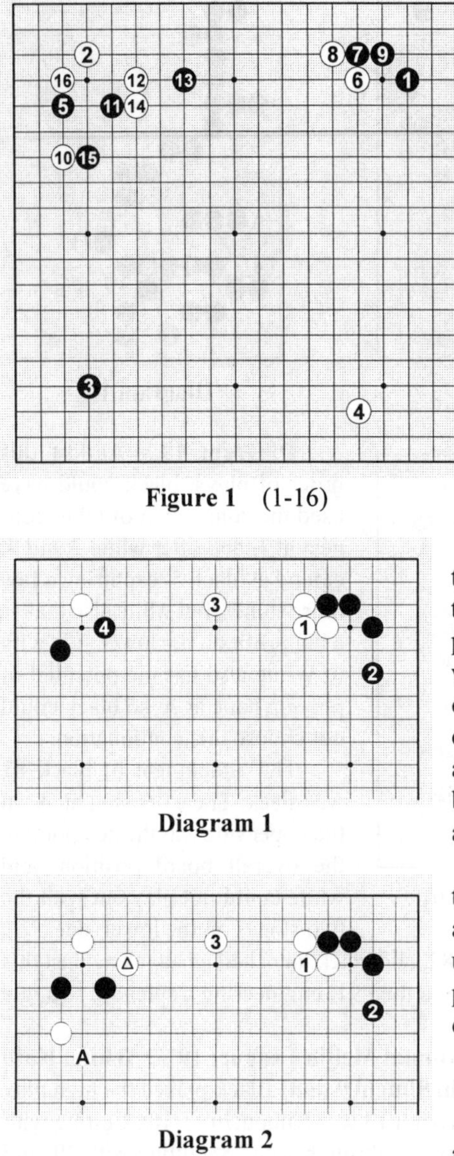

Figure 1 (1-16)

Diagram 1

Diagram 2

Figure 1 - Black 3 on the Star Point [12th Annual Meijin Title Match, Game 4; 1973; White: Rin Kaiho, Meijin; Wins by 1/2 pt; Black: Ishida Shuho, Honinbo]

Black 1 and 3, placed on the diagonal 3-4 and star points in this opening, are played comparatively frequently in contemporary go. The versatility of the star point stone is the distinctive feature that is produced.

White countered with 2 and 4 at 3-4 and 5-3 points.

If, instead of attacking the corner with 5, black enclosed the corner at 7, the game would probably become one in which white also enclosed one of the other corners. White attacked the corner with the high play at 6, and after black attached at 7 and drew back at 9, white left the situation as it was to make the pincer at 10.

Diagram 1 - If white used this play to fix the shape with 1 and made the low extension on the upper side at 3, black would apply pressure with 4, and white's stones duplicate effort.

After black 11, white played 12, and with that,

Diagram 2 - White ideally aimed to play the joseki with 1 and 3, whereupon Δ maintains white's stance. Of course, before that black would make the fencing-in tactic at **A**, and then white would probably play in this area.

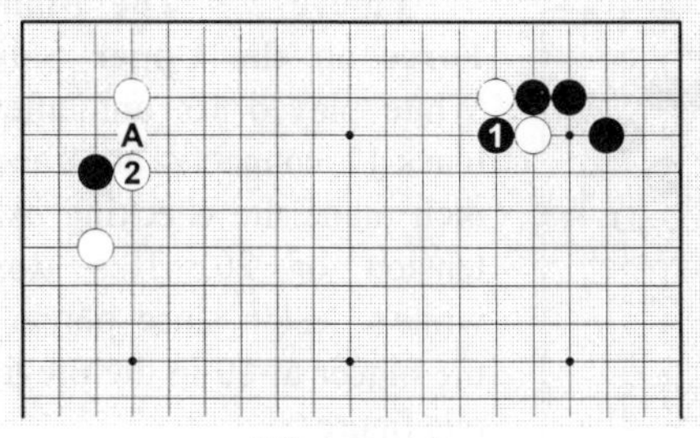

Diagram 3

Diagram 3 - Instead of jumping at 11, if black cut at 1, white would seal off the upper left with 2. Since the ladder following black's hane between white's stones at **A** is unfavorable, this position is no good for black.

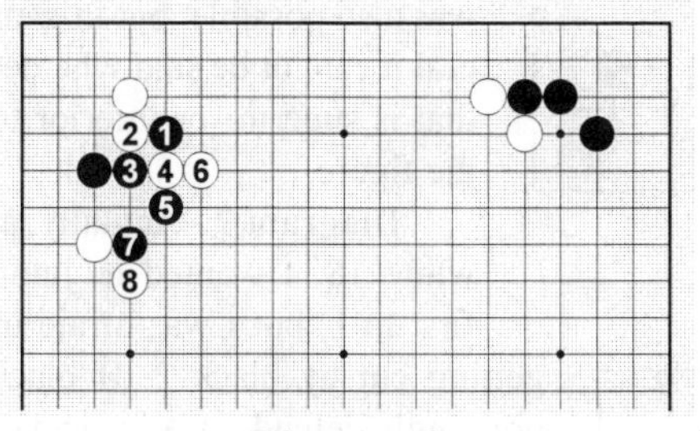

Diagram 4

Diagram 4 - At 11, if black plays the fencing-in tactic at 1, white pokes at 2 and cuts at 4, then initiates a sudden fight with the hane at 8. In that case, there is a strong possibility that white's two stones in the upper right will play a part in the fighting.

Black made the pincer at 13.

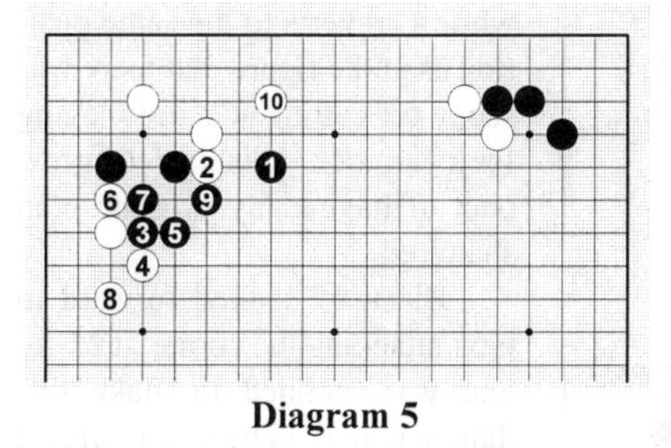

Diagram 5

Diagram 5 - Here, playing high at 1 is another possibility, but with the plays through 10, white builds positions on both sides, and has no cause for dissatisfaction.

In this game, the joseki was chosen where white presses at 14 and makes the diagonal attachment at 16.

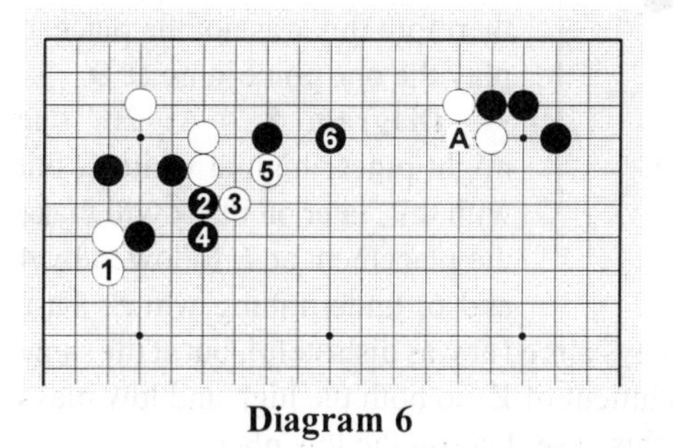

Diagram 6

Diagram 6 - If white used 16 to draw back at 1, the pattern from black 2 through 6 exposes the weak point of the cut at **A**, and so is not an advisable strategy for white.

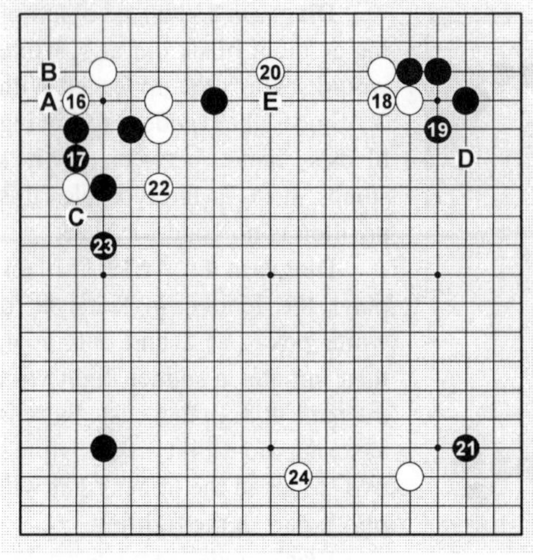

Figure 2 (16-24)

Figure 2 - The Main Force on the Upper Side White played 16, and after black 17, connected at 18 and then made the checking extension of 20. This was white's design since playing the pincer at 10 in the previous figure.

For 17, the pattern with black **A**, white **B** and black **C** was also possible, but in general it cannot be said whether that is superior or inferior to the figure.

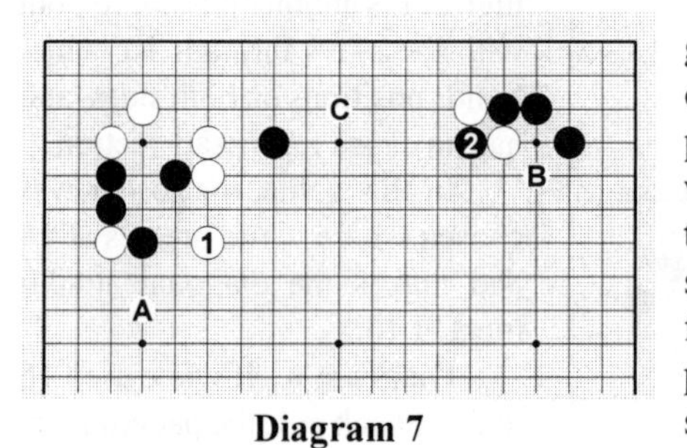

Diagram 7

Diagram 7 - Actually, at white 18, I wanted to jump first to 1, but I was afraid of getting cut by black 2. If black obligingly defends at **A** instead of playing 2, white 2, black **B** and white **C** reverts to the same position as in the figure, but there was scope for cutting at 2 and playing for a variation. I disliked the prospect of having my original plan shattered.

Black 19 looked forward to next attacking the corner at 21, so one was inclined to make this diagonal play. There was also a consciousness of the upper side, therefore this was not the place to play the one point jump at **D**.

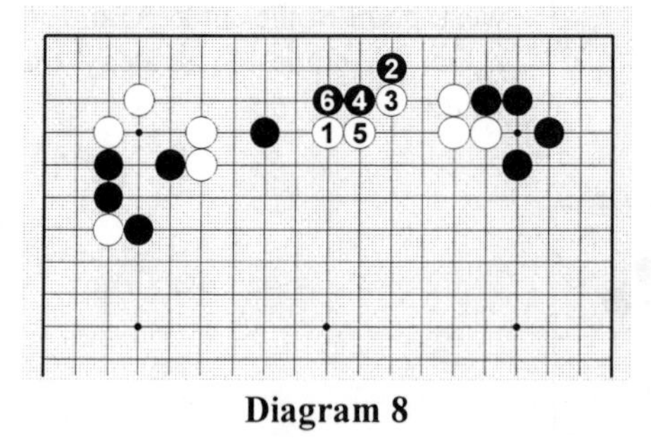

Diagram 8

Diagram 8 - At 20, one might pincer high at white 1, but with this, later on black will make the placement at 2, followed by 4 and 6, undermining white's base while living easily. Having these plays aimed at was distasteful, but at the same time, 20 in the figure left the attachment of **E**, so both the high and low plays had their good and bad points. In this case, I chose the low play.

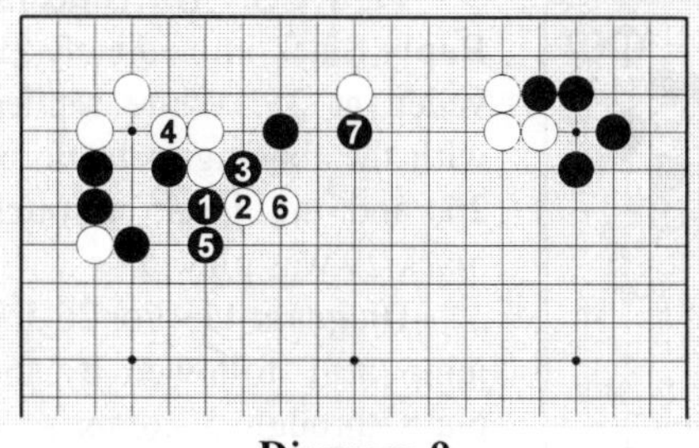

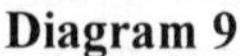

Diagram 9

Since the object was to concentrate forces on the upper side, white jumped to 22 in exchange for black 23. Since black also had to be concerned about having white aim at drawing back at **C**, jumping to 23 was the true play.

Diagram 9 - If 22 was not played, black can aim at playing 1 and cutting at 3, then moving out at 7, which will make it difficult for white to consolidate the upper side.

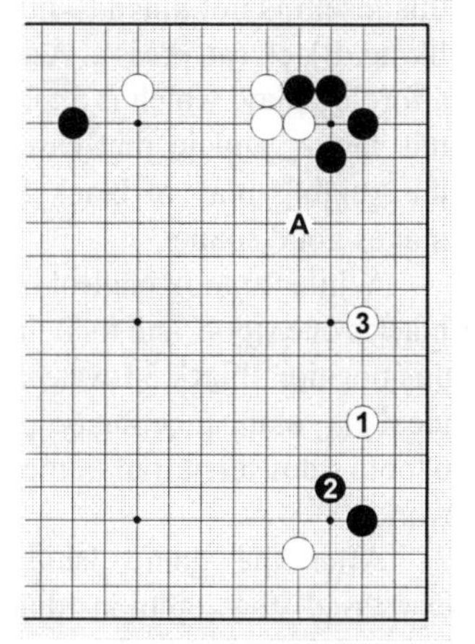

Diagram 10

In response to black 21, white 24 was the extension to make in this position.

Diagram 10 - Playing this to develop on the right with 1 and 3 would be a mistake in direction. In this game, the correct way of thinking may be said to invite black to surround the right, and then expand the upper side with white **A**.

Reference Figure 1 - [Oteai Ranking Tournament, Autumn Session; 1927; White: Inoue Ichiro 3 dan; Black: Murashima Yoshikatsu] The 3-4 and star point diagonal model appeared comparatively early. Murashima: "After the star point at 3, 5 was a play that was not played often, so this was the scheme here." Inoue: "White should have played 16 as the knight's play at **A**. For 36, white should have fixed the shape with **B**, black **C**, white 39 and black **D**."

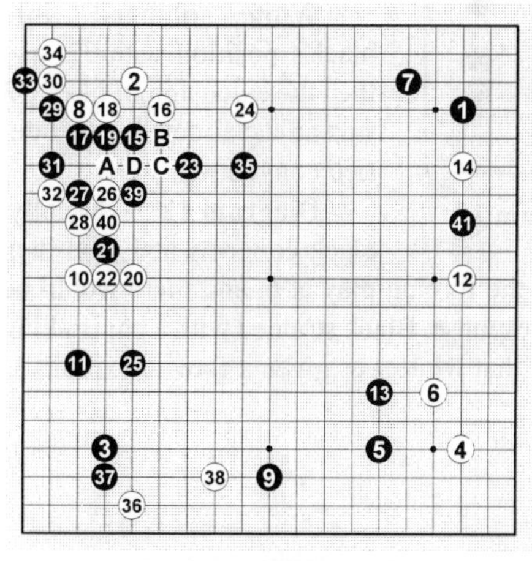

Reference Figure 1

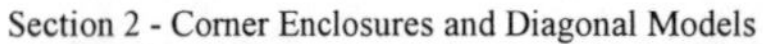

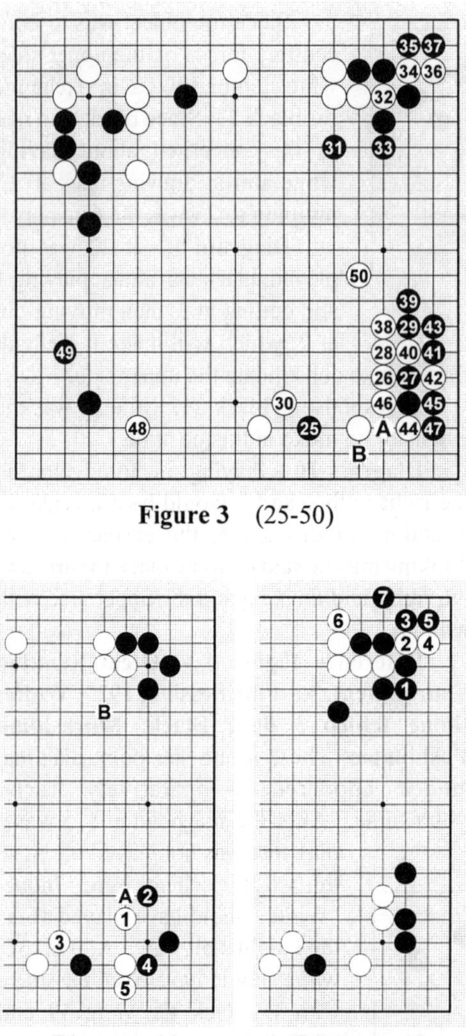

Figure 3 (25-50)

Diagram 11 **Diagram 12**

Figure 3 - An Unusual Reply Black immediately invaded at 25. White replied with the fencing-in tactic of 26, and the joseki through black 29 was played.

Diagram 11 - For 26, the jump at 1 followed by the plays through 5 comprise a shape that is often played, but this joseki is not much to my liking. Black can press at **A** as a forcing play, which is a minus factor, and in that case, the knight's play of black **B** makes good shape.

White 30 took control of black's one stone, and then, in this position, black 31 was an ideal play at the meeting point of both sides' territorial frameworks.

After the game Ishida expressed the opinion that before 31 was played it was better to exchange black **A** for white **B** in the lower right.

White plunged into black's position with 32, and then the extension of black 33 was an usual defense that defied convention.

Diagram 12 - Usually, black connects at 1, and then white plays 2 and 4 before making the forcing play at 6, and there would be nothing out of the normal with this response. Black strained with a painstaking play here, but it was just because of that white was given a flaw to exploit.

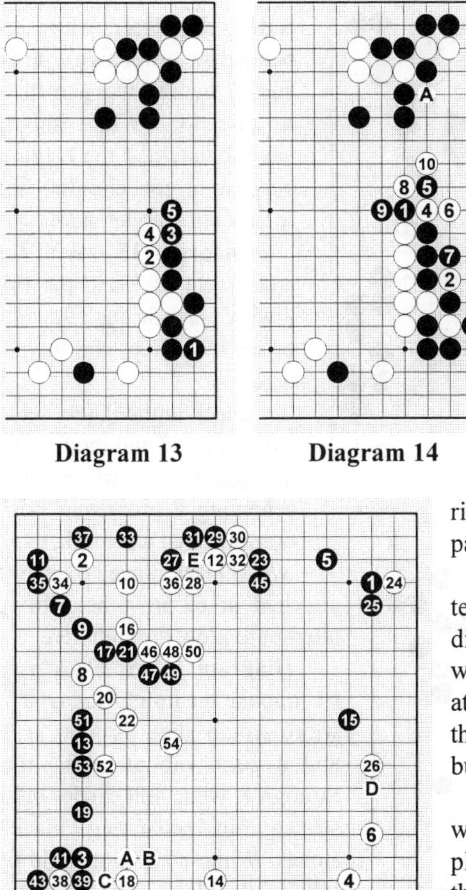

Diagram 13 Diagram 14

Reference Figure 2

Right away, white pressed at 38, and then throwing in the cut here at 42 followed the proper order of plays. Black had no choice but to connect at 43, and then white built thickness and strength with the forcing plays at 44 and 46, putting black into a painful and difficult position.

Diagram 13 - By the same token, if black used 43 to atari at 1, white could press at 2 and 4 as forcing plays, and after black 5 the right side is leveled. This is more pain than was called for.

Diagram 14 - If black counterattacks with 5 in the previous diagram by playing the hane at 1, white answers with 4 through the atari at 10, insuring the life of these stones. The cut at **A** is a burden for black.

White attacked the corner with 48, then made the knight's play at 50, scoring a success with this shape. The bad potential left behind with the extension of black 33 would much later come back to haunt black.

Reference Figure 2 - [21st Annual Honinbo League; 1966; White: Rin Kaiho, Meijin; Black: Otake Hideo 7 dan] After playing the star point at 3, black made a corner enclosure at 5 and white did the same at 6. For 19, black **A**, white **B** and black **C** could have been considered. If white used 26 to defend at 36, black would make the checking extension at **D**. At 27, the attachment of black **E** would have been more unpleasant for white.

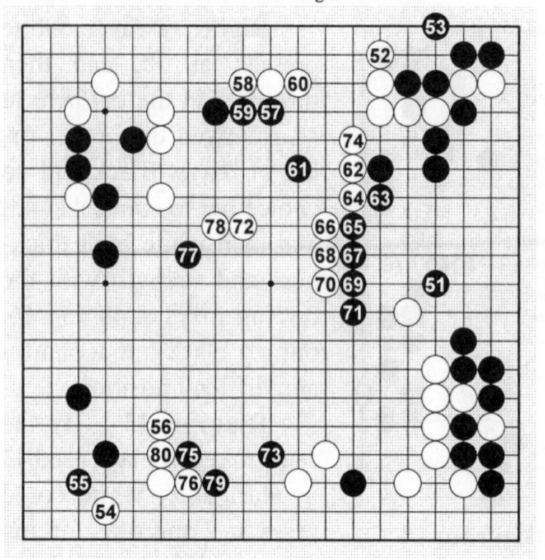

Figure 4 (51-80)

Figure 4 - The Upper Side is Big Here, white expanded the lower side with 54 and 56, but this was a mistake in direction. White should have maintained the original purpose of concentrating the focus on the upper side.

Diagram 15 - With the attachment of 1 and the following plays through 9, white could have kept the advantage.

Black immediately set to work with 57 and the following plays, and white, after achieving a promising position, suffered a setback.

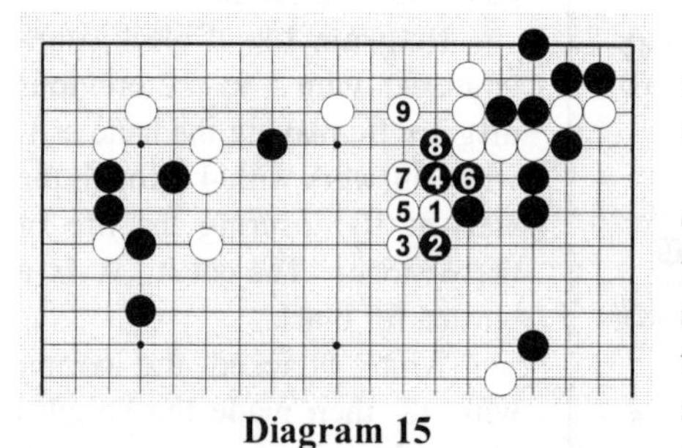

Diagram 15

When black played 61, white attached at 62 in a headstrong attempt to plow through here.

Diagram 16 - If black used 61 to make the knight's play at 1, white would slice through at 2, and it goes without saying that through 8, white still carries out a strategy of separating black's stones. White could not stand by idly while black devastated the upper side.

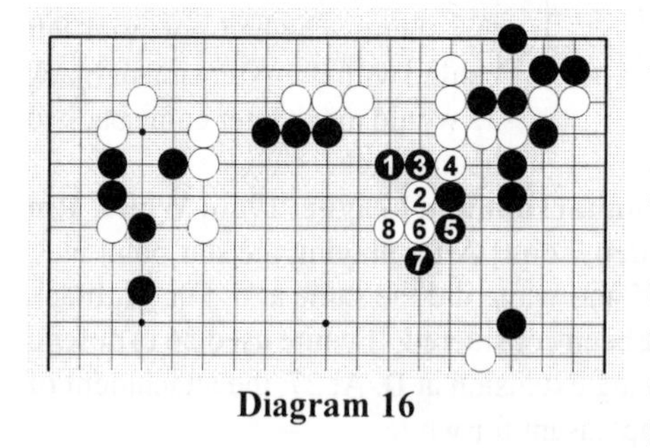

Diagram 16

Black drew back at 63 after seeing that a hane at 64 would not work out well.

Diagram 17 - In response to black 1, white hanes out at 2. After pressing at 6, one way or another white would separate black's groups.

Diagram 18 - If black hanes out with 1 here, white can extend strongly at 2. After black 5 and white 6,

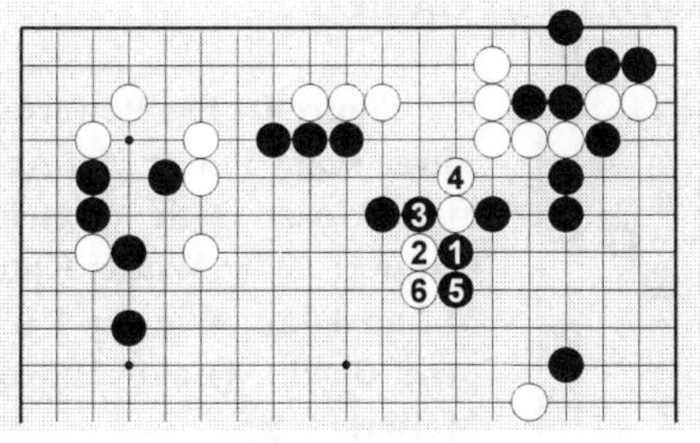
Diagram 17

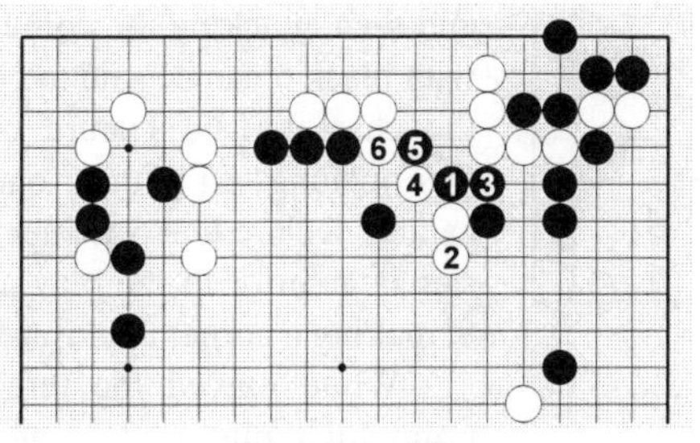
Diagram 18

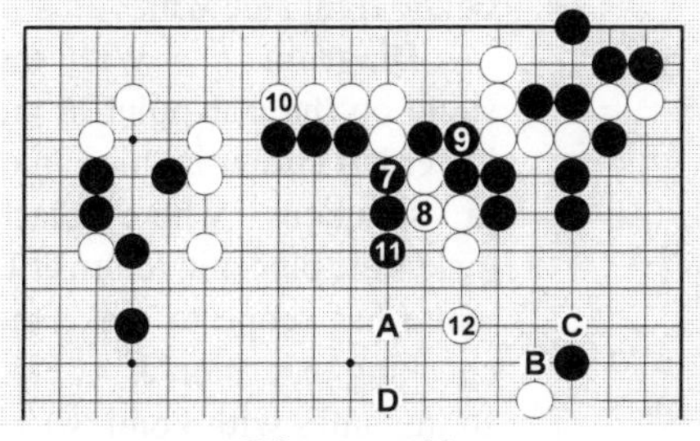

Diagram 19

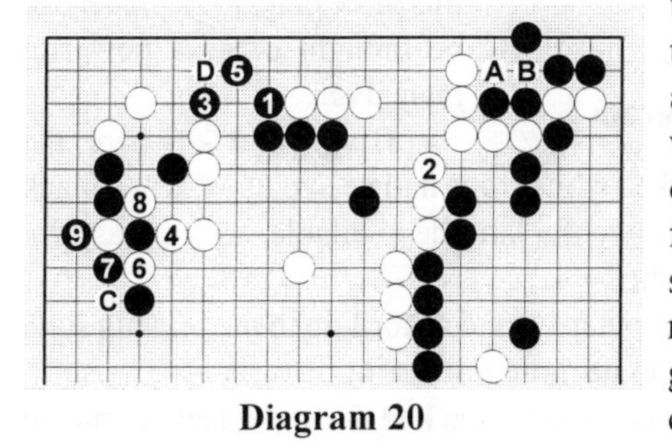

Diagram 20

Diagram 19 - Should black play 7 through 11, white jumps to 12, and then after black **A**, white attacks with **B**, black **C** and white **D**. Since white seems assured of consolidating the lower side, this would have been promising.

White embarked on a strategy of netting black on a large scale by pushing with 64 through 70, then playing 72. After this, the question was how black could live within white's sphere.

Diagram 20 - The conclusion was that with 1 through 5, black could probably survive. With 4 through 6, white captures a stone, and after black 9, white would play **A**, black **B** and tenaciously start a ko fight with white **C**, and the board situation is far from clear. If black 5 at 6, white **D** puts black in trouble.

Black played out on the lower side with 73 and the following plays, and then captured black's stones on a large scale with 78, achieving a big success. White had established an advantage.

After this, white committed several mistakes that led to an unclear position, but a heated battle came down to a fight revolving around an approach play ko which white won, and managed to eke out a half point win. I had lost the first three games of this match, but scored four straight wins to retain my Meijin title, and since this game was the one that started that dramatic reversal, it has a prominent place in my memory.

DIAGONAL MODEL (2) - GAME 2

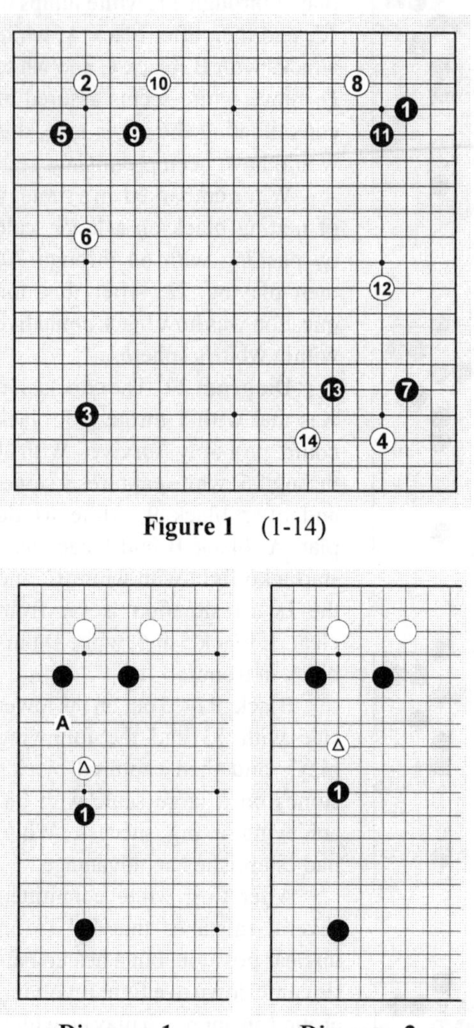

Figure 1 (1-14)

Diagram 1

Diagram 2

Figure 1 - The Powerful Three Point Pincer [1st Annual Gosei Title Match, Game 1; 1976; White: Kato Masao 8 dan; Wins by 1 1/2 pts.; Black: Otake Hideo, Meijin]

The momentum gained from playing at the star point and then attacking the corner with black 5 can be said to be the characteristic feature of this opening. Of course, one cannot declare that 5 is superior or inferior to the play at 8, making a corner enclosure.

White played the three point high pincer at 6, and then used the same maneuver on the right side with 12.

Diagram 1 - With the stone on the star point in the lower left corner in this game, in situations where black makes the pincer in return at 1, white has scope to make the checking extension at **A**, etc., so in games with komi where white aims at a leisurely pace, this three point high pincer can be thought of as a powerful maneuver.

Diagram 2 - If here, the two point high pincer with the marked white stone had been played, when black presses in with 1, white does not have the latitude available, so it is easy for momentum to lead to a sudden fight.

This has gradually gained in popularity, and according to the playing style of those who adopt it, this tactic can be quite interesting.

When black 7 attacked the corner, white attacked the upper right corner at 8, and after black 9, white defended with the two point extension at 10.

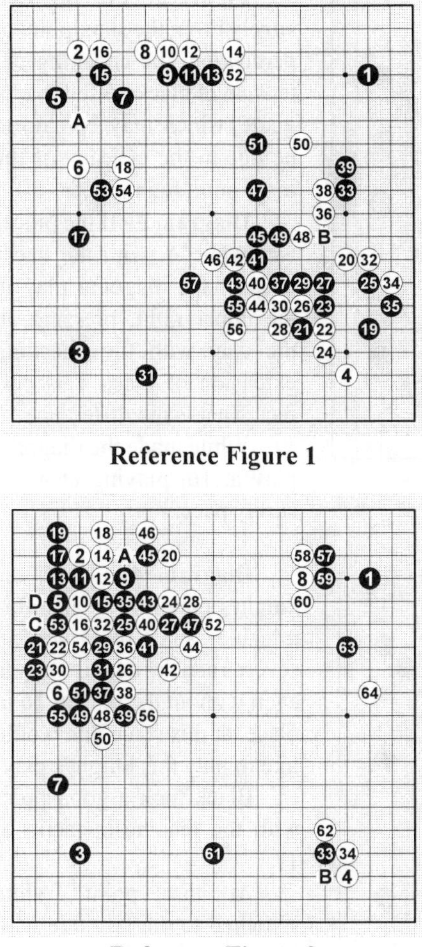
Reference Figure 1

Reference Figure 2

White waited for black to make the diagonal play at 11, then made the three point high pincer at 12, and after black 13 and white 14, the same pattern resulted in diagonal corners.

Reference Figure 1 - [24th Annual Honinbo League; 1969; White: Fujisawa Shuko 9 dan; Black: Kato Masao 5 dan] The two point jumps of black 7 and 21 were in keeping with Kato's taste. That was the period when the diagonal play at **A** was at the height of its popularity. Black played the more restrained pincer at 17, one line farther away. For 31, in this opening pressing at 37 is the vital point. Instead of black 35, sealing white in with **B** was better.

Reference Figure 2 - [26th Annual Honinbo League; 1970; White: Ishida Yoshio 7 dan; Black: Kato Masao 6 dan] White 18 was an unusual maneuver. Here, with **A**, black 35 and the joseki following white 20, 7, enclosing the corner, would have worked effectively. The play at 33 was designed as a ladder breaker after black 35, white 36, black 37, white 40, black 41 and white 43. It would have been interesting to play white 34 at 53, followed by black **B**, white **C**, black **D**, white 36 and black 34, with a swap.

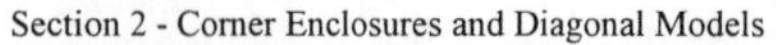

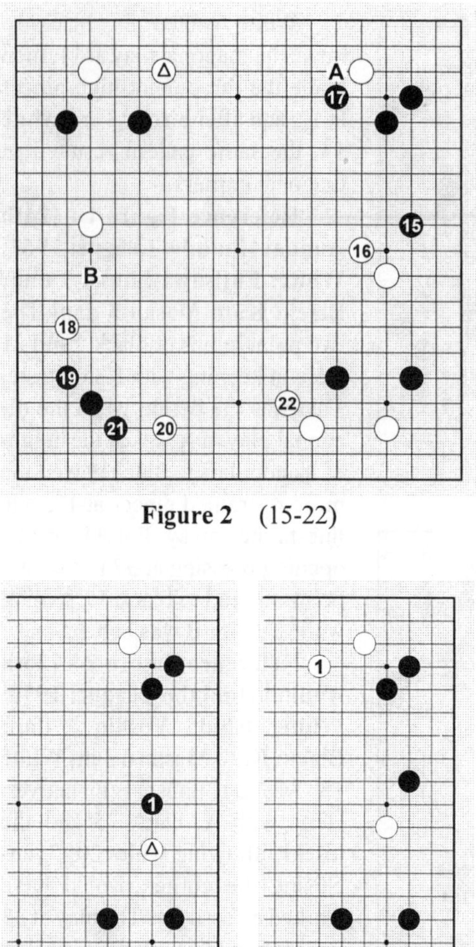

Figure 2 (15-22)

Diagram 3

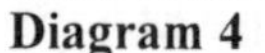
Diagram 4

Figure 2 - Playing Leisurely From the standpoint of perception, the checking extension of black 15 felt inadequate, which may be said to be due to the efficacy of the three point high pincer.

Diagram 3 - If the pincer was white Δ, with the backdrop of the diagonal play in the upper right, pressing all the way with the checking extension of black 1 is perfect. That is the difference.

White made the diagonal play at 16, playing at a leisurely pace.

Diagram 4 - Here, the knight's play of 1 is also formidable. Since there was no severe attack against white even without the play at 16 in place, at this stage one would like to play this knight's play.

Black took a good point with the fencing-in tactic of 17.

At that point, white switched to the left side with 18.

Diagram 5 - With 18, white could defend with 1, but at any time black could make the fencing-in tactic at **A**, meaning that white would be forced into a low posture on both sides. Black would make the pincer at 2, and after white jumps at **B**, the position is no good for white.

Since white had the extension of Δ in place, it was judged that in this position the block of black **A** was not so big. Backtracking, it was better to use the play at black 17 to hurry to make the checking extension at **B** on the left side.

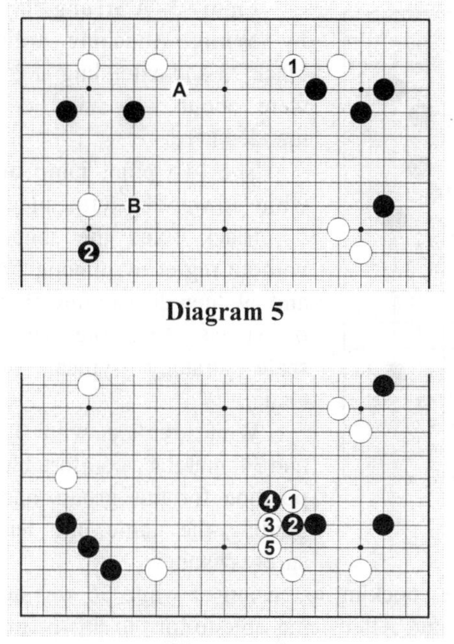

Diagram 5

Diagram 6

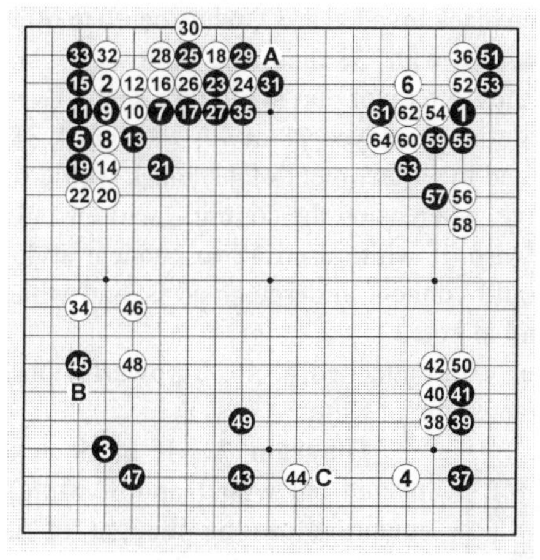

Reference Figure 3

White made the extension at 18, getting a little breathing room. Then, white extended at 20, and black played diagonal plays on both sides, creating the three crows formation in the corner.

The diagonal play of white 22 was played in Kato's leisurely style, and placed the principal focus on the lower side.

Diagram 6 - In addition, with the play, was it not possible to play white 1 at the corner of this position? If black answers at 2, white plays 3 and draws back at 5, and since the diagonal play is in place on the right side, white can probably fight without reserve here. With good conditions in the surrounding area, this resolute method is powerful.

Reference Figure 3 - [1st Annual All Japan First Place Title Match, Game 3; 1970; White: Fujisawa Shuko 9 dan; Black: Otake Hideo, First Place Titleholder] The plays following white's drawing back at 20 comprised a new joseki. If black used 25 to cut at 29, white 25, black **A** and white 35 would produce a disadvantageous fight for black. White 32 was a natural forcing play, but by taking the stone at 35, black built a thick and strong position. Playing white 44 as the attack on the corner at **B**, followed by black **C** and white 50 was better form.

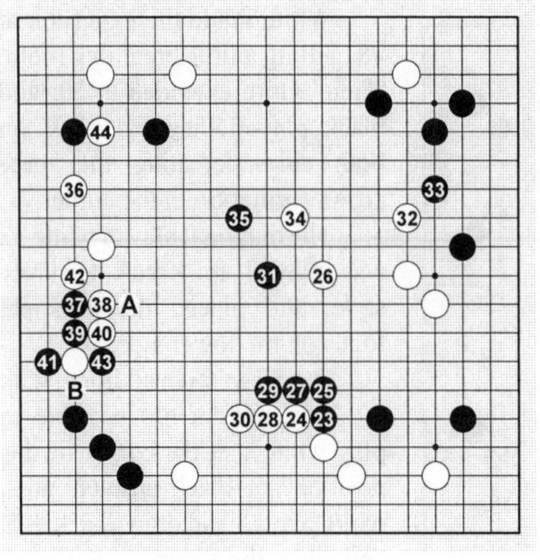

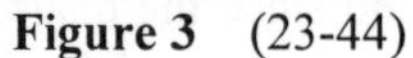

Figure 3 (23-44)

Figure 3 - A Strong Play by White Attaching with black 23 and extending at 25 were about what was demanded here.

The two point jump of white 26 was also a fine play.

Black fixed the shape without regret by playing 27 and 29, then the capping play of 31 was first rate, large scale strategy typical of Otake.

White replied with 32 and 34, making a comfortable position for this group, and guiding the game into leisurely channels.

The checking extension of white 36 was an ideal point. After being able to turn to this point, white could be thought of as having a formidable game.

When black invaded at 37, white dared to offer no resistance with 38 and the following, but adopted the strategy of playing to take sente. Even if white defiantly played 38 at 40, with black 38, white **A** and the attachment of 41, black would be able to live, whereas on the contrary, white would be thin. Also, if white used 42 to connect at 43, black would connect underneath at **B**, and white would end in gote.

Here, white attached at 44, a powerful play characteristic of Kato.

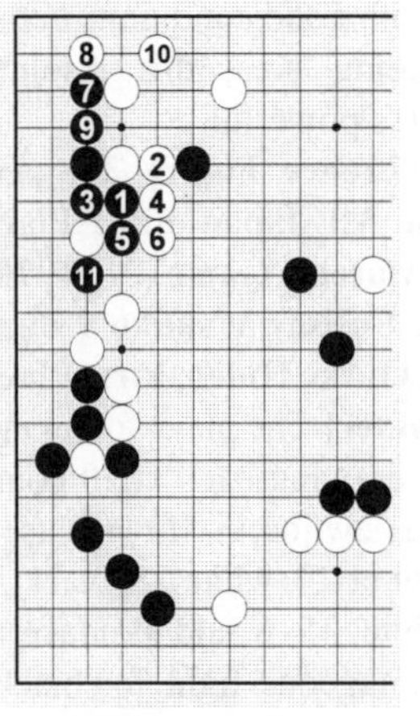

Diagram 7

Diagram 7 - If black next played out with 1 and 3, white's intention can be thought of as pressing with 4 and 6, playing to make the center thick and strong. With black 5 through 11, white incurs a territorial loss, but the aim was to next exploit black's thinness in the center.

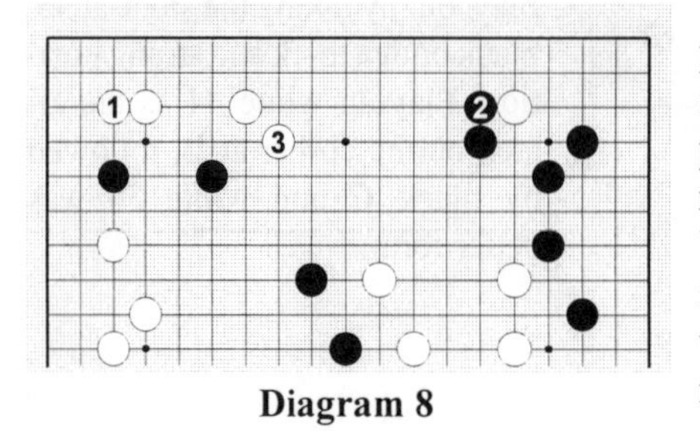

Diagram 8

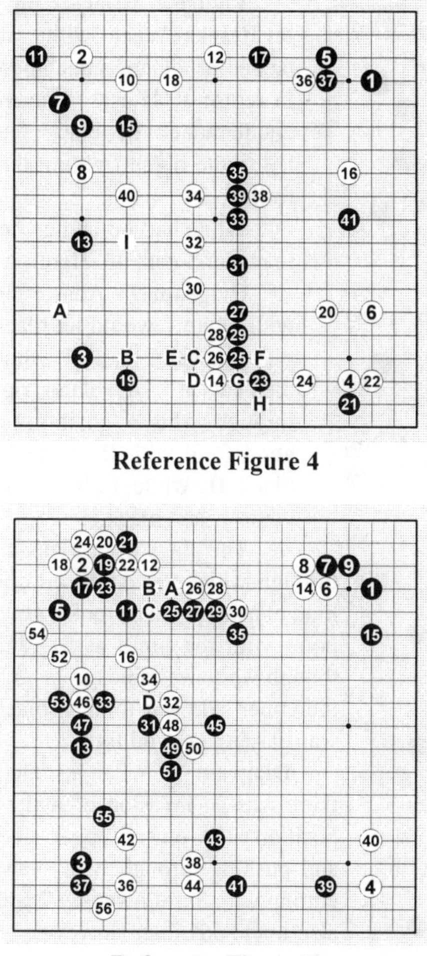

Reference Figure 4

Reference Figure 5

However, Kato, after reflecting on the harrowing course of action in the next figure said that,

Diagram 8 - For 44, descending at 1 was better. Then, black's block at 2 would be standard here, so white could make the good diagonal play at 3.

Reference Figure 4 - [2nd Annual All Japan First Place Title, Final; 1971; White: Kato Masao 7 dan; Black: Yamabe Toshiro 9 dan] With black 5 and white 6, both sides made corner enclosures. Black 13 and white 14 were equivalent options. If black used 13 to extend at 14, white would develop with **A**, black **B** and white 13, producing a different game. For black 25, the strategy with the shoulder hit of **C**, white 26, black 28, white **D**, black **E**, white **F**, black 25, white **G**, black 29, white **H** and black **I** would have been promising.

Reference Figure 5 - [27th Annual Honinbo Title Match, Game 5; 1972; White: Rin Kaiho, Meijin; Black: Ishida Shuho, Honinbo] White played 6 and 8, building up firepower on the upper side. If black played 17 at 23, white intended to play 19 and black **A**, and then push through and cut with white **B**, black **C** and white 25. When faced with the large scale play of black 31, white made the painstaking play at 32. If black had played 33 at 34, white would have pushed through at **D**. This game was rife with diagonal plays at 34, 52 and 54.

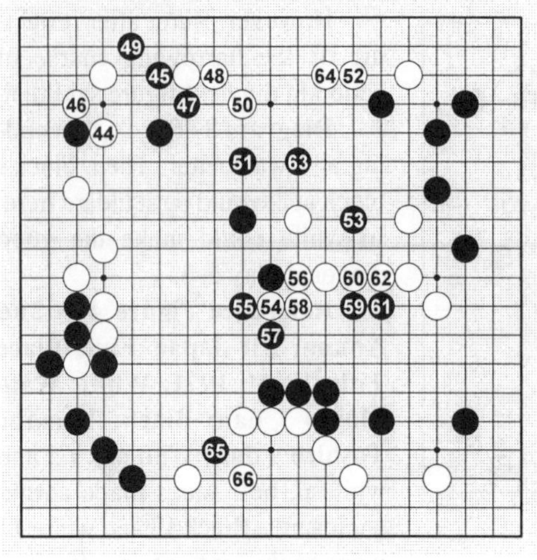

Figure 4 (44-66)

Figure 4 - Black Counterattacks When white attached at 44, the attachment in return at 45 was a severe counterattack by black that led to the fierce fighting that followed.

White had no choice but to respond with 46. Here,

Diagram 9 - Answering with white 1 would let black play out with 2 and 4. If white then cuts at **A**, black rips through white's position in good form with **B**, white **C**, black **D**, white **E**, black **F**, white **G** and black **H**.

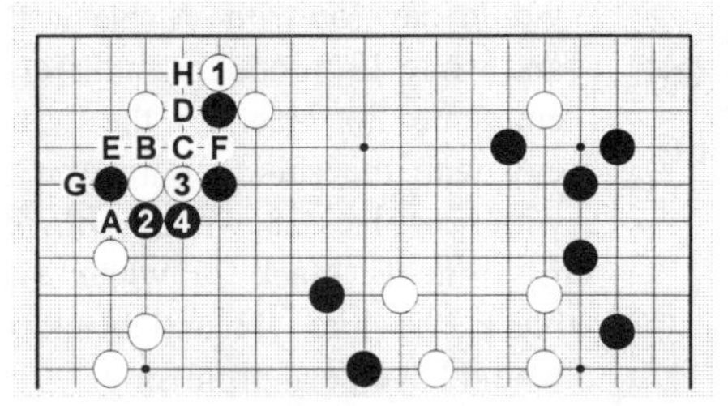

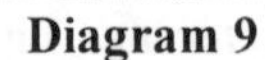
Diagram 9

The plays from black 47 through white 50 comprised one kind of a swap. Black took a good point with the jump at 51, and though white was able to play 52, the upper side was thin, so black was playing in good form.

Diagram 10 - For instance, there was an invasion of white's position at **A** on the upper side, and pushing through with 1 and cutting with 3, followed by 7 was also made possible. However, on white's part, there was the aim of peeping at **B**, and after black **C**, moving out at white **D**, so the position had become difficult for both sides.

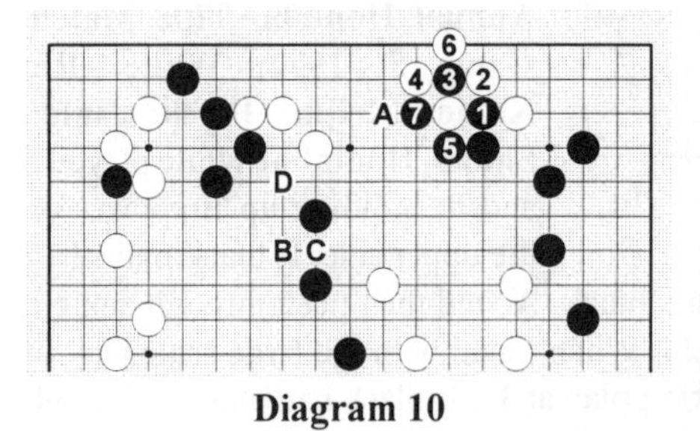

Diagram 10

Changing the field of battle, black 53 pressed in at the vital point of white's group. This was a severe play.

With 54 through 58, white unavoidably fought defensively, playing to create defects in black's shape.

With black 59 and 61, white had no choice but to respond with 60 and 62. Here, bearing down patiently was the only tactic. By defending this way, it was unlikely that this big group of stones would suffer painfully to survive.

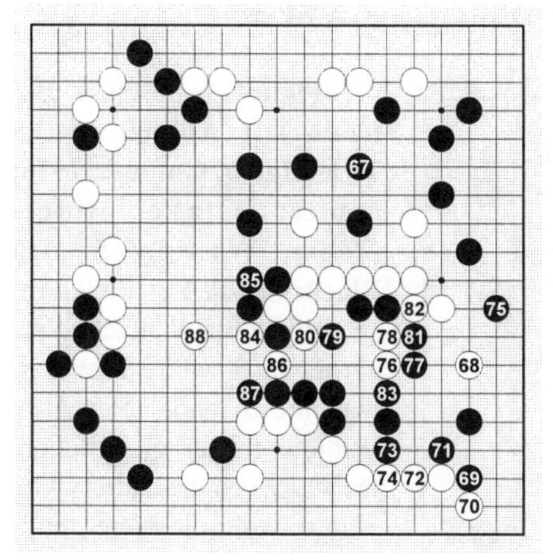

Diagram 11

After black split white's positions above and below with 63, white was able to defend the upper side with 64, easing things a bit. Black could aim at harassing white in the center, but in general, the board position seemed to be close here.

Diagram 11 - This shows the further course of the actual game. Black jumped at 67, but with this play,

Diagram 12 - Black should have extended at 1, preventing white from cutting at **A**, was Otake's opinion after the game.

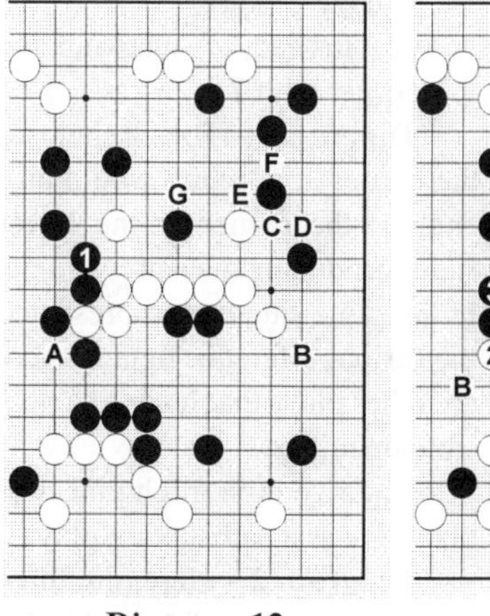

Diagram 12

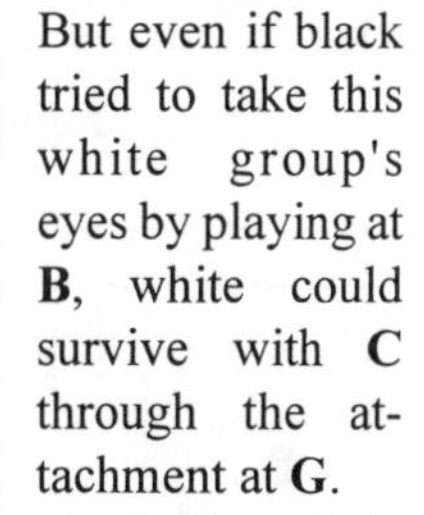

Diagram 13

But even if black tried to take this white group's eyes by playing at **B**, white could survive with **C** through the attachment at **G**.

White's thrust and parry with 68 and the following plays was splendid.

The play at white 76 was played at the vital point.

For black 77,

Diagram 13 - The attack of 1 would be met by white's plays from 2 through 10, which threaten the cut at **A** and creates the possibility of a capturing race with the tactic of white **B**.

With the survival of the group after 88, there was a lull in the action.

This game helped secure Kato's first title.

DIAGONAL MODEL (2) - GAME 3

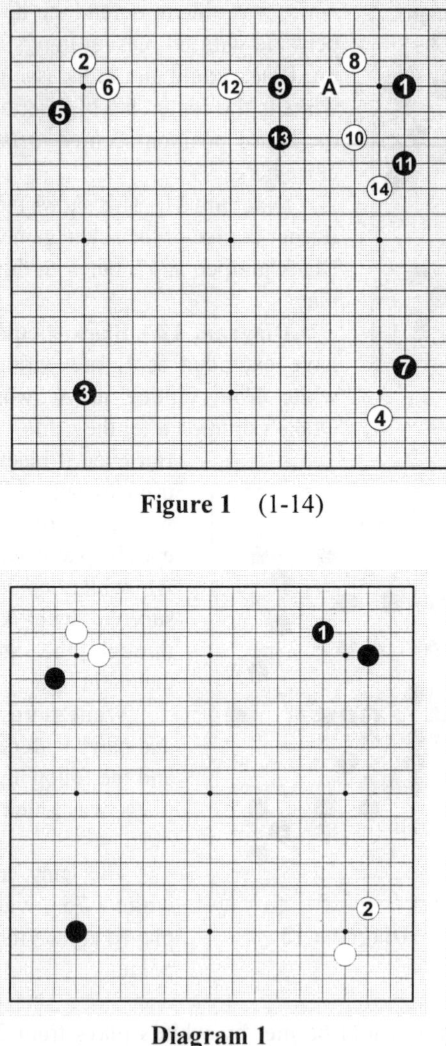

Figure 1 (1-14)

Diagram 1

Figure 1 - White Defends [1st Annual Meijin Title Match, Game 2; 1976; White: Otake Hideo, Meijin; Wins by 5 pts.; Black: Ishida Yoshio 9 dan]

When black attacked the corner at 5, white answered with the diagonal play at 6. Without fluster or agitation, the attacks on the corners with 7 and white 8 were made equivalent options, and one can feel white's intention of starting the game from a defensive posture.

Instead of attacking the corner with 7,

Diagram 1 - If black encloses the corner at 1, white would also enclose the corner in the lower right, producing a leisurely game. In the same situation as presented the various reference figures, there are other plays that leads to a possible openings.

The two point high pincer of black 9 was a painstaking play.

Diagram 2 - Here, the three point low pincer of 1 could also be considered, but in this opening, it was distasteful to have white play the Taisha joseki with the fencing-in tactic at 2, was Ishida's thought during the game. In the position that results after the joseki from black 3 through white 18, white Δ works effectively, so this course of action would not be to black's liking. Depending upon the arrangement of the surrounding stones, the fact is that everyone comes to choose different joseki.

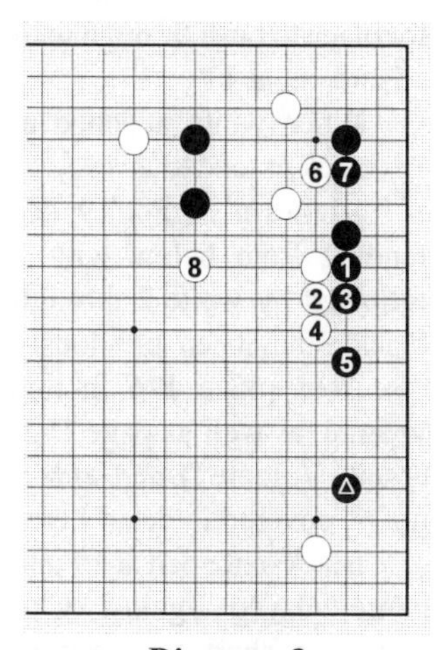

Diagram 3

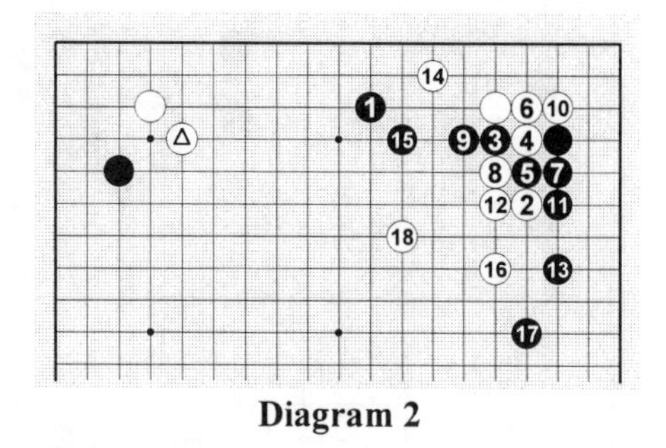

Diagram 2

In response to black's two point high pincer, white jumped to 10 and black defended at 11. According to the age, openings and joseki often revolve in a cycle, and the diagonal play at **A**, which at one time was often played, from a little while before this started to disappear from sight.

Regarding the fencing-in tactic of white 14, next,

Diagram 3 - After black defends at 1 and 3, white expects to play 8. Black ▲ represents a duplication of effort, so naturally black could not adopt this sequence.

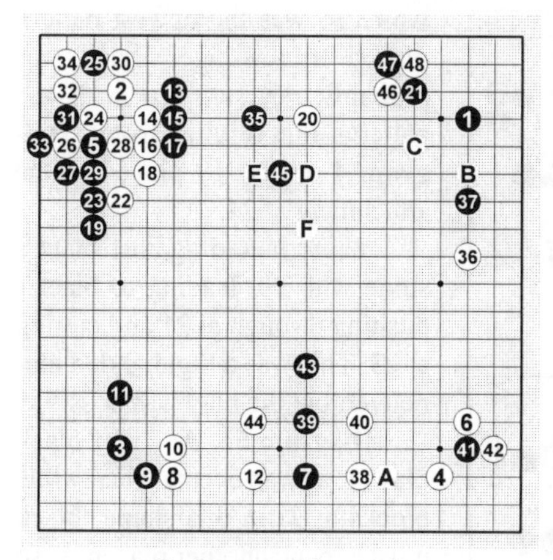

Reference Figure 1

Reference Figure 1 - [13th Annual Meijin League; 1974; White: Fujisawa Shuko 9 dan; Black: Ishida Shuho, Honinbo] The joseki up to 34 was, in the local context, a loss for white, but being able to split the side with the single stone at 20 made this a credible result. In addition, white occupied the good points at 36 and 38. If black 37 was played as the checking extension at **A**, after white **B**, black **C**, white **D**, black **E** and white **F**, black had no good follow-up play, so 37 took precedence.

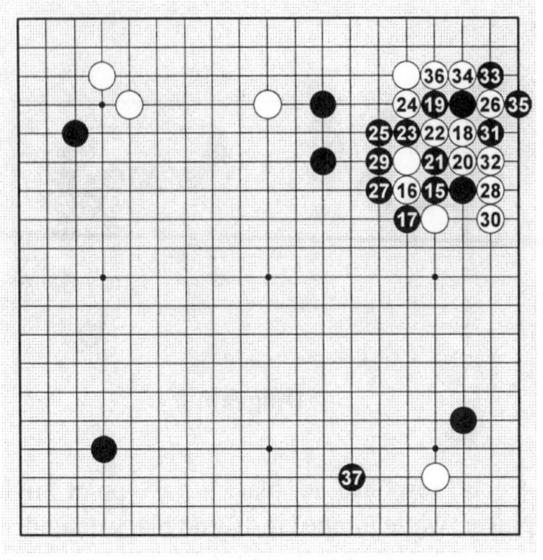

Figure 2 (15-37)

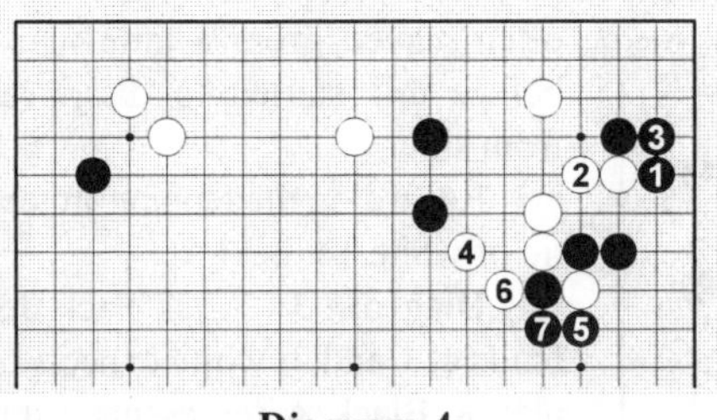

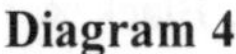
Diagram 4

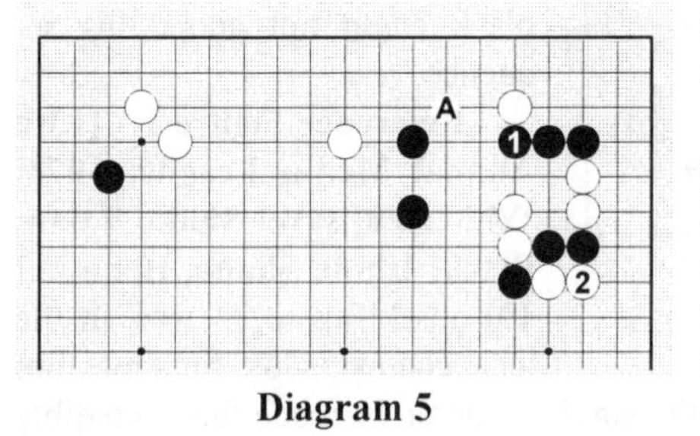

Diagram 5

Figure 2 - Playing a New Pattern It was natural for black to push through with 15 and cut at 17.

When white attached at 18, black extended at 19.

Diagram 4 - For 19, defending from below with 1 followed by white 2 through black 7 has been previously discussed (page 176 in this volume, as well as page 172, et seq., Volume I), and so will not be covered in detail here.

Black extended at 19 in a game played against Cho Chikun a short time before this, and the sequence through white 36 was the newest pattern played in this age. Black was probably not satisfied with the patterns that resulted from **Diagram 4** or else 19 played as the attachment at 24.

White butted against black's stone with 20, leading to black's pushing through at 21 and cutting at 23. This was a highhanded maneuver, but the play was possible.

Diagram 5 - At 21, if black plays 1, a swap occurs when white blocks at 2. In this shape, black must expend another play at **A**, so white has no cause for dissatisfaction.

White played 24 and haned at 26, black played atari at 27, and after 28, white extended at 30.

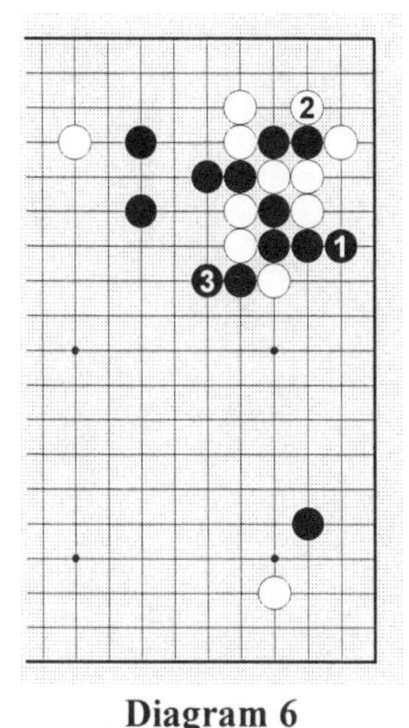

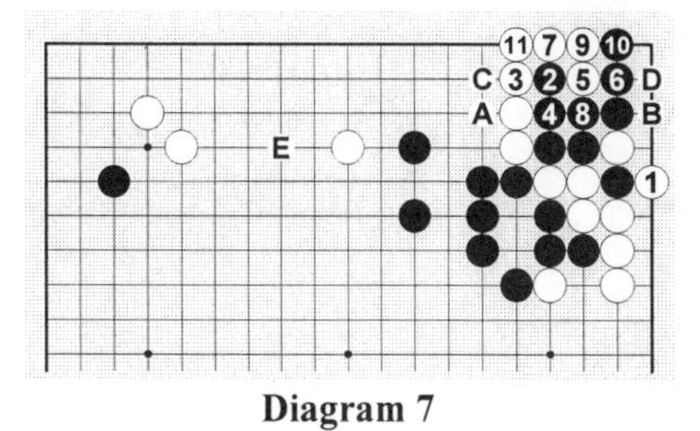

Diagram 7

Diagram 6 - Instead of 27, considering conditions on the right side, it was also feasible to descend at 1, followed by white 2 and black's extending at 3. Potential plays in the corner are eliminated, and I would have probably played this way myself.

Diagram 6

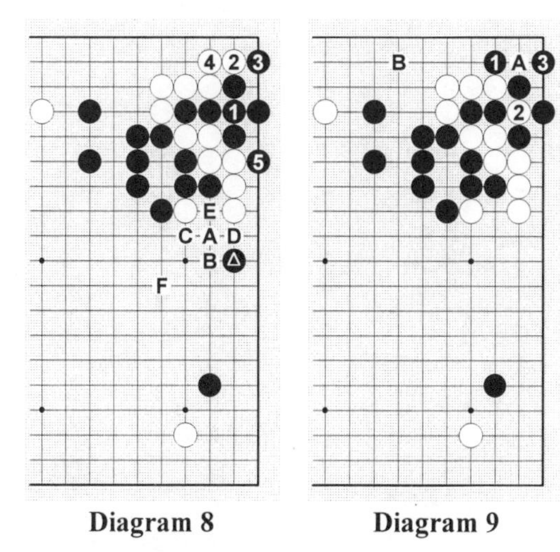

Diagram 8

Diagram 9

After cutting at 31, black played atari at 33 to probe white's response. White 34 and 36 were the norm in this position.

Diagram 7 - White can capture a stone with 1, since the plays through 11 win the race, but black **A** starts a forcing sequence that wraps white up through **D**, and then black invades at **E**, leaving white badly off.

Diagram 8 - In evaluating this joseki, it must be taken into account that if the black ▲ is put in place, 1 through the hane at 5 produce an approach play ko. If white plays out at **A**, black blocks access to the outside with **B** through **F**.

Diagram 9 - Furthermore, the hane at 1 in the corner, probing white's response, is possible. If white replies at 2, the potential of a ko with the tiger link of black 3 remains. Should white use to 2 to make a placement at 3, after black **A** and white 2, black can make a forcing play in the vicinity of **B**. Taking all these factors together, white has a liability of about a half a play. And with a thick and strong position on the outside, this is probably advantageous for black.

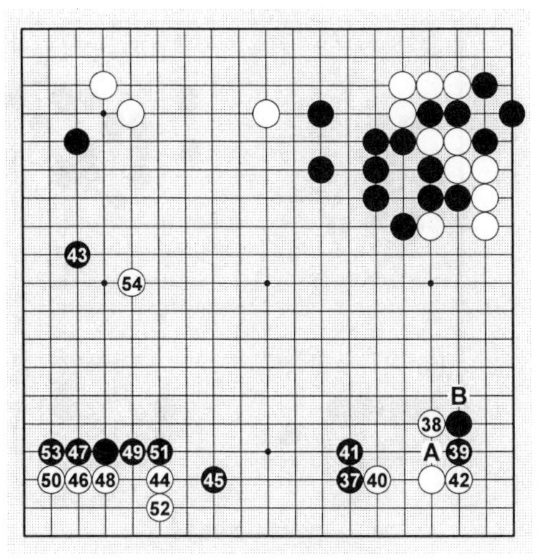

Figure 3 (37-54)

Figure 3 - White Has the Initiative When black made the pincer at 37, white attached on both sides at 38 and 40, then settled the group with 42.

According to Otake, it was better to use 40 to connect at **A**, followed by black 42 and the hane of white **B**.

The low three point extension of black 43 provoked much criticism. That was because after this, white had a perfect erasure play at 54.

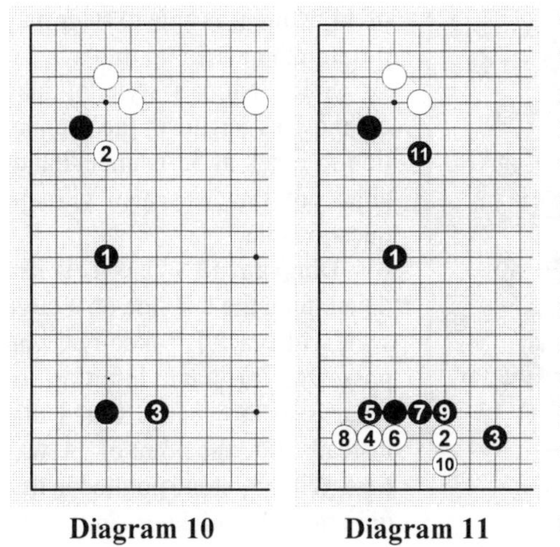

Diagram 10 **Diagram 11**

Diagram 10 - According to Takemiya, it was better for black to occupy the star point with 1, and I have to agree with that assessment. If white makes the fencing-in tactic at 2, black leaves the area to develop ideally with the one point jump at 3.

Diagram 11 - When black plays 1, if white attacks the corner with 2, the sequence from black 3 through white 10 follows, and then black builds up the left side with 11.

Diagram 12 - If white uses 4 in the previous diagram to attach at 1, black exchanges the plays from 2 through white 5, then, here too, the knight's play of black 6 makes fine shape. This was the focal point of the opening of this game.

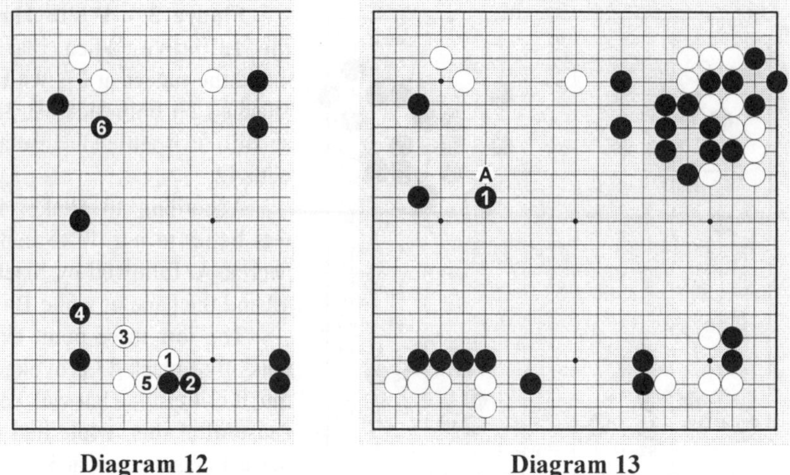

Diagram 12 Diagram 13

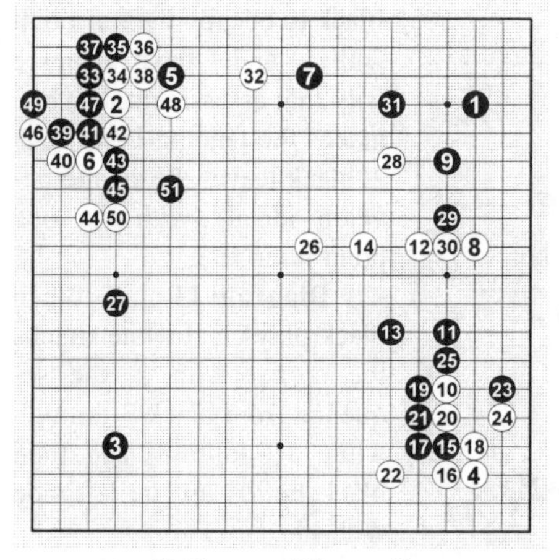

Reference Figure 2

With the attack on the corner of 44, white was able to steer play through the joseki up to black 53.

Since Ishida's style of play emphasizes territory, the inclination to block at 53 is understandable, but this was also perhaps questionable.

Diagram 13 - One feels like developing the left side on a large scale with black 1. Takemiya, who possesses brilliant intuition in regards to the center, stated that instead of 1, the point of **A** was best. With the stone pointed in this direction, the thickness in the upper right works effectively.

White made the knight's play at 54 as an erasure, taking hold of the initiative in the game.

Reference Figure 2 - [1st Annual Meijin League; 1976; White: Rin Kaiho, 10 Dan; Black: Yamabe Toshiro 9 dan] Black played fast-paced plays at 5 and 7. There were many places to play with black 11 and the following plays, but fixing the shape here was Yamabe's style. For black 33, one wants to deal deftly with the situation by playing 34, white 33 and black 37.

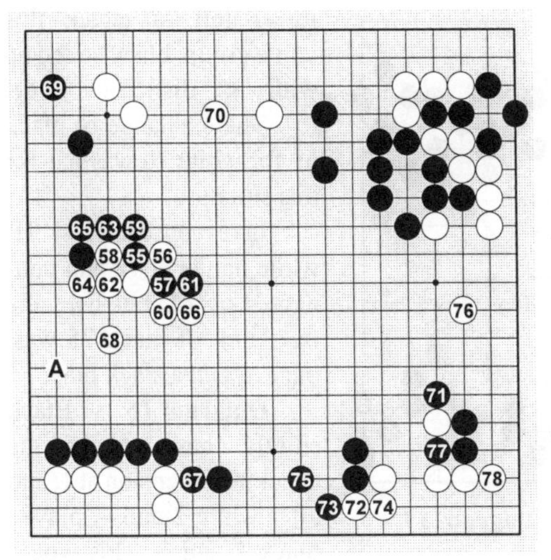

Figure 4 (55-78)

Figure 4 - A Difficult Fight for Black In response to white's erasure play, black attached at 55 and cut at 57, but this, on the contrary, gave white the impetus to deal deftly with the situation, did it not?

Diagram 14 - One wants to attach at 1 and extend at 3 to see how white will respond, setting up an ambush.

When white pressed at 66, black added the play at 67. This was terribly slack.

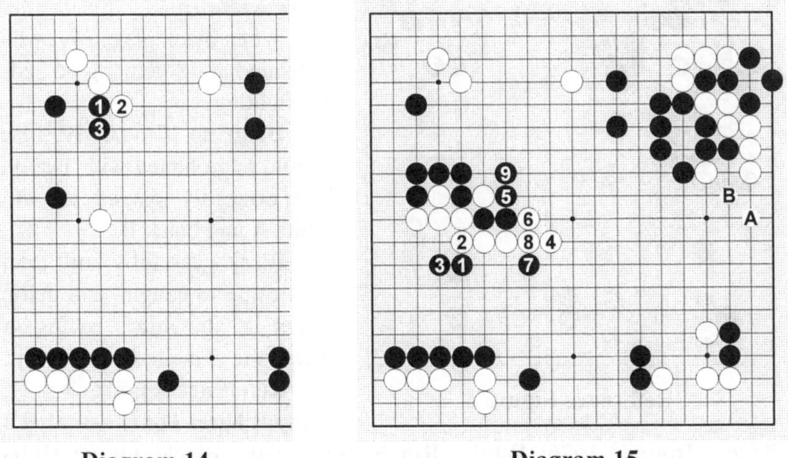

Diagram 14 **Diagram 15**

Diagram 15 - Black 1 and 3 take away white's base, and then 5 through 9 put black's shape in order. Since black can play forcing plays on the right side at **A** or **B**, the position is thick and strong, so white will surely have to go through agony to settle this group of stones.

White developed at the vital point with 68, in general achieving a settled shape. Next, playing at **A** would secure life, so this may be said to have been a big opportunity that was missed. This was the second questionable point in this game. By not using the two sources of thickness in the upper right and

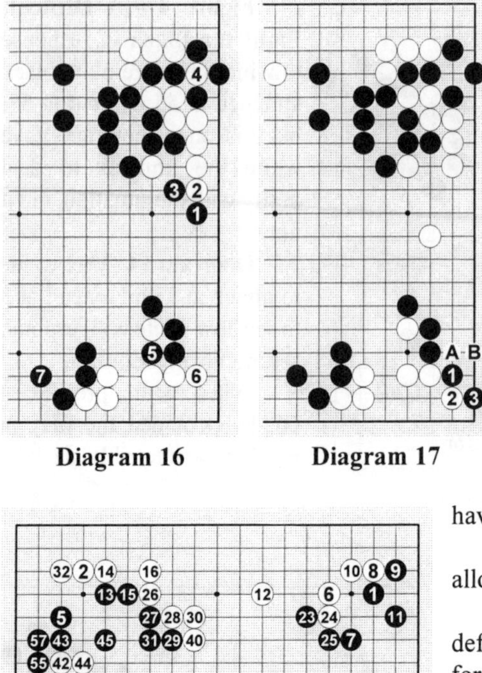

Diagram 16 **Diagram 17**

lower left to attack this white group, black ended up with a difficult game.

The exchange of black 69 for white 70 was par for this situation.

In response to black 71, white haned at 72 and connected at 74, but here the tiger link of black 75 was, once again, a slack play.

Diagram 16 - Black should have made the checking extension at 1, and after white 2 and 4, played black 5 and 7. This would have given black a flicker of hope.

It was a failure for black to allow white 76.

When black played 77, white defended at 78, leaving no scope for fighting.

Diagram 17 - At 77, black should have haned with 1 and 3, and doggedly played ko after white **A** and black **B**.

Black's carefully built thickness came to naught, and getting swept up in white's pacing, allowed the game to be put away.

Reference Figure 3

Reference Figure 3 - [1st Annual Kisei Tournament, Top Players Round; 1976; White: Rin Kaiho 9 dan; Black: Otake Hideo, Meijin] White 12 was played out of consciousness of the fencing-in tactic of black 13. White turned at 40, aiming at the invasion of 42. Black took white's eyes away with 55 and 57, and with 60 and the following plays, the fighting spilled into the center.

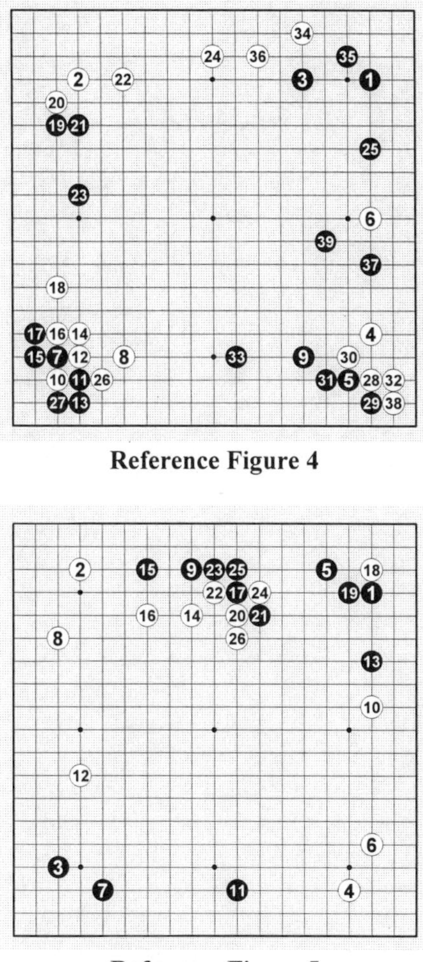

Reference Figure 4

Reference Figure 5

Reference Figure 4 - [Oteai Ranking Tournament, Autumn Session; 1934; White: Iwamoto Kaoru 6 dan; Black: Sekiyama Riichi 5 dan] It was not presented often in the **Corner Enclosure Section**, but the two point high enclosure maneuver of black 1 and 3 is also occasionally used. This was played during the New Opening Era, but at the time, it often happened that 3 at the 6-4 point was played, with black returning to 1 after that. Instead of extending at white 14, blocking at 27 is today's joseki. Black 23 and 33 were played from a sense of achieving a high stance, which gives one an impression of the trend of that time.

Reference Figure 5 - [27th Annual Honinbo League; 1972; White: Takemiya Masaki 6 dan; Black: Rin Kaiho, Meijin] Here is an example of full board corner enclosures, with white 8 being the only large knight corner enclosure. White played 12 one line wider so as not to give black a checking extension, and this was a promising play since it looked to use the upper left corner effectively. In relation to that play, white expanded like a balloon with 14 through 26, embarking on Takemiya's first class large territorial framework strategy.

Books From Yutopian

Sakata Series
1) Killer of Go, 2) Tesuji and Anti-Suji of Go

The Nihon Ki-In Series
A Compendium of Trick Plays
100 Challenging Go Problems for 100 Days of Study
Pro-Pro Handicap Go

Go Handbook Series
1) Go Proverbs, 2) Fuseki, 3) Star Point Joseki

Chinese Professional Series
Nie WeiPing on Go
Thirty-Six Stratagems Applied to Go, by Ma XiaoChun
Beauty and the Beast, Exquisite Play and Go Theory by Shen Guosun
Golden Opportunities by Rin Kaiho
Winning A Won Game, by Go Seigen
Yang Yilun's Ingenious Life and Death Puzzles, vol. 1 and 2
Essential Joseki by Rui Naiwei
Power Builder, vol. 1, by Wang Runan
Strategic Fundamentals in Go, by Guo Tisheng

Art of Go Series
Art of Connecting Stones
Art of Capturing

Pocket Book Series, by Yang Yilun
Rescue and Capture
Tricks in Joseki

Korean Series
Cho HunHyun's Go Techniques, vol. 1
Lee ChangHo's Novel Plays and Shapes

Other Books From Yutopian
Go For Kids
Fighting Ko
Utilizing Outward Influence
Master Go in Ten Days
Dramatic Moments on the Go Board
Igo Hatsuyo-ron, vol. 1